William McClung Paxton

The Marshall Family

William McClung Paxton

The Marshall Family

ISBN/EAN: 9783337379995

Printed in Europe, USA, Canada, Australia, Japan

Cover: Foto ©ninafisch / pixelio.de

More available books at **www.hansebooks.com**

The Marshall Family,

——OR A——

GENEALOGICAL CHART OF THE DESCENDANTS OF
JOHN MARSHALL AND ELIZABETH MARKHAM,
HIS WIFE, SKETCHES OF INDIVIDUALS
AND NOTICES OF FAMILIES
CONNECTED WITH THEM.

By W. M. PAXTON, PLATTE CITY, MO.

Entered according to the Act of Congress, in the year 1885, by
W. M. PAXTON,
In the office of the Librarian of Congress at Washington, D.C.

CINCINNATI:
ROBERT CLARKE & CO.
1885.

STEAM PRESS OF KETCHESON & HUBBELL,
LEAVENWORTH, KANSAS.

INTRODUCTION.

1 (a) This volume is intended for a book of reference. To this end it is furnished with an ample index. I have dealt in facts, rather than panegyric. I have flattered no one, and have written nothing in malice. It has been a labor of love. I have spent two years upon the work, and my expenses are freely contributed. Though pecuniary assistance has been proffered, I have accepted nothing. It cannot be said that my book is written in the interest of one, more than another. To use an apothegm, I have written for mine, not for myself. I admit that kindest words have been bestowed on those I knew and loved. It could not be otherwise. Remember, my book is the tribute of affection, as well as the record of heraldry. Doubtless, there are hundreds whose honors have not been fully given. I did not know them, and their friends failed to notice my repeated calls for information. I knew most of the Kentucky Marshalls well. When I determined to write a memorial of the kindred, in 1884, I issued a Genealogical Chart of the family, and went myself through Kentucky, Virginia and Maryland, that I might meet my relatives and solicit information for my work. I met hundred of noble, generous and hospitable people. I gathered much information on my way, and have since kept up an active correspondence with many of the family.

The chronicles of our family will not be completed by the publication of this volume. The next generation will call for another. I am now too far advanced in life to hope to issue a second memorial; but I trust it will not be regarded presumptuous, if I offer to be the depository of records and information that may be needed by the future herald. So, while I live, I will take pleasure in preserving in good form for future use, every record, ancient or modern, touching any member of our family. I therefore solicit correspondence and genealogical data.

THE CHART.

(b) An important feature in this work is the Genealogical Chart. I have often contemplated the unnatural and unintelligible family tables constructed in various forms, and have thought that something more simple and comprehensive might be invented. After repeated trials and changes of form, I adopted the plan of the chart appended to this volume. It seems to combine more advantages than any form heretofore used. Names may be indexed, and lineages traced with facility. The several generations are distinct. Children appear in the order of birth beneath their parents. With the index, the name of any one may be found in a moment, and his ancestry and posterity may be seen at a glance. If such a form of genealogical table has ever been used, I have not heard of it.

EXPLANATIONS.

(e) *b.* signifies born; *d.*, died; *dr.*, daughter; *s.*, son; $=$, married.

In genealogical tables of families which have intermarried with the Marshalls, such as the Amblers, the Picketts, etc., the first generation indicated by "*A*" in the left hand margin, will be in CAPITALS. The second generation indicated by "*B*" in the margin, will be set to the right three-eighths of an inch. The third generation will be indicated by "*C*" in the margin, and will be set to the right six-eighths of an inch. Brothers and sisters will follow each other in the order of birth, and be numbered 1, 2, 3, etc. Whenever one of the Marshall family is reached, it will be indicated by placing the name in small CAPITALS, followed by the number of the name in the chart, where the posterity, if any, of that person will be found.

The small letters, *a, b, c*, etc., are to facilitate reference by dividing the sections or numbers into paragraphs.

Where the chart contains all the information I possess of an individual, he will not be noticed in the sketches.

(2) THEIR ORIGIN.

(2) THE MARSHALLS—THEIR ORIGIN.

2 Tradition is the only authority the Marshall family have for claiming descent from William le Mareschal, who came over to England with the army of the Norman conqueror. As his name implies, he was a commander in the army of invasion. From him was descended John Marshall, nephew of the great Earl of Pembroke. The estates of the latter were on the border of Wales. After the death of King John, he was Mareschal of England. After the crowning of the infant King Henry III, he was chosen Protector of the Kingdom. He had married a daughter of Richard, Earl of Pembroke, surnamed Strongbow, who in 1172, in the reign of Henry II, had conquered the Irish, and re-instated Dermot, King of Leinster. For his services he had been rewarded with the hand of Eva, the King's daughter. On the death of Strongbow, William, Earl of Pembroke, succeeded to his estates in Ireland. As Protector of England and Guardian of Henry III, he sent his nephew, John Marshall, to Ireland, and constituted him Mareschal of Ireland. This John Marshall is mentioned by Irish historians as the leader of the Irish nobility, in their efforts to gain for that Island the benefits of *Magna Charta*. After the confiscation of the Pembroke estates in Ireland, we hear no more of the Marshall name, until it appears in history in 1558, at the fall of Calais, in the reign of Queen Mary. Capt. John Marshall there distinguished himself, and was severely wounded at the capture of the city. He returned to Ireland, and there died. From him descended John Marshall, who was a Captain at the battle of Edgehill in the reign of Charles I. Being an Episcopalian, he did not follow the fortunes of his deposed Sovereign, but came to America about 1650, and settled, first, at Jamestown, Va., and afterwards removed to Westmoreland County, in the same colony. He became distinguished in the Indian wars. He appears to have left no will. His son Thomas, an humble farmer, here died in 1704. The second son of Thomas was John, known as John Marshall of the "Forest." With him my chart commences.

Perhaps there is no living depository of the traditions of the Marshall family entitled to more credit than Col. Charles A. Marshall (188), of Mason county, Kentucky. He is one of the eight living grandchildren of Col. Thomas Marshall. He was reared at the house where his grandfather had passed the last years of his life,

(2) THEIR ORIGIN.

and was born the very year of his grandmother's death. In 1884 he wrote to me as follows:

(b) Seeing from your last letter to your sister, that you are determined to construct a genealogical tree, and not knowing its scope, I have concluded to give what is, no doubt, the most reliable compend of the traditions of the family. It is the most reliable, because my grandfather (16) led a struggling, active life, until the close of the Revolution, and then came to Kentucky, to spend the closing twenty years of his life among his younger children. My grandmother survived him seven years, dying about the time of my birth. They were then in easy circumstances, and enjoyed abundant leisure. Their minds were relieved of the harrassing cares of life, and their thoughts and conversation would turn to the past. With those younger children, and especially Uncle Louis and Aunts McClung and Daveiss (70, 72, 78), I was an especial favorite, and enjoyed more of their society than any one now living.

(c) Of the origin of the family, the common tradition, both in Kentucky and Virginia, declares that we were descended from William Mareschal, who came over with the Conqueror, and fought at Hastings. Domes-Day-Book shows that his share of the conquered lands was on the Welch border, now Pembrokeshire. Consequently, when, a few years ago, my nephew, Thomas M. Green (648), wrote a sketch of the family, giving our more immediate descent from an Irish Captain, John Marshall, who settled in Virginia in the seventeenth century, Cousin Edward C. Marshall (160) wrote to him suggesting a mistake. He had always heard that the family were Welch. But Mr. Green was undoubtedly right, though it must be admitted the family had passed into Ireland from the border of Wales. Uncle Humphrey (88), who cared little for our high descent from a comrade of William of Normandy, pronounced the claim, as he did others much more holy and divine, to be a myth supported by vanity, yet told me that our ancestor was an Irish Captain, "and a poor one at that." Uncle Louis and Aunts McClung and Daveiss said the same; and they were proud that he had fought for the Stuarts, and had fled from Ireland with his family rather than submit to the stern rule of Cromwell.

(d) Having leisure some years ago, I determined to investigate the matter. Among other books, I consulted Moore's History of Ireland, and learned that in the reign of Henry II, Dermot, one of the Chieftain Kings of Leinster, having, by his vices, disgusted his people, was driven from his throne. Flying to England, he appealed to Henry to re-instate him. But Henry was then at war with France, and declined to interfere; but he allowed such of his barons, as chose, to give the desired help. Consequently, the celebrated Strongbow accompanied Dermot, with some English adventurers, and the King was re-instated. For this service, Strongbow was rewarded by the King with the hand of the only daughter, and the heiress of the grateful sovereign. William Marshall, the great Earl of Pembroke, married the daughter and only child of Strongbow, and succeeded to the Irish estates. This William Marshall, known in history as the elder William, to distinguish him from his son of the same name, was a leader of the barons who exacted *Magna Charta* from King John. But later, the younger William, disgusted with John's falsehood and duplicity, with other barons, rebelled; and calling Louis, the French Dauphin, to England, reduced the King to extremities. But the elder William, the great Earl of Pembroke, was loyal to his King, and John, at his death, made him, by will, the guardian of his son and the Protector of England. He seems to have commanded the confidence of all classes, and won back the discontented barons to their

THE MARSHALL FAMILY. 7

(2) THEIR ORIGIN.

allegiance. John's youngest daughter was given in marriage to the younger William and the French were driven from the kingdom. About this time the Protector sent his nephew, John Marshall, as his representative, to take charge of his estates in Ireland, endowed him with lands, and made him Marshal of Ireland. Through him the benefits of *Magna Charta* were extended to the English residents of Ireland. On the death of the great Earl of Pembroke, and the majority of Henry III, the sons of Pembroke seem to have lost favor at court. The younger William died leaving no heirs, and his widow married DeMonford, Earl of Leinster, who seems to have become a leader of the liberal party in England and an asserter of *Magna Charta*. The other sons of the Earl of Pembroke, having died without issue, Richard, the youngest, succeeded to the title and estates. Being prevailed on by his enemies to visit Ireland at the head of a few knights, he and his attendants were treacherously assassinated. The name was thereupon attainted, and the estates confiscated. The descendants of John Marshall, nephew of Earl Pembroke, still reside in the North of Ireland, and retain the family names of John, Thomas, Humphrey, etc. Since that day none of the family has attained distinction except, first, Captain John Marshall, who distinguished himself at the siege of Calais, and applied unsuccessfully for a restoration of his confiscated estates; and second, our more immediate ancestor, a Captain of the Army of Charles I. But my grandfather, Col. Thomas Marshall, I regard as the greatest man of the name, since the great Earl of Pembroke—the elder William Marshall. I will only add that my great grandmother, Elizabeth Markham [Marshall] (12), survived her husband, John of "the Forest," for many years, and died in Fauquier Co., Va. Her youngest son was undoubtedly known as Markham, not Abraham.

(e) I will conclude my notice of the origin of the Marshall family by an extract from Col. Thos. M. Green's (648) sketch published some years since, in the Cincinnati *Commercial:*

At the siege of Calais in Bloody Mary's time, there fought and was wounded desperately, as the army rolls of the British army show, an Irish Captain, John Marshall by name. After the capture of that port, which cost the murderous Queen her life, Capt. Marshall was retired on half-pay, and spent the remainder of his days on a small landed estate near Dublin. He married late in life, many years after receiving his wound. He claimed descent from one of the nephews of William le Mareschal, the great Earl of Pembroke, who settled in Ireland at the time of Henry III, and that his family had been reduced to the condition of the smaller gentry by their incessant strife with the DeBurghs, to all of which each individual reader may attach whatever belief or importance he chooses. Certain it is, however, that his grand son, also named John Marshall, commanded a troop in King Charles' army, at the battle of Edgehill, and after the overthrow of the power of the Stuarts, preferred seeking his fortune in the New World, rather than remain in Ireland under Cromwellian rule. He settled and died in Virginia, near Dumfries, where his tomb-stone still stood a few years before the war. Of what other offspring he may have had there is no trace; but of his son Thomas Marshall, there remains circumstantial information. He was a Virginia farmer of small fortune, and in no way distinguished from or above his neighbors. The oldest son of this Thomas Marshall was William, one of whose sons was Col. William Marshall, of Mecklenburg, and from him the Andersons of Kentucky and Ohio, the first wife of Hon. James Pryor, of Covington, Capt. Allen, now a Representative

(2) THEIR ORIGIN.

in the Legislature, and the Marshalls of Henderson, Kentucky, are descended. Another son of this Thomas Marshall was John, who was a Captain of Virginia troops in Indian wars, and of whose descendants this sketch will chiefly treat.

We will now trace the Marshall lineage as follows:

1. Capt. John Marshall, emigrant, 1650.
2. His son, Thomas, who died 1704.
3. His son, John of the Forest, who died 1752, and with these we enter the precincts of our Chart.

The Marshalls of Ireland were staunch Presbyterians. Several of them have come to America, bringing with them their family names and their Puritan religion. It will be interesting to notice some of these offshoots of the Emerald tree, and I hope at some time to be in close correspondence with them. The following traces one of these branches:

LINEAGE OF REV. SAMUEL V. MARSHALL.

(*g*) Under date of December 22, 1883, Dr. J. G. Monfort, senior editor of the *Presbyter and Herald*, of Cincinnati, writes me:

Rev. Samuel Marshall and Rev. James Marshall were sons of Rev. Robert Marshall, long pastor at Bethel, eight miles from Lexington, Kentucky. Robert was born in Ireland, and in early life immigrated to Western Pennsylvania, was licensed by Redstone Presbytery, April 23, 1790, and moved to Kentucky about 1790, and died 1832. His first wife was a Miss Vance, mother of James and Samuel V., and his second wife was Elizabeth Glass, a sister of my mother. My father, Francis Monfort, studied with Robert Marshall, and became his brother-in-law. Mr. Marshall was unmarried when he went to Kentucky. His first wife was a Virginian, but I don't think Samuel V. was born in Virginia. Robert was intimate with Dr. Louis Marshall, Alex. K. Humphrey and Mrs. McClung, and they knew they were of the same Scotch-Irish family.

(*c*) In 1884, I addressed letters to fourteen Marshalls, ministers of the Northern branch of the Presbyterian Church, and received courteous replies from all of them. About half the number claimed relationship with our family, but none could trace their lineage to the point of connection. My chart does not embrace one-fourth of the descendants of John of Ireland; and his posterity does not include one-fourth of the name of Marshall in the United States.

(*h*) Rev. A. B. Marshall, of New Lisbon, Ohio, Rev. Alex. S. Marshall, of Marion, Iowa, and Rev. J. H. Marshall, of Hooker, Pennsylvania, Presbyterian ministers, all hail from Western Pennsylvania; and one of that family, Mr. Oscar S. Marshall, of Kittan-

(10) JOHN MARSHALL.

ing, Pennsylvania, in 1884 published a volume of 245 pages, entitled "The Marshall Family — A History of the Descendants of William Marshall, Born 1722, Died 1796." William Marshall was born in the North of Ireland, of Scotch-Irish parents; removed to Scotland when a youth, and there, about 1748, married Elizabeth Armstrong, a native of that country; and shortly thereafter emigrated to Adams county, Pennsylvania. His children were, 1, John, 2, James, 3, Margaret = McGaughey, 4, William, 5, Archibald, and 6, Samuel Marshall. All found homes in Western Pennsylvania, and their posterity are scattered over the West. They are evidently of the same origin as our family, and claim to be of the same blood. This is manifested by the similarity of names, and a strong personal likeness between them, that has been observed. The two families have never intermarried, and have intermingled but little with each other. The Marshalls of Boston and New York are from England and possess none of the characteristics of the more Southern families.

10 JOHN MARSHALL, a Captain of Cavalry, in the reign of Charles I, of England. He was a zealous supporter of the crown and of the Episcopal church. He was born and reared in Ireland. Having raised a cavalry company, he was one of the first to offer his services to Charles; and from the battle of Edgehill until the imprisonment of his sovereign, he was actively engaged in his support. Unwilling to live under the rule of Cromwell, he removed, with his family, about 1650, to Virginia. Here he was employed in the Indian Wars of the colony; and Campbell, in his history of Virginia, gives him credit for the successful termination of hostilities. He may have had other children, but Thomas (11) is the only one whose name has been handed down to us. Capt. John is not mentioned in any of the official records of Westmoreland County, that have been preserved; and Col. Green (648), thinks that he died near Dumfries, and that his tomb-stone, as late as a generation ago, marked his grave. My letters sent to officials at Dumfries were not answered. To show that he had other children, I submit the

LINEAGE OF H. L. MARSHALL, OF MOULTON, IOWA.

1. William Marshall, b. in Virginia, and removed at an early day

(11) THOMAS MARSHALL.

to Mason Co., Ky., said his father was a second cousin of Col. Thos. Marshall (16). He had a brother, Humphrey, of Lewis Co., Ky.

2. William Marshall, b. in Mason Co., Ky., removed to Augusta, Ky., and thence to Brown Co., Ohio.

3. H. L. Marshall, now of Moulton, Iowa, but born in Brown Co., Ohio.

Now William, No. 1 above, always claimed that his father, (name not ascertained) was a second cousin of Col. Thomas Marshall (16). Capt. John, of Ireland, was therefore his great-grandfather, and therefore had other children besides his son Thomas. I think also a daughter must have married a Fontleroy, as tradition names her as a great aunt of Col. Thomas Marshall. Mrs. Royall, (290.) in letters to me, dated 1884, refers to her as her mother's great aunt, and as one who held herself above her relatives of our branch.

11 (*a*) THOMAS MARSHALL, son of Captain John Marshall (10), emigrant, was born in eastern Virginia about 1655, d. May —, 1704, in Washington parish, Westmoreland Co., Va. He was a small farmer and a zealous Episcopalian. His will is of record in Westmoreland County, and I subjoin a copy:

In the name of God, Amen! I, Thomas Marshall, of the County of Westmoreland, of Washington parish, carpenter, being very weak, but of perfect memory, thanks be to God for it, doth ordain this my last will and testament, in the manner and form following:

(*b*) First: I give and bequeath my soul into the hands of my Blessed Creator and Redeemer, hoping, through merits of my Blessed Savior, to receive full pardon and remission of all my sins; and my body to the earth, to be decently buried according to the direction of my executor, which hereafter shall be named.

(*c*) Item: I will and ordain that my well beloved wife, Martha Marshall, shall be my full and whole executrix.

(*d*) Item: I will that my estate shall remain in the hands of my wife as long as she remains single; but in case she marries, then, she is to have her lawful share, and the rest to be taken out of her hands, equally to be divided among my children.

(*e*) Item: I will that if my wife marry, that David Brown, Sr., and John Brown be guardians over my children, and to take the estate into their hands, bringing it to appraisement, giving good security to what it is valued, and to pay my children their dues as they become of age.

(*f*) Item: I will that Elizabeth Rosser is to have a heifer, delivered by my wife, called "Whitebelly," to be delivered as soon as I am deceased.

(*g*) Item: I will that my son William Marshall have my planta-

(11) THOMAS MARSHALL.

tion, as soon as he comes of age, to him and his heirs forever, but in case my son William die before he comes of age, or die without issue, then my plantation is to fall to the next heir apparent at law. (*No date.*)
       THOMAS MARSHALL. [SEAL.]
     Witnesses: EDW'D TAYLOR, JOHN OXFORD
Probated May 31, 1704.   and JOHN TAYLOR.

(*h*) The maiden name of Mrs. Martha Marshall is unknown, and William and John are the only children we can trace. John married Elizabeth Markham, and, with them, I begin my chart. William was the father of the celebrated Col. William Marshall of Mecklenburg, who served in the Revolutionary war, and was one of the patriots who, in 1775, promulgated the Declaration of Independence, which served as a model for the Continental Manifesto. The posterity of Col. William Marshall has already been referred to (10) and it may be useful to trace one branch of his posterity.

1. (*i*) Thomas Marshall, = Martha ——, and d. 1704.
2. William, his oldest son, b. about 1685.
3. Col. William Marshall, of Mecklenburg and of the Revolutionary war, = Lucy Goode, of Powhattan Co., Va.
4. (*j*) William J. Marshall, of Henderson, Ky., = 1824, Sarah Lyne Holloway, daughter of John Holloway, and Anne, eldest daughter of William Starling, and Susanna Lyne, of Mecklenburg Co., Va. Mr. Marshall was a planter and banker, and was highly regarded for his integrity and capacity.
5. (*k*) John Holloway Marshall, the oldest child, = Martha E. Hopkins. The second was William J. Marshall, of Henderson; = Lucy Frances Posey, (9 ch). The third was James B. Marshall; = Harriet E. Hickman. The fourth was Lucy A. Marshall; = Leonard H. Lyne.

(*l*) The above are known as the Henderson Marshalls, and are the only branch of Col. William Marshall's family that I can trace. There are hundreds of others, from this source, scattered over the South; but they cannot trace their connection. I will here give the lineages of several who claim a common ancestry with us.

LINEAGE OF DR. J. M. MARSHALL, OF KNOXVILLE, TENN.

(*m*) He writes: My great grand father came from England, and settled on the Eastern shore of Maryland. His sons were: 1, Isaac, 2, Thomas, 3, William, and 4, John. They were all patriot soldiers in the Revolutionary war.

1. (*n*) Isaac, the oldest, = —— Foote, their son.

(11) THOMAS MARSHALL.

2. Joseph Marshall, of North Carolina.
3. Dr. J. M. Marshall, of Knoxville, b. 1821. He names his brothers, 1, John, 2, Eleazer, 3, Theophilus, 4, Henry, and 5, Richard Marshall. He says his grand father (Isaac) was a cousin of the Chief Justice, and claims kin with Thos. F. Marshall (256), Humphrey (88), and Alex. (68).

LINEAGE OF H. D., FINIS E., AND NEAL B. MARSHALL,

bankers, of Unionville, Mo.
1. (o) Dennis Marshall, of Franklin Co., Va.
2. Louis R. Marshall, = in Va., Mary Ann Nance. They removed to Putnam Co., Mo., in 1836.
3. The three sons above named.
They claim to be of our family.

LINEAGE OF J. W. MARSHALL, OF ROMNEY, W. VA.

1. (p) John Marshall, b. about 1730.
2. John L., b. June 29, 1777 -- d. Nov. 6, 1847.
3. John William Marshall, of Romney.

(q) Mr. Marshall is a highly intellectual gentleman, and was much surprised when he ascertained that his relationship with our branch could not be traced. He was reared at the old family seat in Fairfax Co., Va., some ten or twelve miles from Dumfries, and I think the tombstone of John Marshall near Dumfries, is the monument of the first of the above Johns. The records of Westmoreland County show there was a James Marshall, who died about 1730, and his posterity may have settled in Fairfax. This James was probably a son of Thomas, and brother of William and John.

Mr. M. L. Hutt, the gentlemanly clerk of Westmoreland Co., Va., under date of June 11, 1885, among other statements, says:

> The parish records of this county were destroyed in the Revolution — other records date back to 1652. Thomas Marshall is the oldest of that name on record. He purchased of Francis Wright 200 acres of land. No administration was granted on Thos. Marshall's estate. His 200 acres of land fell to his son William. He is the only child mentioned in the will, but he may have had others. William afterward moved to King and Queen County, Va., and he sold the land to John Marshall, perhaps one of his brothers, by deed dated Oct. 23, 1727. I find inventory and appraisement of John Marshall's estate returned and recorded April 22, 1751. Said John Marshall died before August, 1751 (yet the will is dated 1752, No. 12), from the fact that James Berryman, the administrator, signed the inventory of his property about that time; but said inventory and appraisement were not returned and recorded

THE MARSHALL FAMILY. 13

(12) CAPT. JOHN MARSHALL.

until the 22d of April, 1751, as above stated. (Could this have been another John Marshall, son of John, of Ireland, for Thos. Marshall and Elizabeth Marshall were executors of John Marshall of the Forest, No. 12?) I find inventory and apprisement of James Marshall's estate returned and recorded May 3, 1751. (This may have been another son of Thomas, who died 1704). I find John Marshall's inventory and appraisement returned and recorded July 13, 1752. (Above, it is April 22, 1751). John Marshall's will is dated April 1, 1752. (These discrepancies can be reconciled only by supposing two John Marshalls). John Marshall's widow's name was Elizabeth, and she made a deed of gift for 100 acres to Thomas Marshall, dated May 25, 1752. I can find nothing of Capt. John Marshall, emigrant. The records don't date far enough back. The will of Peter McClanahan is dated January, 1775. His children are 1, Peter, 2, Thomas, 3, James, 4, Mary, 5, John — wife not mentioned. John Smith's will is dated January 7, 1771. Children, 1, Edward, 2, Matthew — wife not named. There is no index to the old marriage bonds, and it would be much trouble to look over them.

12 Capt. John Marshall of the "Forest," was born in Westmoreland Co., Va., about the year 1700; d. April, 1752, = about 1722, Elizabeth Markham, b. perhaps in Alexandria, Va., about 1704, d. in Fauquier Co., 1775. Mr. Marshall was a farmer, possessed of a plantation of 1,200 acres on Appomattox (called Mattox) Creek, in Washington Parish, Westmoreland Co., Va. He was a militia captain, and a man of good reputation and influence in his neighborhood. The records of conveyances in Westmoreland County show that in 1728, William Marshall, of King and Queen Co., Va., conveyed to John Marshall, of Westmoreland Co., 1,200 acres on Appomattox Creek, Washington Parish. This may have been the estate known as "The Forest," and may have been devised to William, the oldest son, by his father Thomas (11), as shown by his will. If so, we ascertain that William, the father of Col. William, of Mecklenburg County, was a resident of King and Queen County in 1728. Other records may be here referred to: 1, Louis Markham died in Washington Parish in 1713, and his estate was divided among eight children; 2, In 1732 William Markham, of Hamilton Parish, Prince William Co., conveys 126 acres on Mattox Creek, to John Price; 3, In 1744, John Smith, jr., and Patience, his wife, sell to John Smith, sr., of Westmoreland County, 160 acres adjoining John Marshall; 4, In 1752, Elizabeth Marshall conveys, by deed of gift, to Thomas Marshall (16), 100 acres of the homestead (The

(12) CAPT. JOHN MARSHALL.

Forest) granted her by the will of her husband; 5, Mrs. Marshall, is referred to as "Lizzie Markham, of Curls Neck, daughter of John Markham." See other references under Nos. 10 and 14.

But the most important and valuable document that has been preserved is:

(a) THE WILL OF JOHN MARSHALL OF "THE FOREST."

The last Will and Testament of John Marshall: Being very sick and weak, but of perfect mind and memory, I first give and recommend my soul to God that gave it, and my body to the ground to be buried in Christianlike and decent manner, at the discretion of my executor, hereinafter mentioned.

(b) Item: I give and bequeath unto my beloved daughter, Sarah Lovell, one negro girl named Rachael, now in possession of Robert Lovell.
Item: I give and bequeath unto my beloved daughter, Ann Smith, one negro boy named Daniel, now in possession of Augustine Smith.
Item: I give and bequeath unto my beloved daughter, Lizzie Smith, one negro boy named Will, now in possession of John Smith.
(c) Item: I give and bequeath unto my well-beloved wife, Elizabeth Marshall, one negro fellow named Joe, and one negro woman named ———, and one negro woman ———, after delivering the next child born of her body, to my son John; until which time she shall remain in the possession of my wife. Likewise I leave my corn and meat to remain for the use of my wife and children. Also I give and bequeath unto my wife one grey mare named "Beauty," and a side-saddle; also six hogs; also I leave her the use of my land during her widowhood, and afterward to fall to my son, Thomas Marshall, and his heirs forever.
Item: I leave my tobacco to pay my debts, and, if any be over, for the clothing of my small children.
(d) Item: I give and bequeath unto my well-beloved son, Thomas Marshall, one negro woman named Hannah, and one negro child named Jacob.
Item: I give and bequeath unto my well-beloved son, John Marshall, one negro fellow named George, and one negro child named Nan.
Item: I give and bequeath unto my well-beloved son, William Marshall, one negro woman named Sall, and one negro boy named Hannibal, to remain in the possession of his mother until he becomes of age of twenty years.
(e) Item: I give and bequeath unto my beloved son, Abraham Marshall, one negro man named Jim, and one negro girl named Bett, to remain in the possession of his mother until he comes to the age of twenty years.
Item: I give and bequeath unto my beloved daughter, Mary Marshall, one negro girl named Kate, and one negro boy, Gus, to remain in possession of her mother until she comes to the age of eighteen years, or until marriage.
Item: I give and bequeath unto my beloved daughter, Peggy Marshall, one negro boy named Joshua, and one negro girl named Liz, to remain in possession of her mother until she comes to the age of eighteen, or until marriage.
(f) Item: I leave my personal estate, except the legacies above mentioned, to be equally divided between my wife and six children above mentioned. (Perhaps his six unmarried children.)

(12) CAPT. JOHN MARSHALL.

Item: I constitute my wife and my two sons, Thomas Marshall and John Marshall, executors of this, my last will and testament.
In witness hereof I hereunto set my hand and seal this 1st day of April, 1752.   JOHN MARSHALL,
Interlined before signing.   [SEAL.]
BENJAMIN ROLLINS, WILLIAM HOUSTON,
AUGUSTINE SMITH, *witnesses.*
Probated May 26, 1752, and Eliza, his relict, and Thomas Marshall qualified as executors.

(*g*) I am indebted to Col. Marshall J. Smith (492), of New Orleans, for a copy of the foregoing will, and for many other favors. The will has proved of great value in determining the names and ages of the children, and in establishing dates. Among the papers left by Mary Isham Colston [Thomas] (164), a genealogical chart was found, of which I have a copy. The children of John Marshall of the "Forest" are named in the order of the will; but Abraham is called Markham; Ann is called Nancy; Lizzie is called Elizabeth, and Peggy is called Margaret. The latter is said to have married —— Smellan.

(*h*) The wife of John Marshall of the Forest was Elizabeth, daughter of John Markham. Tradition has gone wild over the career of John Markham One legend makes him a British peer, another calls him a pirate, a third insists upon his being the buccaneer Blackbeard, but all authority agree in pronouncing him a handsome, dashing and fascinating gentleman, and a daring, cruel and adroit villain. Here again Col. Thomas M. Green (648) shows his skill and power in interpreting traditions, and in deciphering legends. He writes:

There lived near the family, a John Markham, an Englishman with a peculiar history. He was by birth a gentleman, as the term is used in England, and of mixed Anglo-Saxon lineage,—had been an officer in the British Navy, had killed his captain in a duel in the West Indies, and had taken refuge in Virginia, where he had engaged in mercantile pursuits, and had married the widow of a merchant, much older than himself, by whom he had no children, but of whose whole property he managed to obtain possession. His wife died, and he returned to England, sold a small inherited estate which had come down to him from Anglo-Saxon ancestors, who had owned it before the conquest, for which one of his descendants used to say he ought to have been hung, and eloped with and married a young English girl, with whom he returned to Virginia, and by whom he had seventeen daughters and one son. A shrewd, money-getting, out-breaking, lawless, self-witted, large-brained, devil-defying man was this John Markham, if all accounts of him be true, respecting neither God nor man, and fearing neither; and every now and then there breaks out in his race the genuine Markham streak. His son, named John, gobbled up all the paternal estate, and was the father of Commodore James Markham, a distinguished officer of the

(11) CAPT. JOHN MARSHALL.

Virginia Navy during the Revolution. One of the first John Markham's seventeen daughters was the grandmother of the late T. Daviess Carneal, well known in Cincinnati and throughout central Kentucky. Another was the ancestress of Major McRae, formerly Commandant of the Barracks at Newport; of George McRae, of Mississippi, and of the family of that name, of South Carolina. One of the youngest, Elizabeth, married Captain John Marshall.

Mrs. Elizabeth Marshall was living October 15, 1773, for her deed of gift of a negro woman, so dated, is of record in Warrenton, Fauquier Co., Va. She styles herself Elizabeth Marshall of Leeds Manor.

In her latter days, Mrs. Eliza Colston (52), often dwelt on the traditions of the family, and one who, in his early life, sat at her feet, relates:

THE LEGEND OF MARKHAM, OR BLACKBEARD.

(*j*) Blackbeard's correct name was Finch. The scene of his piratical career was the American coast and the West Indies, and the time was the early quarter of the eighteenth century.

Prior to the death of Blackbeard, there lived in Alexandria, Va., a merchant, who had acquired a large fortune by trade. He was a married man, and he and his wife were elderly people. In their employ was a young man named John Markham. The old merchant died, and his widow inherited all his property. Markham persuaded her to marry him, and he thus acquired a large fortune Sometime after the marriage, his business called him to England. The handsome, but unprincipled young man, here met a beautiful young lady, attending a boarding school, and prevailed on her to elope with him, and a mock marriage was imposed on her. On their arrival, the imposition was exposed, and great sympathy was expressed for the lovely girl. Regarding her as free, a gentleman proposed honorable marriage to her. Markham was incensed, and challenged and killed him. His real wife was greatly mortified, and soon died. Markham claimed and appropriated her whole estate, which he had not already squandered. He was now legally married to the young English girl, and a large family of children was born to them. But Markham died, and the widow found herself immensely wealthy. Her beauty was only matured, and her gayety made her a leader in society.

(*k*) At this time there appeared in Alexandria a handsome young Englishman, wearing a rich naval uniform. He seemed to have an abundance of money, and had the address to recommend himself to the good graces of the blooming widow. Infatuated with him, the widow married him, and placed all her fortune under his control. When their honeymoon was ended, and the adventurer had possessed himself of all her property, he threw off restraint, and introduced into her house a set of rough and desperate companions, and made it the scene of boisterous revels. When his wife remonstrated, he struck her, and treated her with brutal contempt. Her children were purposely sent away, or, frightened by the disorderly conduct beneath their mother's roof, fled to Westmoreland County and found protection, from her uncles, William and Lewis. Elizabeth found a home with the widow of Thomas Marshall. She had been finely educated, and possessed not only beauty,

(14) ANN MARSHALL.—[Smith.]

but the highest accomplishments of the day. Her mother now discovered that she had married Blackbeard, the notorious buccaneer. When his identity was exposed, he gathered all and hastily departed to his ship. But female constancy clings to the most brutal and abandoned of husbands. She was often present at his orgies, and on one occasion, when two villains intended to assassinate Blackbeard, and were seated at table, one on his right and the other on his left, she held two pistols beneath the table, and drawing a trigger with each hand at the same moment, the miscreants fell dead at the feet of her unworthy lord. But the ungrateful husband is said to have treated her with such cruelty that she died from the effects of a kick given her in one of his revels. But Blackbeard did not long survive his wife. Lieut. Maynard outwitted him on the North Carolina coast, and his riddled body, hung in chains, was suspended at Williamsburg as a warning to outlaws.

(*l*) I find no mention of John Markham in the records of Westmoreland, but names of William and Lewis frequently appear. This confirms the tradition that John Markham lived in Alexandria, while his brothers resided in Westmoreland County. I have a copy of the will of Lewis Markham, from the records of Westmoreland. He describes himself as of the Parish of Washington, and his plantation on Mattox Creek is given to his widow, Eliza Markham. He refers to his eight minor children, but names none of them. He appoints his widow and Joseph Bayly his executors. It is dated March 15, 1713, and probated June 24, 1713. His personal estate was appraised at £709.

13 SARAH MARSHALL, b. in Washington parish, Westmoreland Co., Va., about the year 1723;=about 1743, ROBERT LOVELL. It is not known what became of this family. The names appear in the will of John Marshall, of the "Forest," (12) and Mrs. Mary I. Colston (Thomas), No. 164, makes Sarah Lovell the oldest child of John and Elizabeth Marshall.

The will of Robert Lovell, Sr., doubtless the father of the husband of Sarah Marshall, is of record in Westmoreland County. It is dated Jan. 15, 1725; probated Feb. 23, 1725; enumerates his children: 1, Elizabeth Lovell=Nicholson, 2, Mary=Harrison, 3, Robert, 4, Daniel, 5 James and 6 Ursula.

14 ANN (or Nancy) MARSHALL, b. in Washington parish, Westmoreland Co., Va., about 1725=about 1745, AUGUSTINE SMITH of the same locality, d. in Fauquier Co., about 1781. Augustine Smith's name appears as one of the witnesses to the will

(14) ANN (or *Nancy*) MARSHALL.—[*Smith*.]

of John Marshall, of the Forest (12), and the will itself virtually names him as the husband of Ann Marshall. After the death of John of the "Forest," in 1752, the Smith's, with Thomas Marshall (11), appear to have removed to the vicinity of Germantown, Fauquier Co., Va. Their property in Westmoreland was disposed of, and land was purchased in Fauquier Co. Mrs. Elizabeth Marshall went with them, and perhaps lived to the beginning of the war. Augustine and John Smith (14 and 15) are supposed to have been brothers, the sons of John Smith, Sr., a native of Bristol, England. He came to Virginia about 1700 and settled on Mattox Creek, Westmoreland County, near to Thomas Marshall. He married Mary Ann Adkins, a relative of the Washington family, of Westmoreland, and from the Washingtons the name, Augustine, was derived. The records of Westmoreland show: 1. In 1723 a Mr. Thompson sells to John Smith land in Washington parish near John Marshall's; 2, In 1735, John Smith sells Triplett a tract on Mattox Creek; 3, In 1743, Thomas Smith of Orange Co., Va., sells to John Smith 200 acres on Mattox Creek; 4, In 1744, John Smith, Jr., and Patience his wife, of Prince William County, sell to John Smith, Sr., of Westmoreland County, 160 acres adjoining John Marshall; 5, In 1752 Hornbuckle sells to John Smith 200 acres in Washington parish. · By the kindness of Col. Marshall J. Smith (492), I am able to present the following:

WILL OF THE FIRST JOHN SMITH.

(*a*) John Smith's will and testament is as follows: I give unto my son Thomas, my land which I now live upon, to him and his heirs and assigns forever. And I give my land which I bought of William Thompson to my son John, to him and his assigns; and in case my son John should die before he comes of lawful age, the land to fall to my son Augustine. Also I give unto my son Thomas a gun and a cow which he calls his. And all the rest of my estate, I give unto my wife Mary, during her widowhood, and then to be equally divided amongst my children. Also I leave my wife Mary and my son Thomas my whole and sole executors. Hereunto I set my hand and fix my seal.

Attest SAMUEL THORNBERRY,   JOHN SMITH; [seal].
       JOHN POPE,
       MARGARET MORRIS.
Probated Aug. 25, 1725.

THE MARSHALL FAMILY.   19

(16) COL. THOMAS MARSHALL.

15 ELIZABETH (*or Lizzie*) MARSHALL, b. in Washington parish, Westmoreland County, Va., about 1727;=about 1747, JOHN SMITH, brother of Augustine Smith, (14) to whose sketch reference is made. John is said to have died in 1783. The following passage of a letter from M. L. Hutt, Dept. Clerk of Westmoreland County, to Col. Marshall J. Smith, dated Aug. 22, 1883, will throw some light on the Smith records:

"I enclose you memorandums of all I can find on the deed-books in this office. They date from 1652. I do not see the names of Mary Ann Adkins, nor of Broadwater, mentioned in the books at all. The name of Fontleroy, just appears in deed-book of 1772. I think they were Richmond County people. The Turners are mentioned only once, in the will-books, though often in the deed-books. In Thomas Turner's will he leaves his farm, "Smith's Mount" to his son Harry Smith Turner, and afterwards H. S. Turner deeds a portion of it to Fontleroy. The Turner family still own the farm. The John Smith mentioned in memorandum 1723, was the father of Thomas, John and Augustine. We have no marriage records nor bonds to show to whom he was married. Probably the marriages at that time were recorded in the church registers, none of which are now in existence in this county."

Lizzie Marshall and John Smith are said to have raised three daughters and one son Mrs. Judith Keith, of Warrensburg, is one of their great-grand daughters.

16 (*a*) COL. THOMAS MARSHALL was b. in Washington parish, Westmoreland Co., Va., April 2, 1730; —d. in Washington, Mason Co., Ky., June 22, 1802;= 1754 in Fauquier Co., Va., MARY RANDOLPH KEITH, b. in Fauquier Co., Va., April 28, 1737; —d. Mason Co., Ky., Sept. 19, 1809.

Col. Marshall is regarded by his posterity with veneration. In sound judgment and depth of native mind he is said to have surpassed all his illustrous children. They, themselves, admitted his superiority of intellect. His posterity are thought to have inherited their mental powers rather from the Markhams and the Marshalls, than from the Keiths.

Col. Marshall is said to have attended, with George Washington, the school of Rev. Archibald Campbell, rector of Washington parish. Here commenced the intimate friendship that continued through life, between Col. Marshall, and the great apostle of liberty. Well instructed and experienced in the surveyors art, he often attended Washington in his surveying excursions for Lord Fairfax

(16) COL. THOMAS MARSHALL.

and others. For these services he received several thousand acres of wild land in Henry Co., W. Va., which were sold and divided among his heirs, as provided in his will. During the French war, he was a Lieutenant of Volunteers. He was not at Braddock's defeat, because he was left behind, employed in building Fort Necessity. His father died in April 1752, and Mr. Marshall, being the oldest son and the heir, qualified as his executor. His brother John, though also appointed an executor, was too young to serve. Shortly after the death of John Marshall of the "Forest," the Marshalls, with their relatives, the Smiths, removed to the vicinity of Germantown, Fauquier Co., Va. Here Thomas accepted the agency, of Lord Fairfax, to superintend his immense landed estate, — to make leases, collect rents, &c. In 1754, he married Mary Isham Keith, daughter of Rev. James Keith and Mary Randolph. Near Germantown his older children were born. In 1765, eleven years after his marriage, he purchased of Thos. L. and R. H. Lee, 350 acres of land on Goose Creek, and removed upon it. His old log house still stands a mile north-east of Markham. In 1773, he sold his farm; and it was, perhaps, at this time that he purchased "Oakhill," or, as he calls it in his will, "The Oaks." Here he built a fine house of wood, which still remains (150). All his younger children were born here. His mother had attended him in all his removals. A little later she disappears, and it is probable she was laid in the graveyard near Germantown, known as "Locust Leavel," where the Marshalls, Keiths and Smiths buried their dead. In 1767, while residing on Goose Creek, he was High Sheriff of Fauquier County. His bond as such still appears of record.

(b) When the war broke out, Col. Marshall was already prepared for it. He was one of that band of early patriots which had resolved to resist the encroachments of the British Crown, at the hazard of all that is dear to man. Their heroic spirit manifested itself in raising a patriotic company known as the Culpepper Minute Men. This was the earliest organization in the cause of freedom. When formed into a regiment under command of Col. Woodford, Capt. Marshall became Major. Major Marshall's esteem for his superior officer was afterwards shown, and his influence manifested, by the County of his residence, in Kentucky, being called Woodford. Major Marshall distinguished himself at the

(16) COL. THOMAS MARSHALL.

battle of the Great Bridge—the first engagement on Virginia's soil. He was frequently elected to the Virginia House of Burgesses, and was a member of the convention that declared the colony independent. He was at Valley Forge, with his sons, John and Thomas. At the battle of Germantown, when Gen. Mercer was killed, he succeeded to the command. A horse was killed under him at Brandywine. Referring to this occasion, Campbell in his history of Virginia writes:

(c) "The Third Virginia Regiment, under command of Col. Thomas Marshall, which had performed severe duty in 1776, was placed in a wood on the right, and in front of Woodford's Brigade and Stephen's Division. Though attacked by superior numbers, the regiment maintained its position until both its flanks were turned, its ammunition nearly expended, and more than half its officers, and one third of the soldiers were killed or wounded. Col. Marshall, whose horse had received two balls, then retired to assume his position on the right of his division, but it had already retreated. Among the wounded in the battle, were Lafayette and Woodford. The enemy passed the night on the field of battle. On the 26th of September 1777, the British entered Philadelphia."

It has been said that at Brandywine, Col. Marshall saved the patriot army from destruction. For such distinguished services, the House of Burgesses through their speaker, Edmund Randolph, presented him a sword. This heirloom descended to his son Capt. Thomas Marshall (56), who by his will bestowed it on his son, Gen. Thomas Marshall, (176). The latter left no male issue, and, on his death, his daughter, Mrs. Bland (632), presented it to the Maysville, Kentucky Historical Society, which preserves it with care.

d. In 1779 Col. Marshall, with his Third Regiment, was sent to reinforce Gen. Lincoln, in South Carolina. He joined Lincoln just in time to be shut up with him in Charleston; and to share in the surrender of that city to the British. But having been parolled, Col. Marshall, with other officers, visited Kentucky in 1780, traveling on horseback through the wilderness. On that trip he located his beautiful farm of "Buckpond," near Versailles.

About the year 1780, Col. Marshall was appointed Surveyor-General of the lands in Kentucky, appropriated to the officers and soldiers of the Virginia State line. The whole territory consisted of

(16) COL. THOMAS MARSHALL.

but one county, known as the County of Kentucky. Nov. 1, 1781 it was divided into three counties — Fayette, Lincoln and Jefferson, and Col. Marshall was made Surveyor of the first. His name appears among the purchases of lots in Lexington, in 1783. In 1785, Col. Marshall returned to Virginia for his family, which he brought west on a flat-boat, down the Ohio river. McClung in his "*Western Adventure*," details the incidents of this trip; which was attended with no trouble, though the voyagers were warned by James Girty, the renegade, of the danger of being decoyed ashore.

In 1787, Col. Marshall represented Fayette County in the Virginia Legislature, and in 1788 was elected to the Danville Convention, to form a State Constitution. He was a zealous Federalist, took an active part in the politics of the day, and was decided in his opposition to the scheme of separating Kentucky from the Eastern States.

(e) In 1795, one of his favorite daughters, Lucy Ambler, died at Jamestown, Va. He was deeply affected by this event, and in a letter to his son, John Marshall, dated Buckpond, Ky., Nov. 6, 1795, he pours forth his sorrows. It shows that, at that time, he held the office of Collector of United States revenue for the State. He writes:

"The death of our dear Lucy is a heavy affliction — perhaps the more so on account of its being the first of the kind which has been felt by your mother and myself. I endeavor to forget it. I have not mentioned her name twice since your letter announced the unfortunate event. But alas, I frequently find myself sighing and moaning on account of her death, without realizing what I am grieving for. But why am I describing my affliction to you who must have felt the same more than once in all its bitterness. God send we feel it no more! Your sister Molly [Mrs. Humphrey Marshall], who had a long fit of illness, I believe knows nothing of our loss as yet. We were afraid to make it known to her. Make our kindest compliments of condolence to Mr. Ambler. I feel for him sensibly, and make not the least doubt but he has his share of the affliction; but no person's can be equal to that of an affectionate father and mother, for the loss of a daughter who never till now was the cause of one painful sensation in the breast of either. Tell Mr. Ambler that we have the firmest confidence in his parental tenderness for the little son, the dear deceased has left with him. Tell him above all to be careful of its health and education — to be careful to sow the seed of virtue and honor early in its breast — to make it virtuous rather than learned, if he can't make it both. That part of what fortune I possess, which I intended for her, I shall leave to him; rather as acknowledgement of parental love and affection, than as an addition to his estate.

(f) We are informed that you are appointed Attorney General for the United States, and that you have accepted the office. Now I

(16) COL. THOMAS MARSHALL.

hope we may be informed why we have no Attorney in this State for the United States. I have complained of this in every letter I have written on the subject of revenue. I cannot possibly have the revenue collected, as no one will comply with the laws without compulsion, and the government has not put it in my power to compel compliance. This I have tried, but without success. What I can do, I know not. I should think that in the present situation of affairs there might be political reasons assigned for the neglect. But if that be the case, why am I repeatedly written to by the Commissioner of Revenue, as if it was expected that I could go on with the business in the same manner as if there were no impediment, &c.

(*g*) From 1780 to 1800, Col. Marshall's home was "Buckpond," one of the most lovely farms in the State of Kentucky. In 1800 his youngest son, Louis, was married to Miss Agatha Smith, and "Buckpond" was given to them. The old people went to live with their son, Thomas, who resided at Washington, Mason Co., Ky. Here June 22, 1802, Mr. Marshall died, and was buried on "The Hill." The inscription on his tomb is now illegible; but, many years ago, I transcribed it, and here reproduce it

"THOMAS MARSHALL, to whom this memorial is inscribed, was born the 2d of April, 1730, intermarried with Mary Keith, in her 17th year, by whom he had fifteen children, who attained maturity; and after distinguishing himself by the performance of his duties as a husband, father, citizen and soldier, died on the 22d of June, 1802, aged 72 years 2 months and 20 days."

(*h*) Col. Marshall's will was executed June 26, 1798, in Woodford Co., Ky., and is found of record in Mason Co., Book B, p. 212. It was probated February 15, 1803. The following is an abstract of its provisions. He gives:

To his son, John: The "Oaks," in Fauquier Co., Va.; two tracts on the Licking, one of which contained 1,000 acres, and the quantity of the other is not stated.

To his son, Thomas: Part of a tract of 14,717 acres, on Clark's run, in Mason Co., and 1,000 acres elsewhere.

To his son, James M.: 6,000 acres from a survey of 15,000 on the North fork of Licking.

To his sons, Charles and William: 13,616 acres on the South side of the North fork.

To his son, Alex. K.: 10,500 acres on Mill creek; 1,800 acres on the Ohio, above the mouth of Salt creek, and 200 acres more at the mouth of Salt creek, and some other lands and three negroes.

To his son, Louis: "Buckpond," containing 575 acres, with the stock thereon, and one-third of my negroes, after the death of my wife. Also a tract adjoining Fitzpatrick's, and my certificates for military services.

(*i*) To Elizabeth Colston: My part of a survey near the Yellowbanks.

To Mary Anne Marshall: 500 acres adjoining Crittenden's preemption; also 400 acres on the Ohio, at the mouth of Hardin creek, and some military lands.

(16) COL. THOMAS MARSHALL.

To Judith Brooke: One-third of my land on the Kentucky river, at the mouth of Gilbert's creek; also one-half of 1,500 acres on the North fork and Cabin creek; also two negroes.
To Thomas Ambler: 3,816 acres on Johnson's fork, and 4,000 acres South of the Licking.
To Susanna McClung: The Blue Spring tract of 2,000 acres, one-third of the Bullitt tract, and four negroes.
To Charlotte Duke: One-third of 2,800 acres in Mason County, Ky.; 500 acres elsewhere, and one negro.
To Jane Taylor: One-third of 8,200 acres, and one-third of my Gilbert creek lands on the Kentucky river, and one-third of my slaves after my wife's death.
(*j*) To Nancy Marshall: The residue of my Ohio lands; the remaining third of my Gilbert creek lands, and one-third of my slaves after my wife's death.
To Elizabeth Colston: 500 acres as a token of my remembrance for her dutiful assistance in raising and supporting my younger children.
To my wife for life: My slaves.
The remainder of his lands are given to his executors, Thomas, Alex. K., and Humphrey Marshall, in trust that they shall sell the same, and make my children equal; and their compensation is to be settled by my son John.
August 8, 1803, the three executors qualified.

(*k*) The wife of Thomas Marshall was Mary Randolph Keith, daughter of Parson James Keith, and Mary Isham Randolph.

The Keiths are descended from Robert Keith, Mareschal of the Scottish army under Bruce. George Keith, born at Kincardine, Scotland, in 1685—died near Potsdam, Prussia, May 25, 1778, was the tenth and last Earl that bore the name. His race had been long Mareschals of Scotland, and were possessed of large estates. The family were adherents of the Stuarts, and took an active part in the Rebellion of 1715, in favor of the Pretender. Alexander, and James afterward Field Marshal of Russia and Prussia, were younger brothers of the Earl. James Keith, afterward known as Parson Keith, a cousin of the Earl, was a son of a professor in the Mareschal College of Aberdeen. The professor was Bishop of the Episcopal church, and the uncle and guardian of the Earl and his brothers. His son James (the Parson) had been educated with his cousins, and in 1715 was a youth of nineteen. The Earl and his brothers took part in the rebellion, and had to leave for the continent. Here, through their cousin James, they still fomented discontent, and in 1719 entered Scotland, and were repulsed. Their secret correspondence with their friends had been conducted through their cousin, James, and he when discovered took refuge in the Colony of Virginia. The Keith estates were confiscated, and their names attainted for treason;

(16) COL. THOMAS MARSHALL.

but afterward, through the solicitations of Frederick of Prussia, a portion of the property was restored. The titles descended in the female line, and are now merged in the united houses of Keith-Elphinstone.

(*l*) James (Parson) Keith, had been educated for the Church. Coming to Virginia, he settled in Fauquier County, and married Mary Isham Randolph, daughter of Thomas Randolph, of Tuckahoe, the second son of William Randolph, of Turkey Island. She was therefore, closely related to John Randolph, of Roanoke, to Thomas Jefferson, and to Richard Henry Lee. Stories are told of this lady that need confirmation. She is said to have first secretly married a subaltern in the British army, and when her marriage and hiding place were discovered, her husband and child were murdered by her brothers. It is charged that her marriage to Parson Keith was concealed from her brothers, and that she stole away to accompany her husband, when he returned to Scotland for orders. Even the name of Parson Keith is blackened by tradition with the charge of licentiousness. But there is better reason to believe that he was a good and holy man. He continued to preach throughout his life, and his name is handed down with veneration. Bishop Meade, vol. 2, p. 216, thus speaks of him:

Of Rev. Mr. Keith and his descendants I have not been able to obtain all the information I desire, or hope for. From all that I can learn, he was a worthy man. He was a native of Scotland. Being involved in the Rebellion in favor of the Pretender, he was forced to fly his country, and to come to Virginia. Returning to England for orders, he was settled in Hamilton parish, and performed the duties of his office there for a long time—probably until 1757 or 1758. A daughter married Col. Thomas Marshall, of "Oakhill," Fauquier County, the seat of the Marshalls to this day (1857).

(*n*) Mrs. Keith long survived her husband, and her wierd form and the wild expression of her eyes, gave color to the ghostly stories told of her. But in her old age she was doubtless deranged.

LEGEND OF THE RANDOLPHS.

The story is told that when Mary Isham Randolph was blooming into womanhood, she was induced by the bailiff upon the estate of Tuckahoe to elope with him. There was great excitement among the family and neighbors, and threats were freely made by the brothers. Some years ago, the Diary of Col. Byrd, who lived at about the period referred to, was published in the *Southern Literary Messenger*, and he records the excitement in the family of the Randolphs, on the occasion of the elopement of one of the daughters. The search for the fugitives for a time was fruitless. At length their retreat was discovered on Elk

THE MARSHALL FAMILY.

(16) COL. THOMAS MARSHALL.

Island, in James river. The angry brothers came upon them by night, murdered the bailiff and the child, and brought their sister home. The deed of blood and cruelty so affected the wife and mother that she became deranged. But care was taken that no allusion should be made to the harrowing scenes she had witnessed, and her reason was at length restored.

(o) Years passed. Mary Randolph married Parson James Keith. A family of children had grown up around them. The tragedy at Elk Island had been forgotten. The bailiff was supposed to be dead. But, one day Mrs. Keith received a letter, and, on opening it, found that it purported to be from the bailiff. It stated that he still lived; that he that was left as dead, had revived, had changed his name, and had fled to foreign countries; after years of wandering had returned to look upon his lawful wife; had found her married and happy; that he would not afflict her by claiming her as his own, but advised her to be happy and forget him, who had more than died for her love, for she should hear no more of him. This letter was perhaps written by some evil-disposed person, or may have been only a practical joke. However that may be, it unhinged the mind of Mrs. Keith. She vainly sought for him, and throughout the remnant of her days her insanity manifested itself by a quiet melancholy, varied by some sudden freak of folly. Mrs. Colston lived with her for many years, and she, and all who met her in her widowhood, testify that she was a lunatic.

THE RANDOLPH FAMILY.

(p) William Randolph is the first of the name who came to Virginia. He possessed Turkey Island, a large estate on the James river. He married Mary Isham, daughter of Henry and Catharine Isham, of Bermuda Hundred, on the opposite side of the James. His children, as far as I have been able to learn, were as follows:

1. William, of Turkey Island, = a Miss Beverly, of Gloucester. He was member of the Council and Treasurer of the Colony.

2. Thomas Randolph, of Tuckahoe, = a Miss Fleming. Their daughter, 1, Mary Isham Randolph, = Parson James Keith.

3. Isham Randolph, of Dungeness, = Miss Rogers, of England; member of the House of Burgesses, 1740, from Goochland, and Adjutant General of the Colony of Virginia.

4. (q) Richard Randolph, of Curls, = Miss Bolling, a descenant of Pocahontas; member of the House of Burgesses, 1740, from Henrico Co., and succeeded his brother as Treasurer. He was grandfather to John Randolph, of Roanoke, b. June 2, 1773, —d. May 24, 1833; several times member of Congress, minister to Russia, &c.

5. Henry Randolph died without issue.

6. Sir John Randolph, of Williamsburg, = Miss Beverly, sister

THE MARSHALL FAMILY. 27

(16) COL. THOMAS MARSHALL.

of his brother William's wife. His son, John, was father of Edmund Randolph, b. August 10, 1753,— d. September 12, 1813. Another son of Sir John was Peyton Randolph, b. 1723, — d. October 22, 1775.

7. Edward Randolph, = Miss Graves, an heiress of England.
8. A Daughter, = Rev. William Yates, of Gloucester.
9. A Daughter, = Rev. Robert Yates.
10. A Daughter, = William Stith, and was mother of the historian of Virginia.

DESCENDANTS OF PARSON JAMES AND MARY I. KEITH.

Their children were: 1, James; 2, John; 3, Thomas; 4, Alexander; 5, Isham; 6, Mary; 7, Elizabeth; 8, Judith.

A 1. JAMES KEITH lived and died in Alexandria, Va. Dr. Anderson Keith, of Augusta, married his youngest daughter. John and James were two of his sons.

2. JOHN KEITH, = a sister of old Dr. Doniphan. Their children were: 1, Thomas, = Judith Key, and left children; 2, Alexander; 3, Peyton; 4, Anderson (above), = 1st, Doniphan; 2d, = George; 3d, = Catherine Keith; 5, George Keith, = McCoy. John Keith also had three daughters.

3. THOMAS, lived in Virginia.
4. ALEXANDER, lived in Fauquier Co., Va.
5. ISHAM, lived in Fauquier Co., Va.
6. MARY RANDOLPH KEITH, = THOMAS MARSHALL (16).
7. ELIZABETH KEITH = Edward Ford, and lived in Bourbon Co., Ky. Issue: 1, Jane Ford, = Thomas Clarke, father of Edward Clarke, of Platte Co., Mo.; 2, Priscilla Ford, = Sangster; 3, Judith Ford, = Simpson; 4, Mary Ford, = Thos.
(r) Winn; 5, Hettie Ford, = Ashmore; 6, Elizabeth Ford, = Clifton Thompson; 7, Susan Ford, = Jas. Rogers; 8, William Ford; 9, James Ford; 10, Thos. Ford; 11, Edward Ford; 12, Chas. Ford; 13, John Ford. Eleven of them lived to be over eighty.
8. JUDITH KEITH, = James Key, and their children were as follows:

(16) COL. THOMAS MARSHALL.

B 1. James Key = Nancy Ireland. They lived in Westmoreland Co., Pa., until 1789, when they removed to Mason Co., Ky. Their children: 1, Judith (now living in Washington, Ky.); 2, Peyton = Rankin, and had two children: 1, James; 2, William.

2. Thomas Key, = Foley. They removed from Westmoreland Co., Pa., to Mason Co., Ky. Issue: 1, Isham; 2, Louisa, = a Thompson, and left two children, Thomas and Sally; 3, Peyton Key, = a Miss Leonard, and has six children: Belle, Anna, Helen, Martha, Richard, Thomas; 4, Thomas Key; 5, Marshall Key, b. 1799, d. 1877, = Carter, and had two children: Martha and Louisa; 6, John Key, = Bullock, and have six children: Lewis, Taliaferro, John, Richard, Mary and Sally. The 7th child of Thomas Key was Richard Key.

3. Alexander Key, = Dawson. Issue: 1, Nancy, who married Shopestate.

4. Judith Key, = Thomas Keith, son of John Keith. Issue: 1, Mary, 2. Susan, 3, James, 4, John, 5, Eliza, 6, Judith, 7, Louisa, 8, Peyton, 9, Harriet. Of these, Mary = Applegate, and after his death, Ginn; Susan = James Claybroke, and her daughter married Bazil Owens; John = Cox; Eliza = Darius Berry; Louisa = Alex. Keith, son of Alex. Keith, of Virginia. Issue: 1, Mary, 2, Thomas, 3, Harriet, 4, Judith, 5, Charlotte Keith.

(s)

5. Peyton (Uncle Peyton) Key, b. in Fauquier Co., Va., January 19, 1776, d. in Washington, Ky., September 19, 1873, in his 98th year He came to Mason Co., Ky, in 1793; in 1803, went to New Orleans, on a flat-boat; was Deputy Sheriff of Fleming County, under William Kennan; served in Capt. Ben. Bayless' company of Kentucky militia in the war of 1812; was at the Battle of the Thames: was a book-keeper in the old Washington, Ky., Bank of Kentucky; farmed for his brother, Marshall Key, for a number of years. His memory was remarkable, and he was often called upon to testify of early times in Kentucky.

(16) COL. THOMAS. MARSHALL.

6. Marshall Key, = Harriet Selman. He died November 16, 1860, in Louisville, Ky. He was born in Fauquier Co., Va., September 8, 1783; removed with his father to Kentucky, 1795. He was for many years Clerk of Mason Co., Ky.; was highly regarded for his hospitality and public spirit. His children were:

1. John James Key, now a distinguished lawyer of Washington City, = Mary Reid, who died childless; = 2d, Miss Rudd, by whom he has two daughters and one son. In 1884 I enjoyed their lavish hospitality.
2. Thomas Key, who was an eminent jurist of Cincinnati, O. Dead.
3. (t) Harriet Key, = Dr. Palmer, and died, leaving, 1, Harriet Palmer, 2, Robert, 3, Marshall.
4. Lizzie Key, now dead, = Hon Thos. Nelson, of Indiana, member of Congress, minister to Mexico, etc. Their children are: 1, Mary, 2, Harriet, 3, Marshall, 4, Lizzie. Mary, = Hannigan; Harriet, = Edward Ashwin, and lives in Brooklyn.
5. Marshall Key, an eminent lawyer of Council Bluffs, Iowa. Died 1884.

Several portraits of Mary R. Keith (Marhsall), are preserved. Miss Mollie Marshall (658), of Washington, Ky., has the likeness preserved by the old lady herself. Mrs. Bullitt (2234), of Louisville, Ky., has the portrait possessed by her grandfather, Dr. Louis Marshall; and Mrs. Alice Carroll, of Leeds, has the third heirloom, handed down from her grandfather, Judge John Marshall. I know of no likeness of Col. Thos. Marshall. The three likenesses of Mrs. Marshall are alike, and represent her dressed with a cap, in the style of an old lady of her generation. Doubtless, the portraits were taken after the death of her husband, or his likeness would have accompanied them.

It was my purpose, when I commenced this work, to eschew all legends, but I find —

'Tis better the past be embellished with story,
Of maiden and lover, or hero and glory,
Than left a dark void which the fancy may fill,
With fiends to affright us, or monsters to kill.

(16) COL. THOMAS MARSHALL.

Then list to my legend:

THE KEITH LEGEND.

(*u*) James Keith (the Parson) was educated at the Mareschal College, at Aberdeen, Scotland. Though a divinity student, yet he was tainted with infidelity, like most of the youth of his day. He had an intimate associate and fellow student, named William Frazier, who also doubted the truth of the Bible, and a state of future rewards and punishments. These youths often talked upon religious topics. In full confidence in each other, they often expressed their doubts. Though they had Moses and the Prophets, yet they thought that if one should return to them from the dead, they would believe. They therefore made to each other the solemn pledge, that he that died first would return to the other and impart the truth or falsity of the Bible. This compact was written and sealed in their own blood.

Years past, and the young men went to opposite extremities of the earth. Keith went to America and Frazier to India. Keith had taken orders in the Episcopal Church. His doubts, however, had not been wholly removed, and his life was not consistent with his professions. In his family was a white servant named McLeod. She attended to the dairy. One evening, after the Parson had grown old, while Mrs. McLeod was employed at her usual duties, a stranger, in military garb, appeared before her and said that he was the spirit of William Frazier, who had just died in India, and who in early life had been the companion of Mr. Keith. He told of the compact, and ordered her to tell her master that the Christian religion was true, and that there was a state of future rewards and punishments. She was further to state that her master would live but one year, and that he should at once prepare for death. The woman was alarmed, and being afraid of her master, failed to make the report as required. The next evening the soldier appeared again, and severely threatening her, exacted a promise that she would tell her master. When Parson Keith heard the story from Mrs. McLeod, and had the description of the man, he was convinced of the reality of the apparition, and was satisfied of the truth of the Bible. He set on foot inquiries for William Frazier, and found that he had died in India only a few days prior to his appearance in America. He changed his mode of life, became an exemplary Christian, and died one year after the apparition.

(*v*) This tradition is supported by the credence of all the older members of the family, and is corroborated by the fact that the McLeod family, of Baltimore, have a record of it in their possession. In 1868, two descendants of Mrs. McLeod came to Kentucky, from Maryland, to confer with Martin P. Marshall and Col. Charles A. Marshall, both of Washington, Ky. They represented that they were descended from Mrs. McLeod, and that their ancestress was an heir to estates in Scotland, and they were in search of evidence to establish their claim. They represented that her Bible was still an heirloom, and reference was there made to the same story. This confirmation of the old legend caused surprise to all parties.

Whether this story may be entitled to our respect or not, it is strange that no descendant of Parson Keith that I have ever known or heard of, has more than temporarily denied the truth of Christian revelation. Dr. Louis Marshall and J. A. McClung, for a time, had their doubts, but both devoted their last years to the Redeemer. Senator Humprey Marshall had no Keith blood in his veins. His wife was a pious believer.

(16) COL. THOMAS MARSHALL.

ARE THE KEITHS DESCENDED FROM POCAHONTAS?

(w) I shall not take sides in the controversy over this question, but shall content myself with presenting the issue. The Randolph lineage has just been stated. The line of Pocahontas is as follows:
1. Pocahontas = John Rolfe.
2. Thomas Rolfe = Miss Poythress.
3. Jane Rolfe = Col. Robert Bolling.
4. Major John Bolling = Miss Blair. Their dr.:
   1. Mary Bolling = Jan. 20, 1727, COL. JOHN FLEMING.
     1. A daughter, Judith = Thomas Randolph, of Curls.
       1. Mary Isham Randolph = Rev. James Keith.
         1. MARY RANDOLPH KEITH = COL. THOMAS MARSHALL.

If this genealogy is correct, the Keiths and Marshalls are *tainted* with Indian blood. It is denied that Thomas Randolph married a Fleming, but confidently asserted that his wife was Judith Churchill,

From my earliest recollection, I have heard it asserted by the aged members of the Keith and Marshall families that the proud and noble blood of Pocahontas coursed their veins. Bishop Meade, and Campbell, the Virginia historian, say that Thomas Randolph's wife was a Fleming. Judge Keith, of Warrenton, so asserts most positively. Col. Thomas M. Green, the best living authority, has no doubt on the question. John Randolph, of Roanoke, who ought to have known, said that his great uncle married a Fleming.

But a writer in the Richmond *Standard*, of September 24, 1881, mentions only two daughters of Col. John Fleming, who married, respectively, Barnard and Branch. The following paper, furnished by Alex. Brown, of Norwood, names a third daughter, and embodies the evidence that Thomas Randolph did not marry a Fleming:

"Extract from the Descendants of Pocahontas, by Ex-Gov. Wyndham Robertson: Mary Bolling, = Col. John Fleming, and had issue, 8 children, of whom two were daughters: 1, Mary Fleming; = William Barnard, and 2, Caroline, = James Deane."

"According to John Randolph, of Roanoke, the wife of Thomas Randolph, of Tuckahoe, second son and child of the emigrant William Randolph, was a Miss Fleming; but according to Richard Randolph, he married Miss Judith Churchill. Mrs. Ellen Wayles Randolph Harrison, of "Edge-Hill," Albemarle Co., Va. ,(a descendant) states that her name was "Judith Churchill," and that no marriage between a Randolph and Fleming took place until a later period.

(17) JOHN MARSHALL.

"Mr. Wilson Miles Cary, of Baltimore, writes in 1883:" In the conflict of authorities as to the wife of Thomas Randolph of Tuckahoe, I have always accepted Richard Randolph's account rather than that of John Randolph, of Roanoke, because the former was a professed antiquary, and more likely to be correct then the eccentric and erratic statesman, who probably took no pains to verify his opinion by general research; — there being no extracts from parish records, there is nothing left but to choose between their statements, aided by such corroborating testimony as one can obtain at this late day.

"Like Mr. Cary, I do not rely on John of Roanoke, as an antiquary. The children of this couple were: 1, William, b. about 1715, d. prior to 1765, = 1736, Maria Judith Page; 2, Judith, b. about 1718, = July 13, 1738, Rev. William Steth, the historian; 3, Mary b. about 1720, = Rev. James Keith of Scotland, who came to Virginia prior to 1730 — in Henrico parish 2d of March, 1733, — said to have removed to Maryland in 1735; but from some time prior to 1745, to about 1758, he was in Hamilton parish, Prince William Co., Va."

17 JOHN MARSHALL was born in Westmoreland Co., Va., about 1732. He is said to have married JANE GUISENBURY. He was appointed an executor of his father's will, but failed to qualify. His father died in 1752, and John was then, perhaps, a minor. He came to Bourbon Co., Ky., at an early day. He must have died about the year 1800. His name does not appear upon the records of Bourbon County. I have found no family records, and his posterity, now living, never heard of him.

18 REV. WILLIAM MARSHALL was born in Washington parish, Westmoreland Co., Va., in the year 1735,— d. 1809 in Ky., = 1766 in Va., MARY ANN PICKETT, daughter of William Pickett and sister of Martin Pickett. His father died in 1752, and the family removed to Fauquier Co., Va., and settled in the vicinity of Germantown. He was a tall, graceful and handsome youth, with dark, piercing eyes and engaging manners, and fond of the fashionable amusements of the day. In 1765, he purchased land two miles west of Markham, Fauquier Co., Va., and his old residence is still pointed out. About 1766 he married, and in 1768 he was brought under the influence of the New Light preachers, and united with the Baptist Church. His gay and festive habits ceased, and in a short time he began to preach. The circumstance of the conversion

(18) REV. WILLIAM MARSHALL.

of one so wild, as well as the earnest words he uttered, brought many under his influence. His preaching was attended with such power that multitudes were converted, and he was God's agent in one of the greatest revivals that ever occurred in Fauquier County. Among the fruits of his ministry were John Taylor and Joseph Reading, who afterwards became zealous apostles of the gospel. He preached for a season in Shenandoah Co., Va., and thousands came out to hear him. Fifty-three persons were at one time baptized in the Shenandoah. Such was his earnestness that some supposed him deranged, and he was apprehended, but released on the solicitation of his brother, Col. Thomas Marshall. He often preached at Happy Creek and Front Royal. In 1780 he removed to Kentucky, and settled in Lincoln County, where his brother Markham had preceded him. A few years later, he removed to Eminence, Henry Co., Ky., and built up "Fox Run" church. His ministry extended to all parts of the State, and he became a devoted evangelist of the Baptist church. His preaching was an efficient agency in bringing about the remarkable revival of the early part of the present century. But a fall from his horse and a broken limb stopped him from preaching for a time. The bone was imperfectly united, and he suffered much pain. During his confinement he studied theology, and, from that time, his preaching was more doctrinal. But the fire, zeal and pathos of his early years still remained with him. It was affecting to see the earnest patriarch assisted to the pulpit, and there propped, that he might preach to dying men. He died at Eminence in 1809. A year before his death he divided among his children a large amount of real estate, which he had located at an early day. Much of it, however, was lost to his heirs by superior titles. No name is more revered, even at this day, throughout Kentucky; and indeed, William Marshall may be said to have been the best, if not the greatest of the family. His will is recorded in Henry Co., Ky., and is as follows:

WILLIAM MARSHALL'S WILL.

(a) In the name of God, Amen: I, William Marshall, of the County of Henry, in the Commonwealth of Kentucky, being weak of body, but sound of mind, memory and understanding, do make and declare this my last will and testament, as follows:
(b) Item: I give and bequeath to my sons, William and Thomas Marshall, a certain tract or parcel of land, containing 300 acres, situate in Shelby County, to them and their heirs forever, according to their

(19) MARKHAM MARSHALL.

division by them heretofore made, it being the land I purchased of James and Thomas Reeves.

(c) Item: I give and bequeath to my daughter, Elizabeth Ballow, a negro girl named Milly, which she now has in possession, to her and to her heirs forever.

I give and bequeath to my wife, Mary Ann, the tract of land upon which I now reside, containing 107 acres, and all the rest and residue of my estate, both real and personal, during her natural life, if she remains a widow, to be used for the support of herself and younger children, so long as they may live with their mother, viz.: Mary Ann, Susanna and Jane; and in case she should marry another man, or at her death, in either case, then the said lands and personal estate to be equally divided among the following children: Hetty Ballow, Martin Marshall, Lucy Booker, Mary Ann, Susanna and Jane Marshall, which shares they and their heirs, are to hold forever; hereby revoking and disannulling all other and former wills, by me heretofore made.

And lastly, I do hereby constitute and appoint my two sons, Lewis and Martin Marshall, my whole and sole executors of this my last will and testament. Dated December 10, 1806. Probated December term, 1809.

(d) Gen. A. W. Doniphan in a letter written to me in 1883, thus notices Mrs. Marshall and her son George:

In the fall of 1821, my mother made a visit to her only brother, Capt. Robert Smith, of Henry Co., Ky., and I accompanied her. The mother of Martin Marshall, of Augusta, resided in the same neighborhood, and Mr. Marshall requested me to deliver her a letter. I found her a sprightly little lady about 80 years old, having no family but her servants. Like many aged persons, she declined a home with any of her children, preferring to live at the old homestead, where her husband had years before, located in the wilderness, and where he lived, died and was buried. I remained several hours—dined with her, and was delighted to answer her many questions about her favorite son and his family. At her request I called to see her son, George Marshall, who owned a good farm near the road back of my uncles. He was a stout, robust and energetic farmer, and talked-fluently. Of his intelligence I was too young to judge.

For the Pickett family see No. 64.

19 MARKHAM MARSHALL, b. in Westmoreland Co., Va., about 1740. He is called "Abraham" in his father's will. He came to Fauquier Co., Va., about 1753, with other members of the family;=ANN BAILEY, removed to Lincoln Co., Ky., about 1779, and engaged in surveying lands; went further south, and I have heard nothing further of him. The name of Markham Marshall frequently; appears on the records of Fauquier Co., Va., but "Abraham" is not found. There are no traces of his posterity except of a daughter who married William Green (116). Gen. Duff Green notices them. See No. 116.

(20) MARY MARSHALL.—(*McClanahan.*)

20 MARY MARSHALL, b. about 1738, = about 1758, Rev. WILLIAM MCCLANAHAN, of the Baptist Church. Mary was unmarried at the time of her father's death, 1752. The McClanahans lived in Westmoreland County, and the early married years of William and Mary were probably spent there. The marriage must have taken place about 1758. At that time the Marshall family were living near Germantown, Fauquier Co., Va. Their oldest son, Thomas, is said to have been born in Westmoreland. At the breaking out of the war in 1776, the McClanahan family were living in Culpepper County. Sometime towards the close of the century, Mr. McClanahan removed to Greenville, N. C., where he died.

Dr. Alex. Marshall Robinson (454), thus enumerates the children of William and Mary McClanahan:

1. Thomas, d. in Bourbon Co., Ky., leaving posterity.
2. William, d. in Fayette County, leaving, 1, Ann, who married a Robinson, and 2, Marshall McClanahan.
3. John, moved from South Carolina to Morgan Co., Mo., where he lived and died.
4. Nancy, = Elizmond Basye, of Bourbon Co., Ky. They married in Culpepper Co., Va., and were early settlers of Kentucky. They left children.
5. Alice, or Ailsey, = 1st, Vaughn, of Virginia, = 2d, Abbott, of Virginia.
6. Mrs. Triplett, wife of Hedgeman Triplett.
7. Susan, = John Robinson, in Culpepper Co., Va., and removed to Greenville District, S. C., in 1810; came to Bourbon Co., Ky., and in 1828 to Boon Co., Mo., where he died. Issue:

    1. John Robinson, d. single, in Ohio, in the service as a soldier of the war of 1812.
    2. Garrard Robinson, = his cousin, Ann McClanahan. Came to Howard Co., Mo., and died, leaving children.
    3. William, came to Howard Co., Mo., = a Sims, and left issue.
    4. Maxamillian, moved to Boon Co., Mo., = a Butler, and left issue.
    5. Sidney Robinson, now (1883) living in Morgan Co., Mo., aged 78, = his cousin, a McClanahan.

(22) PEGGY MARSHALL—(*Smellan*).

 6. Benjamin F. Robinson, now of Texas, = 1st, a McClanahan; 2d, an Alcock.

 7. Louis Marshall Robinson, d. in California, = a Benson, and left issue.

 8. Frances, = Basye, and d. in Jefferson City, Mo., leaving issue.

 9. Richard H. Robinson, = a Sibley; removed to California and left issue.

 10. Elizabeth, = Stephen Bedford; lived in Boon Co., Mo., and left issue.

 11. ALEX. M. ROBINSON, No. 454.

The will of William McClanahan, father of the emigrant to N. Carolina, is found of record in Westmoreland Co., Va. It is dated September 15, 1760; probated October 29, 1771. His wife's name was Margaret; his sons were 1, Thomas, 2, Peter, 3, William, 4, James, and 5, John McClanahan. A daughter married Garland Moore, and their children were, 1, Robert Moore, 2, Garland, 3, Peter, 4, McClanahan, and 5, Martha Moore.

22   PEGGY (*Margaret*) MARSHALL. From the will of her father, she appears to have been the youngest child, and was born about 1745. The Chart of Mrs. Mary I. (Thomas) Colston shows that she married ———— SMELLAN. I have discovered nothing further.

30   JOSEPH SMITH = WEAVER. He was the oldest son of Augustine Smith, (14) but dying without issue before his father, his brother Thomas became the heir.

32   THOMAS SMITH b. in Washington parish, Westmoreland Co., Va., about 1767, d. in Fauquier Co., Va., about 1796; = July 13, 1769, ELIZAEBTH ADAMS. His father removed with Col. Thomas Marshall and other relatives, about 1753, to the neighborhood of Germantown, Fauquier Co., Va. Here Thomas raised a family of twelve children, as follows:

THE MARSHALL FAMILY. 37

(50) JOHN MARSHALL.

1, Susanna Smith, b. December 21, 1770; 2, Ann, b. November 14, 1772; 3, Augustine, b. September 28, 1774; 4, Mollie, b. November 13, 1776; 5, Betsy, b. December 13, 1778; 6, John, b. June 2, 1781; 7, Sarah, b. January 26, 1784; 8, Lucy, b. May 17, 1786; 9, Harriet, b. October 18, 1788; 10, Letetia, b. July 26, 1791; 11, THOMAS MARSHALL. SMITH, Oct 3, 1793 (140); 12, Jane Smith, b. June 3, 1796.

THE ADAMS FAMILY.

1. (b) John Adams, of England, first cousin of Lord Littleton, and educated with him at Oxford, came to St. Charles Co., Md., about 1700, and = Elizabeth Naylor.
2. John Adams, Jr., heir by primogeniture, b. February 19, 1718 = January 3, 1743, Sarah Stacy Gibbons, b. December 19, 1725. He gave his oldest son, John, large possessions in Maryland and removed with his wife and younger childred to Fauquier Co., Va.; about 1757. Issue.
(c) 1. John Adams b. December 3, 1744 = in Maryland.
2. George Adams, b. March 26, 1747 = —— Turner.
3. Littleton Adams, b. February 12, 1752 = Harriet Smith.
4. Elizabeth Adams, b. June 20, 1754 = THOMAS SMITH, No. 32.
5. Ann Adams, b. August 18, 1757 = Frank Ashe.
6. Thomas Adams, b. February 10, 1760 = Rebecca Wood.
7. Josias Adams, b. September 23, 1762 = Sally Burrows.
8. James Adams, b. September 3, 1765 = Betty Brent.
9. Susanna Adams, b. April 1, 1769 = CAPT. THOMAS MARSHALL, No. 56.

50 (a) JOHN MARSHALL, Chief Justice of the United States, from 1801 to 1835, was b. near Germantown, Fauquier Co., Va., September 24, 1755,—d. at Philadelphia, July 6, 1835; = January 3, 1783, at Yorktown, Va., Mary Willis Ambler, b. March 17, 1766;—d. December 25, 1831, at Richmond, Va. The life of Judge Marshall is so interwoven with the administrative, diplomatic and judicial history of the country, that his biography would demand of me a full volume. His life has been written a hundred times, and these pages must be reserved for those whose memory

(50) JOHN MARSHALL.

might perish, if omitted from my record. At the bar and on the bench,—in congress and in cabinet,—in the councils of war and embassies of peace, he proved himself a jurist, a statesman, a soldier, an orator and a patriot. As the expounder of the Federal Constitution and laws, he laid the foundation of a judicial system that has no equal on earth. His public life was a succession of honors and triumphs, while in his private walk, he was an examplar of humility, patience, charity and love. His name is revered by the nation, and adored by his large posterity.

After the death of John Marshall of the "Forest" in Westmoreland Co., Va., April, 1752, the widow and children removed to the vicinity of Germantown, Fauquier Co., Va. Here the eldest son, Thomas Marshall, afterwards Colonel of the Third Virginia Volunteers, was married, in 1754, to Mary Randolph Keith, daughter af Parson James Keith. The following year John Marshall, the Chief Justice was born. In 1765, when John was ten years of age, his father removed to a farm on Goose Creek. Here he resided until 1773, when he purchased the Oakhill estate, situated at the Western foot of Little Cobbler mountain, in Fauquier County. At this day the Midland railroad passes it, and Markham, the Marshall home, has sprung up eight miles to the west. Col. Marshall built a substantial house at "Oakhill," which is still in good repair, though it has passed out of the family. For a century it was the homestead of the Marshalls. Mr. F. W. Maddux, the present proprietor, in October, 1884, wrote me:

(b) The farm contains a thousand acres in good repair. The dwelling is well preserved. Col. Marshall had part of it built more than one hundred and thirty years ago. This part has seven rooms, and is much in the style of houses of that age, and has been but little changed The whole building was painted less than a year ago. Judge Marshall's son Thomas (150), had the other part of the dwelling built, more than sixty years ago, of the very best material, and it shows no sign of decay. There are five large rooms, and two large halls, besides the basement rooms, in this part of the house. I have added the porches and other little improvements. Only seven of the old oaks from which the farm took its name, are standing in the lawn."

(c) It was in this old homestead that John Marshall grew up to manhood. It was afterwards given to him by his father, was long owned by his posterity, and its very soil is hallowed in their memory. Col. Thomas Marshall must have inherited a good patrimony, and, until impoverished by the war was in good circumstances. His children were well instructed at the country schools,

(50) JOHN MARSHALL.

and by private tutors. The Rev. James Thomson came from Scotland about 1767, and was employed by Col. Marshall to teach his children. Mr. Thomson afterwards married, and established a school which was attended by the children of Col. Marshall. But the children owed their well cultivated minds and their proficiency in history, poetry, science and philosophy chiefly to the instructions of their father. Books were put in their hands, and each was critically examined, commended and encouraged. Instead of the silly sports and pass-times of children, they were taught to discuss themes of importance. Books were their companions, and ancient and modern history was their delight. The large household formed a literary society, and intellectual tilts and tournaments were indulged in at all hours, — but chiefly at the table. Habits of observation and thought were encouraged. Col. Marshall himself was a champion, as well as arbiter, in this intellectual chivalry. His profound native mind, extensive reading and varied experience, were superior to the talents of any of his children. Late in life all of them admitted it. For several generations the Marshalls made schools of their families. In my youth, I witnessed and enjoyed the benefits of these family schools. Few of the early members of the family attended college; they were educated at home.

(d) Here at Oakhill, John Marshall's mind was disciplined for the grand achievements of after life. His father's sound judgment, impartial justice, broad statesmanship, unflinching integrity, indomitable courage and ardent patriotism, laid the foundation of the judicial wisdom that made the son illustrious. Confined at home by the duties of the farm and the school room, he was not conscious of his own superiority; and when called into active life, his modesty and diffidence were a great drawback. The prospect of war called him from retiracy. When brought into collision with the first men of his day, his wonderful power was exhibited; but modesty characterized him to the day of his death. But others observed the merits of which he was himself unconscious. He had not read history in vain, and well knew that war was inevitable. He saw a bloody struggle, but a glorious result. In preparing for war, he was chosen the Lieutenant of a company of minute-men. His patriotic addresses fired the zeal of his soldiers. I shall not follow him closely through the war but shall refer to only the leading events.

(50) JOHN MARSHALL.

(e) Mr. Marshall's first experience was at the battle of the Great Bridge, the successful termination of which was due to the gallantry and courage of his command. In July, 1776, he was appointed 1st Lieutenant of a company in the 11th Virginia regiment. In May, 1777, he became a Captain. He was at the battle of Brandywine September 11, 1777; at Germantown October 4, 1777, at Monmouth June 28, 1778; he endured the hardships of Valley Forge. In 1779 he retired from the army to attend a course of law and philosophy at William and Mary College. In the summer of 1780, he was licensed to practice law; but the courts were closed and he returned to the army. After the surrender at Yorktown, he entered on the practice of law. His success was marked from the beginning. In 1782, he was sent to the Legislature from Fauquier County, and was appointed a member of the Council of State. At Yorktown he met with Miss Mary Willis Ambler, daughter of Treasurer Jacquelin Ambler, and they were married January 3, 1783. In 1785 his father removed his family to Kentucky, and gave him "Oakhill." But, to prosecute the practice of law, he removed to Richmond. In 1787 he was again in the Legislature. In 1788 he was a member of the Virginia convention that ratified the U. S. Constitution. In 1789, 1790 and 1791, he represented Richmond in the State Legislature. He now devoted himself assiduously to the practice of law, and became distinguished for his clear and comprehensive grasp, and logical analysis of the legal and political questions of the day. Though gentle, and even humble in his manners, and careless of his dress, his intellectual powers placed him at the head of his profession.

(f) Washington offered Mr. Marshall the place of Attorney General, and afterwards the ministry to France; but both positions were declined, that he might pursue his lucrative practice. But in 1797 he accepted from President Adams the place of Envoy to France. On his return, in 1798, his course received general approval. In 1799, at the request of Washington, he ran for Congress and was elected. At the death of the Father of his Country, it was the sad duty of Mr. Marshall to announce that event, and to prepare the resolutions of respect. In the life of Washington, his remarks on this occasion are given, and have been pronounced the finest eulogium ever written; yet the author modestly suppresses his own name. In 1800, Mr. Marshall was Secretary of State under John Adams,

(50) JOHN MARSHALL.

and January 31, 1801, he was commissioned Chief Justice of the United States, which office he held until his death in 1835. For several years he was engaged on his Life of Washington, which was published from 1804 to 1807, in five volumes. In 1828, he was a delegate to the Internal Improvement Convention at Charlottesville, and in 1829 was a member and presiding officer of the convention to revise the State Constitution.

(g) Judge Marshall for many years suffered from a disease of the bladder. An operation gave temporary relief; but in 1835 a disease of the liver caused him to visit Philadelphia for medical relief, and here he died in his 80th year. His remains were deposited beside his beloved wife at Richmond, Va., and his tomb bears the modest inscription written by himself:

(h) John Marshall, son of Thomas and Mary Marshall, was born the 24th of September, 1755; intermarried with Mary Willis Ambler, the 3d of January, 1783; departed this life the 6th of July, 1835.

(i) Judge Marshall was a sincere believer in the truth of the Bible. Though reared in an age prolific of infidelity, and in a society given to licentiousness, yet his great mind rested serenely on the truth of Christianity. For a time he doubted the divinity of the Savior; but his scruples were soon removed, and the faith of the Episcopal Church was cordially embraced and transmitted to his posterity. He did not unite with the church, but worshipped regularly, and a public profession was in contemplation at the time of his death. His posterity, including husbands and wives from other families, amount to over four hundred souls; and nearly all belong to the Episcopal Church. I never met a people more ardent in their faith and upright in their conduct. They are commendably proud of their ancestry, and their patriotism caused them to follow the fortunes of their beloved Virginia. Nearly every man among them took up arms for the Confederacy, and not one supported the North. When peace was established, the survivors returned to wasted homes and depleted families.

(j) I might fill many pages with interesting anecdotes of Judge Marshall, to show that one possessed of transcendant abilities may be endued with modesty and simplicity; that one whose mind is embellished with rare intellectual garniture, can neglect his person and

(50) JOHN MARSHALL.

give no attention to his clothing; and that the clearest reason, and the most logical analysis of the evidences of Christianity lead to a faith in its divine origin. But these chronicles are not intended to support any doctrine, nor to eulogize the living nor the dead.

(k) Mrs. Marshall has always been commended for her purity and piety. Perhaps the mother was more the agent, than was the father, in bringing their posterity to the house of God. Her husband, though so exalted, was her devoted lover to the last day of her life; and after her death, he sanctified its anniversary by writing a letter to a friend detailing her virtues and commending her memory. Several of these tributes have been preserved and published. Much of her life, she was an invalid; and her husband tenderly nursed her. Few of the living remember her, but tradition plants the lily and the myrtle, the jasmine and the primrose upon her grave.

THE AMBLER FAMILY.

(*l*) Richard, son of John Ambler and Elizabeth Burkadike, of the City of York, England, b. December 24, 1690, d. February —, 1766, came over to Virginia in 1716, = 1724 Elizabeth Jacquelin, b. October, 1709, d. 1756; daughter of Edward Jacquelin, son of John Jacquelin and Elizabeth Craddock, of the County of Kent, England. Edward came over to Virginia in 1697, and married, for his second wife, in 1697, Martha, daughter of William Cary (Gent.), of Warwick Co., Va., by whom he had issue:

A 1. ELIZABETH AMBLER, b. 1731, d. 1740.
    2. EDWARD AMBLER, b. 1733, d. October 30, 1768, = 1754, Mary, dr. of Wilson Cary, Esq. Issue:

B (*m*) 1. *Elizabeth Ambler*, b. 1754, d. June 26, 1756.
    2. *Richard Ambler*, b. September 6, 1756, d. August 26, 1759.
    3. *Edward Cary Ambler*, b. July 2, 1758, d. March 22, 1775.
    4. *Sarah Ambler*, b. September 27, 1760, d, September 11, 1782, = William H. Macon. Issue:

C 1. Mary Macon = WILLIAM MARSHALL (62).
    2. Sarah A. Macon, d. October, 1782.

B 5. *John Ambler*, b. September 25, 1762, d. May 8, 1836, = 1st, Frances, dr. of Gill Armistead and Elizabeth Allen, of New Kent Co., in 1782. Issue:

THE MARSHALL FAMILY. 43

(50) JOHN MARSHALL.

C
    1. Edward Ambler, b. 1783, d. July, 1846.
(n) 2. Mary Cary Ambler, b. 1787, d. 1843.
John Ambler, = 2d LUCY MARSHALL (66).
1. Thomas M. Ambler (242).
John Ambler, = 3d, Catherine Norton, nee Bush, widow of John H. Norton, father of DR. GEO. H. NORTON (564), and dr. of Philip Bush, of Winchester, and Catherine Clough. Issue:

D
    1. John Jacq. Ambler, b. March 9, 1801, d. November, 1854, = February 15, 1828, Elizabeth Barbour, dr. of P. E. Barbour and Elizabeth Johnston, of Orange Co. Issue: 1, John, 2, Phil. B., 3, Ella C. Ambler.

2. Catherine Cary Ambler, b. November 15, 1802, d. November, 1850, = Henry Wood Monceur, son of William Monceur and Elizabeth Henry. Issue: 1, Sarah Ann E. Monceur, b. September 21, 1824; 2, John Ambler Monceur, b. October 2, 1827; 3, Wm. Cary Monceur, b. January 3, 1829; 4, Catherine Ambler Monceur; 5, Charles; 6, Jean W.; 7, Henry W.; 8, W. George; 9, Richard C.; 10, William M.; 11, John Jacq. Monceur.

(o) 3. Elizabeth Bush Ambler, b. April 22, 1804, = April 14, 1825, Robert Carter Nicholas, of Richmond, Va., son of Philip Narbonne Nicholas, of the same city, and Mary Spear, of Baltimore. Issue: 1, Philip N. Nicholas, b. June 22, 1826, and died same year; 2, John Ambler Nicholas, b. January 8, 1828, d. January 17, 1851; 3, Spear Nicholas; 4, Catherine N.; 5, Edward; 6, Mary S.; 7, George; 8, Robert C.; 9, Elizabeth; 10, Mary B. Nicholas.

4. Philip St. G. Ambler, b. September 5, 1806, = August, 1847, Elizabeth Green, of Rappahannock Co. Issue: 1, John Ambler; 2, Charles; 3, Catherine; 4, Philip St. G.; 5, William H. Ambler.

THE MARSHALL FAMILY.

(50) JOHN MARSHALL.

      5. Sarah Jacq. Ambler, b. November 5, 1809.
      6. Richard Cary Ambler, b. December 11, 1807, d. July 16, 1877, = June 8, 1843, SUSAN MARSHALL (202).
      7. Gabriella B. Ambler, b. May 18, 1815, = Frank E. Brooke. Issue: 1, Frank E.; 2, (p) John A.; 3, Charles C.; 4, Catherine A.; 5, Mary C.; 6, Ella Brooke.
      8. William M. Ambler, b. June 25, 1813, = June, 1854, Martha Coleman. Issue: 1, John Ambler.

B   6. Mary Ambler, b. November 4, 1764, d. October 21, 1768.
    7. Martha Ambler, b. December 7, 1766, d. July 17, 1768.

A   3. JOHN AMBLER, 1735—1766.
    4. RICHARD AMBLER, 1736—1745.
    5. MARTHA AMBLER, 1738—1739.
    6. MARY AMBLER, 1740—1763.
    7. JACQUELIN AMBLER, b. August 9, 1742, d. February 10, 1798, = May 24, 1764, Rebecca L. Burwell, b. May 29, 1746, dr. of Louis Burwell and Mary Willis, of Gloucester Co., Va. Issue:

B   1. Elizabeth Jacq. Ambler, b. March 11, 1765, = 1st, William Brent, of Prince William Co., who died without issue; she then married Col. Edward Carrington, who also died without issue.
    (q) 2. Mary Willis Ambler, b. March 18, 1766, d. December 25, 1831, = JOHN MARSHALL, Chief Justice of the United States (50).
      3. Martha Ambler, b. 1767, d. July 1776.
      4. Ann Ambler, b. March 16, 1772, d. June 29, 1832, = November 24, 1795, Geo. Fisher, son of Daniel Fisher, of Brunswick Co. Issue: 1. Alex. B. Fisher, dead; 2, Elizabeth J. Fisher, = THOMAS M. COLSTON (168); 3, Janetta; 4, George; 5, Lucy; 6, Mary Ann; 7, C. T. M. Fisher.
      5, Lucy Nelson Ambler, b. August 4, 1776, d. May 15,

(52) ELIZABETH MARSHALL—(*Colston*).

1797, = Daniel Call, son of Daniel Call, of Dinwiddie Co., Va. Issue: Elizabeth Call, = Daniel W. Norton.

A 8. GEORGE AMBLER, 1744—1750.
9. RICHARD AMBLER, 1748—1749.

52 (*a*) ELIZABETH (ELIZA) MARSHALL, b. near Germantown in Fauquier Co., Va., 1756, d. at "Honeywood," Berkeley Co., Va., in 1842; = October 15, 1785, RAWLEIGH COLSTON, b. May 10, 1749, d. at "Honeywood," Va., 1823. Aunt Colston was the oldest daughter of the family of Col. Marshall, and received her education chiefly from her father. She, in turn, became the teacher of her younger brothers and sisters, and they ever regarded her with deep veneration. Her father in his will (16) makes a special bequest to her, as an expression of his gratitude for her self sacrificing labors for his younger children. In early life she was engaged in marriage to Col. Porterfield, a gallant officer of the Revolutionary army. When he fell in battle, she was sorely distressed, and for years seldom entered into society. This event gave a tinge of pious sadness to the remainder of her life. Her hours of meditation and reading were interpersed with the duties of instructing the younger members of the family. Nature had endowed her with superior mental qualifications, and her diligent study of the best authors of the day, made her a highly accomplished lady. At the age of twenty-seven she was married to the wealthy and accomplished Rawleigh Colston, at the house of her brother John, in Richmond. He died, in 1823, and she survived him nearly twenty years. She continued to reside at Honeywood until her death in 1842. I believe that she never visited Kentucky. Her memory is fragrant in the hearts of all who share her blood. The following obituary notice appeared immediately after her death:

Died at Honeywood, in the County of Berkeley, Va., on Friday, the 24th inst., Mrs. Elizabeth Colston, relict of Rawleigh Colston, Esq., in the 86th year of her age. This lady was the eldest sister of the late Chief Justice Marshall, whom she strongly resembled in many respects, particularly in the directness and perfect simplicity of her character. Of uncommonly clear and vigorous mind, she used every faculty, not to magnify herself, but to humbly direct her to the proper discharge of every social and moral duty. As a wife, parent, mistress, relation, neighbor and friend, she attracted the esteem and love of all who

(52) ELIZABETH MARSHALL—(*Colston*).

approached her. More especially was her christian character marked and decisive, seeming to strengthen as her physical powers decayed. From the middle of the preceding month, she had been confined to her bed, and suffered much pain. Throughout the whole, she was perfectly resigned to the will of God—yet constantly praying that if it were His will, she might be permitted to depart and go hence. It was natural that her devoted family should pray for her recovery, but this she requested them not to do, as her strongest desire was to be with her Lord in whom she trusted."

(*b*) Rawleigh Colston was born at Exeter Lodge, in what is now Northumberland Co., Va., the seat of his father, on Yocomico river. His mother died about 1752, and his father removed with his children to Hornby Manor, an estate on the Rappahannoch, presented to the children, by their Uncle Daniel Hornby. Here the father died after a few months residence. A Scotch gentleman, named Richardson, was employed as tutor for the children. Mr. Richardson, was a scholar and a christian, and the children were well instructed in the languages, and thoroughly indoctrinated in the tenets of the established church. At fourteen, young Rawleigh Colston was a fair Latin scholar. He was then apprenticed to his relative, James Tarpley, a member of an extensive mercantile house, in Williamsburg, Va. Here he remained several years, acquiring little business knowledge, and exposed to the vices of improper associates. On the death of Mr. Tarpley, Rawleigh returned to his guardian, Maj. Traverse Tarpley, in Richmond County. After spending a year or two in idleness, he applied himself to the study of law. For this purpose he returned to Williamsburg, and read with Chancellor George Wythe. After three years he was licensed as an attorney. But before he had fairly entered on the practice, the Revolutionary War broke out, and the courts were closed. Mr. Colston now sold his patrimonial estate, and raised and equipped a company for the war; but being absent when the regiment was organized, another was put in command. He was thereupon appointed a commercial agent to collect military stores abroad, and was sent to Cape Franceois, St. Domingo Here he engaged in mercantile pursuits, and operated for the colonies. He also engaged in adventures on his own account, which were successful, and he amassed a considerable fortune. In 1784, he returned to Virginia, and, next year was married. He returned to Frederick County and engaged in farming. In 1801 he established himself at Honeywood, on the banks of the Potomac. This estate he received as part of the proceeds of

(56) CAPT. THOMAS MARSHALL.

the large purchase of land made of the heirs of Lord Fairfax, see No. 58. Mr. Colston wrote out a short record of his career in life, which has been published for private circulation by his great grandson, Douglas H. Thomas, (1592) of Baltimore.

THE COLSTON FAMILY.

(c) 1. William Colston, of Bristol, England, was a brother of Edward Colston, the great philanthropist, whose marble statute stands in All-Saints Church, Bristol, and, to whose honor and memory, a sermon is annually preached. William, b. about 1618, came to Virginia, about 1645, and was clerk of Rappahannock County.
2. His son William Colston, was b. about 1665.
3. Charles Colston, b. about 1690, =Susan Traverse, daughter of William Traverse.
4. Traverse Colston, b. about 1712, =1st Alice Corbin Griffin; and after her death =2d, Susanna Opie. The latter was mother of RAWLEIGH COLSTON, b. May 10, 1749.

54 MARY MARSHALL, see No. 88.

56 (a) CAPT. THOMAS MARSHALL, b. in Fauquier Co., Va., October 27, 1761; d. in Washington, Ky., March 19, 1817, = 1790, FRANCES MAITLAND KENNAN, b. in Va., July 24, 1773; d. in Washington, Ky·, November 19, 1833. Mr. Marshall received his education from his father, sisters and the tutors employed in the family. At the age of seventeen he volunteered as a private in his father's regiment, and served until the close of the Revolutionary war, at which time he held the commission of a Captain. He saw hard service, and participated in many of the bloody battles of the war of Independence. At the end of the war he married SUSANNA ADAMS, b. April 1, 1769, daughter of John Adams and Sarah Stacy Gibbons. She died childless after one year. See the Adams Gen. (32).

Capt. Marshall spent several years on his farm in Fauquier. In the fall of 1788, or the spring of 1789, he came to Kentucky The following letter, dated June 14, 1789, without postmark, is directed

(56) CAPT. THOMAS MARSHALL.

to his cousin and brother-in-law, Thomas Smith (32). It shows that he was in Kentucky at its date, and its reference to his grain, not yet thrashed, indicates his departure from Virginia was but a few months earlier.

(*b*) DEAR SIR: We are at a very great distance, and opportunities seldom offer for me to write. You, I understand from Susan's letter, do not intend to write until you receive a letter. I have written before; but this, I hope, will remove all obstructions. I hope you will write me by the first opportunity. I have nothing of consequence to write you. So I shall not refer to any particular event. The most of us do as well as we can, but not as well as we wish. I am sorry to learn that my grain has not been thrashed, for I am in great want of money; and I hope you will proceed to settle the small matters you promised to do, against the fall. Without some unforeseen accident should prevent me, I intend to go into Virginia this fall. You must give my respectful compliments to Cousin Betty and family, and my good old neighbors. You are pretty well acquainted with them I esteemed as neighbors, so I need not mention them particularly. I am, dear cousin, affectionately,
THOMAS MARSHALL, JUN.

(*c*) P. S. DEAR SUSAN: (Mrs. Susan Morgan, his late wife's niece). I received yours by my brother. It gives a singular satisfaction to find you still affectionate; for you are the only one of my friends, of either sex, that shows any sensibility. I expect to see you this fall, if please God I live. I wish you all the happiness I can a friend or relation, for as such I esteem you. And I hope that you will act with all the prudence that becomes your sex. Let me hear from you by every opportunity.
THOMAS MARSHALL.

(*d*) Capt. Marshall, as he promised in the above letter, returned to Virginia in the fall of 1789, and in the spring of 1790, we find him descending the Ohio to Maysville, in a flatboat. See 2d Collins, Ky., 569–71. His adventure with the Indians, and his almost miraculous escape, is recorded by McClung in his "Western Adventure." Shortly after Capt. Marshall's arrival, he was married to Miss Fanny M. Kennan. His first residence was on Clark's Run, four miles west of Washington. Here he built a fine log house, with substantial stone chimneys. In the old cupboard he kept the county records for a time. In this old house my childhood was passed, and it was still standing when I last visited it in 1872. Capt. Marshall was the first clerk of Mason County, and was, perhaps, still in office when he died in 1817. He was a member of the convention that formed the first constitution of Kentucky. His father, Col. Thomas Marshall, left "Buckpond" in 1800, and came to Mason to live with his son Thomas. Capt. Marshall had, I think, moved into Washington as early as 1795, and built a frame house on what was, and is, known as "The Hill." But when Col. Mar-

(56) CAPT. THOMAS MARSHALL.

shall came to Washington in 1800, he assisted his son in the erection of the spacious brick mansion, which is still the Marshall homestead. Here, Capt. Marshall, for seventeen years, dispensed his noble charities. Here, "Aunt Fanny," during the sixteen years of her widowhood, entertained her relatives with profuse hospitality, and Judge J. J. Key, Dr. J. A. McClung and Martin P. Marshall made the old residence a home for all who were of their blood. It was sometimes called the "Federal Hill," on account of the political proclivities of Capt. Marshall and his chosen friends. The following letter of Capt. Marshall to his first wife's niece will interest his posterity. It is directed to Mrs. Susanna Morgan, Oakhill, Fauquier Co., Va.,— by the hands of H. W. Barnett, and dated October 12, 1810:

(e) DEAR SUSAN: After a silence of all my friends and acquaintances for nearly twenty years, I was sometime ago agreeably surprised by the receipt of a letter from you, which showed I was not entirely forgotten by the whole of you. But your letter, agreeable and interesting as it was to me, might have been rendered much more so if you had gone more into family details. Things that to you, on the spot, who see them as they pass, appear of no consequence,— to a friend at a distance, who still feels a strong interest in your welfare, things which appear to you as nothing, are of consequence to me. I wish to hear how each of your brothers and sisters are settled, and what they are about — how your mother is doing, and everything relating to all my friends and relatives in your quarter, for I still look upon you all, and feel that you are all my relatives. I am now growing old, fat and clumsy, with a house full of children, and am very sure I shall never go to your country again; and feel angry and hurt at any one's coming to this country without calling on me. I was informed sometime ago, that Jo. Chilton passed through this place without calling on me. I was much surprised at it, as I live in town, and it hurt me very much. Don't expect to have regular answers to your letters from an old fellow like me; but don't let that prevent you from writing, as I really receive a great pleasure from finding myself still remembered by you. I always feel an interest in the welfare of the people of that part of the world, where I have spent so many of my happy, as well as unhappy hours. I still look upon myself as your uncle, and therefore shall subscribe myself as your uncle,
T. MARSHALL.

(f) Aunt Fanny was a short, stout woman, and full of life and energy. She gathered into her large drawing-room the intelligent, the beautiful and the chivalrous of the West. Many interesting and memorable events transpired under her roof, and make her a historic character. In my early days, when homeless and parentless, I found a welcome and motherly attention on "The Hill." Though Aunt Fanny's temper was terrible in threats, she seldom struck a blow. When I would steal her preserves, her short, heavy form would rise on tiptoe, her head would shake, and her trembling

(56) CAPT. THOMAS MARSHALL.

fore-finger would point upon my crouching figure, and wrath and threats would pour as a river; and the next moment the poor orphan child would be led to her larder and treated to delicacies. Her table was prodigal in its abundance, and the more company she had the better she was satisfied. Capt. and Mrs. Marshall lie side by side in the "Hill" cemetery. His epitaph reads:

(g) Thomas Marshall, son of Thomas and Mary Marshall, was born the 27th of October, 1761, and after serving his friends, his family, his country and himself, departed this life the 19th day of March, 1817. To all, especially to the widows and orphans of the poor, to one as a friend, and to the other as a benefactor. To his memory his affectionate widow and children have constructed this monument.

Aunt Fanny was raised an Episcopalian,— was somewhat inclined to the Baptists, but joined the Presbyterian Church, that she might be with her friends. She joined the church in 1818, and from that day her house was the home of all Presbyterian ministers. Her epitaph reads:

Erected to the memory of Mrs. Frances Marshall, who died November 19, 1833, in the 61st year of her age. During the vicissitudes of a long life, chequered, as is the lot of humanity, with much of happiness and more of sorrow, the character of the deceased remained the same. An affectionate wife, a fond mother, an humble but ardent Christian, a warm-hearted and devoted friend, she will long be remembered in that extensive circle of friends and relatives who, for many years met at her hospitable board, and to whom her house was a home. In the bosom of that numerous connection, who had known her worth and shared her affection, she expired calmly, cheerfully, happily, in the full hope of a joyful resurrection.

THE KENNAN FAMILY.

(h) William Kennan married a Gardener, and they had four children:

1. William Kennan, = Sally Berry. He was the first Sheriff and first representative of Fleming Co., Ky., and left posterity. See Collins Ky., and McClung's Western Adventure.

2. Mollie Kennan, = Griffin Taylor. He died in Clarke Co., Va., leaving one son, John D. Taylor, of Saratoga, Va.

3. Sallie Kennan, = John Taylor. Issue: 1, William Taylor, = Harriet Milton, of Clarke Co., Va., and died in Frederick County. Their daughter, Florinda Taylor, = W. S. Jones (804); 2, Benj. Taylor, a merchant of Baltimore; 3, Richard Taylor, died in Winchester, Va.; 4, Griffin Taylor, merchant of Cincinnati, Ohio; 5, Mrs. Ware, of Frederick Co., Va.

4. Fanny Maitland Kennan, = Capt. THOMAS MARSHALL (56).

(58) JAMES MARKHAM MARSHALL.

58 (a) JAMES MARKHAM MARSHALL, b. in Fauquier Co., Va., March 12, 1764; d. at "Fairfield," Fauquier Co., April 26, 1848; =April 9, 1795, HESTER MORRIS, b. July 30, 1774; d, at "Fairfield," April 18, 1816. Both were buried at "Happy Creek."

Mr. Marshall, like his brothers, was thoroughly educated at home. Though quite a youth, he was elected a Lieutenant in one of the companies of Alex. Hamilton's regiment, and served to the close of the Revolutionary War. At the siege of Yorktown, he led the "forlorn hope," in an attack upon the fort. He came to Kentucky with his father, and, on one occasion, went to the field to fight a duel with James Brown, afterward Minister to France and Senator from Louisianna. He returned to Virginia in 1795, and married Hester, daughter of Rob. Morris, the great patriot and financier of the Revolution. He was sent, by Washington, as agent of the government, to negotiate the release of LaFayette, when a prisoner of Austria, at Olmutz; and while in Paris, witnessed the outrages of the Reign of Terror. Several years were spent abroad, and his two oldest children were born on ships of war, on the British coast. While in England, he purchased of the heirs of Lord Fairfax, all their estates in what was called the Northern Neck of Virginia. This purchase was made in the names of John Marshall, (Chief Justice,) Rawleigh Colston, Harry (Light Horse) Lee and James M. Marshall. But the State of Virginia set up title to the lands by confiscation, and a compromise was effected, whereby the company received all the Fairfax lands in Leeds Manor and some other smaller tracts. Their portion embraced about 180,000 acres, and the cost to them was something less than one dollar per acre. James M. Marshall purchased the share of Harry Lee, and Mr. Colston took lands on the Potomac. All the unsold lands in Leeds Manor, therefore, went to John and James Marshall; and here their posterity have found homes. They form a community in and around the little town of Markham, Fauquier County; attend Leeds church, and send their sons to the State University. All are Democrats, and members of the Episcopal church. There is hardly a household that does not have family worship, and they are never seated at their meals until the oldest present, whether male or female,— father, mother or child,—asks a blessing upon them. They are a frugal, honest, upright, hospitable, sensible and pious people; and I venture to say there is no spot on the con-

(58) JAMES MARKHAM MARSHALL.

tinent, that has produced more preachers to the acre, than Leeds Manor; and I am confident that no other portion of the South, of equal population, sent to the Southern army so many heroes.

(b) With a double portion of the lands thus acquired, Mr. Marshall became a large proprietor, and left his children large estates.

Mr. Marshall studied law and practiced in Winchester. He was eminent in his profession, and like all the early members of the family, he was a decided Federalist. Under the tutelage of Alex. Hamilton, he could be nothing else. The last night of the administration of John Adams, Mr. Marshall was appointed one of what is known as the "Midnight Judges;" but the incoming congress was Democratic, and legislated them out of office.

Early in the present century Mr. Marshall left Winchester, and built on his Happy Creek estate, a costly villa, consisting of a baronial castle, and spacious quarters for his servants, tenants and dependants. This massive structure, with its wide halls and lofty ceilings, still affords shelter for half of his posterity, and its broad and fertile acres bring them a good income. About 1816, he yielded possession of this magnificent estate to his oldest son, R. M. Marshall, and retired to Fairfield, where he died. He was a handsome and dignified old gentleman, six feet two inches tall, weighed about 200 pounds, raw-boned, and he wore a cue, stockings and knee-buckles.

Mrs. Hester Marshall is said to have been a lovely woman. In the principal hall at Happy Creek, there hangs a splended painting of a mother and two daughters. One of the latter shows the beautiful face and form of Mrs. Marshall.

THE MORRIS FAMILY.

(c) 1. Robert Morris of Liverpool, and afterwards of Oxford, Md., and agent of the great house of Corncliff & Co., of Liverpool, was b. 1702, d. July 12, 1750. His son,

2. Robert Morris, the patriot and Philadelphia financier, was b. January 31, 1734, = March 2, 1759, Mary White, b. 1749, daughter of Col. Thos. White, and sister of Bishop White, of Pennsylvania, who was the first lawfully consecrated bishop of the American Episcopal Church. He compiled the Prayer Book called by his name.

3. Hester Morris = JAS. M. MARSHALL.

THE MARSHALL FAMILY. 53

(64) CHARLES MARSHALL.

60 JUDITH MARSHALL, b. in Fauquier Co., about 1766; = about 1783, GEORGE BROOKE. Aunt Judith married against the advice of her parents, yet she does not seem to have been cast off by them. Her father in his will, gives her a full share of his property. The will is dated June 26, 1798, and the Brooke family were then perhaps, living in Lewis Co., Ky. Here they spent their latter years. Mrs. Brooke is said to have been a beautiful and lively girl. Mr. Brooke is described as a fine gentleman, of prepossessing person and fascinating manners, but dissipated, idle and profligate. After marriage they had but little intercourse with the rest of the family. When they died, or, specifically, where, I have not learned. Some of the children were left in Kentucky, and others in Virginia. There were seven children. Three of the boys never married. Mary left quite a household of children, and her posterity are numerous. My chart shows a large part of her descendants. Mrs. Nat Whiting of Prince William Co., Va., was a sister of George Brooke. Another sister, Kitty, = a Conrad. George Brooke belonged to the large and worthy Brooke family of Virginia, but I have not been able to trace the connection.

62 WILLIAM MARSHALL (twin brother of Charles), b. in Fauquier Co., Va., January 31, 1767; d. in Richmond, Va., 1815; = 1st ALICE ADAMS (3 ch); = 2nd MARY MACON, (2 ch); = 3d MARIA C. WINSTON [Price]. After Mr. Marshall's death, his widow = Dr. Roper, whom she survived. Mr. Marshall is remembered as a talented, eloquent and successful lawyer, at the Richmond bar. His first wife was a sister of Dr. Adams, remembered for his chimerical projects for improving the city of Richmond, in which he lost much money. His second wife's name will be found on the Ambler chart (50 m).

64 (a) CHARLES MARSHALL, twin brother of William, was b. at "Oakhill," Fauquier Co., Va., January 31, 1767, d. at Warrenton, Va., 1805, = September 13, 1787, LUCY PICKETT, b. May 2, 1767, d. 1825. Both were buried at Old Turkey Church, in Fauquier Co., Va.; but there is nothing left to indicate their graves.

I have found but little material for a sketch of Charles Marshall.

THE MARSHALL FAMILY.

(64) CHARLES MARSHALL.

He is said to have been a man of genius, erudition and eloquence. He practiced law at Warrenton, Va. His son, Martin P. Marshall, always referred to his father as a brilliant orator and a profound jurist. Martin was but seven years old when his father died, but he had a distinct recollection of his being paralyzed by disease, and of his being borne, by his servants, in a chair, to the court house, that he might attend to business.

THE PICKET FAMILY.

(b) William S. Pickett, = —— Cooke. Issue:

A   1. GEORGE PICKETT.

B
1. William Pickett.
2. Reuben Pickett.
3. John Pickett, 1744 — 1805.
4. Martin Pickett, = —— Blackwell.

C
1. Lucy Pickett, May 2, 1767 — 1825, = CHARLES MARSHALL, 1767 — 1805. See No. 64.
2. Ann Pickett, = Brooke.

D
1. Martin P. Brooke, = McClanahan.
3. Judith Pickett, = Stanton Slaughter.
1. Arthur Slaughter, = Jane Pollard.
2. Martin Slaughter, = Martha Bolling.
3. Diana Slaughter, = Henry Field.
4. Ann Slaughter, = Robert R. Stringfellow.

E
    1, Robert S.; 2, Mary; 3, Martin; 4, Frank.
4. Mildred Pickett, June 1, 1777 — March 22, 1805, = William Clarkson, April 3, 1773 — February 2, 1818. See Clarkson family, No. 152.

D
1. Ann Dorcas Clarkson, October 1, 1794.
2. Henry Martin Clarkson, March 18, 1796, = Marian Payne.

E
    1. Mildred P. Clarkson, = William Stribling, b. June 22, 1819, dead; 2, Marian, 3, George.

D
3. Elizabeth L. S. Clarkson, 1798 — 1868, = J. A. MARSHALL, No. 152.

THE MARSHALL FAMILY. 55

(64) CHARLES MARSHALL.

E

4. Caro. Mat. Clarkson, b. February 8, 1800, living, = January 29, 1818, Robert M. Stribling, February 14, 1793 — August 24, 1862.

(c) 1. William Stribling, June 22, 1819, dead, = Mildred Clarkson, No. 152.
2. Elizabeth Stribling, May 20, 1821, dead.
3. Mildred P. Stribling, February 22, 1823, living, = September 17, 1861, JOHN MARSHALL. See No. 552.
4. Thomas Stribling, October 24, 1825, dead.
5. Ann Eliza Stribling, 1832, living, = Withers Waller.
6. Col. R. M. Stribling, December 3, 1833, living, = 1st,, MARY C. AMBLER, see No. 854; = 2d, AGNES DOUTHAT, see No. 1324.
7, Henry C. Stribling, October 4, 1836, = REB. P. MARSHALL, No. 574.

D
5. Mary Lucinda Clarkson, = Dr. Merideth.
6. Judith Mildred Clarkson.

C
5. Lettie Pickett, = Charles Johnston.

D
1. Lucy Johnston, = THOMAS M. AMBLER See No. 242.

C
6. Betsy Pickett, = Judge John Scott.

D
(d) 1. Robert Scott, = Elizabeth Taylor, dr. of Robert I. Taylor, of Alexandria; 2, Maria, = Arthur Morson, son of Judge Morson, of Fredericksburg, Va.; 3, Margaret Scott, = Robert Lee, nephew of Gen. R. E. Lee; 4, Martin Scott; 5, John Scott.

C
7. George B. Pickett, = Courtenay Heron.
8. Steptoe Pickett, = Sallie Chilton.

B
5. Mary Ann Pickett, = REV. WM. MARSHALL, No. 18.
6. George Pickett, = ———.

C
1. Caroline Pickett, = James Currie.

D
(e) 1. Mary Currie, = N. W. DUKE, No. 282.

(64) CHARLES MARSHALL.

C   2. Robert Pickett.
       1. Maj.-Gen. Geo. E. Pickett, C. S. Army.

A   2. JAMES S. PICKETT, = Mildmay.

B   Capt. Wm. S. Pickett, = Elizabeth Metcalfe.

C   1. Pattie Pickett, b. July 15, 1760, = Judge John Fishback.

D   1. Martin Fishback, b. September, 1786.
       2. Alexander Fishback, b. July, 1789.
       3. Owen T. Fishback, 1791.
       4. Thomas, 1796.

C   2. Col. John Pickett, of Rosahill, Mason Co., Ky., b. December, 1763 — January, 1831, = November 21, 1790, Elizabeth Chamberlayne, of Loudoun Co., Va., b. 1769, d. 1842.

D   (*f*) 1. James C. Pickett, February 6, 1793 — July 10, 1872, = October 6, 1818, Ellen Desha.

E   1. Col. John T. Pickett, 1822 — 1884, = Kate Keyworth, of Washington, D. C. Their son, 1, Thomas J. Pickett, lives in Washington City.
         2. J. Desha Pickett, Ph. D., 1820, living, = Lizzie Holton. Their son, William H. Pickett, is a distinguished lawyer of Indianapolis.

D   2. Thos. J. Pickett, 1801 — 1875, = November, 1833, Margaret Madison Campbell (see No. 68 *e*), b. 1806, living in Maysville, Ky., and to her I am chiefly indebted for this notice of the Picketts.

E   (*g*) 1. Dr. Thomas E. Pickett, a graduate of Princeton, N. J.; Fellow of the Am. A. of Medicine, etc., = Abbie Gray. Issue: 1, Rose Gray Pickett, 2, Abbie Gray Pickett, 3, Margaret.
       2. Margaret C. Pickett.

D   3. Benj. O. Pickett, 1803 — 1872, = Margaret L. Bacon, a descendant of Nath'l Bacon, the hero of Bacon's Rebellion in Virginia.

THE MARSHALL FAMILY. 57

(64) CHARLES MARSHALL.

E   1. John B. Pickett; 2, Capt. Jas. C. Pickett, = Ida Osborne; 3, Thomas J. Pickett, = Julia Perrine.

D   4. Cornelia Pickett, 1805 — 1878, = J. B. Desha.

E   (h)   1. Marg't B. Desha, = Dr. Harvie Opie Clarke, of Cincinnati. Issue: 1, Hiram Opie Clarke, of Louisiana; Cornelia's second husband was Rev. R. S. Ricketts.

D   5. Wm. S. Pickett, 1808 — 1855, = Elizabeth Morford. He succeeded N. D. Coleman as P. M. of Maysville. Issue: 1, John M. Pickett, = Susan Miller; 2, Wm. S. Pickett.

6. Darwin Pickett, 1811 — 1848, = Mrs. Mary Scott. No issue.

7. Mary R. Pickett, 1814, = Charles Forman, who d. 1850. Issue: 1, Bettie; 2, John P.; 3, Cornelia.

C   3. Sally M. Pickett, 1769 — 1843, = Eli Metcalfe. Issue:

D ·   (i)   1. Hiram Metcalfe, = Ann Summers.

1. Fannie Metcalfe, = J. M. HARBESON, No. 2156.

2. Sabina Metcalfe, = George Bruce, M. C., b. 1801.

E   1. Eli M. Bruce, b. 1828,= Mrs. Perry Thomas, b. 1830.

D   (j)   3. Maria Metcalfe, b. 1827, = Edwin Pogue.

E   1. Robert E. Pogue, = Lydia Mitchell.

C   4. Mary O. Pickett, b. 1765, = Dempsey Jackson.

D   1. Claiborne F. Jackson, Governor of Missouri.

C   5. Capt. James F. Pickett, 1775 — 1852, = 1800, Nancy Smith.

D   1. Patsy Winn Pickett, b. 1805, = 1824, Philip R. Dawe.

E   1. Eliza M. Dawe, = Thos. R. Hampton.

D   2. Col. Wm. S. Pickett, of Memphis, b. February 2, 1800, d. 1884, = 1842, Mary E. Walker.

(66) LUCY MARSHALL—(*Ambler*).

(*k*) 3. Rev. James T. Pickett, of Holly Springs, = 1852, Lizzie H. Haughton. ·
4. John S. Pickett, b. 1820, living, = Sarah A. Kerfoot.
5. Mary E. Pickett, 1831, = Ralph Wormly.
6. Charles Edward Pickett, 1817—1874, died at San Francisco.

66 LUCY MARSHALL, b. in Fauquier Co., Va., about 1768; d. at Jamestown, Va., 1795, = 1790, JOHN AMBLER, b. at Jamestown, September, 25, 1762; d. May 8, 1836. Mr. Ambler was born and reared in Jamestown, and inherited a large estate. He was finely educated, and was eminently a gentleman. His first wife was Fannie Armistead. She bore him a son, Edward, 1783, and Mary Cary Ambler, 1787—1843. His first wife died in 1787, and in 1790 he married Lucy Marshall, by whom he had one son, Thomas Marshall Ambler (242). Lucy died in 1795. Her death was the first and only one of the family that Col. Marshall was called on to mourn. Read his letter written on the occasion (16 *e.*). Her early death cast a pall of sorrow over the whole family. "Lucy" has become a favorite family name, and attests her loveliness. For many years her name was seldom spoken without a sigh or a tear. Mr. John Ambler afterwards removed to Richmond, Va., and married Mrs. Catherine Norton, *nee* Bush, and raised a large family of children. For his genealogy see the Ambler chart, No. 50 *n*.

68 (*a*) ALEXANDER KEITH MARSHALL, b. at "Oakhill," Fauquier Co., Va., 1770; d. at "Walnut Grove," Mason Co., Ky., February 7, 1825, = 1st, October 10, 1794, at Danville, Ky., MARY MCDOWELL, b. January 11, 1772; died at the house of James A. Paxton, Washington, Ky., January 27, 1822; = 2d, November 3, 1823, Mrs. ELIZA A. BALL, *nee* Lewis, who died July, 1829.

Mr. Marshall came to Kentucky with his father, on his second trip in 1785. Under the tuition of his accomplished sisters, he received at home the classical education for which the Marshalls were remarkable, and breathed the literary atmosphere that enveloped

THE MARSHALL FAMILY. 59

(68) ALEXANDER KEITH MARSHALL.

"Oakhill" and "Buckpond." After marriage, Mr. Marshall removed to Mason Co., Ky., and on the farm now known as "Walnut Grove," erected the quaint brick house which is still owned by his posterity. The locust and walnut groves he cherished have nearly disappeared; but the old-fashioned building, with its high stone steps, double doors, round front windows, and antique carvings, still stands, and will yet for generations resist the encroachments of time. Here Mr. Marshall spent his life, and here he and his first wife are buried.

Mr. Marshall is remembered as a tall, stately, accomplished and exceedingly handsome gentleman. He dressed in the old style of cue, stocking and buckle. He was a fine lawyer and one of the most chaste and fluent speakers of his day. He possessed a large estate, and practiced law rather for the excitement and employment it afforded, than for its income. In my youth his small brick office still stood in the yard, and was the dormitory for boys. His business was chiefly in the Court of Appeals, of which he was clerk for years. From 1797 to 1800, he represented Mason County in the State Legislature. In 1818 he was appointed State Reporter, and edited three volumes of decisions, which are still of high authority. Collins, in his History of Kentucky, refers to him as a "pioneer lawyer, and one of the ablest of his day." The latter years of his life were spent at home. When about to marry a second time, Mr. Marshall, by the advice of Senator J. J. Crittenden, who was an intimate friend and companion, made deeds to his children of his real estate, leaving himself a small portion. His will is short and I copy it in full:

A. K. MARSHALL'S WILL.

(b) I make my present wife my sole executrix, and authorize her to dispose of my property, landed and personal, to pay my debts and finish the house I am now building. I give my wife everything I own for her life,—to be responsible to no person, and, at her pleasure, to dispose of it among my children by my first wife, as she pleases. If my wife has issue by me, and that issue survives her, I give after her death, the whole property to that issue. Should my wife die without disposing of my property, I will that what little I have, go to my son Charles, to the children of Maria Paxton and Jane Sullivant.

A. K. MARSHALL.

The will had no witnesses, but was in his handwriting. It is dated October 28, 1824, and probated at the April term, 1825.

(c) Mrs. Mary Marshall, the first wife of A. K. Marshall, was

(68) ALEXANDER KEITH MARSHALL.

a McDowell, and like all of the name, possessed both beauty and loveliness. Her purity of heart, sweet disposition and Christian graces, made her an universal favorite. She was so much beloved by her nephews and neices, that she was known as their "angel aunt." She inherited the Presbyterian faith from her Scotch-Irish ancestors, and became one of the founders of the Washington Church. See the chart of the McDowells appended to this article.

Mrs. Eliza A. Ball was a Lewis. Her first husband was John Luke, of Alexandria, Va., by whom she had several children. Her second husband was a Ball, who left one child, Spencer Ball, whose life was spent on the Mississippi river, in the steamboat trade. See Lewis chart, No. 870.

THE M'DOWELL FAMILIES — 1ST, SAMUEL.

(d) Ephraim McDowell, emigrant, was born in the North of Ireland, of Scotch parents. He married Margaret Irvin, and they came to America after the birth of their four children: 1, John; 2, Mary E.; 3, Margaretta, and 4, James. The family first settled in Pennsylvania, but after several years sojourn, they removed to Augusta Co., Va., and were among the first settlers of the "Borden Tract" of 10,000 acres. Their son John, born in Ireland, about 1714, married in Pennsylvania, Magdalen Wood, whose mother was of the James Campbell clan, in the service of the Duke of Argyle. In the fall of 1737, the family removed to Virginia, and December 25, 1742, John, the oldest son, was killed when in pursuit of Indians. The children of John and Magdalen were: 1st, Samuel; 2d, James; 3d, Sarah.

A 1. SAMUEL McDOWELL, b. October 29, 1735, in Penna.; d. in Mercer Co., Ky., September 25, 1817; = January 17, 1755, in Rockbridge Co., Va., Mary McClung, dr. of John McClung and Elizabeth Alexander, b. in Ireland, October 28, 1735. She was a dr. of Archibald Alexander, b. at Manor Cunningham, Scotland, and Margaret Parks, who were married in Ireland, December 31, 1734. Samuel and Mary had 11 children:

B 1. *Magdalen McDowell*, b. October 9, 1755, = Andrew Reid.
2. *Sarah McDowell* (twin), b. October 9, 1755, = Caleb Wallace.

(68) ALEXANDER KEITH MARSHALL.

    3. *Maj. John McDowell*, b. December 7, 1757, = 1st, his
(e)   cousin, Sarah, dr of James McDowell; = 2d, Lucy Legrand, who was mother of the celebrated Dr. Nashe McDowell, of St. Louis, who married a dr. of Dr. Daniel Drake, of Cincinnati.

    4. *Col. James McDowell*, b. April 29, 1760, = Polly Lyle, and settled near Lexington, Ky. Their dr., Isabella McDowell, married the distinguished Dr. John P. Campbell, and their dr., Margaret Madison Campbell, married Thos. J. Pickett, son of Col. John Pickett. See 64 *h*.

    5. *Judge William McDowell*, b. in Rockbridge, Va., March 9, 1762, = Margaret Madison, and settled at Bowling Green, Ky. Issue:

C (*f*) 1. John McDowell. See 228 *f*.
       2. Mary, = Geo. C. Thompson.
       3. Lucinda, = Dennis Brashear.
         1. Eliza Brashear, = Jos. Sullivant.
       4. Agatha, = James G. Birney, first'Abolition candidate for President of the U. S., and brother of Anna Reid Birney, who married JOHN J. MARSHALL, the Ky. Reporter. No. 296.
       5. Eliza, = Jas. Gillespie, and was mother of the first wife of DR. ALEX. K. MARSHALL, of Nicholasville, Ky. No. 260.

B   6. *Samuel McDowell*, b. in Va., March 8, 1764, = his relative, Ann Irvin. Issue:

C   1. Mary McDowell, b. June 12, 1787; d. January 28, 1869, = June 13, 1805, William Starling, b. January 25, 1783; d. November, 1840. See Starling chart, No. 254. 4 ch.

(*g*) 2. John Adair McDowell, b. May 12, 1789; d. September 30, 1823, = November 9, 1809, Lucy Todd Starling, b. October 11, 1790; d. September 28, 1870. 6 ch. See Starling chart, 254.

      3. Abram Irvin McDowell, b. April 24, 1793, = 1817, Eliza S. Lord, was father of Gen. Irvin McDowell,

(68) ALEXANNER KEITH MARSHALL.

        b. in Columbus, Ohio, October 15, 1818; d. in San Francisco, May 4, 1885.

       4. Eliza McDowell, = Nath'l Rochester, of Bowling Green, Ky.

B   7. *Martha McDowell*, b. June 20, 1766; d. July 6, 1835, = October 4, 1788, Col. Abram Buford, b. in Va., July 31, 1749; d. in Ky., June 29, 1833.

       8. *Col. Joseph McDowell*, of Danville, Ky., b. September 13, 1768; d. June 27, 1856, = Sarah Irvin, b. March 12, 1773; d. December 20, 1835. Issue:

C   1. Anne McDowell, = Ab'm Caldwell; 2, Charles; 3, Sarah, = Michael L. Sullivant; 4, Margaret, = Jos.
(*h*) Sullivant; 5, Caleb; 6, Magdalen, = Caleb Wallace. She now lives in Danville, Ky.

B   9. *Dr. Ephraim McDowell*, the great surgeon of world-wide reputation, b. November 11, 1771, = Sarah, dr. of Gov. Isaac Shelby.

     10. *Mary McDowell*, b. in Va., January 11, 1772; d. in Mason Co., Ky., January 27, 1823, = 1794, ALEX. K. MARSHALL. No. 68.

     11. *Caleb McDowell*, b. April 17, 1774, = his cousin Betsy, dr. of Maj. Joe McDowell.

A   2. JAMES McDOWELL, b. 1739; d. 1772, son of John and Magdalen, = Elizabeth Cloyd, d. 1810. Issue:

B   1. *Sarah McDowell*, = Maj. John McDowell, son of Samuel. See No. 68, *e. h. n.*

     2. *Elizabeth McDowell*, d. 1803, = David McGavock, son of James McGavock and Mary Cloud.

     3. *Col. James McDowell*, of Va., = Sarah Preston, dr. of Col. William Preston, son of John Preston, emigrant.

C (*i*) 1. James McDowell, only son of Col. James and Sarah; M. C. and Governor of Va., = his cousin Susanna Preston, dr. of Gen. Frances Preston, of Abingdon.

D   1. Dr. James McDowell, = Elizabeth Brant, of St. Louis; went to France where his wife died. Issue: 1, Sallie Benton McDowell, = Wickliffe Preston;

(68) ALEXANDER KEITH MARSHALL.

D

2, Brant McDowell, of St. Louis,—the only male descendant of James McDowell and Elizabeth Cloyd.

2. Sallie Campbell Preston McDowell, = 1st, Gov. Francis Thomas, of Maryland; = 2d, Rev. John Miller, of Princeton, N. J. Issue: 1, Susanna P. Miller; 2, Elizabeth Miller.

3. Mary Benton McDowell, = Rev. Mr. Ross, of Frederick City, Md.; a widow of Richmond, Va.; childless.

4. Sophonisba Preston Benton McDowell, = Col. James Woods Massie; d. 1877; late a professor in the Virginia Military Institute. Issue: 1, James McDowell Massie, b. about 1860, now of Texas.

5. Susan Preston McDowell, = Col. Charles Carrington, of Richmond, Va. Issue: 1, Frank; 2, a daughter.

(j) 6. Margaret Canty McDowell, = Prof. Chas. P. Venable, of the University of Va. Issue: 1, Frank; 2, Mary B.; 3, Lily C.; 4, Natalie Venoble.

7. Thomas Lewis McDowell, = Constance Warwick. He died in the C. S. A., 1862. Issue: 1, Susan McDowell, now of Richmond, Va.

8. Eliza (Lily) P. B. McDowell, = August, 1865, Maj. Barnard Wolffe. He died in 1871. Issue: 1, Lily P. B. Wolffe; 2, Barnard Wolffe. They live near Hampden Sidney College.

C

2. Susan S. McDowell, = Col. Wm. Taylor, of Alexandria, M. C. 1843 to his death, January 17, 1846. Issue: 1, Dr. James McDowell Taylor, of Lexington, Va.; 2, Rev. Robert Taylor, = Elizabeth McNaught, d. 1871. Issue: 1, Susan M.; 2, Margaret P., = Smith of Missouri.

(k)

3. Susan Taylor, = John B. Weller, b. in Ohio, removed to California; U. S. Senator 1852-57; Governor of California 1858-60; Minister to Mexico 1861; d. in N. O., August 7, 1875. Issue: 1, John B. Weller, jr., a lawyer of California.

(68) ALEXANDER KEITH MARSHALL.

C

  4. Edmonia P. Taylor, = Mr. Levy, of Portsmouth. Va. They live in Texas.
  5. William Taylor, a lawyer of California.
  6. Thos. Benton Taylor, = a dr. of Rev. N. L. Rice, D. D. He is a lawyer of Chicago.

 4. Elizabeth (or Eliza) Preston McDowell, = at "Cherry Grove," Thomas H. Benton, for thirty years Senator from Missouri. Issue:

D

  1. Eliza Preston Benton, = William Cary Jones, dead. She resides in Philadelphia. Issue: 1, Betty; 2, Benton; 3, Cary Jones.
  2. Jessie Benton, = Gen. John C. Fremont, the Pathfinder and Abolition candidate for President. Issue: 1, Lily; 2, Charles; 3, Frank Preston Fremont.
  3. Sarah Benton, = Richard T. Jacob, Lieutenant Governor of Kentucky. Issue: 1, Leila Jacob, = D. W. Woolly; 2, Lieutenant Richard Jacob, U. S. Army.
  4. Susan Virginia Benton, = Baron Gauldrie Boilleau, a French diplomat. Issue: 1, Benton; 2, Charles; 3, Philip; 4, Mary Boilleau.

FAMILY OF MARY E. M'DOWELL WHO MARRIED JAMES GREENLEE; AND SOME NOTICE OF HER SISTER, MARGARET, WHO MARRIED JAMES MITCHELL.

 (*l*) As has been stated, Ephriam McDowell came to Pennsylvania prior to 1735, and in 1737 settled on the "Borden Grant," Rockbridge Co., Va. We have traced the posterity of the sons of John McDowell, 1, Samuel and 2, James. We now return and take up Mary E. McDowell, daughter of Ephraim.

A

 1. MARY E. McDOWELL, b. in Ireland, about 1712, d. in Rockbridge Co., Va., 1811; = 1736, in Pennsylvania, James Greenlee. They, with the McDowells were the first settlers on the "Borden Grant," in Rockbridge in 1737. Issue:

B

 1. *John Greenlee*, b. in Rockbridge Co., Va., October 4, 1738; = Hannah, daughter of Elijah McClanahan and and Miss Ewing. Issue:

THE MARSHALL FAMILY. 65

(68) ALEXANDER KEITH MARSHALL.

C   1. James Greenlee, b. January 29, 1769; d. April 20, 1840; = 1812 Mary Paxton, b. 1791, daughter of William Paxton and Jane Griggsby. Issue:

D   1. Hannah M. Greenlee, b. December 14, 1812, living, = May 24, 1832, Jas. D. Davidson.

E   1. Greenlee Dandson, b. June 18, 1834, fell at Chancellorsville, May 3, 1863.
2. Frederick, b. March 18, 1836, fell at 1st Manassas, July 21, 1861.
3. Mary Davidson, b. February 1, 1849.
4. Clara, b. July 29, 1851.

D   (m) 2. Mary J. Greenlee, b. February 25, 1814; = John T. Finley: 3, John F. Greenlee, b. November 4, 1816; 4, Sarah Ann E. Greenlee, b. December 16, 1819; = Jas. L. Watson; 5, Martha T. Greenlee, b, April 20, 1823; = Eben N. Davis; 6, William P. Greenlee, b. May 16, 1825; = Eliza H. Foster; 7, Francis P. Greenlee, b. August 7, 1829; =P. T. Link.

C   2. Elijah Greenlee, b. 1772, d. in Milledgeville, Ga., a surgeon in United States Army.
3. John Greenlee, b. January 25, 1774; d. in Kentucky.
4. Mary Greenlee, b. September 12, 1776; d. November 14, 1840.

B   2. *James Greenlee*, b. October 19, 1740; = *Mary Mitchell*, his cousin.
3. *Mary Greenlee*, b. May 5, 1745.
4. *Margaret Greenlee*, b. June 15, 1748.
5. *Grace Greenlee*, b. June 23, 1750.
6. *David Greenlee*, b. November 1, 1752.
7. *Samuel Greenlee*, b. January 13, 1757; d. 1824.

A   2. MARGARET McDOWELL; =1736 in Pennsylvania, James Mitchell, and removed to Charleston, S. C. Their oldest daughter Mary, = James Greenlee (above).

(68)   ALEXANDER KEITH MARSHALL.

(*n*) INSCRIPTIONS ON THE M'DOWELL MAUSOLEUM IN THE CEMETERY NEAR FAIRFIELD, VA.

NORTH FACE.

Near this spot repose the remains of Ephraim McDowell, the first of his name in America, who died about 1776.

John McDowell, his son, who was killed by the Indians in 1742.

James McDowell, his son, b. 1739, d. 1772, and Elizabeth his wife, who d. about 1810, and also their daughter, Elizabeth McGavock, who died 1803.

EAST FACE.

James McDowell was b. August, 1770, and d. September, 1838. Distinguished by a native talent of a high order, a gallant and fearless spirit, a noble sense of justice, a lofty courage and an invincible power of will, he lived honorably and usefully, discharging with singular ability and fidelity, the trusts, civil and military, committed to him, and died universally regretted. His remains repose here with those of his ancestors for three generations.

WEST FACE.

Sarah McDowell, daughter of Col. Wm. Preston, and wife of James McDowell, was b. May 23, 1768, and d. July 3, 1841. Born in the stormy period of our national history, her character, moulded by the spirit and developed by the struggle of the times, was eminently truthful, patriotic and elevated; yet to these traits she added the gentler qualities of the tender and devoted woman and the sincere christian.

SOUTH FACE.

To commemorate the virtues, to perpetuate the memory; to record the truth, honor, patriotism and public and social fidelity, that impressed the generations to which they belonged and enabled them to transmit an honored name to their descendants; and also to testify the gratitude and reverence of their families.

THIS MOUNMENT,

is erected to their grand parents, James and Sarah McDowell, by the surviving children of Susan P. Taylor, Elizabeth Benton and James McDowell, in the year 1855.

THE MARSHALL FAMILY.

(68) ALEXANDER KEITH MARSHALL.

THE M'DOWELL-REID FAMILY.

(o) Magdalen McDowell, b. in Rockbridge Co., Va., October 9, 1755, daughter of Samuel McDowell and Mary McClung, = Andrew Reid. Issue:

A   1. THE OLDEST DAUGHTER = Gen. Andrew Moore, Member of Congress 1789—97, re-elected 1804; United States Senator 1804—1809; d. May 24, 1821. Issue:

B   1. *Samuel McDowell Moore*, Member of Congress 1833 —35; served in the Confederate Army, d. 1884; = Evilyn Alexander, daughter of Wm. Alexander, of Rockbridge Co., Va. Their daughter Sallie, = her cousin, John Harvey Moore.

     2. *David E. Moore*, = Elizabeth Harvey. Issue:

C   1. Andrew Moore, = Elizabeth McGavock.
     2. J. H. Moore, = Sallie Moore.
     3. David E. Moore, lawyer, Lexington, Va.
     4. Edmond Moore, = —— Allen; 5, Fannie; 6, Sarah.
     7. Virginia Moore, = Tedford Barclay.
(p)   8. Elizabeth Moore, = Prof. Alexander Nelson.

B   3. Andrew Moore went to Georgia.

A   2. A DAUGHTER of Andrew Reid, = a Mr. McCampbell.
     1. Magdalen McCampbell, = a Venable.
     3. A DAUGHTER, = a Venable.
     4. ANOTHER DAUGHTER, = a Venable.
     5. A DAUGHTER, = Judge Abraham Smith of Rockbridge.
     6. A DAUGHTER, = Major John Alexander of Lexington, Va.

B   1. *Their son, Archibald*, = Sallie Dix; 2, John; 3, Bettie; 4, Mary M.; 5, Agnes, = Tucker Lacy.

A   7. NANCY REID; 8, MAGDALEN REID.
     9. SAMUEL McDOWELL REID, = a Miss Hare.
     1. A daughter, = Prof. James White.
     2. Agnes Reid, = Col. John S. H. Ross.

(68) ALEXANDER KEITH MARSHALL.

DESCENDANTS OF SARAH M'DOWELL AND COL. GEORGE MOFFET.

(q) 1. Margaret Moffet, a great beauty, = Gen. Joseph McDowell, of North Carolina, he commanded a portion of the army under his brother Charles, at the Battle of Kings Mountain, October 7, 1780; Member of Congress 1782—88, and again 1793—95.

    1. Joseph J. McDowell, Member of Congress, from North Carolina, 1843—47, = Sallie McCue.

2. Jas. McD. Moffet, = Hannah Miller.

    1. Col. Henry McD. Moffet.

3. George Moffet, = Miss Gilkerson.

4. William Moffet, = 1st, McChesney; = 2d, Jones.

5. Mary Moffet, = Dr. Jos. McDowell. After his death, she = Col. John Carson, and was mother of Samuel P. Carson, Member of Congress from North Carolina, 1825—33.

6. Magdalene Moffet, = Jas. Cochran. They were parents of Geo. M. Cockran, of Staunton, and John Cochran, of Charlottsville.

7. Martha Moffet, = Capt. Robt. Kirk, United States Army.

8. Elizabeth Moffet, = Jas. Miller.

(r) EPITAPHS IN THE DANVILLE, KY., CEMETERY.

1. Samuel McDowell, was b. November 7, 1735, and d. October 25, 1817.

2. Mary McDowell, d. October 27, 1827, aged 93 years.

3. Col. Joseph McDowell, b. September 13, 1768, d. June 22, 1856.

4. Sarah Irvin, his wife, was b. March 21, 1773, d. December 20, 1835.

5. Here lie the remains of Mrs. Margaret Sullivant, b. November 22, 1809, d. June 1, 1831.

6. Caleb W. McDowell, b. April 24, 1811, d. October 2, 1840.

7. Charles C. P. McDowell, b. April 19, 1804; d. March 4, 1883.

(70) DR. LOUIS MARSHALL.

70 (*a*) DR. LOUIS MARSHALL, b. at "Oakhill," Fauquier Co., Va., October 7, 1773; d. at Buckpond, Woodford County, Ky., 1866; = at Frankfort, Ky., 1800, AGATHA SMITH, b. 1782; d. May 1844. Like the other sons of Col. Marshall, Louis received instruction under the parental roof. When the family came to Kentucky in 1785, he was with them, and remembered the events of the perilous voyage down the Ohio, on a flat boat. He was sent to Edinburg, to complete his literary and scientific studies; and thence went to Paris, that he might enjoy all the advantages of that city for instruction in medicine and surgery. But the thrilling events of the French Revolution demanded his attention. He became an ardent Republican, and, with some of his fellow students participated in the attack on the Bastile, — was present at the massacre of the Swiss guard, — witnessed the murder of the Princess De-Lamballe, — was arrested in the Reign of Terror, and lay in prison for several years. He was at one time condemned to death, but was saved by the stratagem of the turnkey. He was at length liberated through the intercession of his brothers, John and James, then in Paris as representatives of the United States. He is said to have fought several duels, not without fatal results to his adversaries. However the truth may be, he would never suffer any one to refer to his career in Paris. He became excited at any allusion to it.

(*b*) Upon the marriage of Dr. Marshall, in 1800, his father surrendered "Buckpond" to him, and retired to Mason County, to dwell with his son, Thomas. Upon this farm Dr. Marshall commenced the practice of medicine, and attained the name of the most learned and successful physician in the State. His extraordinary attainments not only in medicine and surgery, but in every department of knowledge, gave him a high reputation throughout the West. But he inherited the family talent and propensity for teaching, and at his country home, gathered the most promising young men of Kentucky, and formed a private school. Nearly all his nephews in the West were educated by him at "Buckpond." He was a fine linguist, and well read in science, history, philosophy, and bells-letters. His scholars admired and feared him. He was a strict disciplinarian — severe and dogmatic in his style. He treated his scholars often with rudeness, encouraged a combatative style of argumentation, and instilled self-reliance. Among his scholars, the

(70) DR. LOUIS MARSHALL.

following are remembered: F. Blackburn, R. J. Breckinridge, Charles Buford, Basil Buford, Geo. B. Crittenden, Abram Buford, Basil Duke of St. Louis, Gen. Basil W. Duke, James K. Duke, Dr. John M. Duke, Capt. N. W. Duke, William Duke, Charles W. Forman, D. D., W. W. Forman, Dr. Lewis W. Green, Col. John J. Hardin, Geo. B. Kincaid, W. B. Kincaid, Alex. McClung, John A. McClung, D. D., Col. Chas. A. Marshall, Gen. Humphrey Marshall, Louis Marshall, Robt. M. Marshall, Geo. Madison, Joseph Perry, Christopher Tompkins, Charles Walker, Samuel Wallace and Henry Waller. This list with many others who are not recollected, forms an imperishable monument to his name.

(c) In 1838, Dr. Marshall was President of Washington College, Lexington, Va.; and in 1855, he was President of Transylvania University. He died at the age of 93, with a mind little impaired by time. In early life, he was tinctured with infidelity. As he said, himself, he tried hard to disbelieve the Bible. His doubts, however, were overcome, and he became a firm believer. The return of Dr. McClung (272) to the church, was, perhaps, owing largely to his Uncle's influence. I heard several lengthy private discussions between them in 1838 on the prophesies.

(d) Dr. Marshall, even before the death of his wife, spent much of his time in visiting from house to house, among his relatives. The first time I remember meeting him, was in 1835, at the house of his niece and my step-mother, Mary K. Green, near Danville, where I was attending college. I had often heard of his peculiarities, and of his bluff and dictatorial manner, and was prepared for a rebuff. I spoke to him cordially, called him Uncle Louis, and offered him my hand. He threw himself back, folded his arms and exclaimed: "Who the d—l are you, presuming to call me uncle!" I explained my relationship, and told my name. He thereupon became gracious, enquired into my studies, and ordered me to bring my Cæsar, that he might see if I had any sense. Fortunately, he selected a passage with which I was familiar. I translated it correctly; but he said otherwise; and pronounced me a fool. I was then ordered to parse a passage. He laughed at me and asked what sort of teachers I was under. Knowing his disposition I turned on him, and expressed my surprise at his want of scholarship and good breeding. This impertinence pleased him, and he always treated me kindly afterward.

THE MARSHALL FAMILY. 71

(70) DR. LOUIS MARSHALL.

Many stories are told of Uncle Louis's whims and peculiarities, as well as of his towering intellect and sublime scholarship. But he was more feared than respected,—more admired than loved.

Aunt Agatha Marshall was said to have been a lovely woman. Her husband was never rough to her. His scholars esteemed her highly, and she was generally beloved. She and her husband were buried at "Buckpond" but afterward removed to Frankfort. Chancellor Logan (264) and his wife were also interred at Frankfort.

THE PRESTON AND BRECKINRIDGE FAMILIES.

(*f*) John Preston, a native of County Derry, and a shipmaster of Dublin, married in Ireland Elizabeth Patton, and emigrated to Virginia, settling about 1743, near Staunton. Issue:

A   1. LETITIA PRESTON, = July 10, 1758, Col. Robt. Breckinridge. The Breckinridge family originated in the highlands of Braidalbane, Scotland; moved to the north of Ireland, whence Alexander Breckinridge emigrated to America early in the 18th century, bringing with him his son Robert. He settled at the West fork of the Blue Ridge, in what became Augusta Co., Va. He was twice married: 1st, to a Miss Pogue, by whom he had two sons, 1, Alexander; 2, Robert; both company officers in the Virginia line of the Revolutionary army, and among the first surveyors of Ky. They are frequently mentioned in Collins' Ky. Alexander = Jane Buchanan, widow of John Floyd, and left four sons, all men of importance in their communities. Robert lived in Louisville, never married, but left an honored name. Col. Robert Breckinridge, Sr., married Letitia Preston as his second wife. He died about 1770, leaving a widow with six small children, as follows:

B   1. *William Breckinridge*, b. May 2, 1759, lived to a great
(*g*)   age in Fayette Co., Ky., and left several children.

2. *John Breckinridge*, b. December 2, 1760, = June 28, 1785, Mary Hopkins Cabell, of Buckingham Co., Va., dr. of Col. Jos. Cabell, and Mary Hopkins. Issue:

C   1. Letitia Preston Breckinridge, b. June 13, 1786,= 1805, Alfred W. S. Grayson (issue); = 2d, Peter B. Porter, of New York (issue).

THE MARSHALL FAMILY.

(70) DR. LOUIS MARSHALL.

C   2. Joseph Cabell Breckinridge, b. July 24, 1788, = Mary C. Smith, dr. of Samuel Stanhope Smith, President of Princeton College, N. J., and Ann Witherspoon, dr. of Dr. Witherspoon, a signer of the Declaration of Independence. Issue:

D

       1. Frances Ann Breckinridge, = Dr. John C. Young, President of Centre College (issue).

(h)   2. Caroline Breckinridge, = Rev. Dr. Joseph Bullock (issue).

       3. Mary Breckinridge, = Dr. Thomas P. Satterwhite, of Louisville (issue).

       4. John C. Breckinridge, Vice-President of the U.S., = Mary C. Burch, dr. of Clifton R. Burch and Aletha Viley. Issue:

E   1. Cabell Clifton Breckinridge, now M. C. from Arkansas.

          2. Fanny, = John Steel.

          3. John; 4, Owen, of California.

          5. Mary Desha Breckinridge, b. March 31, 1854, = December 20, 1877, ANSON MALTBY, No. 1704.

D   5. Letitia P. Breckinridge, = Charles Parkhill.

       6. Mary Ann C. Breckinridge.

B   3. *Mary Ann Breckinridge*, b. February 4, 1795, = 1812, David Castleman.

(i) 4. *John Breckinridge*, D. D., b. July 4, 1797, = 1st, Margaret Miller; = 2d, Miss Babcock.

      5. *Robert J. Breckinridge*, D. D. L. L. D., b. March 8, 1800, = March 11, 1823, Ann Sophronia Preston. (Issue.)

      6. *William L. Breckinridge*, D. D. L. L. D., b. July 22, 1803, President of Centre College, Kentucky, and of University of Mississippi; = May 10, 1824, Frances Caro. Prevost. Issue.

C   1. Cabell Breckinridge, b. March 11, 1825.

        2. John B. Breckinridge, b. October 27, 1826.

        3. Robt. James Breckinridge, b. December 2, 1828.

(72) SUSAN TARLETON MARSHALL—(McClung).

C
    4. Marcus P. Breckinridge, b. October 17, 1830.
    5. Wm. L. Breckinridge, b. November 12, 1832.
    6. Lewis G. Breckinridge, b. September 19, 1834.
    7. Fannie P. Breckinridge, b. October 12, 1836.
    8. Mary H. Breckinridge, b. February 1, 1839.
    9. Stanhope P. Breckinridge, b. April 20, 1841.
    10. Theodosia P. Breckidridge, b. August 11, 1843.
    11. Cabell Breckinridge, b. November 22, 1846, = October 7, 1868, JULIA S. MARSHALL, No. 2430, b. October 20, 1843.
    12. Letitia P. Breckinridge, b. August 24, 1849.

A   (k) 2. A DAUGHTER, = Rev. John Brown.

    3. WILLIAM PRESTON, = Susanna Smith.

B   1 *Francis Preston*, = Sarah B. Campbell.

C   1. Sophronia Preston, =R. J. Breckinridge.

A   4. ANNE PRESTON, = Francis Smith.

B   1. *Agatha Smith*, = DR. LOUIS MARSHALL, No. 70.

A   5. A DAUGHTER, = John Howard.

72 (a) SUSAN TARLETON MARSHALL, b. at "Oakhill," Fauquier Co., Va., May 12, 1774, d. in Marysville, Ky., 1858, = at Buckpond, Woodford Co., Ky., May 25, 1793, JUDGE WILLIAM MCCLUNG, b. in Rockbridge Co., Va., July 12, 1758, d. in Mason Co., Ky., 1811. William McClung was graduated at Washington College, Va., in 1785; studied law with Thomas Jefferson; about the year 1791, emigrated to Kentucky with his cousin, Joe McDowell, and settled at Bardstown; was a member of the Virginia legislature from Kentucky; represented Nelson County in the Kentucky Senate from 1796 to 1800; was a member of the Constitutional Convention that met in Danville, Ky., in 1787; was one of the midnight judges appointed by President Adams, March 3, 1800; but was legislated out of office by the abolition of the circuit of Ken-

(72) SUSAN TARLETON MARSHALL — (*McClung*).

tucky, over which he presided; he then removed with my father, Jas. A. Paxton, to Mason Co., Ky.; was appointed Circuit Judge, and died in office in 1811. In Mason, Judge McClung resided near Washington, Ky., and then purchased the Orr farm, in Charleston bottom, three miles below Marysville. He was attacked with a malignant fever while holding court at Augusta, and was brought up home in a skiff. He was buried on the farm, about 300 yards southeast of the family mansion.

(*b*) Judge McClung was a man of superior legal and literary attainments, and unblemished morals. His logical mind, with his training and erudition, made him almost irresistable in argument. Collins (2d Ky., 576) says, that "he was distinguished for his high attainments as a lawyer, but most eminently for his unapproachable integrity as a judge." My father studied law with him and named me for him.

Aunt McClung was, perhaps, the most intellectual of the daughters of Col. Thos. Marshall. Her mind possessed masculine powers, and she delighted to associate with people of culture. She combined intelligence with sweetness of temper, purity of thought and tenderness of heart. In the days of my childhood and orphanage, she was a mother to me. I delighted to read to her, and hear her comments. She was dignified and imposing in her manner; yet everybody loved her. Her reading was extensive, her information varied, and her conversation exceedingly interesting. When, in 1831 and 1832, I lived at the old haunted Orr mansion, perched on the Ohio bluff, with its solitary halls, lofty ceilings, and spacious corridors, she kindly took me to her room of nights, to allay my boyish fears of ghosts. In her long widowhood of 47 years, she was a welcome and honored visitor among her kindred.

(*c*) THE M'CLUNGS AND ALEXANDERS.

1. Archibald Alexander, of Manor Cunningham, County Donegal, Scotland, descended from the houses of McAlexander, of Tarbert and of Kintyre.

2. William Alexander had four sons: 1, Archibald; 2, William; 3, Robert; 4, Peter.

3. Archibald, b. at Manor Cunningham, February 4, 1708, = December 31, 1734, his cousin, Margaret, dr. of Joseph Parks, of County Donegal. She died July, 1753. With his brother,

THE MARSHALL FAMILY. 75

(72) SUSAN TARLETON MARSHALL—(*McClung*).

Robert, he came to America in 1736, and settled in New Providence, Pa. About 1747, Archibald removed to Rockbridge Co., Va., whither his brother Robert had preceded him. Issue:

A 1. ELIZABETH ALEXANDER, b. in Scotland, October 28, 1735, = John McClung, of Timber Ridge, b. in Ireland in 1731, and came to Rockbridge in 1747. He died in 1817. Issue:

B (d) 1. *William McClung*, = SUSAN MARSHALL.
     2. *Margaret McClung*, = Robert Tate.
     3. *John McClung*, = Mary Stuart.
     4. *Archibald McClung*.
     5. *Elizabeth McClung*, = Robert Stuart.
     6. *Phoebe McClung*, = March 23, 1786, James Paxton.

C   1. Jas. A. Paxton, b. in Rockbridge Co., Va., September 13, 1788, d. in Washington, Ky., October 23, 1825, = May 2, 1811, MARIA MARSHALL. No. 244.

B   7. *Dr. James McClung*.
     8. *Rebecca McClung*, = Wm. Steele.
     9. *Joseph McClung*, b. 1775, d. 1867.
     10. *Esther McClung*.
     11. *Polly McClung*.

A 2. WILLIAM ALEXANDER, = Agnes Ann Reid.

B (e) 1. *Archibald Alexander, D. D.*, President of Princeton College, b. April 17, 1772, in Rockbridge Co., Va.

A 3. ANNE ALEXANDER, b. at New Providence, Pa., September 17, 1740, = Rev. Caruthers.

    4. JOSEPH ALEXANDER, b. at New Providence, Pa., February 9, 1742, = Sarah Reid.

    5. HANNAH ALEXANDER, b. at New Providence, Pa., April 21, 1745, = Joseph Lyle.

    5. PHOEBE ALEXANDER, b. in Augusta Co., Va., August 12, 1749, = John Paxton. Issue:

(74) CHARLOTTE MARSHALL — (*Duke*).

B   1. *James Paxton*, = his cousin (above) Phoebe McClung. Issue:

C   1. Jas. Alex. Paxton, = MARIA MARSHALL. 244.

THE M'CLUNGS.

(*f*) Four brothers and two sisters came from Ireland in 1747 :

A   1. MATHEW McCLUNG, settled in Lancaster Co., Pa., = Martha Cunningham.

     2. JOHN McCLUNG, settled in Augusta Co., Va., = Elizabeth Alexander, and they were parents of JUDGE WM. McCLUNG (above).

     3. A BROTHER, name not remembered, settled in Wilmington, Delaware.

     4. JAMES McCLUNG, settled in Augusta Co., Va.

     5. MARY McCLUNG, = Capt. Samuel McDowell (uncertain). See the McDowells. No. 68 *d*.

     6. A SISTER, married an Alexander.

74   CHARLOTTE MARSHALL, b. at "Oakhill," Fauquier Co., Va., 1777, d. in Washington, Ky., April 17, 1817, = at "Buckpond," Woodford Co., Ky., 1794, Dr. BASIL DUKE, b. in Calvert Co., Md., 1766, d. in Washington, Ky., 1828. Dr. Duke = 2d, MARGARET CHINN, dr. of Raleigh Chinn, of Mayslick, Ky. She survived him, and after his death returned to her relatives.

I know little of Aunt Charlotte She died before my birth. The little I have heard of her is to her credit. The second marriage of Dr. Duke was unfortunate. The children all left the parental roof, and all records and memorials were lost. Dr. Duke's pedigree is unknown to his posterity, but the Duke family, to which he belonged, is still found in Calvert Co., Md.

Dr. Duke received a superior education, under the tuition of a Scotchman, eminent for his scholorship. After studying medicine, and practicing for some years in Baltimore, he removed about 1791 to Lexington, Ky., where he enjoyed a large practice. In 1798, he removed to Washington, Ky., and, while practicing, was extensively engaged in the mercantile pursuits, in company with Judge John

(76) JANE MARSHALL—(*Taylor*).

Coburn and Capt. Nath'l Wilson. Their dry goods store was kept in a frame building opposite the house now occupied by James Marshall. Dr. Duke and Judge Coburn built the old Duke House, southeast of the Court house, and their families occupied separate apartments of it. Capt. Wilson built the Dr. Johnston house, south of the Court house.

Dr. Duke was the first physician in Kentucky that had independence and faith to recommend vaccination, and to this circumstance, as well as to his medical skill, he owes the high regard shown to his name by the profession. But he is also honored for his enterprise, integrity and kindness of heart.

76 JANE MARSHALL, b. at "Oakhill," Fauquier Co., Va., July 29, 1779, d. at Mt. Ephraim, Fauquier.Co., Va., September 13, 1766, = December 22, 1799, GEORGE KEITH TAYLOR, b. March 16, 1769, d. November 10, 1815. Aunt Taylor was handsome, dignified, intelligent and amiable. She received her education chiefly in the family circle, and teaching was the theme of her thoughts and the business of her life. The death of her husband gave her intense anguish. The strain upon her mind was so severe as to cause apprehensions of insanity. Her physician recommended some employment to turn her thoughts from her bereavement. She engaged in teaching, and opened a large school in Petersburg, Va. Her mind became absorbed with her new duties, and she succeeded admirably. After a time she removed her school to Richmond. About 1837, after the marriage of her oldest daughter, she visited her relatives in Kentucky, in company with her two younger daughters, Sallie and Georgianna. I met her at the house of her niece, Mary K. Green (180), near Danville. She spent several weeks with the family. All were highly pleased with mother and daughters. The latter were remarkable for their skill in music. On her return to Virginia, she continued to teach, and her friends claim that her system of education was new and admirable. But her eyesight began to fail, and she finally became totally blind, after having overtaxed her eyes by reading small print. But she still preserved her cheerfulness, and learned to read by touch, as the blind are taught. She died at "Mt. Ephraim," the seat of the Royalls.

(78) NANCY MARSHALL—(*Daviess*).

George Keith Taylor was the oldest child of Richard Taylor, a wealthy merchant of Petersburg, Va., and his wife, Mary Field. By the marriage settlement between his parents, the oldest son was to be named George K. Taylor, and a large estate was settled upon him. He was descended from the celebrated Quaker, and was named for him before birth. He was in no way related to Parson Jas. Keith. Geo. K. Taylor was born, lived and died at "Spring Garden," the seat of the Taylors, in Petersburg, Va.

78 NANCY MARSHALL, b. at "Oakhill," Fauquier Co., Va., about 1781; = 1803, COL. JOE HAMILTON DAVIESS, son of Joseph and Jean Daviess, b. in Bedford Co., Va., March 4, 1774; killed at the battle of Tippecanoe, November 8, 1811. About 1779, his parents moved to the vicinity of Danville, Ky. He received from tutors a good classical education. In 1792 he had his first experience in Indian warfare, under Gen. Adair, who crossed the Ohio and made an incursion as far as Fort St. Clair. Upon his return, he studied law with the celebrated George Nicholas. He was a laborious and indefatigable student, and when, in 1795, he was licensed, took a high position at the bar; settled at Danville, but being appointed United States Attorney for the district of Kentucky, removed to Frankfort; thence to Owensboro, and lastly to Lexington. In 1806 he distinguished himself by his spirited prosecution of Aaron Burr, for treason. In 1811, he accompanied Gen. Harrison in his expedition to the Wabash, and at Tippecanoe fell, in a charge upon the Indians. Col. Daviess was of tall and commanding person — a brilliant orator, and a profound lawyer His death spread a cloud of gloom over Kentucky. He was greatly beloved, and was regarded as the most promising young man of the West.

Aunt Nancy, I remember, when, in my childhood, she visited her friends in Mason. She was cross-eyed, but intelligent and spirited. Her patrimonial estate was on the lower Ohio, and she found society chiefly in Louisville. She married as her second husband, William Pollard. He lived but a short time. Late in life she married a Mr. Cox, and after a few unhappy months experience, was divorced. She was a member of the Christian (Disciples) church. She had no children.

[84] JANE MARSHALL.

80 JAMES MARSHALL, son of John Marshall, lived in Boon Co., Ky., and some of his posterity still reside there. He was a tall, raw-boned, plain and ugly man, and his descendants, on account of their black hair and eyes, were called the Black Marshalls. One of his daughters had a legacy from her aunt Jane Marshall. (84.)

82 JOHN MARSHALL removed to Missouri, and his posterity is unknown to the rest of the family. In 1844, I attended the great Whig Convention at Lexington, Mo., and an old man was introduced on the stand, as a brother of Humphrey Marshall, the Kentucky Senator. I then felt no interest in him, and have never since heard of him.

84 JANE MARSHALL, a maiden sister of Senator Humphrey Marshall, lived and died in Paris, Ky., and is well remembered by old people there. Her will is perhaps the best record, extant, of her life. It was probated September 5, 1836. She gives to:

1. Jane Catlett, a lot in East Maysville and a negro.
2. Frances M. Wall, her niece, several negroes for life, and remainder to her children, if any; and if none, to revert, and go to Jane Marshall, her brother James' daughter, to Jane Whittington, daughter of Thomas and Mary Whittington, to Anna Maria and Catherine Morrison, her nieces. No. 1030, 1032.
3. Samuel G. Wall, her "dear little nephew," a negro, &c.
4. George W. Wall, her "little nephew," a bed for the benefit of his mother for life, and then to go to him.
5. Anna Marshall, daughter of Judge Marshall, a negro, &c. No. 1020.
6. I bequeath $50 to my sister January, &c. She authorizes a slave Robert to buy himself, and the proceeds to go to Matilda E. January, daughter of Peter and Isabella January. She gives to Ann Breeden certain notes.

The will is witnessed by Jos. Stephens, D. R. Williams, and Thos. A. Marshall. Geo. W. Wall appears to have administrated, and in settlement, November 5, 1837, shows assets $223.64, from which he paid to John M. Breeden, husband and administrator of

(86) NANCY MARSHALL.

Ann Breeden, $75; to W. H. Cummins, who had married Charlotte Whittington, $75; and to Elizabeth January $40; leaving in his hands $33.64.

86 NANCY MARSHALL was a daughter of John Marshall. She seems to have died in Paris, Ky., about 1860. She left no will, but her administrator, Geo. W. Williams, made settlement of her estate in 1862, which I copy in full as the only record I have of her heirs. She was never married:

Amount for distribution $4,155 00

CREDITS.

Elizabeth Whittington	$113 40
C. Wall	88 59
Jesse Price	59 05
Jacob McGettan	59 06
Lewis Whittington	28 34
J. and M. Marr	59 06
H. Marshall	88 54
M. Jeffries, et. al	59 05
Elizabeth Stephens	59 06
J. M. Breeden	141 75
A. and M. Kidd	59 06
W. H. and C. D. Cummins	141 74
Jas. Deering	47 25
T. A. Marshall	54 36
J. M. Whittington	47 24
E. J Davis	47 24
Nancy Marshall	59 06
G. W. Grant	47 25
J. J. Marshall	88 59
Chas. Marshall	59 05
Thomas A. Marshall	300 00
J. B. Marshall	88 59
M. A. Ballinger	47 24
F. M. Clark	88 59
	$1,931 16
Balance in Administrator's hands	$2,224 45

88 HUMPHREY MARSHALL, b. in Virginia, about 1756, d. in Frankfort, Ky., July 1, 1841 = in Virginia, about 1784, MARY MARSHALL (54), b. at "Oakhill," Fauquier Co., Va., about 1757, d. about 1827; both buried at Frankfort. Mr. Marshall came to Kentucky prior to 1783, as his name appears on the list of purchasers of lots in Lexington that year. He was a member of the convention at

HUMPHREY MARSHALL.

Danville, in 1787, preliminary to the formation of State constitution; also a member of the Virginia convention that ratified the U.S. constitution; he represented Woodford County in the State legislature in 1793, and Franklin County in 1807, 1808, 1809 and 1823; was one of the first U. S. Senators from Kentucky, 1795–1801: near Frankfort, he fought his celebrated duel with Henry Clay, in which the latter received a slight flesh wound. In 1812, he published the first history of Kentucky, in one octavo volume of 407 pages. In 1824, he revised the work, and published it in two volumes, 502 and 524 pages. It is able and interesting, but prejudice and partizanship appear on every page. He was an overweening Federalist, and wrote more as a politician than as an impartial historian.

Senator Humphrey Marshall was violent, profane and irreligious. He had but little respect for God or man. But his wife was an ardent Episcopalian and a lovely Christian lady. She was called the Hannah More of the family, and her memory is cherished as much by her collateral kindred as by her descendants. Col. Green thus notices the Senator:

"Mr. Marshall took an active part in frustrating the Spanish conspiracy and that of Aaron Burr; was one of the first Senators in Congress from this State, and was many times in both branches of the legislature; he was hated more than any other man of his day by the early Republicans of the State, and he never failed to carry with him the people when he chose to seek their suffrages;—a Captain in the Revolutionary army; an emigrant to Kentucky in 1780; bitterly prejudiced, and sometimes, though not often, unjust; six feet two inches in height, a grand-looking, eagle-eyed old man, and as fearless a man as ever breathed. Gov. Charles Scott at one time offered a free pardon to any one who would kill the old Federalist, and a young man to whom Humphrey Marshall had given some offense, embraced the occasion of a visit to Lexington, to win the eternal gratitude of the Republicans, by doing so. A large crowd was in the town to see the job well done, and, among others, was Gov. Scott himself. After concluding the business which had brought him, Marshall mounted his horse and rode leisurely off\ the young sprig galloping after him. Presenting his pistol, he told Marshall he had come to kill him. "Well," said the old man very coolly, "but you have not come to assassinate me, have you."

(90) MARY MARSHALL—(*Whittington*).

"No," replied the young buck, "here is another for you." Marshall took the offered weapon, and, with a quick blow, knocked the other out of his antagonist's hand, saying: "Now, d—m you, march;" and with that, made him ride back before him, in the presence of the crowd assembled. Scott roared "I have never seen such a defeat since the battle of Monmouth, (where Tarleton had flaxed him)."

90   MARY MARSHALL, daughter of John Marshall, = THOMAS WHITTINGTON and probably lived in Woodford Co., Ky.

92   ELIZABETH MARSHALL, daughter of John Marshall, = SAMUEL JANUARY, and lived many years in East Maysville, Ky., in the house now occupied by Col. Stanton. Mr. January was interred in the private burying ground near his house. I examined the lot in 1884, and could find no stone to the memory of any of the family. When a child, I remember visiting the family with my mother. After the death of Mr. January, his widow removed to Cynthianna, which became the home of his posterity.

94   GEORGE MARSHALL, b. in Henry Co., Ky., = O. VARDEMAN. He was a farmer and a man of intelligence. He resided near Eminence, Henry Co., Ky. See Gen. Doniphan's notice of him. No. 102.

96   LEWIS MARSHALL removed in early life to Alabama, and I have learned nothing further of him.

98   WILLIAM MARSHALL, b. in Henry Co., Ky.: = Rebecca Johnson, a relative of Col. Richard M. Johnson, Vice-President of the United States. His father, Rev. William Marshall, about 1806, deeded him valuable lands, which were lost to him and his children by adverse titles.

(102) MARTIN MARSHALL.

102 (a) MARTIN MARSHALL of Augusta, b. in Fauquier Co., Va., September 11, 1777, d. in Augusta, Ky., September 19, 1853; = in Bracken Co., Ky., March 16, 1803, MATILDA TALIAFERRO, b. in Virginia, September 30, 1787; d. in Augusta, Ky., March 1, 1843. Martin Marshall was a distinguished lawyer and the only one of the family of Rev. William Marshall that associated with the descendants of Col. Thomas Marshall. He represented Bracken County in the Kentucky Legislature 1805 and 1806. In 1829 and 1830, while attending Augusta College, I became familiar with his children. Gen. A. W. Doniphan, now of Richmond, Mo., studied law with him, and thus writes of his old preceptor:

"I regret that knowledge of one I admired and venerated more than any man I ever knew, should be so meagre. Pardon what I feel constrained to offer, as one of the principal reasons why I never learned more of him and his ancestors. The Marshalls generally, indeed, universally, were proud of their family. It would have been unnatural not to have been so;—indeed it was a theme of conversation with many of them. But Mr. Marshall, on the contrary, rarely spoke of himself or his family, during the two years I was reading in his office. I cannot recall a single word he said touching either. He was reticent and dignified; and at the same time he was courteous to others and of gentle manners."

(b) The following passage from a latter of Mrs. M. T. Soward, dated Augusta, Ky., July 17, 1885, will give information on the Taliaferro pedigree:

"I have a copy of the family bible, kept by my grandfather, Nicholas Taliaferro. He married Ann Taliaferro, daughter of Col. John Taliaferro, and Ann Taliaferro, his cousin. His father, William Taliaferro, married Mary Battaille, daughter of Capt. Nicholas and Mary Battaille, of Caroline Co., Va. His grandmother's maiden name was Thornton. My grandfather's father married a second time a daughter of Francis Taliaferro. All of them lived in Virginia. My grandfather was a Revolutionary officer, and served throughout the entire war. He moved from Culpeper Co., Va., to Kentucky, in 1797, with his wife and five children, and settled in Bracken Co. Uncle Martin Marshall married his second daughter, Matilda Battaille Taliaferro. I also find in the record the names of Col. John Thornton and Reubin Thornton, —but their relationship is not shown. We have never known of any relationship to the Washingtons and the Gregorys.

(c) Uncle Martin Marshall wrote in the clerks office, and studied law with Capt. Thomas Marshall (56), in Washington, Ky., and married my aunt whilst there, and remained until he removed to Augusta. He named a daughter, Francis Kennan, after Mrs. Thomas Marshall. They named another child Thornton Francis Louis Marshall, for Mrs. Thos. Marshall and his brother, Dr. Louis Marshall.

FAMILY OF JOHN TALIAFERRO.

(d) Two brothers, John and Richard, are said to have come from Italy? about the beginning of the last century. The descen-

(102) MARTIN MARSHALL.

dants of John, only, intermarried with the Marshalls, and hence I trace his line. He was born 1687, and died in Spotsylvania Co., Va., May 3, 1744. His wife was Mary Catlett. Issue:

A   1. LAWRENCE TALIAFERRO, b. September 8, 1721; d. May 1, 1748; = Susanna Power.

B   1. *Sarah Taliaferro* b. October 18, 1746; = Wm. Dangerfield.

A   2. WILLIAM TALIAFERRO, b. at "Snow Creek," Spotsylvania Co., Va., August 9, 1726; d. April 24, 1798; = October 4, 1751, Mary, daughter of Capt. Nicholas Battaille, and Mary Thornton of "Hay," Coroline Co., Va.

B   1. *Nicholas Taliaferro*, b. October 30, 1757; d. February, 1812; = November 3, 1781, his cousin Ann Taliaferro, b. April 7, 1756; d. February, 3, 1798, in Kentucky. They came in 1797 to Bracken Co., Ky. Issue:

C   (*e*) 1. Lucy Mary Taliaferro, b. August 6, 1782; = Capt. William Buckner, of Augusta, Ky.

2. John Champe Taliaferro, b. October 12, 1784; = Susan Buckner.

3. Matilda B. Taliaferro, b. September 3, 1787; = MARTIN MARSHALL. See No. 102.

4. Mary Willis Taliaferro, b. August 11, 1789; d. January 25, 1797.

5. George Catlett Taliferro, b. March 21, 1792; d. March 23, 1823; = June 17, 1813, Mary King; d. 1820. Issue:

D   1. Matilda Ann Taliaferro, b. December 28, 1814; = December 22, 1852, Col. Alf. Soward, d. December 22, 1879, son of Gen. Richard Soward, of Mason Co., Ky.

C   (*f*) 6. Dr. William Thornton Taliaferro, the distinguished Oculist of Cincinnati, b. January 16, 1795; = in advanced age, Eliza Ramsey. No issue.

B   1. *Nicholas Taliaferro*, = 2d, Frances Blassingame, and had three sons:

THE MARSHALL FAMILY. 85

(102) MARTIN MARSHALL.

C   1. Lawrence W. Taliaferro, b. October 28, 1800.
       2. Nicholas Taliaferro, b. August 14, 1806.
       3. Marshall Taliaferro, b. March 9, 1809.

B   2. *John Taliaferro*, b. July 31, 1753; = Ann Stockdell.
       3. *Lucy Taliaferro*, b. December 15, 1755.

A   3. MARTHA TALIAFERRO, b. June 24, 1724, = William Hunter, d. January 25, 1754.

B   1. *James Taliaferro*, b. November 6, 1746.
       2. *Martha Taliaferro*, b. October 20, 1749.

A   4. COL. JOHN TALIAFERRO, of "Dissington," = —— Hannon.

B   1. 1, *John* ; 2, *Richard* = Baldwin; 3, *a daughter* = Chancellor Geo. Wythe, 1726,— June 8, 1806; 4, *Ann Taliaferro*, = her cousin Nicholas (above).

A   5. PHILIP TALIAFERRO, = Lucy, daughter of Col. Thos. Baytop, and grand-daughter of "King" Carter.

B   1. *Dr. William Taliaferro*, = Harriet Throckmorton, daughter of Phillip Throckmorton and Mary Langborn. He was educated abroad. Issue:

C   (*g*) 1. Warner Taliaferro, father of Maj. Gen. William B. Taliaferro, C. S. A.
         2. Dr. William Taliaferro, educated in England and Germany.
         3. Gen. Alex. G. Taliaferro, = AGNES H. MARSHALL. No. 502.

B   2. *James Taliaferro*, = 1st, Kate Booth; = 2d, Betsy Thornton.
       3. *Rev. Philip Taliaferro*, = Oliver.
       4. *Richard Taliaferro*, = Betsy Wedderbane.
       5. *Thomas Taliaferro*, = Sarah Oliver.

THE FOLLOWING TRANSCRIPT OF AN OLD FAMILY BIBLE IS FURNISHED BY J. S. PITCHER, OF NASHVILLE, TENN.

Richard Taliaferro, = Rose Berryman, June 10, 1726, and died September 27, 1748. Issue:

(116) MRS. WILLIAM GREEN.

(h) 1. Sarah Taliaferro, b. June 7, 1727.
2. Benjamin Taliaferro, b. November 21, 1728.
3. Zacharias Taliaferro, b. August 29, 1730.
4. Richard Taliaferro, b. February 15, 1731, d. the 26th of the same month.
5. John Taliaferro, b. April 7, 1733.
6. Charles Taliaferro, b. July 16, 1735.
7. Beheathland Taliaferro, b. August 20, 1738.
8. Peter Taliaferro, b. February 12, 1740.
9. 10. Elizabeth Taliaferro and Rose (twins), b. November 2, 1741.
11. Mary Taliaferro, b. October 6, 1743.
12. Francis Taliaferro, b. December 9, 1745.
13. Richard Taliaferro, b. September 2, 1747.

CHILDREN OF CHARLES TALIAFERRO, b. July 16, 1735, = Isabel McCulloch, April 13, 1758, and d. April 11, 1798.

(i) 1. Richard Taliaferro, b. May 23, 1759.
2. Charles, b. March 29, 1761.
3. Peter, b. March 4, 1763; d. July 4, 1782.
4. John, b. May 4, 1765; d. November 4, 1809.
5. Zacharias Taliaferro, b. September 23, 1767; d. September 12, 1823.
6. Benjamin, b. January 9, 1770.
7. William, b. March 17, 1772.
8. Sarah, b. August 16, 1774.
9. Roderick, b. May 16, 1777.
10. James, b. April 12, 1779.
11. Rose, b. January 2, 1783.

116 (a) MRS. WILLIAM GREEN was born in Virginia in 1769. She was the only child of Markham Marshall, of whom there is any knowledge in the family. Her christian name has not come down to us. Gen. Duff. Green, in his volume entitled " Facts and Suggestions," thus notices the family:

THE MARSHALL FAMILY. 87

(116) MRS. WILLIAM GREEN.

"My parental grandfather left seven sons: 1, William Green; 2, Robert; 3, Duff; 4, John; 5, Nicholas; 6, James, and 7, Moses.

(*b*) "My grandfather, with his cousin, Sir William Duff, and a Mr. Hite, were, as I have frequently heard my father say, joint owners of large tracts of choice land, some situated on James river, and others in the valley of the Shenandoah. My grandfather, Duff Green, married first, a Miss Barbour, who died leaving a son and daughter, — John and Elizabeth. He then married a sister of Col. Lewis Willis, of Fredericksburg. She was a cousin of Gen. Washington, and nearly related to the Lewises, Henrys and Lees, of Virginia. My grandfather died before the Revolution. My grandmother had three sons, Willis, Henry and William, and one daughter, Eleanor. My father, William, the youngest son, was a volunteer in the army of the Revolution, and when fifteen years of age, was with Morgan in the battle of the Cowpens.

(*c*) "As the eldest son, John, was heir under the law of primogeniture, and took the greater part of the property. The three younger sons, through the influence of friends and relatives of the family, made contracts to locate land-warrants in Kentucky. Under this arrangement Willis and Henry went to Kentucky soon after the termination of the war, leaving my father in charge of mother and sister. Willis was elected a delegate from Kentucky to the Legislature of Virginia, and was appointed Register of the Land Office. He then relinquished his interest in the land-warrants to his brothers and sister. Henry having made his locations, returned to Virginia, sickened and died. This made it necessary that my father should remove to Kentucky, taking his mother and sister with him. My aunt soon thereafter married John Smith.

(*d*) "My maternal grandfather was Markham Marshall, who married Ann Bailey. They resided on the Shenandoah, until my mother, who was their second child, was about ten years of age. He removed to Kentucky in the fall of 1779, and settled near Knoblick, in Lincoln County., My father after his marriage, resided in Woodford County, until I, his eldest child, was about fourteen years old, when he removed to a large tract of land on the Cumberland river, in Wayne County. When I was about six years of age, I was sent to a neighborhood school. Most of the scholars were the children of my father's tenants, or persons holding lands under an ad-

(118) THOMAS M'CLANAHAN.

verse title. Humphrey Marshall, my mother's cousin, was my father's counsel, and Henry Clay opposed him. Mr Marshall had married his cousin, the eldest sister of the Chief Justice, and she and my mother were intimate friends. He had been Senator in Congress from Kentucky, and voted for "Jay's treaty," which was bitterly denounced by Mr. Clay and others. Mrs. Humphrey Marshall gave me the use of books from her library, and, after my returning them, examined me on what I had read. My parents were both of the Baptist Church. My mother was my companion and friend. Her intelligent comments on the lessons in history, which I read to her, and upon the events of the war of the Revolution, and her description of frontier life, did much to form my character. She had a happy faculty of illustrating her advice by anecdotes, &c." See Green chart, 180 *h*.

118 THOMAS MCCLANAHAN, b. in Fauquier Co., Va., about 1758, d. in Bourbon Co., Ky., 1809, = in Va., about 1780, NANCY GREEN. In boyhood, Thomas was remarkable for strength and activity. Many of his adventures are recorded by his kinsman, T. Marshall Smith, in his volume of " Legends." Fifty pages of the book are devoted to the courtship, marriage and achievements of Thomas McClanahan. After displaying his physical prowess in unnumbered fights, the boy-hero entered the regiment of his uncle, Col. Thomas Marshall, and proved himself a daring and chivalrous soldier. About the end of the war, he fell in love with Miss Nancy Green, but found a bitter enemy in her brother, Col. Robt. Green, of Revolutionary fame. But in spite of all opposition, they marry, and after a short time are reconciled with Col. Green. They settle on New river, near Abington, Va.; in 1782 remove to Kentucky, and settle near Boon's Station; he becomes a hardy woodsman; has many perilous adventures with the Indians; follows them to Ohio and Indiana, and becomes noted for his heroic exploits. Mr. Smith, in his " Legends," records many acts of daring, all of which are crowned with success. Though generous and chivalrous, yet his fighting propensities gave him the character of a desperado. He settled in Bourbon Co., Ky., and was elected to the Legislature in 1793.

Thomas McClanahan's will is recorded in Bourbon Co., Ky., Will Book, C, p. 476. It is dated May 4, 1807, probated at the

(144) THOMAS MARSHALL SMITH.

February term, 1809; recites, 1st, the names of the heirs of his son William, as follows: Thomas, William, Lucy Brown, Elizabeth Harrison, Aga Pullen, Sally and Polly. William's widow is called Elizabeth; 2d, Thomas McClanahan; 3d, Clary, wife of David Hickman; 4th, Peggy, wife of Robt. Johnstone; mentions his grandson, William Johnstone, also Maurice Langhorne, Samuel Elgin and Aggy his wife, Thomas Ashford and Sally his wife, and Josiah Elkins and Ann his wife. He seems to have had seven children, but the will does not name them distinctly. The will of Thomas McClanahan, Jr., is dated November 18, 1833, and probated October 6, 1834.

140 THOMAS MARSHALL SMITH, b. in Fauquier Co., Va., October 3, 1793; = FELITIA CHILTON; went to Missouri, and reared a large family of children.

142 JOHN ADAMS WASHINGTON SMITH, b. in Fauquier Co., Va., June 2, 1781; d. September 1, 1832; = February 2, 1806, MARIA LOVE HAWKINS, b. 1789, d. July 18, 1826; = 2d, October 18, 1827, Julia A. M. Chapin, who died October 5, 1828; = 3d, Sarah O. Hall, of Loudon Co., Va. Mr. Smith was educated in Richmond; studied law with his relative, William Marshall; settled in Warrenton, and engaged in the practice of law until 1808, when he was appointed clerk of Fauquier County, and remained in office until his death in 1832. His first wife was a daughter of Capt. John Hawkins, Adjutant of Col. Thos. Marshall's Third Virginia Regiment. He was descended from Ralph Hawkins, who settled in Charles Co., Md., about 1650. On the female side she came from the Lees of Maryland.

144 THOMAS MARSHALL SMITH, b. in Logan Co., Ky., or perhaps in Virginia, before his parents came, to Kentucky,—d. in Louisville, Ky., about 1859. He married twice, — the second time to MRS. EMMIT, mother of Guy N. Emmet, Secretary and Treasurer of the American Aid Society of Louisville, Ky. He preached and practiced law by turns. We first find him at Frank-

(150) THOMAS MARSHALL.

lin, Simpson Co., Ky. In 1838,—then old and gray,—he removed to Russellville, Ky.,—he next appears at Louisville, and here he died. In 1855 J. F. Branan, of Louisville, published for him a volume entitled, "Legends of the War of Independence and the early Settlements of the West," by T. Marshall Smith. The remainder of his life was devoted to the recommendation and sale of this book to every household he entered. He was a fluent writer, but every page of his book proves his mind unhinged. His chief purpose was to prove that tedious details would make the most common-place topic interesting. His hatred of Calvinism was intense, and he buried it under mountains of denunciation. The Witness of the Spirit was the cardinal doctrine of his religion. He was connected with the Methodist church, and, though intensely sectarian in his views, gave poor satisfaction to his members; and, in the practice of law, he gave less satisfaction to his clients. He was a ready talker, but was generally regarded as flighty.

150 (a) THOMAS MARSHALL was b. in Richmond, Va., July 21, 1784; d. in Baltimore, June 29, 1835; = October 19, 1809, MARGARET W. LEWIS, b. 1792, at Weyanoke, Charles City Co., Va.; d. at "Oakhill," Fauquier Co., Va., February 2, 1829. From an early age, Mr. Marshall manifested uncommon talent. The following ode on the death of Washington, was written in his boyhood, and is preserved in the family;

> The brave, illustrous Washington is gone!
> Henceforth, Virginia, mourn your noble son,
> The voice of death has called a deathless name
> To shine immortal on the roll of fame.
> His manly virtues and his heart, sincere,
> Demand the priceless tribute of a tear.
> Who now, when war shall desolate the land,
> Remains to save us from a tyrant's band?
>
> And where's the man like him, both wise and brave,
> His country from despotic rule to save!
> His dazzling merit and superior parts,
> In spite of faction and her envious arts,
> Unrivalled shine, his great and honored name,
> Borne on the wings of everlasting fame,
> Until remotest ages, shall be known;
> And man forever will his loss bemoan.

(150) THOMAS MARSHALL.

(b) Mr. Marshall completed his literary education at Princeton College, graduating with the degree of A. M., at the age of nineteen. After studying law, he engaged in its practice at Richmond. He married in 1809 Miss Margaret W. Lewis, of Weyanoke, who had just completed her education at Williamsburg. She was beautiful in person and lovely in disposition, and made a happy home for her husband and children. Mr. Marshall's health failed, and he retired to "Oakhill." The remainder of his days were spent in farming. He found the soil of his ancestral estate exhausted, and its improvements out of repair. But by judicious management and the introduction of marl as a fertilizer, he changed the sterile farm into a garden. He became a zealous member of the Episcopal church, and nearly all his posterity have followed him in religious sentiment. At "Oakhill" his children were born, and until the war scattered and impoverished them, they formed a happy community. His living descendants, counting wives and husbands, are now 137. Mr. Marshall was a man of literary taste and culture. He was a connoisseur in art,—fond of music and painting, and an interested observer of the progress of science and civilization. He was a member of the Virginia Constitutional Convention of 1829, over which his father presided. He was no aspirant for honor or office, but found his delight in the quiet seclusion of home, in the entertainment of choice friends, and the education of his children. Bishop Meade, Vol. 2, p. 220, thus kindly notices him:

(c) Mr. Thomas Marshall, eldest son of the Chief Justice, lived at the old homestead of the Marshalls, "Oakhill," on the road to Warrensburg and Fredericksburg. · He was one of my earliest and dearest friends. He became a communicant at an early day. He often begged that, in my efforts for the promotion of religion which required pecuniary aid, I would consider him as ready to afford it. Mr. Thomas Ambler, a nephew of Judge Marshall's, and an old schoolmate of my early years, lived in the same neighborhood. Cool-Spring meeting house lay between them. The Marshalls and Amblers continued to settle in this neighborhood, until they have become two small congregations, or rather important parts of two congregations. The children of my esteemed friend, Thomas Marshall, six in number, settled in sight of each other, on the estate of their father, and are all living (1857).

(d) In June, 1835, Mr. Marshall was summoned to the bed of his dying father, at Philadelphia. On his way at Baltimore, in company with his relative, the late Dr. John Hanson Thomas, (610) a storm compelled them to take shelter under the scaffolding of the court house, which was undergoing repair. While there, the house was struck by lightning, and a dislodged brick fell, striking and fracturing Mr. Marshall's skull. He never regained consciousness, though he lived a week.

Mr. Marshall's wife preceeded him to the grave, and her epitaph, written by her husband, is a touching tribute to her virtues:

(e) Sacred to the memory of Mrs. MARGARET MARSHALL, consort of Thomas Marshall of "Oakhill." She died February 2, 1829, in the 37th year of her age. Admired without envy; beloved without hypocricy; candid, kind and considerate; every look and every word denoted equal dignity and sweetness; earnest yet exempt from selfishness, her sympathy, generosity, sacrifice of ease, health and comfort, were not often equalled. An humble follower of the Blessed Jesus, she made His word the rule of her life on earth, and trusted to his blood as her passport to the life above.

> In vain would language labor to impart
> The deep-felt anguish of her husbands heart,
> That heart which owned no bliss while she was here,
> But her loved smile or sympathizing tear.
> Oh gracious Father look with pitying eye,
> Forgive the error of idolatry.
> With humble lips I kiss thy chastening rod,
> And own Thee Sovereign, Father, God.

By her side lies her affectionate husband, and his slab bears the following inscription:

Reared to the memory of THOMAS MARSHALL, ESQ., who died in Baltimore, on the 29th of June, 1835, in the 51st year of his age, while on his way to see his venerable father, then ill in Philadelphia. He has left seven motherless children to mourn his untimely end. In him were united all the virtues which rendered him eminent in the discharge of every duty. By this stroke of death, has fallen the ripe scholar, the devoted patriot, the liberal philanthropist, and the humble servant of God. In the atonement of the Blessed Savior, he placed his whole hope of happiness beyond the grave. Blessed are the dead who die in the Lord. Born July 21, 1784.

(f) On the opposite side of Mrs. Marshall, lies her mother. Her slab bears the following inscription;

Sacred to the memory of MRS. AGNES LEWIS, consort of Fielding Lewis, Esq., of Weyanoke, who departed this life on the 11th of August, 1822, aged 53 years. She died surrounded by her family. In their hearts, her memory is embalmed, and in the hearts of all who knew her, will be cherished; for to all she manifested a kindness so touching, and a disinterestedness so noble, that the recollection can never be effaced.

There are perhaps a dozen other graves at Oakhill Cemetery,

(150) THOMAS MARSHALL.

but no other stones bear inscriptions. No one has been buried there since the property passed from the family, and the ground and the inclosure have been neglected.

THE ROBERT LEWIS FAMILY.

(g) 1. Gen'l Robert Lewis, of Beecon, Wales, came to America about 1640, with a grant of land from the crown. He settled in Gloucester Co., Va. His children were: 1st, Major William Lewis, and 2d, John Lewis.

2. John Lewis, Sr., was born about 1645; was educated in England, where he married in 1666, Isabella, or Catherine Warner, daughter of a rich East Indian merchant. He built and named for his wife, "Warner Hall," an ancient structure of twenty-six rooms. Whether there was one or two Johns has long been controverted.

3. His son John Lewis, Jr., was born in Gloucester Co., Va., November 30, 1669, d. November 14, 1745. He was a member of the Virginia Council, and married Elizabeth Warner. Issue:

A   1. COL. FIELDING LEWIS, = 1747, 1st, Catherine Washington, daughter of John Washington, and cousin of Gen. George Washington. Issue:

B   1. *John Lewis*, b. June 22, 1747; d. November 23, 1825; = 5 times. His first and second wives were Lucy Thornton and her cousin, —— Thornton, neither of whom left issue. His third wife was Elizabeth Jones, daughter of Gabriel Jones, the "Valley Lawyer." Issue.

C   1. Warner Lewis, d. young.
     2. Fielding Lewis d. young.
     3. Gabriel J. Lewis, b. September 16, 1775; d. February 7, 1864; = November 24, 1807, Mary Bibb. Issue:

D   1. Elizabeth Lewis, b. November 11, 1813, = September 29, 1831, Col. Sam'l McDowell Starling. Issue:

E   1. Mary Starling, = R. W. Payne.

B   1. *John Lewis*, = 4th, Mary Ann Fontaine, (Mrs. Armstead). Issue:

(150) THOMAS MARSHALL.

C   1. A daughter, = Keeling Terrill. Issue:

D   1. Mary F.; 2, Narcissa, = Smith; 3, Mrs. Trotter.

B   1. *John Lewis*, = 5th time, Mrs. Mercer, *nee* Carter. No issue.

A   1. COL. FIELDING LEWIS married 2d, 1750, Bettie Washington, dr. of Augustine, and sister of President Washington. Issue:

B (h)   1. *Col. Fielding Lewis*, b. February 14, 1751, = —— Alexander. Issue:

C   1, Austin; 2, George; 3, Mrs. Spotswood.

B   2. *Maj. George Lewis*, b. March 14, 1757, = Katie Dangerfield. Issue:

C   1. Dangerfield Lewis.

        2. Samuel Lewis, = ? Issue:

D   1. Alloway Lewis, = John Putnam.

           2. Henry Howell Lewis, now of Baltimore.

           3. Mary, now of Morganfield, Ky., = John Casey.

           4. George; 5, Thomas; 6, John Lewis.

C   3. Mary Lewis, = Byrd Willis. Issue:

D   1. Fanny, 1805–67, lived in Florida, = Achille Murat, son of Caroline Bonaparte, and enjoyed a pension from the Emperor, Napoleon III. No issue.

        2. Mrs. Botts; 3, Lewis Willis; 4, Murat; 5, George.

B   3. *Charles Lewis*, b. October 3, 1760; d. single.

    4. *Bettie*, b. February 23, 1765, = Charles Carter.

    5. *Lawrence*, b. April 4, 1767, = Eleanor Custis. Issue:

C (i)   1. Judith Lewis, = Rev. E. C. McGuire. Issue:

D   1. Bettie McGuire, = Rev. Chas. E. Ambler. No. 848.

(150) THOMAS MARSHALL.

B 6. *Robert Lewis*, b. January 25, 1769, = Miss Brown.
   7. *Howell Lewis*, b. December 12, 1771, = Miss Pollard, a great beauty. He died in Kanawha Co., Va. Issue:
    1. Fanny, = Brooke Gwathmey.

A 2. WARNER LEWIS, = Eleanor Bowles, widow of William, son of Gov. Gooch. Issue:

B   1. *Warner Lewis*, = Mary Chesswell. Issue:

C   1. Warner Lewis, = Courtenay Norton, dr. of J. H. Norton and Ann Nicholas. Issue:

D   1. Mary C. Lewis, = 1, John Peyton, son of Sir John Peyton. Issue:

E   1. Rebecca C. Peyton, = EDWARD C. MARSHALL, No. 160.

D   2. Elizabeth Lewis, = Mathew Brooke.

E   1. Elizabeth Brooke, = H. M. MARSHALL, No. 200.
      2. Courtenay W. Brooke, = Robert Selden.
      3. Mary L. Brooke, = Dr. S. P. Byrd.
      4. John L. Brooke, = M. L. Ashby.

C   2. John Lewis, = Ann C. Griffin.
    3. Elizabeth Lewis.
    4. Eleanor, = 1st, Fox, = 2d, Oliver.

B   1. *Warner Lewis*, = 2d, Mary Fleming, a descendant of Pocahontas. Issue:

C (j)   1. Philip Lewis, = Charles Barnet.
    2. Julia Lewis, = Thomas Throckmorton.

B   2. *Fielding Lewis*, of Weyanoke, = Agnes Harwood. Issue:

C   1. Nancy Lewis.
    2. Fanny F. Lewis, = Archibald Taylor. Issue:

D   1. Col. F. L. Taylor, = E. F. Fontleroy.
     2. Dr. Archibald Taylor, = Martha Fontleroy.
     3. Robert Taylor; 4, Thomas Taylor.

96   THE MARSHALL FAMILY.

(150) THOMAS MARSHALL.

C
      3. Margaret Lewis, 1792—1829, = 1809, THOMAS MARSHALL, No. 150.
      4. Eleanor Lewis, = Robert Douthat. Issue:

D
          1. Robert Douthat, = MARY A. MARSHALL, No. 514.
          2. Jane Douthat, = Dr. Selden.
          3. Agnes Douthat, = Robt. L. McGuire. Issue:
               1. Jane S. McGuire, = JAS. F. JONES, No. 1300.
          4. Fielding L. Douthat, = M. W. MARSHALL, N. 550.

B
      3. James Lewis, = Miss Thornton. Issue:

C
          1. Eleanor Lewis.
(k)   2. Sally Lewis, = Dr. Griffin. Issue:

D
               1. James Griffin; 2, Cyrus Griffin.
               3. Louisa Griffin, = Dr. Wright. Issue:
                    1. Sallie Wright, = Capt. Ball.

B
      4. Addison Lewis, = Sue Fleming, sister of Mary Fleming (above). They were daughters of John Fleming, son of Charles Fleming, son of Thomas Fleming, who married, January 20, 1727, Mary, dr. of Maj. John Bolling, of "Cobbs," who was a son of Robert Bolling and Jane Rolfe, dr. of Thomas, son of John, who was son of Pocahontas. See No. 16 w. Issue:

C
          1. Susan Lewis, b. March 7, 1782, d. November 12, 1865, = Wm. Byrd, son of Col. Wm. Byrd. Issue:

D
              1. Addison Byrd, = Sue Coke.
(l)   2. Mary W. Byrd, = Richard C. Coke. Issue:

E
               1. Rebecca F. Coke, = F. L. MARSHALL, No. 506.

D
          3. Jane O. Byrd, = G. W. McCandlish.
          4. Samuel P. Byrd, = Cath. C. Corbin. Issue:

E
               1. Richard Byrd, = ANN G. MARSHALL, No. 1240.
            Samuel = 2d, Mary L. Brooke (above).

THE MARSHALL FAMILY. 97

(150) THOMAS MARSHALL.

B
    5. *John Lewis*, d. single.
    6. *Rebecca Lewis*, = Dr. Robert Innis. No issue.
    7. *Thomas Lewis*, = Nannie Harwood.

A   3. CHARLES LEWIS, b. 1696; settled in Goochland Co., Va., 1733, = 1st, Mary Howell. Issue:

B
    1. *John Lewis*, b. October 8, 1720.
    2. *Charles Lewis*, b. March 14, 1721; d. May 14, 1782, = Mary Randolph.
    3. *Elizabeth Lewis*, b. April 23, 1724, = May 3, 1744, William Kennon.
(m)   4. *James Lewis*, b. October 6, 1726; d. May 1, 1764.
    5. *Howell Lewis*, b. September 13, 1731.
    6. *Ann Lewis*, b. March 2, 1733.
    7. *Robert Lewis*, b. May 29, 1739, = February 20, 1790, Jane Woodson.
    8. *Frances Lewis*, b. August 1, 1744; d. September 3, 1760.

A   3. CHARLES LEWIS, = 2d, Lucy Taliaferro. (This is denied). Issue:

B   1. *John T. Lewis*, = Warring. 2, Charles; 3, Mary W. Lewis.

A   4. ROBERT LEWIS, of Albemarle Co., Va., b. about 1694, = Jane Meriwether, dr. of Nicholas Meriwether. His will was recorded in Albemarle County, 1756. Issue:

B
    1. *Robert Lewis*, = Miss Fontleroy and settled in North Carolina.
    2. *John Lewis*, went to North Carolina.
(n)   3. *Charles Lewis*, = Mary Lewis, dr. of Charles Lewis and Mary Randolph.
    4. *Nicholas Lewis*, = Mary Walker; lived in Chancellorsville, Va.
    5. *Capt. William Lewis*, = Lucy Meriwether; lived in Albemarle. Issue:

C
    1. Meriwether Lewis, of Lewis & Clarke's Expedition.
    2. Dr. Reuben Lewis, = Mildred Dabney.
    3. Jane Lewis, = Edmund Anderson.

THE MARSHALL FAMILY.

(150) THOMAS MARSHALL.

B   6. *Mildred Lewis*, = John Lewis, of Fredericksburg, son of Zachariah Lewis and Mary Walker.

7. *Sarah Lewis*, = Dr. Walker Lewis, brother of John (above) and son of Zachariah.

8. *Mary Lewis*, = Samuel Cobb. Went to Georgia.

9. *Elizabeth Lewis*, = Barret, of Richmond.

(o)   10. *Mary Lewis*, = John Lewis, son of Charles; or as others say, Thomas Meriwether.

THE WARNERS, THE LEWISES AND THE WASHINGTONS.

A   1. LAWRENCE WASHINGTON, Mayor of Northampton, 1533 and 1546.

2. ROBERT WASHINGTON.

3. LAWRENCE WASHINGTON, = Margaret Butler.

4. SIR JOHN WASHINGTON, = Ann Pope. Came to America in 1657; d. 1675.

5. LAWRENCE WASHINTON, d. 1697, = Mildred Warner, sister of Isabella Warner, wife of John Lewis, Sr., and daughter of Col. Augustine Warner and Mildred Reade, daughter of George Reade, Governor of Virginia, and Secretary of the Colony, 1693-97. Issue of Lawrence and Mildred:

B   1. *Mildred Washington*, = 3 times: 1, a Lewis; no issue; = 2d, Roger Gregory, by whom she had three daughters who married three brothers, named Thornton. She = 3d, Col. Harry Willis. Issue:

C   1. Anne Willis, = Duff Green. See Green chart, 180 *h*.

2. Lewis Willis.

1. Byrd Willis, = a dr. of George Lewis.

B   2. *John Washington*, = Catherine Whiting.

C   1. Catherine Washington, = Col. Fielding Lewis, (See Lewis chart, 150), son of John Lewis, Jr., and Elizabeth Warner. He was therefore related to both his wives, through the Warners.

(152) DR. JACQUELIN AMBLER MARSHALL.

B   3. *Augustine Washington*, b. 1694, = 1st, Jane Butler, of Westmoreland Co., Va., and had four children. He = 2d, Mary Ball. Issue:

C   1. Bettie Washington, = as his second wife Col. Fielding Lewis. See Lewis chart, No. 150.
2. President George Washington and others.

152 (*a*) Dr. Jacquelin Ambler Marshall, b. in Richmond, Va., December 3, 1787, d. in Fauquier Co., July 7, 1852,= January 1, 1819, Eliza L. S. Clarkson, b. January 1, 1798, d. July 2, 1868. Dr. Marshall was well educated and deeply read in medicine, theology and general literature. He did not practice as a physician, but was often consulted in uncommon diseases. His life was spent at "Prospect Hill," his residence, ten miles south of Markham, in Fauquier Co. His attainments in every department of knowledge were put to no use. With little ambition, he was satisfied to superintend his farm and to entertain his select friends. He and his wife were buried at Leeds' Church. Their epitaphs are as follows:

'(*b*) Sacred to the memory of Jacquelin A. Marshall, who was born on the 3d day of December, 1787, and died on the 7th day of July, 1852, in the 65th year of his age. Blessed are the dead which die in the lord from henceforth; yea, saith the Spirit, that they may rest from their labors, and their works do follow them.

Sacred to the memory of Mrs. E. L. S. Marshall, born January 1, 1798, died July 27, 1868. Those things which ye have both learned and received and heard and seen in me, do; and the Lord of Peace shall be with you.

(*c*) THE CLARKSON FAMILY.

Henry and Dorcas Clarkson had three children:

A   1. WILLIAM CLARKSON, b. April 3, 1773, d. February 22, 1818, = January 9, 1794, Mildred Pickett, b. October 30, 1777, d. March 22, 1805.

B   1. *Ann Dorcas Clarkson*, b. October 1, 1794.
2. *Henry M. Clarkson*, b. March 18, 1796.

(154) MARY MARSHALL—(*Harvie*).

B
  3. *Eliza L. S. Clarkson,* = JACQ. A. MARSHALL, No. 152.
  4. *Caro. M. Clarkson,* b. February 8, 1800 (living), = January 29, 1818, Dr. Robert M. Stribling, b. February 14, 1793, d. August 24, 1862.

C (*d*) 1. Dr. William Stribling, = Mildred Clarkson, his first cousin.

D
    1. Col. Robert M. Stribling, = 1st, MARY C. AMBLER; = 2d, AGNES DOUTHAT. See Nos. 854 and 1324.
    2. Mildred Pickett Stribling, = JOHN MARSHALL. See No. 552. See Pickett Chart, No. 64 *b.*

A 2. HENRY CLARKSON, b. January 20, 1775.

B 1. *Mildred Clarkson,* above.

A 3. MARTHA CLARKSON, b. December 20, 1778.

154 MARY MARSHALL, b. in Richmond, Va., September 17, 1795, d. April 29, 1841, = September 18, 1813, at "Oakhill," GEN. JACQUELIN BURWELL HARVIE, b. in Richmond, Va., October 9, 1788. Mrs Harvie was the Chief Justice's only daughter, and was more intimately associated with him than any other of his children. She lived within a stone's throw of his dwelling, and enjoyed his society almost daily. In mind and person she is said to have resembled him. She inherited his virtues, and was both admired and beloved.

  Gen. Harvie was prepared for the navy, and was serving as a midshipman, when the terrible tragedy of the burning of the Richmond theatre occurred. On that occasion, he lost a brother, a sister and a niece. The condition of his mother required him to resign, that he might assist in the management of the estate. During his life he filled many places of honor and trust; was for many years a State Senator, and at the time of his death was Major-General of Militia for the Eastern District of Virginia. He was full of enterprise, and the Richmond Dock and Water Works, and Belle-Isle Nail Factory still attest his public spirit. His father was Col. John

(158) JAMES KEITH MARSHALL.

Harvie, a delegate from Virginia to the Continental Congress, 1778-79, and an army officer during the Revolutionary war. He was an intimate friend of Washington, and advanced large sums of money to the struggling government. In return he received lands in Virginia and Kentucky, which were lost to his heirs. Gen. Harvie's mother was Margaret, daughter of Gabriel Jones, the "Valley Lawyer." But see 228 d.

156 JOHN MARSHALL, b. at Richmond, Va., January 15, 1798, d. at "Mt. Blanc," Fauquier Co., Va., November 25, 1833, = Febrary 3, 1820, ELIZABETH M. ALEXANDER, b. August 20, 1802, d. January, 1847. Mr. Marshall was a graduate of Harvard College, was well read in all solid learning; merry, jovial and sprightly, a boon companion, of fine address and exceedingly popular manners; was several times elected to the State Legislature; spent his married life at "Mt. Blanc," a large farm five miles southeast of Markham, in Fauquier Co., Va. He managed well, but his social temperament often led him into excess. Mrs. Marshall was a daughter of Dr. Ashton Alexander and Catherine Hanson Thomas, of Baltimore.

158 (a) JAMES KEITH MARSHALL, b. in Richmond, Va., February 13, 1800, d. at his residence, "Leeds," in Fauquier Co., Va., December 2, 1862, = December 22, 1821, CLAUDIA HAMILTON BURWELL, b. January 9, 1804, d. March 4, 1884, at "Leeds." Mr. Marshall was a graduate of Harvard College, but led the life of a farmer and country gentleman, at "Leeds," situated six miles south of Markham. He was highly esteemed for his literary attainments and social virtues. A gentleman of fine address and genial manners, he possessed the graces of both heart and mind that called for veneration as well as love. He was several times elected to the State Senate, and the civil war found him in office. He was one of those Senators who ineffectually opposed the ordinance of secession, but who, when the deed was accomplished, gave their cordial adhesion to the Confederacy. He was charitable to the poor, social, hospitable and generous, both in sentiment and action. After going to Richmond to aid in the organization of the new government, he

(158) JAMES KEITH MARSHALL.

returned and died early in the war. His revered wife survived him twenty-one years, and now lies beside her husband, in "Leeds" church yard. When I visited her grave, in August, 1884, I found on the green sod a fresh wreath of flowers. Before her death she became both blind and deaf. Her memory is cherished by her posterity. No stone has yet been erected to her memory, but the epitaphs of her husband and aunt are as follows:

(b) SACRED to the memory of JAMES KEITH MARSHALL, son of John Marshall and Mary Willis Marshall, born February 13, 1800, died December 2, 1862. I know in whom I have believed.

SACRED to the memory of MARIA WILLIS, born September 23, 1784, in Gloucester Co., Va., and died October 5, 1835. I know my Redeemer liveth.

(c) THE BURWELL LINEAGE.

1. *Ancestor:* Major Lewis Burwell, of the County of Gloucester, Va., (Gent.), descended from the ancient family of the Burwell's, of the Counties of Bedford and Northampton, in England, b. 1625, d. 1658, = Lucy, dr. of Robert Higginson, d. 1675. Their son:

2. Major Nathaniel Burwell, d. 1721, = Elizabeth, dr. of Robert (King) Carter. Issue:

A
1. ELIZABETH BURWELL, = President William Nelson, and was mother of Gen. Thomas Nelson.

2. ROBERT C. BURWELL, of Isle of Wight Co., father of Nathaniel Burwell, and of Fanny Burwell, who =
(d) Gov. John Page.

3. CARTER BURWELL, of "The Grove,"=Lucy Grymes, sister of Alice, wife of Manu Page, and dr. of Hon. John Grymes. Issue:

B
1. *Nathaniel Burwell,* of Carter Hall,= Susanna Grymes. Issue:

C
1. Lewis Burwell, b. in Gloucester Co., Va., July 4, 1764, d. in Richmond, Va., August 24, 1834, = Judith Kennon, b. in Charlotte, N. C., February 24, 1770, d. in Richmond, July 20, 1849.

(160) EDWARD CARRINGTON MARSHALL.

C
  2. Nathaniel Burwell, = Ann R. Willis, b. March 17, 1766, dr. of Frank Willis, of "White Hall," Gloucester Co.
   1. Claudia H. Burwell, = JAMES K. MARSHALL, No. 158.

B
  2. *Rebecca Burwell*, b. May 29, 1746, = 1764, Jacquelin Ambler, son of Richard, b. August, 1742, d. February 10, 1798. (7 ch. See Ambler Chart, 50.) Among others:

C
   1. Mary Willis Ambler, = JOHN MARSHALL, No. 50.

D (e)
   1. James K. Marshall, = CLAUDIA H. BURWELL, No. 158.

B
  1. *Nathaniel Burwell*, of Carter Hall, married a second wife, Lucy Page (Baylor), and, among other issue had:

C
   1. William N. Burwell, b. 1793, d. August 12, 1822, = 1812, MARY BROOKE (214).

160 EDWARD CARRINGTON MARSHALL, b. at Richmond, Va., January 13, 1805, d. at "Innis," Fauquier Co., Va., February 8, 1882, = February 12, 1829, REBECCA COURTENAY PEYTON, b. December 19, 1810, living. Mr. Marshall graduated at Harvard College in 1826, married in 1829, settled at Carrington, in Fauquier Co., Va., and engaged in Agriculture; for four successive terms, from 1834 to 1838, was the representative from Fauquier County to the Virginia Legislature. In 1850, Mr. Marshall removed to Markham, and subsequently to "Innis," a mile north of Markham. In 1836, an injury to one of his ankles confined him to his couch for several years; by a fall from his horse, the injured limb was broken, and a second fall made him almost helpless for thirteen years; yet with crutch, staff or an iron frame made for his support, he managed to get about. In 1832, he united with the Episcopal Church, at Alexandria, and became an ardent member and a zealous laborer in every good cause, for fifty years. He attended Sabbath School regularly, often traveling six miles that he might give his personal

(160) EDWARD CARRINGTON MARSHALL.

superintendence to his school. His public spirit and generous nature were not restrained by his crippled limb and uncertain health. The Manassas-Gap R. R. owes its existence to his energy and influence. With untiring zeal he pressed the measure on the Legislature, and, accepting the presidency of the company, he made the road a success. Too old to give his personal aid to the South, his sympathies were with his people. But fire, war and Confederate money impoverished him, and as a personal compliment, he was granted a place in the Pension office, by which he earned a support. This favor was granted during the administrations of Grant and Hayes, with a distinct understanding that his political sentiments should thereby be untrammelled. While performing his clerical duties at Washington, he often found time to visit his family at "Innis."

(b) Mr. Marshall was fond of the classics, and delighted to quote from ancient authors. His profound scholarship, his literary acquirements and cordial manners made him a welcome companion in the most learned circles of society. He was fond of the game of chess, and enjoyed conversation on scientific, literary and religious topics. He was cheerful, hopeful and cordial, and was regarded as a model of the old Virginia gentleman. When not otherwise engaged, he found employment for his active mind in assisting his relative, Dr. Jacq. Ambler, in the labors of his school at "Clifton."

Cousin Rebecca C. Marshall still lives to gladden the hearts of her numerous posterity. She possesses the vivacity and sprightliness of youth. In 1884 I found her living at "Innis," with her daughter Courtenay (590), taking an active interest in the happiness of the family and guests, and in performing a share of the household duties. My daughter and I shall never forget her kind attentions and generous hospitality.

THE CARRINGTONS.

(c) George Carrington, son of Paul Carrington, came from the Barbadoes, about the year 1727, and settled at the falls of James River. About 1732, in his 21st year, he married Anne, the daughter of William Mayo, then in her 20th year. Both died in February, 1785. They settled in Cumberland County, and had eleven children, of whom Edward Carrington was the eighth. He was a gallant officer in the Revolution. He was born February 11, 1748, and died October 28, 1810. He married Elizabeth Jacquelin Am-

(162) EDWARD COLSTON.

bler, sister of Mr. Marshall's mother, (See Ambler chart, No. 50). He was, therefore, by marriage, the uncle of Mr. Marshall, and he was named for him. As to the progenitors of Mrs. Marshall, see the Lewis chart (150). Her parents were Mary C. Lewis and John Peyton. She was an only child. After her father's death, her mother married Thomas Nelson. She lies in Leeds church-yard, and on her beautiful monument we read:

(d) MARY C. NELSON, born January 1, 1791, died November 14, 1853. In the way of righteousness there is life, and in the pathway thereof there is no death. Prov., 12: 28.

162 (a) EDWARD COLSTON, b. near Winchester, Va., Dec. 25, 1786; d. at "Honeywood, Berkley Co., Va., April 23d, 1851; = 1st, May, 1814, JANE MARSHALL, b. in Warrenton, Va., August 28, 1794, d. at Honeywood, childless, March, 1815, = 2d, May 2, 1825, SARAH JANE BROCKENBROUGH, b. 1805, yet living with her sons at Martinsburg, W. Va. At the time of Edward's birth, Rawleigh Colston was living at "Hill and Dale," near Winchester, Va. In 1801 the family removed to "Honeywood," in Berkely County, and built a fine mansion overlooking the Potomac river. Here Edward was raised in the midst of affluence, with one of the noblest of women for a mother. At Honeywood Edward lived and died. Having graduated with honor at Princeton College in 1806, he prepared himself for business and usefulness, by studying law. He was a Federalist by birth, education and conviction, and as such, was elected, in 1821, to the Virginia House of Delegates, and in 1817 was elected to Congress. There he found among his comrades, Henry Clay, W. H. Harrison, Henry Baldwin, John Floyd, R. M. Johnson, Geo. Tucker, and other honored names; yet Mr. Colston was able to take an active and highly influential part in the debates on the important questions before them. Upon the expiration of his term in Congress, Mr. Colston found it necessary to give his personal attention and counsel to his aged mother; and, as her agent, took charge of large estates situated in Virginia and Kentucky. But in 1826 and 1827, 1833 and 1834 he was again in the House of Delegates. While in Richmond, he was married to Miss Sarah Jane Brockenbrough, who is the mother of all his

(162) EDWARD COLSTON.

children. Mr. Colston was a magistrate for many years, and in 1845, was High Sheriff of Berkely County. Though a Federalist, he entered the army in 1812, and, as a Lieutenant, did service in Norfolk, and other exposed points. He was an ardent Episcopalian, and often, as a delegate, attended the Conventions of the Church. His legal acquirements and business qualifications made his counsel and service valuable to the Church. At home he was the counsellor of his neighbors, and often had occasion to render assistance to the poor and defenseless people around him. His death was sudden and painless. While examining some books for his children, he fell lifeless. His will gives his estate, which was large, to his widow. His brother-in-law, Willoughby Newton, and Hon. Chas. J. Faulconer were appointed his executors. But fire and the reverses of war have taken "Honeywood" from the family; the hands of Vandals appropriated their valuable library, and the widow has a bare competency. Mr. Colston was a noble specimen of the enlightened country gentleman. His manner was courteous and dignified; his conversation interesting and instructive; his hospitality large and free; and in scholarship he had few superiors. He had a noble inheritance and his charities were boundless.

(b) I have many letters from cousin Jane Colston. Though eighty winters have furrowed her brow, yet her mind and her pen are vigorous and cordial. She came of a noble race, and belongs to a generation of pure, pious and patriotic matrons, that will soon be extinct.

(c) THE BROCKENBROUGH FAMILY.

Col. William Brockenbrough, emigrant, settled in Richmond Co., Va. By his second wife, a Miss Fontleroy, he had issue:

A   1. NEWMAN BROCKENBROUGH, left no children.

    2. DR. JOHN BROCKENBROUGH, of Tappahannoch, = Sarah Roane.

B   1. *Judge William Brockenbrough*, of Richmond, = Miss White.

C   1. Judge John White Brockenbrough, of Lexington, = April 15, 1835, Mary C. Bowyer, of Lexington.

THE MARSHALL FAMILY.

(162) EDWARD COLSTON.

D   (d) 1. John B. Brockenbrough, = October 12, 1864, Lucy A. Murrell, daughter of William Murrell, of Lynchburg.

E   1. Alice Brockenbrough; 2, John W.; 3, William M; 4, Edward; 5, Robert L.; 6, James; 7, Marian W.

D   2. Wm. Brockenbrough, = Lucy W. Major, of Rockbridge County.

E   1. William N. Brockenbrough; 2, John B.; 3, Lucille B.; 4, Edward C.; 5, Emily B.; 6, Mary B.

D   3. Edward C. Brockenbrough.
     4. Willoughby N. Brockenbrough, Columbia, Mo., = Alice Thomas.

E   1. Eleanor Brockenbrough; 2, James T.; 3, Mary B.; 4, John W.; 5, Thomas S.

D   (e) 5. Louisa G. Brockenbrough, = Thos. M. Semmes, Virginia Military Institute.

E   1. Bernard B. Semmes; 2, Mary B.; 3, Eliza V.; 4, Louisa R. Semmes.

D   6. Robert L. Brockenbrough, = Mary A. Grasty, of Austin, Texas,—now of St. Louis.

E   1. Mary L. Brockenbrough; 2, Robt. S.

D   7. Francis H. Brockenbrough.

C   2. Judith White Brockenbrough, = Rev. J. P. McGuire.
     3. Mary S. Brockenbrough, = Hon. Willoughby Newton, of Westmoreland Co., Va.

D   (f) 1. William B. Newton, = Mary Page;• 2d, Sallie, = Phil. Smith, of Winchester; 3, Willoughby Newton, = ELIZABETH MARSHALL. See No. 586.
     4. John B. Newton, = Robuta Williamson.
     5. Robert Newton, = Annie Arnett.
     6. Judith W. Newton, = Edwin Claybrooke.
     7. Edward C. Newton, = Lucy Y. Tyler.

(162) EDWARD COLSTON.

C
 4. Elizabeth Brockenbrough, = Phelps.
 5. Sarah Jane Brockenbrough, = EDWARD COLSTON. No. 162.
 (g) 6. Dr. William S. R. Brockenbrough, d. December 2, 1880, in Westmoreland Co., Va., = Nelson.

B
 2. *Arthur S. Brockenbrough*, 2d son of John and Sarah, = Lucy Gray.

C
 1. Judge William Brockenbrough, Senator from Florida, = Byrd. No issue.
 2. Thos. W. Brockenbrough, = Sarah Wharton, of Orange Co.

D
  1. Benj. W., = Flora B. Johnson, of Norfolk.
  2. Sallie M., = Wm. A. Brockenbrough.
  3. John C.; 4, George; 5, Mary C. Brockenbrough.

C
 3. John N. Brockenbrough.
 (h) 4. Austin Brockenbrough.
 5. George L. Brockenbrough, = Mrs. McAdams, of Florida.
 6. Arthur S. Brockenbrough.
 7. Sarah R., = Maxwell, of Florida; 3 children.
 8. Mary R., = Judge Hawkins, of Florida.

B
 3. *Dr. John Brockenbrough*, of Warm Springs, = Gabriella Randolph.
 4. *Dr. Austin Brockenbrough*, of Tappahannoch, = 1st, Lettice Lee Fontleroy.

C
 1. Dr. William A. Brockenbrough, = 1st, Mary C. Gray.

D .
  1. Lucy Y. Brockenbrough.
  2. William A., = Lulu B. Beadles; 7 children.
  3. Maria C.; 4, Thomas; 5, Catherine W.; 6, Lettice L.
  7. John F.; 8, Mary R., = Dr. T. T. Arnold.
  9. Henrietta N.; 10, Elizabeth, = M. Fontleroy.
  11. Judith B., = R. H. Montgomery.

(162) EDWARD COLSTON.

C (i) 2. John F. Brockenbrough, = Fannie Carter, daughter of Frances R. Ball, who was a daughter of Col. James Ball, youngest brother of Mary Ball, mother of George Washington.

D 1. Ella Brockenbrough, = Bishop John W. Beckweth, of Georgia.

E 1. John F. B. Beckweth; 2, Ella S.; 3, Bessie.

D 2. Eugenia, = S. G. Compton, of Louisiana.
3. Fannie R., = John A. Barbour, of Georgetown, D. C.
4. Lettie F., = M. Thompson, of Md.
5. Austin, = M. Williams, of Baltimore.
6. Louisa C., = 1872, Alf. Price, of Md.
7. Johnella; 8, Alice B.

C 3. Henrietta Brockenbrough, = Dr. Benj. Nelson, of Hanover County.

D 1. Catherine Nelson, = John Pollard.
2. Lettice L. Nelson, = Dr. D. B. Benson.
3. Thomas Cary Nelson, killed in the war.

B Dr. Austin Brockenbrough, = 2d, Frances Blake.

C 1. Elizabeth Brockenbrough, = S. F. Hammond.
2. Eliza C., = Dr. L. H. Robinson, of Norfolk: 2 children.
3. Fanny B., = Wm. G. Gordon; 6 children.
4. Austina B., = Gen. John M. Brockenbrough.
(k) 5. Gabriella, = Jos. W. Chinn, of Richmond County; 3 children.
6. Austin, killed at Gettysburg.
7. Benj. B. Brockenbrough, = Anne Nelson.

A 3. MOORE FONTLEROY BROCKENBROUGH, = Mrs. Lucy Barnes, nee Roane, sister to his brother's wife.

B 1. Lucy Brockenbrough, = Vincent Shackelford, of King and Queen Co., Va.; 6 children.

(164) MARY ISHAM COLSTON—(*Thomas*).

B
    2. *Mary Brockenbrough*, = John Luckie; 3 children.
    3. *Elizabeth*, = Phil. Woodward, 3 children.
    4. *Moore F.*, = Ball, and after her death, = 2d, Sarah Smith. Her issue:

C
        1. Benj. W. Brockenbrough.
        2. William, = Eliza B. Smith; 7 children.
    (*l*) 3. Gen. Geo. M. Brockenbrough, = Austina Brockenbrough. Issue: 9 children; = 2d, Kate Mallory, 2 children.

C
        4. Littleton Brockenbrough, = his cousin Lucy C. Shackelford.

D
        1. Moore F. Brockenbrough.
        2. Littleton W. Brockenbrough.
    (*m*) 3. JOHN LYNE BROCKENBROUGH, b. November 23, 1855, = February 10, 1880, ELIZA M. BRAXTON. No. 1354.

C
        5. Edward Brockenbrough.
        6. Alice R. Brockenbrough, = Col. Wm. Aylett; 10 children.
        7. Etta Brockenbrough, = November 10, 1868, Lieut. Rob. Knox; 6 children.

To him, Lieut. Knox, of Fredericksburg, Va., I am indebted for the foregoing table:

164 MARY ISHAM COLSTON, b. June 23, 1789, d. December 11, 1844, = October 5, 1809, J. HANSON THOMAS, b. May 16, 1779, d. May 2, 1815. Mrs. Thomas was a lady of culture and refinement. She possessed at the same time remarkable beauty of person and amiability of character, Her society was eagerly sought by the highest social circles of Baltimore, Richmond and Washington. She was the intimate friend of Mrs. and President Madison, and made frequent visits to "Montpelier" as a welcome guest.

Hon. John Hanson Thomas was the son of Philip Thomas, of Frederick, Md., and Jane Contee Hanson, daughter of Hon. John Hanson, President of the Continental Congress 1781-2. He was

(166) SUSANNA COLSTON — (Leigh).

educated at St. John's College, Annapolis, Md., and read law in the office of the learned Robert Goodloe Harper, of Baltimore. But his inclination was not in the direction of law, but rather to belles lettres, history, philosophy and politics. His mind was discriminating and reflective, and his excellent education and extensive reading prepared him for political life. Modest and unassuming, he did not seek the paths of ambition; but at the earnest solicitation of friends he entered on his short but brilliant career. In 1812-14, he was a member of the State Legislature, and was at once acknowledged as a leading statesman, orator and patriot. His course upon the embargo, and the able State papers prepared by him, attest the clearness, precision and strength of his mind. But Mr. Thomas was also an intelligent and faithful Christian. Brilliant as were the scenes through which he passed, and fresh as were the laurels he wore, he never appeared so transcendantly great as at the death bed of his venerable father. The dying man having expressed a desire for the offices of a clergyman, and in fear of his failure to arrive in time, the affectionate son fell on his knees, and with fervor poured forth a stream of comfort and supplication that was cheering to the parent. But the excitement, anxiety and exposure of that sad occasion were, perhaps, the cause of his own death. Exactly a week after his father's death, he himself fell asleep.

166 SUSANNA (*Susan*) COLSTON, b. November 27, 1792, d. —— = BENJ. WATKINS LEIGH, b. in Chesterfield Co., Va., June 18, 1781, d. at Richmond, February 2, 1849; graduated at William and Mary College, in 1802; studied law, and in 1802 was admitted to the bar; practiced law in Petersburg until 1813, when he removed to Richmond; was a member of the State Legislature and of the State Constitutional Convention of 1829-30; was official Reporter, and issued twelve volumes of Virginia Reports, 1829—1841; was elected to the U. S. Senate in 1834, as a Whig, to fill a vacancy; was re-elected, but resigned rather than obey instructions. He was a lawyer and statesman of national repute.

Susanna Colston was Mr. Leigh's second wife. She was remarkable for her beauty and amiability — qualities seldom united.

(168) THOMAS MARSHALL COLSTON.

168 THOMAS MARSHALL COLSTON, b. in Richmond, Va., November 11, 1794, d. in Fauquier Co., Va., April 30, 1840, = May 25, 1820, ELIZA J. FISHER, d. 1845. He was educated at Yale College; studied law with his brother-in-law, B. Watkins Leigh. After marriage, he settled on a large landed estate left him by his father, in Fauquier County, and here he pursued the business of agriculture with zeal and success. He died of pneumonia after a life of Christian usefulness. For the Fishers, see Ambler chart, 50 *q*.

170 (*a*) DR. RALEIGH COLSTON, b. near Shamadella Springs, Va., October 29, 1796, d. in New York City, September 21, 1881, = 1st, about 1820, in Paris, France, MARIA THERESA, DUCHESS OF VALMEY, b. about 1775, at Bologna, Italy. She died in Paris in 1845. He = 2d, URANIE DE GRAND, b. at Grenoble, France. After graduating at Yale College, Dr. Colston spent two years with his uncle, Dr. Louis Marshall, at "Buckpond," Ky. He then graduated in medicine at the University of Pennsylvania. Still further to perfect himself in medicine and surgery, he visited Europe, and after spending sometime in Scotland, he proceeded to the continent. In Paris, he was the guest of Lafayette and the American Consul. But the young physician was taken sick and his life despaired of. In a state of delirium he spoke in the English language. Some one was sought to interpret his ravings. In the same hotel the Duchess of Valmey was boarding. She was the divorced wife of Gen. Kellermann, who had inherited the title of Duc de Valmey, conferred on his father by the first Napoleon for gallantry on the battle field of Valmey. She was the daughter of an Italian nobleman, and possessed beauty, accomplishments and wealth. She was able to speak the English language, and cheered the sufferer by her sympathy and attention. She removed him to her own apartment, called her servants to her aid, and, by her affectionate care and generous solicitude, won the handsome and accomplished youth back to health. But in the contest she lost her own heart. She fell deeply in love with the agreeable and talented stranger. When he prepared to return to America, her tears and entreaties held him in Paris. Her age was the only obstacle to marriage. But love soon removed this objection, and they were married. Still his heart yearned for his Western home. But being of a kind, gentle and submissive nature, her strong will held him in Paris.

(170) DR. RALEIGH COLSTON.

(b) In 1824, young John M. Colston, on account of declining health, was sent over to France to his brother, Dr. Colston. When somewhat improved, they took ship in 1825, for America; but were becalmed at sea, and the delicate youth could not live on the salt provisions to which he was reduced. He died, and was buried at sea (174). Dr. Colston remained in America eleven months.

(c) The Duchess was sorely distressed that by reason of age she could not bear children for her beloved husband. On one occasion, when he had been long from home, with the assistance of a physician in her confidence and pay, she palmed off upon him as her own a boy child, who was reared to manhood as a legitimate son. He received a finished education, and was universally received and honored as the son of Dr. Colston. Like Moses, he was nursed by his own mother, and the boy and his father believed that the poor couple who often visited the mansion, regarded themselves as only the foster parents of the boy. At his baptism he was named Raleigh Edward Colston. He came to Virginia and was educated at Washington College. He married the sister of the wife of Judge Brockenbrough. He discovered the secret himself, but revealed it to no one. But in her last illness, the Duchess was conscience stricken, and sent for a minister, a notary, and the real parents of the boy; and, in the presence of Mr. Colston the imposition was confessed by all the guilty parties. The parents, who were of the name of Boucher, produced the evidence that their son, Victor, was born in an almshouse in 1825. Mr. Colston was greatly incensed, and never afterward would recognize the youth as a son. But he became the distinguished Gen. Colston, of the Confederate army, and has borne himself in a way that would have done credit to any name. He has shown abilities of no ordinary character, and in civil life has displayed honor, capacity and integrity. He is in Washington, in the office of the Surgeon-General, where he has proved himself a useful assistant. He lives honorably, and speaks but little of his romantic career. A year or two after the death of his first wife, Dr. Colston visited London, with a purpose of offering himself as a missionary to Africa. Here he met Marie Sophie Olympie Uranie dé Grand Fonlepaisse, a daughter of an officer of the French army and a nobleman from Dauphine, France. She was in financial distress. His sympathies were enlisted, and he offered assistance. Shortly afterward he married her. After staying in England and Scotland for

(172) LUCY ANN COLSTON.

four years, they came to America. He had inherited 14,000 acres of land. It yielded him but little income, because of faithless agents and want of tact on his own part. During the first years of the war, the family stayed in Georgia. In 1863 they returned to Staunton. In want of means of support, Mrs. Colston went to Philadelphia, and engaged in teaching French. The Doctor was not willing to go North, and remained in Staunton. His land was sold for Confederate money, and treacherous friends robbed him of his estate. But he found others more kind, who ministered to all his wants. At Winchester he found a home and sympathetic friends at the house of Mrs. Ward. In 1881 he was boarding in New York City, and became alarmed by a cry of "fire." His landlady told him to be quiet and lie down, that she would inquire into the matter. On her return he was dead.

(d) Dr. Colston was a surgeon of skill and learning. He was a kind and sympathizing friend, a sincere Christian and a refined and cultivated gentleman. He was much beloved, and his strange and affecting story engendered tenderness wherever it was told. His confidence was often misplaced, and this, with his want of business capacity, was his ruin.

Mrs. Colston is teaching French in Washington City. I have never heard an adequate reason for her desertion of her husband. She has two daughters, one of whom is married.

172 LUCY ANN COLSTON, b. September 15, 1798, at Richmond; d. 1839. Her niece, Mrs. Conway Robinson, (614) says of her: She was for years my fond and faithful guide and teacher — taking the child of her dear sister (herself) near to her heart. Her memory is dear to me, but this I can say truly of each of my uncles and aunts.

174 JOHN MARSHALL COLSTON, b. at Honeywood, Berkeley Co., W. Va., July 15, 1802; died at sea in 1825. By hard riding on horseback, he had produced some disease of the kidneys, and for medical relief, was sent to his brother, Dr. Raleigh Colston, in Paris. A cure was supposed to have been effected, and, in 1825,

(176) GEN. THOMAS MARSHALL.

Dr. Colston started home in a sailing vessel. But on the homeward voyage, the ship was becalmed, and the passengers and crew were reduced to the use of salt provisions. These produced a disorder that caused death in a few days, and his remains were committed to the sea. Though greatly beloved by his kindred, yet the chief mourner was Miss Mary Ann Nicholson, of Baltimore, to whom he was engaged in marriage. She was remembered in his will, and a large part of his fortune was left to her. She herself has joined him in the circle of glorified saints. And it is said that even while on earth, she was an angel.

176 (a) GEN. THOMAS MARSHALL, b. in Mason Co., Ky., April 13, 1793; d. in Lewis Co., Ky., March 28, 1853; = about 1819, in Virginia, KATHERINE TAYLOR, who died in Kentucky in 1820; = 2d, in Washington City, November 6, 1821, JULIANNA WINCHESTER WHETCROFT, b. at Annapolis, Maryland, 1805, died in Fleming Co., Ky., October, 1860. Mr. Marshall received the best education the West, in his day, afforded, and he was prepared for his future career by the study of law. His frame was large and muscular, his eyes were black and piercing, his voice was loud and commanding, and his courage quailed before neither man nor demon. Yet withal, he was a true and generous friend, a skillful and successful politician, an able statesman, a sincere patriot and a fearless soldier. His temperament suited the times when the duel was the arbiter of all disputes. April 19, 1812, Mr. Marshall fought his celebrated duel with Chas. S. Mitchell, on the banks of the Ohio, above Maysville. He challenged Mitchell for some insult offered his father, Capt. Marshall. Mitchell was an expert with the pistol, and at the first fire, shot Mr. Marshall in the hip. But the latter was not satisfied, and wanted a second round. This was refused by his friends.

Mr. Marshall received from his father a tract of three thousand acres of land in Lewis Co., Ky., and here he lived from his marriage until his death. He lorded over a large number of tenants. Though overbearing and profane, he was liberal in his charities. His tenants loved him in spite of his faults, and they found him a powerful protector. No one near him was permitted to suffer, if relief was in his power. His irritability was increased by the occasional torture pro-

(176) GEN. THOMAS MARSHALL.

duced by a broken ankle, caused by his fall from a horse. He was a decided Democrat, and frequently a candidate for the Legislature. He represented Lewis County for six terms, 1817, 1828, 1836, 1839, 1842 and 1844. At one time he was Speaker of the House. When the Mexican war broke out, President Polk appointed him Brigadier General of volunteers, and he served from July 1, 1846, to July 20, 1848. He was with Gen. Taylor in the Buena Vista campaign, and was with Gen. Scott in his invasion of Mexico. During the last six months of the war, he was the Military Governor of Mexico. His daughter, Mrs. Bland, (632) just before her death, wrote me her version of her father's life and death, from which I make some extracts:

(b) "My father went to the Mexican war when about 52 years of age. I remember one instance of his promptness, which I will relate: He had been ordered to guard a very dangerous pass between Monterey and Buena Vista, and had labored twenty-four hours to throw up immense breastworks, when, just at dark, he received a peremptory order to hasten on to Buena Vista under cover of night and darkness, with his heavy artillery. He called his officers together, and informed them of the command he had received, and the necessity of immediate relief to their endangered comrades. Each man hastily swallowed a cup of coffee, and eagerly commenced his rugged march of thirty miles. Frequently they would have to dismount, and push the heavy guns up the mountains. The General himself assisted in this work. The Mexicans had heard that Gen. Marshall's command consisted of six thousand men, when, in truth, he had only one thousand. When he reached the summit overlooking the bloody field of Buena Vista, he announced to his men that it was either victory or death for them, and he gave orders that the first man that faltered should be shot down by his comrades. The cannon were posted, and the cavalry charged down on the enemy. The Mexicans supposing the Americans were reinforced by a large army, fled in confusion. On reaching the bloody battle ground, Gen. Marshall found no enemy. In his bitter disappointment he is said to have wept the only tears that ever moistened his eyes. The battle of Buena Vista was gained by father's stratagem and by his prompt and heroic obedience. But of this he never had the credit. He always complained of injustice from both Taylor and Scott."

(c) Gen. Marshall always claimed to have been the "Blucher" of Buena Vista, and often cursed his fate in having been placed behind, where he could not share the glory of the victory he achieved without striking a blow. Mrs. Bland thus details the circumstances of Gen. Marshall's death:

My father was murdered by a desperado named Tyler, of Mt. Carmel, Fleming Co., Ky. Tyler attempted to ingratiate father's favor by telling on the tenants. He bought a piece of land of father, and made only one payment. He proved very troublesome, and father, trying to get rid of him, got another tenant to buy Tyler out. Learning the facts Tyler became exasperated, and threatened to kill father. With an ac-

THE MARSHALL FAMILY. 117

(178) JOHN MARSHALL.

complice, Tyler attacked father on the highway one dark night, when coming home. But this attempt at assassination failed. Tyler then burned, as is believed, a new distillery of my father's, containing several thousand bushels of grain. Tyler told the neighbors that he intended to insult Gen. Marshall, so that he might have a pretext to shoot him. This he did, when Gen. Marshall was in his field measuring corn; but my father struck and choked him. Tyler went off muttering revenge. He procured a double-barrel shotgun, and went to a tenant's, where father was, and called for him. Father went to the door, and Tyler asked "Are you ready?" My father answered "Yes," as he went down the steps into the yard. Some one then offered him an empty rifle, saying, "Take this, General; it will scare him." My father remarked, "Let's have fair shooting, Tyler. Don't get behind a tree. We have carried this thing far enough." Just then Tyler fired both barrels into father's breast. Without speaking, he fell on his knees and died. Tyler escaped to Ohio and died there.

(d) Mrs. Marshall left her husband some years before his death, and lived with her daughter, Mrs. Fleming. She was a lovely woman. Her soft, sweet temper, contrasted with the violent nature of her husband. She was a daughter of William Whetcroft and Anne Winchester, of Annapolis, Md. She had two sisters and a brother: 1, Mary F. Whetcroft, = Samuel Chase, of New York; 2, Sarah Ann Whetcroft, = Judge Alfred Cavalry; 3, William Whetcroft, who died single. Gen. Marshall was buried at Washington, Ky. His wife was interred at Maysville, Ky.

178 JOHN MARSHALL, b. at Washington, Ky., January 1, 1795, d. at his home on Mill Creek, Mason Co., Ky., September 3, 1859, = 1818, his cousin, LUCY MARSHALL, b. at "Walnut Grove," Mason Co., Ky., September 17, 1796, d. January 24, 1835. Uncle John was a gentleman of native intellect and cultivated mind. Upon his marriage, his father gave him his Clark's Run estate, four miles west of Washington, Ky. Here he lived in the indulgence of his literary tastes and hospitable nature until 1833, when his reduced fortunes required him to sell. He then removed to his wife's property on Mill Creek. He was at times intemperate, but during the latter years of his life he refrained from liquor, and seldom left home. He was a Democrat in politics, and though his party was in a decided minority in the County, yet his personal popularity, on one occasion, came very near electing him to the Legislature. His information was varied, his reading general and his judgment sound. He read every book that came in his way. His proficiency in history,

(180) MARY KEITH MARSHALL—(*Green*).

philosophy, politics any other branches of information, made him an interesting and instructive companion; but from indolence, his capabilities were never improved, so as to raise him to distinction. His brilliant talents and independent fortune caused him to prepare for no profession, and the man that might have adorned the bench, the bar or the legislative forum, spent his life in privacy.

Aunt Lucy was an amiable and interesting lady, an indulgent mother and a discreet housekeeper. From my father's death, in 1825, until the family removed to Mill Creek, in 1833, the orphan children of my parents found a home beneath the roof of Uncle John and Aunt Lucy, and a warm place in their hearts. Both were interred on the "Hill," at Washington, Ky.

180 (*a*) MARY KEITH MARSHALL, b. at Washington, Ky., January 13, 1797, yet living, = 1st, March 1, 1825, JAMES A. PAXTON (244), who d. October 25, 1825; = 2d, January 29, 1835, at Frankfort, Ky., JUDGE JOHN GREEN, b. in Virginia, January 4, 1786, d. at "Waveland," near Danville, Ky., September 30, 1838.

My step-mother was reared at Washington, Ky., in its golden age. Perhaps no town in the West possessed a more literary and enlightened population, than was found in Washington the early part of this century. I have known no female that surpassed my step-mother in intelligence, knowledge, vivacity and spirit. Her energy was a passion; her versatility was taken for frenzy, and her animation suggested insanity. She sought excitement, moved from place to place, read every new book that came out, was ardent in her piety, enlightened in her views, and could maintain her sentiments against jurists, statesmen and theologians. Upon her marriage with my father, she went with him to Columbus, Ohio. But while on a visit to Kentucky, my father died in the old drawing-room on "The Hill," and in the graveyard there, he lies buried. One child, Mary F. E. Paxton, was the fruit of the marriage. She was the widowed mother's pride and darling, her joy and hope. But the little one, when three years old, wasted and died, and the mother was disconsolate. Its remains lie beside its father's, and its epitaph reads: "Born December 19, 1825, died April 18, 1829. Of such is the Kingdom of Heaven."

(180) MARY KEITH MARSHALL—(*Green*).

(*b*) Her step-children now demanded her care. She took us to Uncle John's (178), and had a room built for our accommodation. She herself became our teacher. Never was a mother more faithful. But it was a religious rather than a parental instinct that impelled her. Her conscience was her supreme ruler. In fulfilling her duties she had a martyr's firmness. It was not love to us, but her obligation to God. It was not tenderness, but a moral impulse. In 1830, she rented a house in Augusta, that she might take boarders, and send my brother and me to college. A few months experience disgusted her, and she went to Cincinnati. After sending me to Dr. John A. McClung's for a year, she took me to Cincinnati and put me in the Catholic school known as the "Athenæum." Here I remained until December, 1834, when she went with me to Danville, Ky., and entered me in the Freshman Class of Centre College. Here she met Judge John Green, and in a short time they were married. Judge Green's palatial home was known as "Waveland," and is one mile from Danville. I lived with them throughout my college course. If Judge Green was ever paid a cent for my board, I do not know it.

(*c*) Mr. Green was a tall and broad-shouldered man, of commanding person and dignified address. He was a profound lawyer and a conscientious judge. His reading was extensive, but the Bible was his favorite study. His large household was regularly gathered for prayer. He was a patriarch, rather than a master, among his servants. His first wife was Sarah Fry, daughter of the distinguished teacher, Joshua Fry. The children of his first wife were: 1, Willis Green, who married a daughter of Bishop Smith and became a missionary to India; 2, Sally, who married a Barclay; 3, Peachy, married Rev. Mr. Johnstone, and now lives in Danville, Ky.; 4, Joshua, the apostle of Presbyterianism in Arkansas; 5, Susan, married James Weir; and 6, William, married a Weir, and was a Presbyterian minister in Leavenworth, Kansas, some years ago.

I regard it as one of the great blessings of my life, that I was brought under the influence of so great and good a man as Judge Green. Though he seldom spoke specially to me, yet his virtues had a wide-spread influence. His associates were the learned and pious men of his day. Dr. Young, Dr. Lewis W. Green, Dr. W. L. Breckenridge, Dr. Nelson, the author of the work on Infidel-

(180) MARY KEITH MARSHALL—(*Green*).

ity, Dr. Louis Marshall, and other good men often met in his parlor, and we were encouraged to be present to enjoy their learned conversation.

(*d*) Mr. Green was one of the noble band of early emancipationists in Kentucky. He placed on record a paper liberating all his slaves, some forty in number, as they became of age; and, long before the war, they were free. His views on the slavery question were severely criticised, and caused him much vexation. He was an elder in the Presbyterian Church, and represented Lincoln Co., in the State Legislature for seven terms, as follows: 1818, 1820, 1821, 1822, 1824, 1825 and 1832. He died in 1838, and his widow returned to Mason County. She lived a number of years in Covington, and is now with her son, Col. Thomas M. Green, in Maysville. She is the oldest of the eight surviving grand children of Col. Thos. Marshall. The seven others are Nos. 200, 202, 188, 262, 266, 286 and 288. She is very deaf, and quite helpless; yet she walks around and speaks intelligently. Perhaps I have the last long letter written by her own hand, and as I prize it, maybe others will be interested in it. It is as follows:

(*e*)   MAYSVILLE, KENTUCKY, November 1, 1875.
W. M. Paxton, Platte City, Mo.:

MY DEAR SON:—I received your letter sometime ago, and would have answered it sooner, but was told you were expected in Washington.

I was born on the 13th of January, 1797. Your father was born the 13th of September, nine years before. He was seventeen years old when he came to Uncle McClung's (72) to read history and study law. He was about twenty-two when he was married to your mother. About a month later your Aunt Lucy (178) and I were sent to Virginia. Your father inherited a fortune of ten thousand dollars from his Grandmother Paxton, a very old woman. With that money he built the house you children were born in. John McDowell read law at the same time with Uncle Alexander (68). They met Saturdays in town, and slept at the office with Cousin Marshall Key (16 s), and eat at my father's, who was always called Uncle Tom by both of them. Sometimes they got into scrapes, writing against some of the candidates, and my father had to get them out.

The summer after your father was married, his mother and stepfather, Mr. Moore, came to see them. They brought his half-brother and half-sister, William and Jane Moore, and remained two years. Jane went to school with my sisters, to old Mrs. Lee, and William went to school to Mann Butler. Jane was homely, but a girl of fine sense. I do not remember hearing your father speak of his Paxton kin; but he was very proud of his step-father.

I met with a letter written by your father when twenty-one, and sent it to your brother, Marshall. There were letters besides, but when

THE MARSHALL FAMILY.

(180) MARY KEITH MARSHALL—(*Green*).

I settled with the court, I gave up the property and with it the letters. I retained nothing excepting yourself; nor did I ever give you up until I saw you married to Mary Forman.

(*f*) I got a letter from William Green (her step-son). I will answer it next week. He talks of coming to see me sometime this winter. Paxton (690) will be at home with his wife this week. Lizzie Waller (686) is at home. I hope I shall be able to get to see them, but the house will be very full. I have seven grand-children, and a very fine family. Nannie (648) is a fine manager of them.

Give my love to Mary and the girls. I met with old Mr. Paxton [John D. Paxton, D. D.,] after the death of my baby. He was related to your father. Gen. Houston was a cousin. There is a family of Paxtons living in Lincoln County, who are related to you.

Your affectionate mother,

MARY K. GREEN.

God bless the old lady, and may death come as a messenger of peace.

(*g*) In 1884, I visited the grave of Judge Green in Danville cemetery, and copied from his monument the following inscription:

"In memory of John Green, who was born June 4, 1786, and died September 30, 1838, in the 52d year of his age. And I heard a voice from heaven saying unto me, write, Blessed are the dead which die in the Lord, from henceforth—Yea, saith the Spirit, that they may rest from their labors, and their works do follow them."

THE GREEN FAMILY.

(*h*) William Green, a Captain in the body-guard of William III, = Eleanor Duff. Their son, Robert Green, = Eleanor Dunn. Robert was born in England about 1695, crossed to America about 1712, and settled in Culpeper Co., Va. His mother's brother, Sir William Duff, came with them, but returned to England. They had seven children:

A 1. WILLIAM GREEN, = a Miss Coleman, of Caroline Co., Va. 8 ch: of whom

B 1. *William Green,* = his cousin, Elizabeth Green.

2. *Frances Wyatt Green,* = Strother.

1. *Joseph Green* was father of Dr. N. Green, President of the W. U. Tel. Co.

A 2. ROBERT GREEN, = Pattie Ball, of Northumberland Co.

3. DUFF GREEN, = 1st a Miss Thomas, (But See 116 b.) and was mother of Elizabeth Green, who married her cousin William Green. Duff Green = 2d, Ann, dr. of Col. Harry Willis, of Fredericksburg, Va., and Mildred Washington, aunt of George Washington. She was a dr. of Lawrence Washington and Mildred Warner. (150 p.). Issue:

(180) MARY KEITH MARSHALL—(*Green*).

B 1. *Willis Green*, = Sarah Read. 7 ch.

C   1. Duff Green, = Mrs. Crecy, *nee* Kenton, a niece of Simon Kenton.

D (*i*)   1. Dr. Willis Duff Green, of Mt. Vernon, Ill.
   2. Mrs. Gray, of Bloomington, Ill.
   3. Mrs. Havely, of Bloomington, Ill.
   4. Judge W. H. Green, of Cairo, Ill., = two sisters, Hughes.

C   2. Judge John Green, = Sarah A. Fry. (See Fry Chart, No. 180). Issue: 1, Willis Green; 2, Peachy, = Johnstone; 3, Sally, = Barclay; 4, Rev. Joshua Green; 5, Susan, = Weir, and 6, William, = Weir. Judge Green's 2d wife was MARY K. MARSHALL. See No. 180.

C   3. Letitia Green, = Maj. James Barbour, and was mother of Dr. Lewis G. Barbour, of Richmond, Ky., and Col. James Barbour, a banker of Maysville, Ky.

  4. Elizabeth Green, = Dr. Benj. Edwards, brother of Gov. Edwards, of Ill., and of Lucretia Edwards, who married Gen. Duff Green, No. 424. They had ten ch.: 1, Sarah Edwards, = Col. Lewis Parsons; 2, Dr. Willis G. Edwards; 3, Benj. Edwards; 4, Letitia, = Whitaker; 5, Presley, = Tunstall; 6, Frank; 7, Pedgy; 8, Julia, second wife of Col. Lewis Parsons; 9, Cyrus, and 10, Martha, = Robert Todd, of Lexington, Mo.

  5. Martha, or Patsy, = Dr. William Craig. 6 ch: 1, Eliza; 2, John J., = Amanda Goodloe, dr. of Judge Wm. C. Goodloe, and grand dr. of Gov. Wm. Owsley; 3, Willis G. Craig, now Prof. in the Theo. Seminary of the N. W. at Chicago — an eloquent pulpit orator, = Amelia Owsley, 8 ch.; 4, Lettie Craig, = Dr. George Cowan; 5, Martha Ellen (Pattie) Craig, = her cousin, COL. THOS. GREEN, No. 648; 6, Lewis G. Craig, d..

(*j*)

(180) MARY KEITH MARSHALL—(*Green*).

C 6. Dr. Lewis Warner Green, = 1st, a dr. of Judge William Montgomery; = 2d, Mrs. Mary Lawrence, nee Fry. (See Fry chart, 180 *n*). Issue: 1, Julia, = Mat. T. Scott, live in Bloomington, Ill.; 2, Letitia Green, = Hon. A. E. Stevenson, live in Bloomington, Ill., 4 ch.
   7. Sarah Green, = Sneed and died young.

B 2. *William Green,* = a daughter of MARKHAM MARSHALL, No. 19. See No. 116.

C 1. Gen. Duff Green, of Jackson's Cabinet (No. 424), = Lucretia Edwards (above).
   1, Laura Green, = J. S. Reed, 6 ch.; 2, Margaret Green, = Andrew Calhoun; 3, Benj. Green, = Lizzie Waters; 4, Lizzie; 5, Mary, = Maynard; 6, Duff, = Pickins; 7, Florine.
   2. Willis Green; 3, William, = Stone; 4, Henry Green, was a missionary; 5, Nancy, known as long Nancy, being upwards of six feet tall; 6, Betsy, = Huling; 7, Ellen Green, = Gen. James Semple; 8, Sarah, = Rev. Neal.

A 4. COL. JOHN GREEN, = Susanna Blackwell. He was distinguished at the Battles of Brandywine and Guilford. Issue:

B 1. *William Green,* = Lucy Williams, dr. of William Williams and Lucy Clayton.

C 1. John W. Green, b. November 9, 1781, d. February 4, 1834; War of 1812; Judge of Virginia Court of Appeals, = December 24, 1805, Mary
(*k*) Brown. Issue: 1, William Green, D. D.; 2, Raleigh, 1808–41; 3, Daniel S., b. February 29, 1812; 4, Philip Green, 1814–15. The second wife of John W. Green was Million Cooke. Issue: 1, John C. Green, 1818; 2, Thomas C., 1820; 3, George M., 1822; 4, James W. Green, 1824.

B 2. *Gen. Moses Green,* = Fanny Richards. Issue; 1, Amanda Green, = Gen. Barnard Peyton; 2, Thomas Green, married 3 times; 3, William, = a Saunders; 4, Archibald Magill Green, = Eleanor F. Farish. Issue: 1, Moses Magill Green, = LILY T. MARSHALL, No. 832.

(180) MARY KEITH MARSHALL—(*Green*).

A   5. NICHOLAS GREEN, = Miss Price.
     6. JAMES GREEN, = Jones, perhaps a daughter of Gabriel Jones, ancestors of Grant Green, of Frankfort, and the Greens of Henderson, of Cassius and Brutus Clay, and of Green Clay Smith (954), and of Nannie Lewis (966)
     7. MOSES GREEN, = a Blackwell, sister to his brother John's wife.

THE FRY FAMILY.

(*l*) Col. Joshua Fry, emigrant, = a Miss Micon. Their son, John Fry, = Sarah Adams, dr. of Col. Richard Adams, and they were the parents of the celebrated teacher.

A   1. JOSHUA FRY, = Peachy Walker, b. February 6, 1767, dr. of Dr. Thomas and Mildred Walker. Issue:

B   1. *A Daughter*, = Thomas Speed. Issue:

C   1, James Speed; 2, Joshua Speed; 3, Philip Speed; 4, Smith Speed.

B   (*m*) 2. *Sarah Adams Fry*, = John Green, whose second wife was MARY K. MARSHALL (Paxton). See full gen., No. 180, *i*.

      3. *Patsy Fry*, = David Bell.

C   1, Hon. Joshua F. Bell; 2, James Bell; 3, Ann Bell = Dr. Ormond Beatty, President of Centre College.

B   4. *Mildred Ann Fry*, = William Christian Bullitt.
         1. Col. T. W. Bullitt, = ANNE P. LOGAN, No. 900.
      5. *John Fry*, = Judith Cary Harrison. See Laughorne chart, No. 1012.
      6. *Thomas Fry*, = Betsy Smith. Issue:

C   (*n*)   1. Gen. Speed Smith Fry.
         2. Mary Fry, = Dr. L. W. Green. See Green chart, No. 180 *i*.
         3. Nancy Fry, = Thos. Barbee. Issue:
             1. Thos. Fry Barbee, = HENRIETTA BUFORD, No. 980.
         4. Frank Fry; 5, David; 6, Lucy; 7, Sarah.

(182) ELIZA COLSTON MARSHALL — (*Marshall*).

182 ELIZA COLSTON MARSHALL, b. at Washington, Ky., March 17, 1801; d. July 19, 1874; = September 19, 1819, her cousin MARTIN PICKET MARSHALL, b. in Warrenton, Va., February 10, 1798; d. in Washington, Ky., May 9, 1883. See No. 234. I knew cousin Eliza in her prime. Tall, handsome, stately and commanding, she was perhaps the most radiant of the daughters of Capt. Marshall. It was my delight in my college vacations, to visit Belle-Grove, the charming villa in Fleming Co., Ky., where she presided. And when the family removed to Washington, and established themselves in the old homestead, I was often entertained and instructed by the brilliance and power of her conversation. But in her latter years her intellect was clouded, her vivacity hushed, and her spirit veiled.

Cousin Martin was one of the most superb old gentlemen that I ever met. He lost his father when he was a boy, and his uncle, Chief Justice Marshal, took him into his family at Richmond. Here he remained several years, reading history and philosophy. I will let him tell his own story. In 1876 I had a long conference with him, in his private study, in which he remarked:

In 1816, I left my mother in Virginia, determined to work out my own destiny. Uncle John proffered to send me to college, but I desired rather, to build on my own resources, I had nothing but poverty for my inheritance, and energy for my capital. With this independent spirit, I made my way to Kentucky. I brought no letters of introduction, and my coming was unannounced. I had no acquaintance on whom I could call for assistance. I first saw my uncle, Alex. K. Marshall, (68) and told him I was a son of his brother Charles, and that his brother John would write in my behalf. He embraced me with affection, and told me his brother's son had no call for recommendations to him. Under his guidance, I resumed the study of law. When on my first visit, I presented myself to my uncle Thomas, he asked why I had come to Kentucky. I told him I was on my father's business, and in search of his wild lands. Aunts Fanny Marshall and Susan McClung met me kindly. Behind them, I saw a sweet face, and, at Aunt McClung's command, Eliza modestly advanced and saluted me with a kiss. I now devoted myself to the study of law, with Uncle Alexander. My diligence was untiring. Of Saturday nights, I would go in to see Eliza, and would return Sunday evenings. But I had an enemy in

(182) ELIZA COLSTON MARSHALL—(*Marshall*).

Eliza's brother, Thomas. He poisoned her mind against me, and she rejected me, much to the chagrin of her mother. I visited her no more, and our engagement was forgotten. In 1818, I was licensed to practice, and settled in Paris, where Uncle Humphrey was living. In six months I had earned $500, and was greatly elated. In April 1818, I visited Washington, and my suit for Eliza's hand was renewed. I was accepted, and we were married. Owing to an epidemic that broke out in Paris, about the date of my marriage, I determined to adopt the suggestion of Cabell Breckenridge, and settle in Cincinnati. Eliza and I rode to the city on horseback, and remained there eleven months. Our prospects were good, but my health broke down, and we concluded to return. After spending several years in Washington, we went in 1823 to Fleming.

Seeing that Cousin Martin was feeble, I suggested that he lie down and rest, while I visited my father's grave. "Go William," he exclaimed, "and you will find there a fresh and unmarked grave. There lies my sainted Eliza. I am waiting for my own death, when one stone shall cover us both." In speaking these words the tears rolled down his cheeks, and the long white locks of hair fell over his face. Exhausted, he fell upon his bed.

Mr. Marshall was prosecuting attorney for Fleming County, and prosecuted Isaac Desha, for murder. He represented the County in 1825 and 1827. He was twice elector for Harrison and for Clay. He was a member of the Convention of 1849, that framed the present Constitution of Kentucky; and was elected Senator from Mason in 1861. He opposed secession, and was a prominent supporter of the Union cause.

Cousin Martin had a large and well selected library, and the children were expected and required to use it. Cousin Eliza delighted in young company, and her parlors were a favorite resort of numbers of the most accomplished of both sexes. Many a week have I spent at their hospital mansion when the halls and dining room presented the appearance of a lasting reception. With private tutors for the children, and educated and accomplished visitors, books were the theme of constant discussion. Cousin Eliza presided as a goddess surrounded by nymphs.

Cousin Martin was my *beau-ideal* of a patriarch. An orator by

THE MARSHALL FAMILY. 127

(182) ELIZA COLSTON MARSHALL—(*Marshall*).

nature, he announced his opinions with emphasis, and sustained them with earnestness. Upwards of six feet tall, and erect as a soldier, he bore in his left hand a lofty staff, whose ponderous thud clinched his arguments. His well combed locks fell far down on his shoulders, and gave him a venerable appearance. He and his family united with the Methodist Church, and to his death he was a liberal supporter of every christian and benevolent cause. He was a friend of Henry Clay, and espoused gradual emancipation. Though he had not practiced law for fifty years, yet the Maysville bar was called together, and complimentary resolutions were passed on the occasion of his death.

Mr. Marshall's will is recorded in Maysville. It is dated in 1868 and ten codicils were added at different times. His children are made equal, and his son Charles is appointed executor. The homestead and appurtenant lands are granted to Mary and Phoebe. The shares of his daughters and of the sons of Lucy McKnight are settled on trustees. The library and pictures are given to Mary. A marble slab is to be placed over the graves of himself and wife, and the graveyard is to be enclosed with an iron fence.

Before Mr. Marshall's death, I desired to show him my veneration, and sent him the following tribute:

TO HON. MARTIN P. MARSHALL, OF MASON COUNTY, KENTUCKY, PRESENTED ON HIS 84TH BIRTH-DAY.

I.

Dear kinsman, and friend of my father, I hail thee,
  With homage and love that are true;
And yet I am conscious that language will fail me
  To give thee the honor that's due.
Thy eighty-four years have made tremulous fingers,
  And hair that is silvery white;
But health, in both body and spirit, still lingers,
  And hope, for the future, is bright.

II.

How well I remember, in days of my childhood,
  The welcome I found at thy home!
Where fish in the streamlet, and game in the wildwood,
  Invited me often to roam.
Your library, furnished with lore of all ages,
  My youthful ambition inspired;
And here with philosophers, poets and sages,
  My fondness for books was acquired.

(182) ELIZA COLSTON MARSHALL—(*Marshall*).

III.

Profuse hospitality, friendship and learning,
  With art and religion combined,
Are now an appropriate harvest returning,
  In children well read and refined.
Your house was a home, where the laden and weary
  Could find, on their pilgrimage, rest,—
Where friends, when the world was upbraiding or dreary,
  With aid and good counsel were blest.

IV.

Where now you reside, from my first recollection,
  Has been the dear home of your race;
'Tis hallowed by time, and my early affection,
  And Marshalls delight in the place.
The art of the Muses and taste of the Graces,
  Its halls with luxuriance, store;
The guest "Hospitality" everywhere traces,
  And "Welcome" is found on the door.

V.

Thy kindred, to-day, as a father, revere thee,
  And deem thee a type of the past:
The children, with filial affection, draw near thee,
  And glances of reverence cast.
We hope, that in health, for long years you may flourish,
  And five generations behold;
And pray you may live, as a shepherd, to nourish,
  And gather your flock to the fold.

VI.

The surname of Marshall is loved and respected;
  And thou art its prophet and sage;
We'd find thee the first, were the kindred collected,
  In stature, in wisdom and age;
And if the relations could meet in reunion,
  And fill the old family rooms,
How pleasant and sacred would be their communion,
  Beside their progenitors tombs.

VII.

The bones of thy grandsire, Tom Marshall, here slumber,
  With those of his wife, by his side;
Their children, who married, were fifteen in number,
  And all were of note, ere they died.
And here is the tomb where my father reposes,
  With others for whom I yet weep;
A mantle of ivy, with myrtle and roses,
  Apparel the ground where they sleep.

VIII.

As Orator, Warrior, Statesman and Jurist,
  Thy kindred have honored the name;
Their deeds were the noblest, their lives were the purest,
  And time will their merits proclaim.

(182) ELIZA COLSTON MARSHALL—(*Marshall*).

Thy uncle, Chief Justice John Marshall, forever,
   With laurel and palm will be decked;
And you, as his favorite pupil, can never,
   His precepts and honor neglect.

IX.

The name of thy father, with pure veneration,
   Virginians still mention with pride;
He rose on the sky, as a bright constellation,
   And just at his zenith, he died.
That genius—Tom Marshall—Kentucky's proud scion—
   The idol and child of the West,
And John A. McClung, the true soldier of Zion,
   The blood the Marshalls attest.

X.

While John J. and Thomas A. Marshall were noted,
   And honored, on bench and at bar,
The family name was still further promoted,
   By Humphrey's career in the war,
And scores of good men, from the Marshalls descended,
   Still strive in the battle of life,
And yet will be crowned, when the conflict is ended,
   With laurels achieved in the strife.

XI.

Thy sainted companion, Eliza, the gifted,
   With thee shall eternity spend;
Her grave for thy body, ere long, shall be rifted,
   And thou to her side shall descend.
Her wisdom and grace, from my first recollection,
   Were such as few women possess;
Her husband could trust in her truth and affection;
   Her children, her memory will bless.

XII.

You love the green graves where your ancestors pillow,
   And often commune with the dead,
And over their tombs, like the twigs of the willow,
   Your hoary hair hangs from your head.
And sometimes, when low, at their graves, you are kneeling,
   The eyes of your faith look above;
And there you behold a bright vision, revealing
   The bliss of the dead whom you love.

XIII.

Among them, you see, in elysian enjoyment,
   Dear Lucy, whose grave is yet new;
Her eyes are oft turned, from her blissful employment,
   To look, to the portal, for you.
To part from thy friends upon earth, will bring sorrow,
   Though few of them linger below;
But when, in God's likeness, you wake on the morrow,
   Vast numbers their love will bestow.

(184) LUCY AMBLER MARSHALL—(*Coleman*).

184 (*a*) LUCY AMBLER MARSHALL, b. in Washington, Ky., December 30, 1802, d. in Vicksburg, Miss., July 3, 1858, = October 19, 1826, NICHOLAS D. COLEMAN, b. April 22, 1800, d. at Vicksburg, May 11, 1874. Cousin Lucy was a pleasant, and amiable lady. Her wedding was the first I ever witnessed. After the removal of the family from Washington, I never met her. She died in Vicksburg, and was brought home for burial.

Mr. Coleman was raised in Harrison Co., Ky.; was well educated, studied law, represented Harrison County in the State Legislature in 1824 and 1825; was elected to Congress in 1829, as a Jackson Democrat, from the Mason District. The next election he was defeated by his wife's cousin, Thomas A. Marshall. He was then appointed postmaster at Maysville, Ky. About 1840, he was appointed postmaster at Vicksburg, Miss. While superintending the performance of official duties, Col. Coleman contined the practice of law, and was an ardent advocate of many laudable enterprises. The Maysville and Lexington Turnpike was his earliest scheme, and chiefly through his powerful advocacy Congress made a liberal appropriation for the road; but the bill, greatly to Mr. Coleman's chagrin, was vetoed by President Jackson. Another of his projects was a Southern Pacific Railroad, by way of Vicksburg, Shreveport and El Paso. He was overjoyed when ground was broken for his darling enterprise, and for a time accepted the presidency of the DeSoto road. In 1855, Col. Coleman removed to New Orleans; was in the Senate of Louisiana when the war broke out; opposed secession, but when the State went out of the Union, he gave an ardent support to the Southren cause. His three sons were in the army; two of them lost their lives, and all were covered with martial chaplets. After the war Col. Coleman found himself impoverished, and engaged in life insurance. He died at the house of his son, Major James T. Coleman, of Vicksburg. He died of disease of the heart. Col. Coleman was a handsome, accomplished and agreeable gentleman. His iron honor and adamantine integrity were joined with agreeable condescension and polished grace. He was equally loved and admired.

THE COLEMAN FAMILY.

(*b*) Burbridge Coleman and Daniel Coleman, of Caroline Co., Va., were brothers.

THE MARSHALL FAMILY. 131

(184) LUCY AMBLER MARSHALL—(*Coleman*).

A 1. CAPT. THOMAS B. COLEMAN was a son of Burbridge Coleman. He married Mary O. Coleman, daughter of Robert Coleman, of Hanover Co. After the death of Thomas B. Coleman, she married George Fleming. Issue of Capt. Thomas and Mary O. Coleman:

B 1. Col. *Lewis Minor Coleman,* = MARY A. MARSHALL, No. 560.

A 2. GEN. JAMES COLEMAN, son of Daniel Coleman, b. in Caroline Co., Va., November 27, 1773, d. 1828, = August 3, 1797, Elizabeth Warfield, b. June 27, 1779, d. 1857. Issue:

B 1. *Nicholas D. Coleman,* = LUCY MARSHALL, No. 184.

(c) 2. *Lloyd R. Coleman,* b. July 25, 1819, = July 13, 1841, Harriet L. Moore, b. April 29, 1823, d. March 2, 1871. Issue:

C 1. Nicholas D. Coleman, b. August 10, 1851, = October 6, 1875, ELIZA M. BROWNING, No. 2288.

THE WARFIELD FAMILY.

A (*d*) RICHARD WARFIELD of Shropshire, England, emigrated to America about 1639, and settled at the Blackhouse farm, nine miles from Annapolis, Md. He left six children.

B JOHN WARFIELD, his fourth and last son, resided near Indian Landing, Md., = Ruth Saither, and left six sons and two daughters.

C BENJAMIN WARFIELD, his second son, = Rebecca Ridgeley, daughter of Nicholas Ridgeley, one of the early Judges of the Supreme Court of Delaware, and Sarah Worthington, his wife.

D ELISHA WARFIELD, fourth son of Benjamin and Rebecca, was born November 29, 1741, emigrated to Kentucky, 1790, and died July 16, 1818. He married, 1st, August 11, 1771, Eliza Dorsey, by whom he had three children. He married 2d, August 22, 1778, Ruth Burgess, by whom he had twelve children.

E (*e*) 1. ELIZABETH [*Betsy*] WARFIELD, first child of Elisha and Ruth, was born June 27, 1779, d. 1857, = August 3, 1797, Gen. James Coleman, b. November 27, 1773, d. 1828. They left eleven children, two of whom:

THE MARSHALL FAMILY.

(186) JAMES WILLIAM MARSHALL.

F 1. NICHOLAS D. COLEMAN, b. April 22, 1800, d. 1874, = October 19, 1826, LUCY A. MARSHALL, b. December 30, 1802, d. July 3, 1858.

F 2. LLOYD RUFFIN COLEMAN, youngest child of Elizabeth and James Coleman, was born July 25, 1819, = July 13, 1841, Harriet L. Moore, daughter of Col. William Moore, of Norfolk, Va., b. April 29, 1823, d. March 2, 1871. Their son:

G NICHOLAS D. COLEMAN, b. August 10, 1851, = October 6, 1875, LIZZIE McCLUNG BROWNING, b. June 9, 1854. See No. 2288.

E Benjamin Warfield, son of Elisha and Ruth, = Sallie Caldwell. Issue:

1. William Warfield, = Mary C. Breckenridge. Issue:
    1. Benjamin B. Warfield, D. D.
    2. E. D. Warfield.

186 JAMES WILLIAM MARSHALL, named for two brothers who had died before his birth; b. in Washington, Ky., March 9, 1807; died near Tollsboro, Ky., at the house of his niece, Julianna Bland, December 6, 1877, and buried, by his request, in the Baptist churchyard, Washington, Ky. He was educated at the U. S. Naval School, at Annapolis, Md.; in early life was a brilliant and spirited gentleman; when on the death of his mother, he received his patrimony, it was squandered in extravagance; became slightly insane, and spent some time at the Kentucky lunatic asylum; was discharged as harmless, and was sustained by relatives for the rest of his life; in his latter years, was somewhat restored to reason; united with the Baptist Church, and led a quiet and exemplary life.

188 COL. CHARLES ALEXANDER MARSHALL, b. in Washington, Ky., May 2, 1809; = September 12, 1833, PHŒBE A. PAXTON, b. in Washington, Ky., February 2, 1818. They are now living at " Walnut Grove," one mile from Washington, Ky. Col. Marshall was educated at " Buckpond," at the private school of his uncle, Dr. Louis Marshall. Under the tutelage of his father and

THE MARSHALL FAMILY. 133

(188) COL. CHARLES ALEXANDER MARSHALL.

older sisters, he read at home history, philosophy and belles letters. After marriage he purchased "Walnut Grove" of the descendants of his wife's grandfather, A. K. Marshall (68); and here he has spent his useful life, in the quiet pursuits of agriculture. His home has long been the center of refinement, literature and religion. Beneath his hospitable roof I have always found a welcome and generous entertainment. Ten years my senior, I have always found Col. Marshall a wise counsellor and a powerful protector. Of tall and ungainly person, his bodily activity, mental power and moral courage give him even yet a commanding influence. His boiling Kennan blood is assuaged by Marshall pride, sober thought, and the curtain lectures of his good wife. By nature, a "rough ashler," his wide experience, social culture and extensive reading, have polished him into brilliant marble. I have seldom met with one better versed in English and American history, and the politics and literature of the day. His associates have been the leading men of Kentucky. He is liberal in his views, and takes a lively interest in every reform.

Mr. Marshall has been successively a Whig, American and Democrat. He represented Mason Co., Ky., in the State Legislature in 1840 and 1855–1859. When the war broke out he was a decided Union man, and opposed secession with all his powers. Though too old for active service, his energy and influence caused him to be selected to raise a regiment of infantry in Northern Kentucky. He had hardly commenced the work of enlistment before he was ordered to join Gen. Nelson in the mountains of Eastern Kentucky. Ou the 19th of October, 1861, he started with 350 men. On the march of Nelson's brigade up the Big Sandy, Marshall was placed in the advance. Scouts were thrown out, but Nelson demanded more haste. Col. Marshall pressed forward rapidly, and suddenly found himself attacked by the enemy. His men were in a narrow defile, with the river on one side, and the bluff upon the other. A deadly fire was poured on him from the bluffs in front, and from the opposite side of the river. The men were ordered under cover of the rocks, and for an hour an equal battle raged. Col. Marshall's horse was killed under him, and his cap and clothing were perforated with balls. The combatants suffered about equal loss. When reinforcements appeared on the bluffs, the enemy fled. Having accomplished their purpose the brigade returned. The Sixteenth Kentucky was completed, and did signal service in the war. But Col. Mar-

(188) COL. CHARLES ALEXANDER MARSHALL.

shall found that age and rheumatism unfitted him for service, and he resigned.

Col. Marshall's wife is my sister. Bright, merry and joyous in her youth, she is yet full of life, energy and enterprise. She rules her own department, which extends over house, yard and garden. No one has earlier vegetables, or more beautiful or rare flowers. Her hearty welcome and large and cordial hospitality, have made "Walnut Grove," with its antique and aristocratic surroundings, a favorite resort for a large circle of friends.

My sister, in early life, joined the Presbyterian Church, and, years afterward, her husband followed her to the house of God. He has long been an elder, and a zealous supporter of the church. A family alter is erected, and the voice of prayer is daily heard at the evening sacrifice. I will conclude this article with two poetic tributes I have paid to him and his family:

TO COL. CHAS. A. MARSHALL, OF MASON COUNTY, KENTUCKY.

When first ambition seized my soul,
  And hope its pæons chanted,
True excellence I made my goal,
  And for it toiled and panted;
But those I thought were good and pure
  Proved false in half their dealing,
And, in their schemes to rise and soar,
  Lost honor, truth and feeling.

I therefore sought some paregon —
  Some wise and genial Mentor,—
To point the way and urge me on,
  In virtue's paths to enter.
At length I found that guide in you —
  That friend and elder brother;
You bade me wisdom's ways pursue,
  And turn from every other.

I found in you a generous heart,—
  Benignant, meek and tender.
You always took the wronged one's part,
  And proved a true defender.
When innocence or virtue wept,
  You sighed in tender yearning;
For Mercy's lamp was always kept
  Within your bosom burning.

In times that made the strongest quail,
  You did not cringe nor waver;
You never learned to catch the gale
  Of shifting public favor.
No tyrant's threat — no maddened throng
  Could drive you from your duty;

(188) COL. CHARLES ALEXANDER MARSHALL.

No bribe could make you do a wrong,
  Nor could the smile of beauty.

In times of peace, the olive bough
  Thy worthy deeds attested;
In times of war, upon thy brow
  A laurel chaplet rested.
But nobler deeds of Christian love,
  Your useful life pervading,
Assures to you, in heaven above,
  A crown of life unfading.

Your firm decision, faith and zeal—
  Your truth and self-denial;
Your love of right and nerve of steel
  Have won in many a trial;
Your good example often nerved
  And cheered me in temptation:
And when from duty I have swerved,
  I met your condemnation.

You walk in academic groves—
  By bright poetic fountains;
Through Tempe's vale your fancy roves,
  Or climbs Parnassian mountains;
Political and civil lore
  Your daily thought engages,
And history holds for you in store
  The wisdom of the ages.

I looked into your inmost heart,
  And found no envy burning—
No jealousy, with poisoned dart,
  Nor scorn—the humble spurning;
But justice, with impartial scales,
  Gives equal rights to others,
And tender charity prevails,
  To make all men thy brothers.

That patient, genial heart of thine—
  So void of selfish feeling—
A wondrous power to work on mine,
  Was year by year revealing;
I tried to equal, not excel,
  Your justice, truth and meekness,
But far below my model fell,
  And proved my empty weakness.

Although to three score years and ten,
  Thy pilgrimage is lengthened,
Yet thou art still revered by men,
  And all thy powers are strengthened;
And we will hope, as years increase,
  Thy burden will be lighter,
And when earth's lights grow pale and cease,
  You'll find a world that's brighter.

(188) COL. CHARLES ALEXANDER MARSHALL.

GODLEN WEDDING—TO MY SISTER, MRS. P. A. MARSHALL, AND HER HUSBAND, COL. C. A. MARSHALL, OF MASON COUNTY, KENTUCKY, ON THE OCCASION OF THE FIFTIETH ANNIVERSARY OF THEIR MARRIAGE, SEPTEMBER 12, 1833—1883.

    Dear Sister, I see in the tints of your hair,
        And lines of your radiant face,
    That time is morose, and unwilling to spare
        The purest and best of the race.
    But pitiless age cannot take from your life
        The graces the Spirit bestows:—
    The faith of a mother, the love of a wife,
        And peace that the pardoned one knows.

    'Tis fifty long years, since, in maidenly glee,
        You made all around you rejoice:
    As waves you were wild, and as winds you were free,
        And sadness withdrew at your voice.
    Health glowed in your features, and flushed on your cheek,
        And happiness beamed from your eye;
    Your presence brought hope to the lowly and meek,
        And pleasure and mirth to the high.

    Though nature vouchsafed you a form that was fair,
        And virtues of mind and of heart,
    Yet training had added accomplishments, rare,
        In literature, science and art.
    And you were endowed with the graces, in youth,
        Expressed by the lily and rose,—
    With modesty, diffidence, coyness and truth,
        The timorous violet shows.

    The lover that gathered the beautiful flower,
        Still wears it, in love, on his breast:
    To him it's as fresh as when plucked from the bower,
        And first on his heart was caressed.
    Its incense assures him her prayers are sincere,
        And rise to the heavenly dome,—
    Its roseate leaves tell of sunshine and cheer,
        She brings to his heart and his home.

    'Tis said that good angels companions select
        For those whom they love upon earth;
    And surely their choice, in your case, was correct,
        And you were well mated from birth.
    Your marriage, like Eve's, was arranged in the skies,
        And angels stood sponsors below;
    And loving immortals, unseen by your eyes,
        Still guard you wherever you go.

    My Sister, the partner you chose for your life,
        Yet faithfully stands at your side;
    In fond admiration, he clings to his wife,
        As when you were first made his bride.
    His form is yet stately,—his arm is still strong,
        And wisdom increases with age;
    Around him his children and grandchildren throng,
        With reverence due to a sage.

(188) COL. CHARLES ALEXANDER MARSHALL.

In youth he could charm by his tongue or his pen,—
  Was generous, handsome and gay,—
Beloved by the women, and envied by men,
  And honored by all at that day.
His name on the halls of the State is engraved;
  His voice in the forum was heard;
The flag of his country in triumph he waved,
  Though dangers and toils were incurred.

But when the glad era of peace had returned,
  No more of earth's honors he'd seek:—
Content with the laurel and palm he had earned,
  He bowed with the lowly and meek.
And now that his heart has been mellowed by years.
  And cleansed by the gospel of peace,
The joy of his Lord more attractive appears,
  And sanctified pleasures increase.

'Tis fifty long years, since, arrayed as a bride,
  You pledged your devotion and truth,
To him, who as husband, has walked at your side,
  Fulfilling the vows of his youth.
And now in each other's full love you repose,
  With faith that is boundless and free;
For love, which, at first, as a rivulet flows,
  Becomes a broad, fathomless sea.

For one generation together you've trod
  The paths of the humble and just;
You've fully devoted your hearts unto God,
  And put in your Savior your trust;
And daily at God's holy altar you meet,
  For family service and praise;
And find in the Bible a lamp for your feet,
  Illuming your path by its rays.

Your sons and your daughters, though scattered afar,
  Are strangers wherever they roam;
For filial regard, like the mariner's star,
  Still points them to parents and home.
And now, in reunion, they've gathered to-day,
  Around the dear hearthstone of yore,
Their pure veneration and love to display,
  To parents they almost adore.

Here, Thomas, your first-born, who dwells in the west,—
  Has come over mountain and plain;
And William, my namesake, his love to attest,
  Now treads the old homestead again.
And Paxton and Benjamin, though they may seem
  To you, as but boys, are now grown,—
And bow to your call or command as supreme,
  And make all your pleasure their own.

Here's Fanny, the child whom I knew in her youth,
  And nursed in her infantile days;
She clings to you closely,—commending your truth,
  And mingling devotion with praise.

(190) THOMAS MARSHALL.

And Lizzie and Lucy now sit at your feet,
   And there would remain evermore;
While Sallie conceives that her home is so sweet,
   She'll never depart from its door.

But one is not here:—'tis Maria the blest—
   The daughter so noble and true!
She sits at the banquet above, as a guest,
   And waits a reunion with you.
Her heart was all kindness,—her spirit all love;
   Her soul was on usefulness bent;
As wholly unselfish as angels above,—
   Her life in God's service was spent.

This chair at the table is placed for her seat;
   For truly her spirit is here;
And three other chairs make the circle complete,
   Of children whose spirits are near.
And thus all the living and dead, of the name,
   Are here, and united in love,—
And soon they shall gather, as saints to proclaim.
   A diamond wedding above.

The fiftieth year of your marriage has past,
   And mercies untold have been yours;
For two generations your lots have been cast,
   Where plenty has emptied its stores;
Your sons have proved trustworthy, honest and true:
   Your daughters in marriage are blest;
And lovely grandchildren come fondly to you,
   And wait to be kissed and caressed.

Believe not your usefulness ended below,
   Nor think that your mission is done;
For just as your age and experience grow,
   So judgment and wisdom are won;
And like as the patriarch, prophet and sage,
   Imparted instruction of old,
So you shall distribute the precepts of age,
   And counsel more precious than gold.

And now, let the richest of blessings descend
   From Him whom you worship as Lord;
For neither your comforts nor duties shall end,
   Till called to your final reward.
And there in the presence of Him you adore,
   May pleasures unending abound,
And perfect enjoyment and life evermore,
   By all your descendants be found.

190 THOMAS MARSHALL, was born on a man-of-war, in the Thames, February 6, 1796, d. at Winchester, Va., in 1826, = 1822, CATHERINE, dr. of FRANK THORNTON, of Fredericksburg, Va., and a dr. of Judge Harry Innes, of Kentucky. She was born

(196) JOHN MARSHALL.

about 1800, and died in 1826. Mr. Marshall was educated for the law, and was practicing in Winchester, Va., when an epidemic broke out and carried off the whole family. The parents died in the same hour, and one of their children preceded them, and the other followed with the intermission of only twenty hours.

192 ROBERT MORRIS MARSHALL, b. on a U. S. vessel, on the coast of England, January 20, 1797, d. at Happy Creek, Warren Co., Va., February 10, 1870,= January 20, 1819, his cousin, LUCY MARSHALL (232), b. August 15, 1796, d. December 24, 1844, at Happy Creek. Mr. Marshall was educated at Yale College, and was a gentleman of superior literary attainments. After living several years at "Mt. Morris," Fauquier Co., Va., his father relinquished to him, as the oldest son, the Happy Creek estate, where he spent the life of a genial and hospitable Virginia gentleman. In politics he was a Whig, and in religion an Episcopalian. Too old to take up arms, he opposed secession; but when his State withdrew from the Union, his whole soul became enlisted in the cause. Four of his sons entered the Southern Army, and the only remaining one was in India. Mrs. Marshall was born and educated in Warrenton, Va. She was a lovely, pure and Christian woman.

194 JAMES MARSHALL, b. at Happy Creek, October 21, 1802, d. at Winchester, Va., February 11, 1880, and buried there. Mr. Marshall was an eminent lawyer. His patrimony was increased by the income of his profession. He was a member from Fauquier to the State convention in 1861, and opposed secession with all his powers. But when defeated, he gave his adhesion to the State. He died precisely ten years after his brother Robert. His liberality and generous endorsements for failing friends, swallowed up his estate and reduced him to a bare competency. He was amiable in disposition, and much beloved. He was highly esteemed as a statesman and as a lawyer. He never married.

196 JOHN MARSHALL [Navy John], b. at Happy Creek, Warren Co., Va., June 27, 1804, d. at Edgeworth, Fauquier Co., Va., September 18, 1855, = 1st, 1837, MARY PAYNE, nee SHACKEL-

(196) JOHN MARSHALL.

FORD, sister of the late Dr. John Shackelford of Maysville, Ky. She was born February 6, 1811, d. August 7, 1849, and buried at Leeds Church. Mr. Marshall = 2d, October 24, 1850, REBECCA BOYD SMITH, b. December 21, 1822, living.

(*b*) Lieut. Marshall visited Mason Co., Ky., before his first marriage, and I remember him as a noble, gallant and chivalrous young gentleman. He was much courted for his handsome person and agreeable manners. His naval voyages introduced him to the wide world, and his knowledge of foreign races and countries made him an interesting companion. After marriage, he resigned his position in the Navy, and settled at "Edgeworth," nine miles south of Markham, in Fauquier Co., Va. Here he erected a spacious and quaintly fashioned mansion, and expended much labor on the grounds. He lived the luxurious life of a learned, independent, genial and hospitable farmer, never aspiring to higher distinction than that of a generous friend, a charitable neighbor or patriotic citizen. The following letter to his sister Mary, dated Marseilles, France, September 2, 1832, will give a sunny view of his life on the seas:

(*c*) "MY DEAR SISTER:—Our ship has just anchored at Marseilles, having on board Com. Biddle, who intends to return by way of Havre, in such ill health as to make us fear he will not live to get home. He will be a greater loss to the service than any officer in it, not even excepting Com. Warrington. I know of no officer from whom I have received more gentlemanly attention than from Com. Biddle; and I believe there is a general feeling of extreme regret, at his being forced, by his ill health, to ask his relief;—I mean among those officers who know him well, for there are some who have unavoidably been employed in distant parts of the station, and who were dissatisfied at being ordered off, without being permitted to visit and idle away eight or ten months in Italy or France, and who disliked him because they had no opportunity to get acquainted with him.

I received your letter by the frigate "United States," and am surprised to hear of your having written before, as this is the first letter I have received from you since I left home. From Susan, I have received two, and I have written often. But as I generally had to send through Spain to Gibraltar, or through France to Havre,

(196) JOHN MARSHALL.

I calculated on one-half, at least, miscarrying. I did not write to William Leigh, as I was nearly one hundred and eighty miles from Syracuse when he sailed, being on a visit to Mt. Ætna and Palermo, and did not arrive until two days after the sailing of the Ontario.

(d) It is probable the Concord will return this fall to the United States, but I shall not return in her, as it is possible I may be made First Lieutenant of the John Adams, and that will be so advantageous to me, professionally, that I will be willing to stay a year or two longer to procure the place.

I received rather a melancholy letter from Henry Morris (200) inclosing yours, and am gratified to hear from him that he intended to come out in the Delaware. I hope it may be more pleasant to him than his last cruise, which was wretched enough, as you must have heard.

If Congress decides to give us the swords presented to the officers of this ship by the Pasha of Egypt, I wish father to get mine, and to have it put away until my return.

I do not give you an account of our cruise in the Archipelago, and our visit to Greece, Egypt and Asia Minor, as I wrote to Sue from Smyrna, in detail, I believe. I shall send this by my friend, Harry Ingersoll, of Philadelphia, aid-de-camp of Com. Biddle, who returns with him. God bless you. J. MARSHALL."

(e) Cousin Rececca, widow of First Lieutenant John Marshall, lives with her daughter, Hester, wife of Paxton Marshall, in Mason Co., Ky. She possesses the vigor and sprightliness of middle life, corresponds extensively among her kindred, and enjoys the service of the Episcopal Church, of which she is a devoted member. I have received from her many letters, sparkling with intelligence, piety and truth.

(f) EPITAPHS IN LEEDS CHURCH YARD.

JOHN MARSHALL, born June 27, 1804, died September 18, 1855. The gift of God is eternal life through Jesus Christ our Lord.

MARY JANE MARSHALL, born February 6, 1811, died August 7, 1849. There remaineth, therefore, a rest for the people of God.

THE SMITH FAMILY.

1. John Jacquelin, of England, = Elizabeth Craddock.
2. Edward Jacquelin, of the County of Kent, came to Warwick

(198) CHARLES LOUIS MARSHALL.

(g) Co., Va., in 1697, and married as his second wife, Martha, daughter of Wm. Cary.
3. Mary Jacquelin, b. March, 1714, d. 1764, = John Smith.
4. Gen. John Smith, of Frederick Co., Va.,= Anna Bull, of Pennsylvania.
5. Col. Augustin Charles Smith, of the war of 1812, = Elizabeth Dangerfield Magill, dr. of Col. Chas. Magill, and Mary, dr. of Col. Chas. Mynn Thruston, of Virginia and Louisiana. Issue:
    1. Rebecca Boyd Smith, = JOHN MARSHALL.
    2. Elizabeth Augusta Smith, = Cornelius Baldwin Hite, son of Isaac Hite, of Frederick County, and Ann T. Maury, cousin of Com. Maury. Issue:
        1. Cornelius B. Hite, = MARGARET L. MARSHALL, (1266).

198 CHARLES LOUIS MARSHALL, b. at Happy Creek, Warren, Co., Va., April 14, 1809; studied law and died at Fairfield, Fauquier Co., Va., in 1831, just as he was commencing to practice.

200 HENRY MORRIS MARSHALL, b. at Happy Creek, Warren Co., Va., June 13, 1811; = May 16, 1834, ELIZABETH BROOKE, b. October, 1813. They live at Rockland Mills, 9 miles southwest of Markham. Their postoffice is Linden, Va. Mr. Marshall was a graduate of the University of Virginia; has pursued the calling of a farmer; has declined office, and all public honors, preferring private life, and the quiet pursuits and pleasures of home; was too old to take part in the war, but his sons were active in support of the lost cause. I met him in 1884, and found him a pleasant and intelligent old gentleman, five feet ten inches in height and weighing 144 pounds. He is one of the eight surviving grand children of Col. Thomas Marshall. For Mrs. Marshall's lineage see the Lewis chart. No. 150 i.

202 SUSAN MARSHALL, b. at "Happy Creek," Warren Co., Va., October 11, 1812; = June 8, 1843, DR. RICHARD CARY AMBLER, b. November 8, 1810, d. July 16, 1877. Cousin

(210) LOUIS BROOKE.

Susan Ambler, with her unmarried children, lives at "The Dell," six miles southwest of Markham, Va. "The Dell" is an estate of 3,100 acres of timbered land and pasture. She has other landed estates, and enjoys a large income. I visited her in 1884, and found a hale, handsome and dignified matron; hospitable, generous, intelligent and reserved; altogether, she is a grand old lady. A friend writes me: "She is one of the most elegant women I ever knew. Her trials and sorrors have only served to enhance the beauties of her character."

After receiving a liberal education and studying medicine at Paris, Dr. Ambler settled in Richmond, Va., and practiced successfully for some years. After his marriage he returned to "The Dell," and while superintending his large estate, became an amatuer in history, science and philosophy. He read extensively and became a proficient in literature and art. He enjoyed the esteem of all who knew him, and was revered for his learning and medical skill. His monument is found in the Leeds church-yard. The inscription reads: "Richard Cary Ambler, third son of John Ambler and Katherine (*nee*) Bush, his wife, born November 8, 1810; died July 16, 1877." I am indebted to him chiefly for the Ambler Chart, found No. 50 *o*.

204   HUMPHREY BROOKE, d. single before his father, and was buried on "The Hill," Washington, Ky.

206   WHITING BROOKE is said to have been a rough customer. He went to the Florida war and died.

208   GEORGE BROOKE lived in Fauquier Co., Va.; was a hatter; = Rachel ——, raised a family; collected money; went off to purchase furs and never returned.

210   LOUIS BROOKE was a tailor; made garments for the families of his relatives, going from house to house; was very deaf; d. single.

(212) LUCY BROOKE—(*Davis*).

212 LUCY BROOKE = Pres. Davis; lived in Shelby Co., Ky. d. childless.

214 MARY BROOKE, b. about 1796; d. 1838; = 1812, William Nathaniel Burwell; b. 1793; d. August 12, 1822. After her first husband's death, Mary married William Newman, of Wheeling, a politician of distinction. He was several times in the Virginia legislature. There were children by the second marriage, but I have not found them. Mary was a lovely girl as were all the females of the Brooke family. Her descendants are excellent people.

216 FANNY BROOKE, b. in Kentucky, about 1804; d. about 1844; = 1st, WILLIAM IRVING, who d. a year after marriage, without issue; = 2d, GILBERT ADAMS, b. March 29, 1798; d. January 20, 1872. After the death of her parents, cousin Fanny was raised by her Uncle Humphrey Marshall. Under the tuition of her aunt, Mollie Marshall, she grew up into a charming womanhood. She married first, in Woodford. During her widowhood, I often saw her. She spent much of her time in Mason, and was admired for both beauty and accomplishments. Mr. Adams was a widower of Pittsburg, with several daughters, one of whom married Dr. Alex. K. Marshall (636). Mr. Adams' father left quite an estate to the children of his son Gilbert. The latter was at one time a merchant in Washington, Ky., and subsequently at Mt. Carmel. He died at the latter place and was buried on "The Hill," in Washington. A handsome monument marks his grave, with only his name and dates of birth and death.

218 ELIZA A. MARSHALL, b. in Richmond, Va., = at Happy Creek, William D. Taylor. The family bible was burned at Taylorsville, Va., and the family record lost. Mrs. Taylor was revered for her charities and her faithful work in the church. She was the second wife of her husband, and raised and cherished her step-children with all the love and tenderness of a mother. Her faithfulness and zeal for the church, and her labors in her narrow

THE MARSHALL FAMILY. 145

(228) ANNA MARIA MARSHALL — (*Jones*).

sphere for the poor, secured for her the complimentary title of "The Bishop." All her posterity yet attend the church in Taylorsville, where she worshipped.

220 WILLIAM MARSHALL, d. 1824. He was a handsome youth of agreeable manners and gay and festive habits. He studied law, but became dissipated, and died of consumption in early manhood, at the house of his brother-in-law, W. D. Taylor.

222 THOMAS G. MARSHALL, b. in Richmond, Va., April 26, 1800, d. in Fauquier County, July 8, 1880, = April 15, 1824, ANN E. HARRIS, dr. of George and Mary Harris, of Tonisa Co., Va., b. August 14, 1804, d. June 28, 1853. He was a farmer, and a man of intelligence and influence.

224 LUCY M. MARSHALL, b. at Richmond, Va., d. at "Belle Grove," Fleming Co., Ky., 1830,= January 7, 1824, EDWIN BURNLEY, b. February 23, 1796, d. in Copiah County, Miss., June 23, 1868.

228 ANNA MARIA MARSHALL, b. at Warrenton, Va., August 8, 1788, d. in Frederick Co., Va., November 25, 1823, = Jan'y 31, 1806, WILLIAM STROTHER JONES, b. in Frederick Co., Va., October 7, 1783, d. at "Vaucluse," near Winchester, in 1845. An Episcopalian, a Federalist and a Whig. He was educated at Chapel Hill, N. C. He was a gentleman of unbounded hospitality, strikingly handsome and a splendid horseman. After the death of his wife, Anna Maria, he married a Miss Randolph, who raised some of his younger children, and was much beloved by the family. Mr. Jones was a farmer, and spent his life at "Vaucluse." There he lies buried, with the dust of his ancestors. The name of his first wife, *Maria*, is much revered, and she is said to have been exceedingly lively in her manners, and brilliant in her conversation.

(*b*) THE JONES FAMILY.

1. Gabriel Jones, the "Valley Lawyer," was born six miles from Williamsburg, of English parents, May, 1724. On the death of his

(228) ANNA MARIA MARSHALL — (*Jones*).

father, his mother, with Gabriel returned to London, and he entered a solicitor's office. On attaining his majority, he returned to America. His patrimony was in Frederick Co., Va., and after a short stay, all his property, except " Vaucluse," in Frederick County, was sold, and he removed to Rockingham County. In 1750, he married as her second husband, Margaret Strother, the oldest of thirteen children of William Strother and Margaret Watts, in Stafford County. Bishop Meade, vol. 2, p. 325, and all her descendants, speak of her in reverential terms. Their only son was

(*c*) 2. Col. Strother Jones. He was educated at William and Mary College; was commissioned as a Captain in the Colonial army; resigned in 1774, to marry Mary Frances Thornton, of "Tall Hill," near Fredericksburg, daughter of Francis Thornton and Miss Iunis. Her pedigree is traced to the Duke of Ormond. He was commissioned as a Colonel of Militia. At the age of thirty-two he died at "Vaucluse." Issue:

3. William Strother Jones, = ANNA MARIA MARSHALL.

(*d*) THE STROTHER FAMILY.

A 1. WILLIAM STROTHER, of Stafford Co., Va., = Margaret Watts, and had thirteen daughters, of which the following are mentioned.

    1. Jane Strother, = Thomas Lewis.
    2. Margaret Strother, = 1st, Harvie (doubtful).
        1. John Harvie, of the Continental Congress, 1778–1779, and father of Gen. Jacq. B. Harvie, No. 154.
(*e*)   Margaret = 2d, Gabriel Jones, see No. 228.

B   3. *Agatha Strother*, = John Madison, cousin of President Madison. Issue:

C   1. Bishop James Madison, b. 1749, = Miss James.
        2. Richard Madison, = Preston.
        3. Thomas Madison, = Susanna Henry, sister of Patrick Henry.
        4. Gabriel Madison, d. 1804, = Meriam Lewis, b. 1759, d. 1845, in Jessamine Co., Ky.
        5. Roland Madison, = a daughter of Gen. Andrew Lewis.

(236) CHARLES COATSWORTH MARSHALL.

C
(f)

    6. George Madison, Governor of Kentucky,= Jane Smith. Their daughter Myra = an Alexander, and was mother of Appoline Alexander, who = Gen. F. P. Blair.
    7. Eliza Madison, = Lewis.
    8. Lucy Madison, = Lewis.
    9. Margaret Madison, 1765, = Gen. William McDowell, of Bowling Green. See No. 68 i.

B
    4. *Sarah Strother*, = Col. Richard Taylor, and was mother of President Zack. Taylor.
    5. *Anna G. Strother*, = John Hawkins.
    6. *A daughter*, = Capt. John Frog.

230   JANE L. MARSHAL. See No. 162.

232   LUCY MARSHALL. See No. 192.

234   MARTIN P. MARSHALL. See No, 182.

236   CHARLES COATSWORTH MARSHALL, b. in Warrenton, Va., August 10, 1799; d. April, 1849; = November 1, 1821, JUDITH STEPTOE BALL, b. in Lancaster Co., Va., March 21, 1805; d. in Mississippi, November 2, 1865. Mr. Marshall lived some years after his marriage in Lancaster Co., Va. About 1830, he removed to Kentucky, and spent a few years in Fleming County, near his brother Martin. He then went to "Woodburn," on the Ohio, in Lewis County, and farmed and kept a woodyard. About 1847, the family removed to Mississippi, near Charleston. In 1849, he paid a visit to Kentucky and Virginia, and, on his return, he was taken with cholera at Memphis, and there died. He was buried at Memphis, and a handsome stone attests his grave. I remember Cousin Charles as a tall and handsome gentleman. On one occasion I visited his family, when they resided in Fleming. Mrs. Marshall sur-

(238) ALEXANDER J. MARSHALL.

vived her husband, and died at Charleston. She was a daughter of the distinguished William L. Ball, of Lancaster Co., Va., who represented his district in Congress for four consecutive terms, and died in office, February 28, 1824. Her mother was Mary Pierce.

238 ALEXANDER J. MARSHALL, b. at Warrenton, Va., February 21, 1803; d. at Baltimore, February 21, 1882; buried in Warrenton; = 1st, December 6, 1827, MARIA R. TAYLOR, b. November 30, 1808; d. January 8, 1844; = 2d, ANN ROBB, who yet lives in Warrenton. Mr. Marshall was a lawyer of fine promise in early life, but ceased to practice on his election as Clerk of Fauquier. He filled this place for years. During the war he was in the Confederate State Senate. After the war he removed to Baltimore, where he died. The first Mrs. Marshall was a daughter of Robert Johnstone Taylor, an eminent lawyer of Alexandria, Va. The second wife was a daughter of Charles Gartz Robb and Sarah G. McGlenachan, of Warrenton. Mr. Marshall was a learned and polite gentleman,— an agreeable companion,— of fine conversational powers, and sober, yet festive in his habits. His great heart and open hand wasted his estate, and left him in humble circumstances. His wit and fund of anecdotes made him agreeable and popular.

240 SUSAN MARSHALL, b. October 18, 1805; d. April 23, 1828, = 1827, THOMAS SKENKER. She died childless a year after marriage. Her husband lives in St. Louis, and is highly respected.

242 MAJOR THOMAS MARSHALL AMBLER, b. in Jamestown, Va., May 1, 1791; d. at "Morven," Fauquier Co., Va., September 4, 1875, = April 15, 1819, LUCY JOHNSTON, b. October 31, 1800, (living). Mr. Ambler's mother died soon after his birth. He graduated at William and Mary College; studied law, but never practiced; married at Lynchburg, Va.; settled at "Morven," three miles south of Markham, in Fauquier County, and spent his life in agriculture. He served a short time in the war of 1812; united with the Episcopal Church at Warrenton, under the preaching of Rev. Geo. Lemon, and continued a zealous disciple of the Lord to

(244) MARIA MARSHALL—(*Paxton*).

his death. He was buried at Leed's Church, where a stone records his name, birth and death. He was a man of remarkable faith and piety, and was venerated for his virtues. Three of his sons became Episcopal preachers. Cousin Lucy Ambler lives at "Church Hill," Markham. Her health is good, and her memory remarkable. I am indebted to her for much genealogical lore. I visited her in 1884, and had long conferences about early times. She was a daughter of Charles Johnson and Lettie Pickett. The latter was a daughter of Martin Pickett, and sister of Lucy Pickett. See Pickett chart, No. 64 c.

244 (a) MARIA MARSHALL, b. at "Walnut Grove," Mason Co., Ky., July 20, 1795; d. in Columbus, O., February 6, 1824; = May 2, 1811, JAMES A. PAXTON, b. in Rockbridge Co., Va., September 13, 1788; d. in Washington, Ky., October 23, 1825. My mother died when I was but four years old; yet I remember ome of the circumstances, and can recall the sad pageant of her burial. She was buried in the Franklinton Cemetery, but, a few years ago, we had her dust removed to the Columbus Cemetery, and laid beside her sister, Mrs. Sullivant. We erected a neat monument, to preserve her memory. I have often heard my mother praised for her lovely yet fragile form, and for her amiable disposition. Her house was the home of her relatives. She inherited from the McDowell's sweetness, modesty and purity, and from the Marshalls intelligence, vivacity and spirit.

(b) My grandfather, James Paxton, was killed in Rockbridge Co., Va., shortly after his marriage, by an accidental shot from the gun of a companion, with whom he was hunting. My father was the only child of the marriage; but his mother married a Mr. Moore, removed to southwestern Kentucky, and raised a large family, none of whom I remember ever meeting. (See No. 180 e.) When a youth, my father followed his uncle, William McClung, to Kentucky, and lived for a few years near Bardstown. About 1803, the uncle and nephew came to Mason Co., Ky. Under the instructions of Judge McClung (72), my father pursued a long course of reading and studied law. His learning, as well as his handsome person and brilliant oratory, introduced him into a wide practice. Raised in the Federal school of politics, he became a zealous Whig,

(244) MARIA MARSHALL—(*Paxton*).

and a sincere Emancipationist. In 1822, he determined to sacrifice his well established practice and rear his children upon free soil. He accordingly removed to Columbus, then a small but rising city, and was received by the McDowells, and other friends, that had preceded him with open arms. There he started on a professional and political career that would have brought distinction. But my mother died, and his heart and children were in Kentucky. His second wife was a cousin of my mother. (See No. 180.) He lived but a few months after his second marriage. He died while on a visit to Washington, Ky. He was thrown from his buggy at the Blue-Licks, his head struck a log, and he died from some affection of the brain.

(c) I was six years old when my father died. He was portly, six feet high, and weighed 175 pounds. As a lawyer and orator he had few superiors. An intelligent, genial and urbane gentleman, he was beloved by a large circle of intimate friends, and was very popular with all classes. His commanding military person, as well as his coolness and courage, called him forth in the Indian Wars; and, as aide to Generals Shelby and Harrison, he filled his proper place. He was an enthusiastic Mason, and was buried with all the "pomp and circumstance" of the Mystic Order. He lies in the cemetery on the "Hill," in Washington, and his broad slab bears the following legend, written by Dr. Edgar:

(d) "REARED to the memory of James A. Paxton, the son of James Paxton and Phœbe McClung, b. September 13, 1788, in Rockbridge Co., Va., d. October 23, 1825, aged 37 years. No one has fallen a victim to death of more incorruptable integrity. To pre-eminent talents and attainments, he united the social and domestic virtues in a degree seldom if ever, surpassed by a friend or husband, a father or brother. Though learned and eloquent as a jurist, yet his main attractions were found in his sympathetic heart, his disinterested benevolence, and his moral delicacy of sentiment and action."

"His home was the retreat of peace and plenty, where, supporting and supported, polished friends and dear relatives met and mingled into bliss."

(e) My father's will was made September 11, 1825. It gives his lands to his executors, with power of sale, in trust for his widow and children. The widow was to have received a child's part, but this she would not take from the children, having enough property in her own right. The will appoints his widow and my uncle, James K. Marshall, his executors. It is witnessed by Marshall Key, Susan McClung, Frances Marshall and John A. McClung.

THE MARSHALL FAMILY. 151

(244) MARIA MARSHALL—(*Paxton*).

The descent of my father from the Alexanders and McClungs will be found No. 72.

The following poem, I addressed some years ago to my sister: (860.)

(*f*)   TO MY SISTER, MRS. CHARLES A. MARSHALL.

Dear sister, three score years have passed
Since our good mother breathed her last.
I then in age was only four,
And you were scarcely two years more;
Our brother's age was only seven,
And sister Mary's not eleven.
  Our father took us to his heart,
And would not let the nestlings part.
By mutual love we cheered each other;
But what was home without a mother.
As youngest, I was father's pet;
For me his cheeks were often wet;
By day I followed as he led;
At night I slept upon his bed.
But two years more, when father died,
We lost our only friend and guide.
This caused our infant hearts to bleed;
For we were orphans, now, indeed.
Though friends were many and were kind,
A parents love we did not find.
No tender father's gentle hand
With pride led forth a merry band;
No mother quelled our rising fears,
Nor kissed away our welling tears;
And when some happy mother smiled,
And fondly pressed her darling child,
I've often thought a mother's kiss
Would fill my heart with perfect bliss.

  But while the outside world was cold,
Our uncle's house became our fold,
Where all our wants were well supplied,
And sympathy alone denied.
Since no one loved us as before,
We loved each other all the more.

  But bitter partings came at last,
And we were far asunder cast;
And since that day, so fraught with pain,
The four have never met again,—
Nor can we ever meet before
We join in heaven to part no more.
Yes, half our band have gone above,
And now enjoy eternal love.
But you and I must stay below,
Until the Master bids us go.

  Now let us speak of those above,
And burnish all our words with love.

(244) MARIA MARSHALL—(Paxton).

(g)　　　　　OUR MOTHER—MARIA PAXTON.

Our mother quit this earthly stage
When only thirty years of age.
I was her pet and darling child;
On me she always fondly smiled.
Her face, by memory's native art,
Is photographed upon my heart.
Her brow was as the lily, fair;
Her cheek would with the rose compare:
The music of her tender voice
Made all within its reach, rejoice.
'Tis said she had the Marshall mind,
With rich McDowell heart combind.
The wisdom of her father's race
Was linked to all her mothers grace,—
That mother whom her nephews named
Their "Angel Aunt," because they claimed
No earth-born being could compare
With one so pure, so chaste and fair.
As pure, as lovely, and as true,
Our mother was an angel too.
Her charity was broad and free;
So, too, her hospitality.
Around her hearth her kindred met,
Her board was with abundance set;
Her door forever, open stood,
To welcome there the poor and good;
Her home became the glad retreat
Where welcome friends would daily meet
To spend the dewy twilight hour
In festal ease in hall or bower.

At father's grave, through many years,
We've paid the tribute of our tears;
But mother's grave is far away,
And no one kneels by it to pray;
And though we've built a handsome tomb,
And roses on her bosom bloom,—
Yet, Sister, shall we never lave,
With tears the sod upon her grave?

(h)　　　　　OUR FATHER—JAMES A. PAXTON.

At thirty-seven, our father died;
He then was just in manhood's pride.
An orphan boy, without a home,
He left Virginia's vale to roam.
He crossed the mountains—wandered west,
And in Kentucky's wilds found rest.
The boy was handsome and refined,
Of cultivated heart and mind;—
His diligence prepared the way,
By which his genius gained the day;
His eloquence and words of fire,
To noble deeds all hearts inspire:
Success secured him wealth and fame,
With high position, friends and name;

(244) MARIA MARSHALL—(*Paxton*).

In person, portly, tall and straight—
Of stately mien and measured gait;
An eye that photographed the soul;
A voice adapted to control;
A mind with full, well-ordered store
Of legal and historic lore—
He wielded power in peace or war—
In tented field or courtly bar.

To every eager, worthy youth,
Possessed of energy and truth,
He ever proved a sterling friend,
To aid, encourage or defend.*
In manners social and polite,
A Mason and a generous Knight;
A soldier in his country's cause;
A Jurist, deeply versed in laws;
And last,—and this is praise sublime—
A gentleman of olden time.
Our father was not yet content;
On higher ends his soul was bent.
Alas, he did not fill his dreams,
For death disorganized his schemes.
The first act scarcely closed, before
The curtain fell to rise no more.

The leaves of ivy, fern and moss,
Our father's sacred tomb emboss,
And no one now can read the half
Of what was once his epitaph;—
So sister, we, as children true,
Must 'grave that epitaph anew.

(i)   OUR BROTHER—MARSHALL PAXTON.

My Sister, when our father died,
Four hapless orphans wept and sighed;
Now two the heavenly harvest reap,
While you and I are left to weep.
But, Sister, 'tis a cheering thought,
That all in Christian love were taught,
And all possessed that faith whose power
Consoled our mother's dying hour.

Our brother, Marshall, from a child
Was frank, affectionate and mild.

---

*I hope my filial pride will be pardoned for introducing the following passage from a letter to me, of the venerable Lewis Collins, author of the History of Kentucky, dated Maysville, Ky., February 21, 1860: "I suppose you were too young to have a very distinct recollection of your father. He was a man of very superior talents—remarkably bland and courteous in his manners, and possessed of remarkably strong sympathies for poor young men, who were moral in their habits, and of persevering and energetic characters; and those sympathies seemed to be still stronger when such young men had been left orphans in childhood. When I bought the *Eagle* establishment in 1820,—then a very poor, struggling boy, he encouraged me, not only with excellent counsel and kind and hearty shake of the hand, when I met him, but freely opened his purse to me. On one occasion when severely pressed, I asked him for the loan of $50 for a week. He instantly pulled out his pocket book, and said: 'Here are $50, and you shall have fifty more—or a hundred more, not for a week only, but for six weeks, or six months, if you need it.' Such kindness, my young friend, is rare. I shall never forget your father.

(244) MARIA MARSHALL—(*Paxton*).

By nature generous and true,—
His soul no selfish instinct knew.
No envy, jealousy, nor pride
Could in his humble heart abide;
But right and conscience governed there,
And made his dealings just and fair.
Designed by nature to succeed,
He chose a merchant's life to lead.
Success crowned every venture made,
And showed new avenues of trade.
His diligence secured him wealth,
But with it came the loss of health.
From active life he sought for rest,
And found it on his Savior's breast.
His sainted wife, heart-broken here,
Soon joined him in the upper sphere.
Their only daughter, young and fair,
Received no more a parent's care;
But good grand-parents kindly smiled,
And as their darling reared the child.

   Ah, gentle Lydia, sweet and fair, (2164)
Thou art the child of many a prayer!
Though thou art now in widow's weeds,
And thy dear heart in sorrow bleeds,
Yet cheering light ere long shall shine,
Upon those noble sons of thine,
Whose good and brilliant deeds shall claim
New lustre for the "Blackburn" name.

(*j*)   OUR SISTER—MARY HARBESON.

In memory's first and earliest place,
I see a form of sylph-like grace—
I hear a soft melodious voice,
That makes my raptured soul rejoice;
And even now that figure seems
The beau-ideal of my dreams.
'Tis thus, within my heart, I find
My sister Mary's form enshrined.
The angel mantle mother wore,
Her first-born daughter meekly bore;
Her comely form and shining face
Her gentle words and polished grace
Were sure her visitors to please,
And make the timid feel at ease.
Her meek-dark eye, with silent prayer,
Asked trust, affection, help and care.
A charmed enthusiast in flowers,
Her home was hid with fragrant bowers.
The choicest fruits, the season round,
Were in her teeming garden found;
And at her table, richly spread,
Her welcome friends and kindred fed.
She loved her home—she loved the noise
Of romping, laughing girls and boys;
But loved still more the house of prayer,

(244) MARIA MARSHALL—(*Paxton*).

And longed to meet her brethren there.
Her faith and zeal were uniform;
When others failed, her love grew warm;
When waves of unbelief increase,
Her anchored spirit rides in peace;
And when death's angry waters roll,
The oil of peace sustains her soul.

Our sister Mary's memory needs
No stone to tell her noble deeds,
For every heart that shared her alms,
Her name and memory embalms.
Her children rise, her name to bless,
And give her praise for their success.
And you and I, while life shall last,
On memory's shrine will incense cast;
And at her grave, and on her urn,
Love's vestal lamp shall always burn.

Now sister, wipe away that tear;
The glad reunion day is near.
For three-score years the cross we've borne;
But soon we'll cease to toil and mourn,
Our longing spirits soon shall rise
To join the loved ones in the skies.
And even now, my raptured eye
Beholds a scene performed on high:

Our father sits at Adam's feet,
And hears the patriarch repeat
The story of his early bliss,
When Eve first thrilled him with her kiss.
There, mother, near the Savior stands,
To claim a blessing from His hands.
He sweetly smiles and bids her bow,
And sets a crown upon her brow.
Contentment, hope and trust I trace
In Brother Marshall's beaming face,
As in the Book of Life he reads
The names of loved ones and their deeds.
And there I see, 'mid fragrant bowers,
Our Sister Mary crowned with flowers;—
Her duty is, with angel throngs,
To pass the days in sports and songs.

But lo! I hear a gladsome voice
That makes the listening saints rejoice;
The guardian angels who, on earth,
Have watched our pathway from our birth,
Their duties done, to heaven have sped,
Announcing you and I are dead,
And that our happy spirits wait
Our friends and kindred at the gate.

Our mother casts her crown away,
Our sister leaves her comrades gay,
Our father springs upon his feet,
Our brother leaves in haste his seat,

(244) MARIA MARSHALL—(*Paxton*)

   And all, in ecstacies of joy,
   Their never-tiring wings employ,
   To bear them to the pearly door,
   And glad reunion ever-more.

   If, Sister, half of this is true,
   And if, by death, we may renew
   The broken ties of earthly love,
   And all the dear ones find above;
   And there while endless ages roll,
   Unbounded love shall fill the soul,—
   Then Death, thou hast no sting for me,
   And grave, thou hast no victory.

(*k*)   THE PAXTON FAMILY.

About 1730 the Paxtons, with the Houstons and others settled in Pennsylvania. They were from the North of Ireland, and Presbyterians. When the "Borden Tract," in Augusta, now Rockbridge County, was opened for settlement about 1740, a widow with five children removed to Rockbridge. Two of her children died young, and her three sons 1, John; 2, William, and 3, Thomas Paxton survived. These are the progenitors of the Virginia Paxtons.

A 1. JOHN PAXTON, b. in Ireland or Pennsylvania, about 1721, came to Rockbridge Co., Va., about 1740, = about 1742, Martha Blair. Children:

B   1. *Captain John Paxton*, b. in Rockbridge Co., Va., about 1743, d. October 3, 1787, from the effects of a musket-ball received at the head of his company, at the battle of Guilford, March 15, 1782, = Phebe Alexander, of Rockbridge Co., dr. of Capt. John Alexander, uncle of Dr. Archibald Alexander, President of Princeton Seminary. Phebe Paxton d. February 13, 1821. Issue:

C   1. John Paxton, b. in Rockbridge Co., Va., emigrated to Lincoln Co., Ky., d. 1807, = 1791, Elizabeth Logan, d. 1840. Issue:

D   1. James A. Paxton, b. 1793, d. 1828, = Mary Hoff. Issue: 1, Elizabeth P.; 2, Martha,= Pearson; 3, John A.; 4, Luke H. Paxton,
(*l*)   = Mary·A. Prewett; 5, James R. Paxton.
    2. Joseph Paxton.
    3. William Paxton.
    4. Phebe, = Love.
     1. James Love, of Liberty, Mo. = ——.
    5. Margaret = Behond.

(244) MARIA MARSHALL—(*Paxton*).

C
    2. Archibald Paxton.
    3. William.
    4. Joseph.
    5. Polly Paxton, b. 1784, d. July 13, 1859, = Col. William Paxton.
    6. Alexander Paxton, d. s. May 15, 1847, aged 60.
    7. Isabella Paxton, d. October 13, 1835, aged 53, = Hugh Paxton, d. November 4, 1838, aged 60. Issue:

D
        1. John A. Paxton, now a wealthy banker of San Francisco.
        2. Aurelia, = 1st, Peter A. Salling, = 2d, Jacob Mohler.
        3. Mary Jane Paxton.
        4. Margaret Paxton, = Cornelius C. Baldwin, lawyer and editor, of Balcony Falls, Va.

E
            1. John; 2, Aurelia; 3, Dr. Joseph S. Baldwin.

D
        5. John A. Paxton.
        6. Elizabeth Ann Paxton.
(m)   7. Peggy, d. July 12, 1838, aged 66.

B
    2. *William Paxton*, = Elizabeth Stuart. Issue:

C
        1, William; 2, Bessie; 3, Isabella; 4, Jane; 5, James; 6, Joseph Paxton.

B
    3. *Joseph Paxton*, = —— Barclay. Issue:

C
        1, Hannah; 2, Mrs. Coalter; 3, Harriet, = Philpot.

B
    4. *James Paxton*, = March 23, 1786, in Rockbridge Co., Va., Phœbe McClung, dr. of John McClung and Elizabeth Alexander. He was accidentally killed by a companion while hunting, about 1788. Their only child was

C
        1. James Alexander Paxton, b. September 13, 1788, d. in Mason Co., Ky., October 23, 1825, = MARIA MARSHALL, No. 244.

(244) MARIA MARSHALL—(Paxton).

B
    5. *Isabella Paxton*, = Capt. Lyle. Three children.
    6. *Betsy Paxton*, = Maj. Samuel Houston. Issue:

C
        1, Paxton Houston; 2, Robert; 3, James; 4, John;
(*n*)   5, Gen. Samuel Houston, President of Texas; 6, William; 7, Isabella; 8, Mary; 9, Elizabeth.

B
    7. *Hannah Paxton*, = Maj. James Caruthers. Issue:
        1, John P. Caruthers; 2, William H.; 3, Frank; 4, Polly; 5, Margaret; 6, Betsy Caruthers.
    8. *Mary Paxton*, = Cowan.

A   2. **WILLIAM PAXTON**, b. in Ireland or Pennsylvania, in 1732, = Ellen Hay.

B   1. *Joseph Paxton*, = Esther Lyle.

C
       1. Lyle Paxton, = Cummings.
       2. Mary Paxton, = Robert Campbell.
          1, Alexander Campbell; 2, Esther; 3, Eliza J.;
(*o*)   4, Prof. John Campbell, of W. and L. University, = Harriet Baily; 5, Rev. William Campbell; 6, Rev. Samuel Campbell.
       3. Sallie, = Samuel Cummings.

B   2. *John Paxton*, died single.
    3. *William Paxton*, = his cousin, Mary Paxton.

C
       1. Archibald H. Paxton (lawyer)
       2. Mary E. Paxton, = Col. Alex. T. Barclay.

D
          1, Agnes M. Barclay. = Judge James Paxton, seven children; 2, Sallie, = M. Woods; 3, Hannah, = William P. Houston, a lawyer, of Lexington, Va.; 4, Alex. T.,= Virginia Moore; 5, Elihu, = Margaret Roane; 6, Dr. James P., = Emma Moore.

C   3. Col. James H. Paxton, = Kate Glasgow. Six children.
(*p*)   4. Phœbe A. Paxton, = Dr. James McClung, n. i.
       5. Margaret Park Paxton, = Rev. Samuel R. Houston, D. D. Issue: 1, Wm. P. Houston, = 1st, Edith McClung, two children; = 2d, Hannah M.

(244) MARIA MARSHALL — (*Paxton*).

C
    Barclay; 2, Samuel Adger Houston; 3, A. Corey Houston; 4, Mary Margaret Houston; 5, Ellen A.; 6, Bessie; 7, Janet, a missionary to Mexico; 8, J. Barnard Houston, and 9, Hubert T. Houston.
    6. Dr. William B. Paxton, removed to Kentucky,= Fanny Offutt.

B   4. *Maj. James Paxton,* = Catherine Jordan.

C
    1. Jordan Paxton, = Eliza Lane. Issue: 1, Douglas; 2, Kate; 3, Cora; 4, Clifton; 5, Laura Lee Paxton.
    2. William Paxton, = Lou Eagan; two children.
    3. Catherine, = Jos. Gilmore.
    4. Bettie, = Wm. Burks.
    5. Estaline, = S. Robinson.
(*q*)   6. Maria, = John Roland.
    7. Melancthon.
    8. Isabella, = Allen Stalnaker.

B   5. *Elisha Paxton,* = Margaret McNutt.
    1, William Paxton, = Barnard, six children; 2, Alexander, = Eller, seven children; 3, Jackson, = Beesly, six children; 4, Gardner, = Anna White, four children; 5, Rachael, = William Buckner, four children; 6, E. Frank Paxton, Brigadier-General, C. S. A., fell at Chancellorsville, May 2, 1863, = Lizzie White, three children; 7, Gallatin Paxton, lawyer.
    6. *Sally Paxton,* = Prior, one child.
    7. *Mary Paxton,* = Samuel Greenlee, no issue.
    8. *Susan,* = Jos. Gilmore.
(*r*)   1, Madison Gilmore, = Jenett Houston; 2, Paxton Gilmore, = Sallie Irvine, four children; 3, James Gilmore.
    9. *Betsy,* = Sawyer, one child.
    10. *Isabella Paxton,* = Andrew Alexander. Issue: 1, Sallie Alexander, = Jas. McClung; 2, Archibald; 3, Isabella, = Andrew Cummings; 4, Phœbe, = Samuel Cummings; 5, Amanda Alexander.

THE MARSHALL FAMILY.

(244) MARIA MARSHALL—(*Paxton*).

A   3. THOMAS PAXTON, b. in Ireland, about 1720, d. 1788, = in Rockbridge Co., Va., Betsy McClung.

B   1. *John Paxton,* = Sarah Walker.

C   1. Joseph Paxton, = Sally Edmondson; seven children.

           2. Dr. James Paxton, = Bessie S. Houston.

              1. Dr. John Paxton, = Campbell.

              3. Rev. John D. Paxton, D. D.,= 1st, Carr; = 2d, Dodge.

              4. Nancy Paxton, = John Donald; two children.

(*s*)   5. Sally, = Cowan.

B   2. *Samuel Paxton,* = Coalter.

      3. *William Paxton,* = Jane Grigsby.

C   1. Joseph Grigsby; 2, Elizabeth Grigsby; 3, Mary Grigsby, = James Greenlee. Issue:

D   1, Hannah M. Greenlee,= James D. Davidson, eight children; 2, Mary J.,= J. T. Finley, five children; 3, Martha, = Eb. Davis; 4, J. Franklin Greenlee; 5, Sallie A. E., = James L. Watson; 6, Fannie, = P. T. Link;

(*t*)   7, William P., = Lizzie Foster; 8, Martha.

C   4, Martha Greenlee, = Joseph Steele, seven children; 5, Sarah, = Templeton; 6, Rachael; 7, Thomas Greenlee,= Anderson; 8, John; 9, Samuel; 10, Benjamin P.; 11, William Greenlee, = Sarah P. Burks; 12, Frances J.; 13, Agnes A. C. Greenlee,= Alf. Douglas, one child; 14, Hannah, = Wm. Crawford; 15, Verlinda.

B   4. *James Paxton.*

      5. *Thomas Paxton,* = Hogshead.

      6. *Sally Paxton,* = Edmondson; nine children.

      7. *Mary Paxton,* = Teaford.

      8. *Jane Paxton,* = Cummings.

A   3. THOMAS PAXTON, = 2d, Polly Barclay.

      1. Joseph.

      2. Hugh (see above), = Isabella Paxton.

THE MARSHALL FAMILY.

(248) CHARLES THOMAS MARSHALL.

A
   3. Hannah Paxton, = Cor. Goodwin.
   4. David.
   5. Isaac.
   6. Bessie Paxton, = Joseph Cousins, of Kentucky.
   7. Rachael Paxton, = Col. Jos. Blair; five children.

INSCRIPTION ON TOMBSTONE AT BUFFALO FORGE, ROCKBRIDGE CO., VIRGINIA.

(*u*) Here lies the body of Thomas Paxton, who departed this life September 27, 1788 (?), aged 69 (?) years. [Dates almost illegible.]

INSCRIPTIONS AT FALLING SPRING CEMETERY.

In memory of William Paxton, sr., who was born April 7, 1757, and died December 27, 1838.

SACRED to the memory of Jane [Grigsby] Paxton, wife of William Paxton, was born October 19, 1769, and died November 15, 1832.

(*v*) SACRED to the memory of John Grigsby, who was born ——, 1720, and departed this life April 7, 1794.

    Pause, reader, here, and look with solemn dread
    Upon the last lone dwelling of the dead.
    Though numerous graves appear on every hand,
    This was the first of all the silent band.

SACRED to the memory of Elizabeth Grigsby, who was born February 22, 1734, and departed this life October 7, 1807.

246 LUCY MARSHALL. See No. 178.

248 CHARLES THOMAS MARSHALL, (known as Black Dan), b. at "Walnut Grove," Mason Co., Ky., July 14, 1800; d. at his home, near Lewisburg, Ky., March 5, 1846, = 1827, JANE LOVE LUKE, b. April 16, 1808; d. July 5, 1876. Uncle Charles was a sensible and agreeable gentleman, and a skillful and successful farmer. He was domestic in his habits and his delight was in the privacy of his happy home and the society of his family. He

(248) CHARLES THOMAS MARSHALL.

cultivated a large farm, and transmitted a fine estate to his children. He did not trouble himself about politics, and had no ambition for office. Aunt Jane was his step-sister, daughter of his father's second wife. Aunt Jane was an intelligent and accomplished lady, and like Solomon's "virtuous woman" devoted her attention to her prosperous household. I do not now remember having ever met her away from her home. Uncle Charles was my guardian, and I could not have had a better one. He charged no commission for his services. His will grants all his property to his widow, and, at her death, to be divided among his children.

THE ANDREW LEWIS AND THE LUKE FAMILIES.

(b) John Lewis, "pioneer," son of Andrew Lewis and Mary Calhoun, born in Ireland, and died in Hanover Co., Va.; settled near Staunton, Va.; = Margaret Lynn, descendant of the Laird of Loch Lynn. Issue:

A
1. THOMAS LEWIS, Surveyor of Augusta Co., Va., = Jane Strother.

2. SAMUEL LEWIS.

3. WILLIAM LEWIS, = Ann Montgomery.

4. GEN. ANDREW LEWIS, of Botatout Co., Va., the hero of Point Pleasant, = Elizabeth Givens, of Augusta Co., Va., in 1749. Their son

B
    1. *John Lewis*, = Patty Love of Alexandria, Va. Their fourth child was,

C
    (c) 1. Eliza Lewis, who = 1st, a Mr. Luke, of Alex'a; = 2d, a Mr. Ball, of Kentucky, and = 3d, ALEX. K. MARSHALL, of Kentucky, being his second wife. See No. 68. Her daughter, Jane Luke, = CHAS. T. MARSHALL, and another daughter, Ann Luke, was the mother of G. W. ANDERSON, Nos. 248 and 870.

A
5. COL. CHARLES LEWIS, of Augusta Co., Va., fell at battle of Point Pleasant, = Sarah Murray.

6. JOHN LEWIS.

(252) SAMUEL M. MARSHALL.

250 JAMES KEITH MARSHALL, b. at "Walnut Grove," Mason Co., Ky., March 2, 1802; d. July 4, 1866; = 1827 CATHERINE CALLOWAY HICKMAN, b. Jan. 12, 1812; yet living in Louisville, Ky. Uncle James was six feet three inches tall, and was called "Long James," to distinguish him from a cousin of the same name. When I saw him last, about 1864, he weighed about 225 pounds, and was as handsome an old gentleman as I ever met. His urbane manners and interesting conversation greatly attracted me. He studied law in Columbus, with my father, but never practiced. His father granted his two sons, James and Samuel, their shares of his property undivided, and by deed provided that the survivor should take the whole. Upon the death of Samuel, Uncle James, therefore, took a double portion. After marriage, he spent a short time in Paris, and then removed to his fine estate on Mill Creek, in Mason County. Here he built a fine house, and lived until about 1836, when he returned to Paris, and engaged in milling and other pursuits. But his large estate melted away through improvidence and the gaming table. In 1852 he found himself impoverished, and removed with his family, to Milwaukee. But finding himself rather a burden than a support to his family, he left them, returned to Kentucky and taught school for a support on the property he once owned. Honest and generous to a fault, he wronged no one but himself and family. His children are intelligent and capable, and will rise from their embarrassments. Aunt Catherine was regarded as one of the most beautiful women of Kentucky, and her children are remarkable for the same quality. She is now old and embecile. Her daughter, Kate, takes care of her. I visited her in 1884, and found her body and mind were a wreck, and her voice was scarcely audible. She is the daughter of John L. Hickman and Mary Calloway, of Bourbon Co., Ky. It is fortunate that she has in her old age, children whose care and affection can sustain her. May God bless them.

252 SAMUEL M. MARSHALL, b. at "Walnut Grove," Mason Co., Ky., July 19, 1804; d. at sea, 1824. He was educated for the navy, and died of yellow fever while on a cruise. His patrimony being in joint tenancy with his brother James, the latter inherited a double portion of his father's estate.

THE MARSHALL FAMILY.

(254) JANE MARSHALL — (*Sullivant*).

254 (*a*) JANE MARSHALL, b. at "Walnut Grove," Mason Co., Ky., January 7, 1808; d. in Franklinton, Ohio, January 7, 1825, = in Columbus, Ohio, April 7, 1824, WILLIAM STARLING SULLIVANT, b. January 15, 1803; d. in Columbus, April 30, 1873. Aunt Jane was a delicate, pure, fair and lovely girl. She went with my mother to Columbus, was married and lived in Franklinton. Seventeen days after the birth of her first and only child, the fragile flower was crushed; but the fragrance of her memory still cheers many hearts. The child — as sweet and seraphic as her mother — yet lives to honor and adorn the name that both bore.

William S. Sullivant was educated at Ohio University, and finished his literary course at Yale College. As a classical and scientific scholar, he had few superiors. The degree of L. L. D. was conferred on him by Kenyon College. In the department of Botany, he was a proficient. The study of this science was his life-work, and the numerous dissertations published by him testify to his diligence and ability. He was handsome, dignified and courteous; took an active part in the educational enterprises of his times, and by his public spirit and munificence, did much to advance the material interests of Columbus. As the husband of my aunt, I often visited his house in my boyhood, and venerated him as a scholar, financier, scientist and gentleman.

Mr. Sullivant was three times married, and his brother Joseph, now dead, in 1874, published a "Family Memorial," which is a treasure-house of heraldic lore, and an imperishable monument to many distinguished families. On its classic pages and ancient records I have often drawn.

THE SULLIVANT FAMILY.

(*b*) Michael Sullivant, of Mecklinburg Co., Va., is the first of the name that distinctly appears. He married Hannah Lucas, and left three children: 1, Lucas; 2, Michael, and 3, Anne. The latter married a Lucas; Michael was drowned, unmarried, and Lucas was left to transmit the name. He was born in Mecklenburg Co., Va., September, 1765; removed, when a youth, to Kentucky; engaged in surveying; became an enterprising backwoodsman; removed to Ohio in 1797, and settled on the Sciota; laid off Franklinton; engaged in many enterprises for the public good; laid the foundation for the future wealth of his family, and died August 8, 1823. H*

THE MARSHALL FAMILY. 165

(254) JANE MARSHALL — (*Sullivant*).

married Sarah Starling, b. July 17, 1781, in Virginia, died in Franklinton, April, 1814. They had three sons: 1, William; 2, Michael, and 3, Joseph.

(c) 1. WILLIAM S. SULLIVANT, b. in Franklinton, Ohio, January 15, 1803; d. in Columbus, April 30, 1873, = April 7, 1824, JANE MARSHALL. He married his second wife, Eliza G. Wheeler, November 29, 1834, and his third wife, Caroline E. Sutton, September 1, 1851.

(d) 2. MICHAEL LUCAS SULLIVANT, b. August 6, 1807; d. about 1875, = 1st, June 27, 1827, Sarah L. McDowell, dr. of Col. Joe McDowell, of Danville, Ky. His second wife was Fanny Willes, b. June 22, 1832, = October 10, 1854. Michael L. Sullivant was the great agriculturist, and the possessor of the two experimental farms in Illinois, "Broadlands," and "Bur-Oaks," the latter containing 40,000 acres of land. His experiments were failures, and he died in reduced circumstances.

(e) 3. JOSEPH SULLIVANT, b. in Franklinton, Ohio, December 3, 1809; d. 1884, = 1st, Margaret I. McDowell, 1810–1831; = 2d, Mary Eliza Brashear, 1814–1850; = 3d, December 8, 1852, Elizabeth Underhill, b. 1831.

(f) STARLING LINEAGE.

1. Sir William Starling, knighted 1661; Lord Mayor of London, 1670.
2. William Starling.
3. Roderic Starling, = Miss Hubbard.
4. William Starling, = Jane Gordon. Issue:
    1. William Starling, b. September 4, 1756; d. December 25, 1826; = 1774, Susanna Lyne, b. 1757; d. September 7, 1802.
    2. Sally Starling, b. 1758; d. 1797, = Abram Archer.
    3. Roderic Starling, b. 1760; d. February 15, 1828, = Miss Hill.

(g) CHILDREN OF WILLIAM AND SUSANNA STARLING.

1. Thomas Starling, b. December 5, 1775; d. 1798.
2. Anne Starling, b. September 21, 1777; d. August 2, 1840.
3. Thomas Starling, b. September 3, 1779; d. October, 1852.

(256) THOMAS FRANCIS MARSHALL.

4. Sarah, b. July 17, 1781; d. April, 1814, = Lucas Sullivant. See Sullivant family above.
5. William Starling, b. January 25, 1783; d. November, 1840.
6. Lyne Starling, b. December 27, 1784; d. November 21, 1848.
7. Susanna C. Starling, b. November 8, 1786; d. August 16, 1801.
8. Jane Starling, b. June 23, 1788; d. May 28, 1863.
9. Lucy Starling, b. October 11, 1790; d. September 28, 1870.
10. John H. Starling, b. October 8, 1792; d. 1795.
11. Edward L. Starling, b. May 9, 1795; d. August 30, 1869.

256 THOMAS FRANCIS MARSHALL, b. in Frankfort, Ky., June 7, 1801, d. near Versailes, Ky., September 22, 1864, = BETTIE YOST. Mr. Marshall's career is a part of the history of Kentucky, and I shall notice only the leading events of his life. He was educated at home, by his learned father; went in 1821, to Virginia, to pursue the studies of law and philosophy, but failing health caused him to return. In 1826, he resumed the study of law, under Gov. John J. Crittenden, and in 1828 was admitted to the bar; settled at Versailes; in 1829, went to Richmond, Va., to attend the debates of the celebrated Constitutional Convention, over which his uncle, John Marshall, presided; in 1830, went to Washington to witness the proceedings of Congress; represented Woodford County in the State Legislature, 1832, 1838, 1839 and 1851–53; represented the City of Louisville, 1835 and 1836. In 1833, he removed to Louisville, but in 1837 was beaten for Congress by Graves, and, in disgust, returned to Woodford. In the Legislature he distinguished himself as an orator, and did himself honor by his energetic opposition to the Cincinnati and Lexington R. R. bill, contending for Louisville as the proper terminus. In 1841, he was elected to Congress from the Ashland District. Here he distinguished himself by his erratic course, as much as by his wonderful oratorical powers. In 1844, he deserted Mr. Clay, and voted for Polk; in 1849, he was beaten for Congress by Garret Davis. In 1846, he raised a volunteer company and went to the Mexican war. In 1856, he removed to Chicago, but soon returned. The remainder of his life was devoted to the practice of law, and to the delivery of public lectures

THE MARSHALL FAMILY.

(260) DR. ALEXANDER KEITH MARSHALL.

on various topics. His great vice was intemperance; yet at times he abstained from spirits, and some of his noblest efforts were in the cause of sobriety. As an orator, he was unrivalled. As a statesman, he had few equals. His brilliant literary discourses, replete with classic and historic lore, filled his hearers with admiration. His eloquence consisted not only of flowers of rhetoric, but of the fruit of untiring thought and logical analysis. His choicest passages were bolts forged in seclusion, and thoroughly burnished for the occasion. Though his wit, humor and pathos seemed only on the surface, yet in truth they were drawn patiently from the deepest mines, and refined in the crucible of profoundest thought. Mr. Marshall was six feet two inches tall, erect, and well proportioned. His speeches and writings were gathered by W. L. Barre, and published before his death. He was buried on the "Buckpond" estate, under a tree that he had pointed out.

Mr. Marshall married late in life, and his widow is, perhaps, yet alive; but I have inquired in vain for her home.

258 WILLIAM LOUIS MARSHALL, b. at Buckpond, Woodford Co., Ky., September 26, 1803; d. in California, October 5, 1869; = 1825, ANN K. LEE, b. in Va., about 1806, d. in Baltimore, February 20, 1864. After receiving instruction at his father's private school, Mr. Marshall spent several years with his Aunt Trigg, near Frankfort, Ky. Visiting Virginia, he married Ann, daughter of Gen. Henry Lee, (Lighthorse Harry) and settled in Baltimore, first as a preacher, and then as a lawyer; was Chancellor of the city; United States District Attorney; was regarded as one of the most able jurists of the day; was a Republican in politics. After his wife's death in 1864, he removed to Missouri, and purchased a farm near Wakesha; after a few years, removed to California, and purchased a ranche, where he died. Mrs. Bullitt, (900) his niece spent several years with him in Baltimore, and pronounces him the most intellectual, as well as the most moral and unimpeachable member of the family.

260 DR. ALEXANDER KEITH MARSHALL, b. February 11, 1808; d. in Fayette Co., Ky., April 28, 1884; = February 5, 1832, LUCY McDOWELL, she is still living with her only child at East

(262) JOHN CAMPBELL MARSHALL.

Hickman, Fayette Co., Ky. He married in early life Miss ELIZA GILLESPIE, (see No. 68 ƒ) who died childless, one year after marriage. Dr. Marshall was a handsome gentleman, and a chaste and forcible speaker. Under his father's tuition he became a classical scholar. His scientific and medical course commenced under the celebrated Surgeon, Dr. Ephraim McDowell, and was finished at Transylvania University. In the medical department of Transylvania, he, at one time, filled a chair. He settled in Nicholasville, and for many years, was a leading physician and politician. He was a member of the State Constitutional Convention of 1849; held the office of Grand Master of the I. O. O. F.; was elected to Congress 1855. In 1848 he left Nicholasville, and lived for a time, on a farm on the road to Lexington, Jessamine County; removed to the vicinity of St. Louis; here his son John was killed by a horse; removed to the vicinity of Independence, Mo.; when the war broke out he returned to Kentucky, and spent the remainder of his life with his son Louis, on a farm in Fayette County. He was buried at Lexington.

For the McDowells see No. 68 ƒ.

262 JOHN CAMPBELL MARSHALL, b. at "Buckpond," Woodford Co., Ky., about 1813; = REBECCA WOOD, of Ohio. Both yet live on a farm in the vicinity of Independence, Mo. Cousin John lived with his father until about 1857. I knew him well in his early manhood. Like his father he liked to visit around among his relatives. He was a plain, sensible and agreeable man, devoid of ambition; and was regarded as an old bachelor from his boyhood. But, that he might have a home, he actually got married. When I was at Danville in 1836–38, he paid us several visits. He had just enough of life in him to make us a pleasant companion at the fireside. I sometimes hear of the old gentleman at Independence, but he wont reply to my letters. He is one of the eight grandchildren of Col. Thomas Marshall, yet living.

I will here remark that between Dr. Alex and John, there was another son of Dr. Louis Marshall, named Charles, who attained his majority, studied law, and died before he entered on the practice. He was a brilliant youth.

(266) EDWARD COLSTON MARSHALL.

264 AGATHA MADISON MARSHALL, b. at "Buckpond," Woodford Co., Ky., July 1, 1818; d. there July 18, 1858, = there, October 24, 1843, CALEB W. LOGAN, b. July 15, 1819; d. August 1, 1864. I remember Cousin Agatha as a lovely young lady. She married a classmate of mine at Center College. After graduating at Danville in 1838, he attended the law department of Transylvania University; settled in Louisville, and practiced law; represented the city in the Legislature in 1850; was Judge of the City Chancery Court; held a professorship in the Louisville Law School. He was a member of the Chamberlain Literary Society at Danville, and took a zealous and active part in its exercises. He was regarded as a talented and promising young man, but he entered but little into society. He appeared too much absorbed in his own meditations to be an agreeable companion. With his wife, he was buried at Frankfort.

266 EDWARD (*Ned*) COLSTON MARSHALL, b. at "Buckpond," Woodford Co., Ky., about 1820, = about 1852, JOSEPHINE CHALFANT, of Ohio, sister of the wife of Senator Pugh. Both are living in San Francisco. Edward received a general, or perhaps universal education—if he was ever educated at all—at home, at Washington College, Virginia, at Center College, Kentucky, and at Transylvania, Lexington, Ky.; practiced at Nicholasville, Ky.; went to Cincinnati; was wounded in a duel with a Mr. Ward, of Missouri, January 19, 1847; appointed First Lieutenant 1st U. S. Infantry, April 9, 1847; went to the Mexican war; made Captain, May 6, 1848, dismissed May 22, 1848; went with the first flood of emigrants to California in 1849; in 1851 was elected to Congress; returned to Kentucky in 1856; purchased "Buckpond," of his father, and still owns it; October 6, 1870, commenced, with others, the Lexington Daily *Press*; ran as an independent candidate for Congress, and was defeated by Joe Blackburn; returned to California, and was Attorney General of the State.

In 1837, Ned was my room and bed-mate at Judge Green's mansion, near Danville, Ky. He was an "irregular" in College, as he has been everywhere; he attended to everything but his duties; seldom looked at his lessons, but always had a plausible excuse, until

(270) CHARLOTTE J. M'CLUNG—(*Woolfolk*).

President Young told him that one that was good at making excuses was good at nothing else; issued in manuscript, a weekly paper called the "College Review," which produced a wonderful sensation among the students; I was myself implicated as publisher. At length he was called before the faculty, and admonished that his " tenure " at college was very " precarious "; he used these terms, repeating them constantly for several days; their definitions were his first lessons in law. He was one of the brightest, readiest and wittiest youths I ever met; was perfectly independent of rules and laws; though indolent in his habits, he was active and energetic under excitement; was the sprightliest boy in college; studied nothing, but took in knowledge by intuition. In extemporary oratory, he was more brilliant than his brother, Thomas F. Marshall; the difference was, that the latter was a student, and the former not. I have written four times to him, but have no reply. Laziness accounts for the neglect.

270 CHARLOTTE J. MCCLUNG, b. near Washington, Ky., in 1803; d. in Woodford Co., Ky., in 1840, = 1828, THOS. H. WOOLFOLK, b. 1795; d. July 3, 1850. I do not remember ever seeing Cousin Charlotte, but have often heard her spoken of as a brilliant woman, but possessed of many idiosyncrasies. Her son Lucien thus writes of her: "I remember her well as surpassing all women I have ever known in mental grasp, eloquent expression, warm natural affection, and lofty aspiration. But above all, she was remarkable for the most delicate, quick and sensitive intuition, manifesting itself in prevision, bordering on prophesy. My father told me (and he was a good judge) that she was the most brilliant conversationalist he ever met. He regarded her as mentally superior to any woman he had ever known; and, as he said, superior to her brothers."

Another son, Alexander M. Woolfolk, thus writes of his father: " He (T. H. Woolfolk) was the youngest of a large family born in Woodford Co., Ky. He was a lawyer by profession, but I believe never practiced after his marriage. He is said to have been a very promising young lawyer—being a ready and eloquent speaker; but having come into the possession of a handsome fortune by inheritance and marriage, the promising lawyer degenerated into a very poor farmer. His literary tastes hindered, rather than helped him,

(272) REV. JOHN A. M'CLUNG, D. D.

in his new calling. The result was that he gradually ran through his patrimony. He died of cholera in 1850, at the age of 56 years, on his farm in Trimble Co., Ky. He was a fine conversationalist, with a remarkable power of social fascination, and of great personal influence. It was his misfortune to have possessed an ample estate."

272 REV. JOHN A. McCLUNG, D. D., b. near Washington, Ky., September 25, 1804; d. at Niagara Falls, August 6, 1859, = at Washington, Ky., November 25, 1825, ELIZA JOHNTSON, b. about 1806; d. at St. Paul, Minnesota, December 28, 1860. The life of Dr. McClung has been ably written by Hon. Henry Waller, of Maysville and Chicago. Mr. Waller practiced law at the Washington and Maysville bars, and sat under Mr. McClung's ministry, after he entered the pulpit, and his biography is a brilliant, as well as a pious, tribute to a truly great man. It will be found as an introduction to Collins' last edition of McClung's "Western Adventure." Dr. McClung was educated at "Buckpond," by his uncle Louis Marshall, and while there, united with the Presbyterian Church. In 1823, he went to Princeton Seminary; graduated, and was licensed in 1828. After preaching several years in Washington, Ky., he became unsettled in his religious views, and leaving the church, retired to his large farm in the Ohio bottom, below Maysville. Here he was engaged in literary pursuits until 1835. In 1830, he published a novel entitled "Camden, a tale of the South." This book brought him a world-wide reputation, but was severely criticised for the profanity of some of its characters. In 1832, he wrote the "Western Adventure," a book of thrilling interest, that has enjoyed, and still enjoys, extensive sale. I was living with him, as a pupil, when this volume was written, and remember his interviews with old settlers of Kentucky. He contributed largely to Collins' first edition of the History of Kentucky, and was esteemed as one of the most chaste and forcible writers of his day.

(b) In 1835, after studying law in private, Dr. McClung removed to Washington, and at once took a front place at the bar, then adorned by such names as Governor John Chambers, Francis T. Hord, Henry Waller, Thomas Payne, Henry Reeder, Harrison Taylor and John D. Taylor, with Judges Adam Beatty and Walker

Reid. In 1838 and 1839, Dr. McClung represented Mason County in the State Legislature, and was regarded as a leading orator and statesman. In 1838, I entered the office of McClung & Taylor as a student of law. I knew Dr. McClung best while under the cloud of infidelity. I do not remember ever hearing from him an infidel sentiment; not even in his discussions with his uncle, Lewis Marshall. Indeed, he regularly asked a blessing at his table, and no man was more exemplary in his words and conduct. His tender conscience and childlike simplicity, with his intelligence and scholarship, inspired his young friends with reverential awe. His health was bad, and required peculiar diet and regular exercise. He would walk for miles daily, always taking the middle of the turnpike, and with three foot strides he distanced all competitors. This was his favorite time for reflection and meditation, and the teams he met in the way had to take care of themselves. He often sat in meditative mood for hours, twirling with his right hand, the long lock of hair behind his ear, and clearing his throat at regular intervals. These hours of abstraction were the times at which he forged the bolts of eloquence and argument that afterward fell from his lips. I have heard him after an hour's meditation, recite a long poem to his wife, who was his only adviser; yet I do not know that he ever polished a line of poetry. When aroused, he was genial and polite, but he cared little for company, and had no intimate friend. Chess was his only pastime, and at this game he seldom found his match.

(c) When the county seat of Mason was removed to Maysville, Mr. McClung removed there. In 1849, Drs. Rice and Grundy held, in that city, a protracted meeting. No one knew of Mr. McClung's change of sentiment, and there was sincere joy among his old friends when, at the close of the exercises, a call was made for applicants for church membership, and Mr. McClung walked deliberately forward and extended his hand. A meeting of session was immediately called, and the religious views of McClung were found to fully conform to the tenets of the Presbyterian church. With the congratulations of thousands, and to the sore discomfiture of disbelievers, he was re-admitted to the church. It was a triumph of christianity when the most learned theologian, the most rigid logician, the most sincere searcher after truth, and the brightest intellect of the State, renounced infidelity, ceased his wanderings, and, as a long lost lamb, returned to the fold. There was rejoicing on earth and in

(272) REV. JOHN A. M'CLUNG, D. D.

heaven. In the far West I heard of it with tears of delight, and my faith was strengthened. He was ordained a second time, and preached for a few months to crowded houses in Louisville. He then accepted a call to the First Presbyterian Church at Indianapolis, and preached there for several years. South Hanover College conferred on him the degree of D. D. and offered him the presidency of the institution. He declined the place. But his old complaint, dyspepsia, the Nemesis of his life, demanded a change of climate, and he visited St. Paul. After preaching at St. Paul until 1857 he found his health improved, and accepted a call from his old church, at Maysville, Ky. But his former disease returned in a more terrible form. His jaundiced complexion and plaintful countenance betrayed his suffering. He again went north for relief, announcing his purpose of trying a water cure establishment. He was traced to a hotel some miles above Niagara falls, and his naked body was found below the cataract. His remains were brought home for interment. I visited his grave in Maysville cemetery in 1884, and copied the following inscription:

(d) "In memory of Rev. John A. McClung, D. D., late pastor of the Presbyterian Church, at Maysville, Ky.; born September 25, 1804, died August 6, 1859. How is the strong staff broken, and the beautiful rod. Jer. xlviii; 17, This monument is erected by members of the church, and by friends of his youth and mature years, to whom he was endeared by every quality that can sanctify friendship and dignify and adorn manly character."

Dr. McClung's will is characteristic, and I transcribe it in full:

As life is very uncertain, I do hereby declare my wife, Eliza McClung, sole devisee and legatee of all my property, real and personal, with all the authority of an executrix. My real estate is mortgaged for the payment of my debts, with a power of sale in the mortagees. Whatever may remain after payment of said debts I give to my wife as her own property. I recommend to her to sell instantly, all personality, including furniture, books, &c., upon a credit of six months, with bond and security; and with the proceeds pay my debts in Maysville; and with what may remain in money, to remove with Nanny to St. Paul. I think she had better live with her sister. May God bless the widow and orphans, for Christ's sake; Amen.

Dated March 7, 1859; probated September 12, 1859.

(272) REV. JOHN A. M'CLUNG, D. D.

(e) Cousin John McClung was the most conscientious man I ever knew. Judge John Green, of Danville, Ky., stands next to him in purity. Both of them liberated their slaves, and by their nobility of character incurred the odium of an unappreciative world. Mr. McClung was a friend and supporter of Henry Clay, and advocated his system of gradual emancipation. He was a proficient in the use of words, and expressed himself so concisely and pointedly, that his mere statement of a case carried conviction. He was a master in logic. He followed his convictions, and no danger would cause him to swerve from duty. As an orator he was more logical than eloquent. He did not work upon the affections, but appealed to the judgment. Truth was his aim, and conviction his purpose. In speaking, he rose above his natural timidity, and throwing himself back, with his thumbs in the arm holes of his vest, he poured out with earnestness a pure and powerful stream of argument. What others would expand into a volume, he would compress into a page. He never used a sophism — never violated truth, nor resorted to artifice to secure success. He therefore possessed the boundless confidence of the people. Though his patrimony was large and his practice extensive, yet he seldom charged for his service one half their value, and dispensed with a liberal hand; so that in age and affliction he found himself impoverished. I never heard him preach after his return to the church. Even yet, after his body has lain in the grave more than a quarter of a century, the fragrance of his memory cheers many hearts. When I visited his grave in 1884, a stranger overheard me ask the sexton to point out to me Dr. McClung's monument. As I was transcribing the epitaph, that stranger saluted me, and inquired who it was that visited the grave of his beloved pastor. He detained me a half hour to pour forth in tears the praises of his spirtual father.

(f) Cousin Eliza McClung was a lovely woman. She possessed the literary taste and the womanly accomplishments that her learned husband required of a companion. She was a kind mother to me, in the months of loneliness I spent at the old Orr mansion.

(g)   THE JOHNSTON LINEAGE.

1. Archibald Johnston, of Connecticut.
2. Dr. John Johnston, of Lexington, and afterward of Washington, Ky., = Abigail, daughter of Edward Harris. Issue:

THE MARSHALL FAMILY. 175

(274) COL. ALEXANDER KEITH M'CLUNG.

1. Gen. Albert Sidney Johnston, C. S. A.
2. Eliza Johnston, = DR. J. A. McCLUNG. Stoddard Johnston, Senator from Louisiana, was Mrs. McClung's half brother.

274 (a) COL. ALEXANDER KEITH McCLUNG, b. in Mason Co., Ky., 1811, committed suicide at Jackson, Miss., March 23, 1855. He was a scholar, orator and soldier, but noted chiefly as a duelist. He attended the school of his uncle, Louis Marshall (70), but at the age of fourteen, escaped punishment by leaping from a window and flying to his home; served as a midshipman in the navy; studied law, and at the age of twenty went to Mississippi; went to the Mexican war as Lieutenant Colonel of a Mississippi regiment; was severely wounded at the assault of Monterey, by a minie ball penetrating his hip, from which he suffered the remainder of his life; was Charge d'Affairs to Bolivia in 1843-51; resumed practice in Jackson, Miss.; became celebrated as an orator and statesman, and admired as an elegant writer. His eulogy of Henry Clay is regarded as a masterpiece of chaste rhetoric and pure composition. Tall, dignified and reserved, he united the soft timidity of the gazelle with the fearless intrepidity of the tiger. As a friend he was true, and as an enemy he was relentless. One of his nephews has kindly furnished me with an account of several of his duels:

"While in the navy, Midshipman McClung, when only sixteen, accepted a challenge, which resulted in his receiving a broken arm. His antagonist was known as a " dead shot." He knew that his only chance of life was for the bone of his arm to catch the ball intended for his heart, he therefore fired from his hip and let his arm be broken. At eighteen he fought his second duel; received the fire of his challenger, and he himself fired in the air. I know little of the circumstances under which he killed Baker. But I have been told of his magnanimous avoidance of a duel when nineteen years of age. At a party of young men, high words passed between Mr. McClung and a friend. The latter was the aggressor, but had been rebuffed and placed in the attitude that, by the code, he had to challenge, or be disgraced. To avoid trouble and relieve his friend, McClung presumed on his well-known character for courage, and went late at night to his adversary's room, and knocked for admittance. "Who

(274) COL. ALEXANDER KEITH M'CLUNG.

is there," came from within. "I am Alex. McClung," was the answer. "What do you want?" was sternly demanded. "I want to sleep with you," was the reply. The door was opened; without a word of explanation they slept together, breakfasted side by side in the morning, and appeared arm in arm on the street.

He went to Mississippi at twenty years of age, where every man of spirit had to fight. He was soon, though not by his fault, involved in a duel which he never ceased to regret. Col. Allen was a chivalrous gentleman and a noted duelist. He showed many courtesies to young McClung, and they were cordial friends. But a difficulty arose between a desperado and a young man lately arrived. The youth was challenged, and was advised that the companions of the challenger would murder him in case he killed their friend. The young man could get no second until advised to ask McClung, who accepted, with the determination to see a fair duel. The parties met. A crowd of desperate men were standing around. McClung told them that, by the terms agreed on, they were excluded, and requested all to retire beyond a neighboring fence. After some hesitation all started, except Col. Allen. He swore that he would stand where he was. McClung held the pistols, charged and cocked for the duel. He stepped up to Allen, and placing both pistols to his breast, ordered him to retire. This he did, swearing vengeance. A challenge came, and with it time, place and weapons were fixed. They were to meet in an eighty acre lot full of bushes, each armed with four pistols and a bowie knife. At the word they were to advance, using their weapons at pleasure. McClung accepted both challenge and terms. He remarked that he would shoot Allen in the head, and the result proved his markmanship. At the word McClung advanced slowly, but Allen rushed precipitately. McClung waited until Allen raised his pistol and then fired. Throwing down the empty weapon, a second pistol was presented; but before he drew the trigger, Allen plunged forward and fell. The ball had entered his mouth, and he died a few days later.

McClung's duel with John Menifee occurred at Vicksburg, Miss., December 29, 1839. The weapons were rifles, and the distance thirty paces. It grew out of a youthful frolic. Some boys had stolen, in mischief, their clothes while bathing. Menifee caught one of them and was beating him unmercifully, when McClung interfered. Menifee's rage was turned on him, but McClung, being an expert

(274) COL. ALEXANDER KEITH M'CLUNG.

pugilist, warded off the blows. After he had sufficiently put up with Menifee's violence, he gave him a severe blow, which ended the combat. A week later Menifee came on him with a club, and taking him unawares, beat him frightfully. Bystanders interfered, and picked up the almost lifeless form and bore it away. As he was led off, Menifee kicked him in contempt. This last indignity was more than McClung could bear. McClung had promised his mother he would never again give a challenge. He therefore notified Menifee that he would shoot him whenever they might meet. His known dexterity with the pistol, and his physical power, required Menifee to challenge him. McClung therefore chose rifles, as he did not desire to take any advantage of Menifee's inexperience with the pistol. At the second shot, the ball from McClung's gun hit the cock of Menifee's gun and divided, one portion striking his forehead, and passing around under the scalp. He died a few days afterward, from concussion of the brain. In after years McClung expressed no regret for Menifee's death, but he felt a life-long anguish for the fate of Allen.

After the age of twenty-two McClung fought no more duels. His formidable reputation saved him from being challenged. But in Bolivia he killed an over-bearing Englishman. Once when the sheriff and posse were held at bay by an armed ruffian, he deliberately walked up to him and took the pistol from his hand. In 1840 he edited a brilliant campaign paper, and Harrison made him Marshal of the Northern District of the State. He afterward ran for Congress, but the Democratic majority was too strong to be overcome.

McClung was noble, generous and chivalrous. The public sentiment of the times, and the lawless condition of Mississippi, made the falsely named "code of honor" more imperative than the criminal law, and McClung was its victim. When a boy, I often met him. He was the cousin of both my father and my mother, and I loved him dearly. He was possessed of a sweet, gentle nature, that seemed imperturbable; but under excitement, his temper knew no law. His sensitive regard to public censure, and the rebellious voice of conscience drove him nearly mad. Life became a galling burden. Remorseful and despairing thoughts drove sleep from his couch. His feelings are fully expressed in an ode which he wrote in contempla-

(276) JUDGE THOMAS MARSHALL DUKE.

tion of the end of his sufferings. A Mississippi paper thus alludes to him and his poem:

McClung had a genius of the first order; was honored, loved and almost worshipped. Wearied of life, disappointed and satiated, he wooed the embraces of death. With the hope of being slain, he enlisted in the Mexican war. His gallantry on the battle field of Monterey is known to all. He was severely wounded, but death came not to his relief. At Buena Vista, he was carried on a litter to the battle-field, and he exposed his life again. But death still eluded him, and refused to recognize his earnest votary. Despairing of finding death on the battle field, he returned to Mississippi and lived until life became a burden to him, and then committed suicide by blowing out his brains. A few months before his death, he wrote the following lines, overflowing with vocal and rythmic liquidity. It is the melody of despair,—the last lay of the minstrel:

ODE TO DEATH.

Swiftly speed o'er the waves of time,
    Spirit of Death;
In manhood's home, in youthful prime,
    I woo thy breath.
For the fading hues of hope have fled,
    Like the dolphin's light;
And dark are the clouds above my head,
    As the starless night.
Oh, vainly the voyager sighs for the rest
    Of the peaceful haven,—
The pilgrim saint for the homes of the blest,
    And the calm of heaven;
The galley slave for the night-winds breath,
    At burning noon;
But more gladly I'd spring to thy arms, O, Death,
    Come soon, come soon!

276 JUDGE THOMAS MARSHALL DUKE, b. in Lexington, Ky., 1795; d. in Texas, about 1870, = 1st, BETTIE TAYLOR, of Newport, Ky. After her death he married 2d, 1827, NANCY ASHBY, of Lexington, Ky. She died in Texas, and he married 3d, —— MCCORMICK, of Texas. Thomas Duke at one time had a store in Washington, Ky., at the southwest corner of the Court House Square. He went to Refugio, Texas, then a part of Mexico, and was an Alcalde; and hence the title of "Judge" given to him. The notorious Isaac Desha was tried before him, and condemned to death, but escaped from his place of confinement. He visited Kentucky about 1858. One of his sons was killed in the late civil war. His last wife left six children, but I have failed in my efforts to get into correspondence with them.

THE MARSHALL FAMILY. 179

(280) JAMES K. DUKE.

278 MARY WILSON DUKE, b. in Lexington, Ky., February, 1797; d. in Missouri, September, 1823, = May 7, 1818, DR. JOHN F. HENRY, b. January 17, 1793, in Scott Co., Ky.; d. November 12, 1883, in Iowa. Mary Duke married in Washington, Ky., and removed to Perry Co., Mo. Her only child died in 1823, and the mother died two weeks later. Dr. Henry afterwards removed to Hopkinsville, Ky.; married a Miss Ridgley; was elected to Congress in 1826. He is said to have been a splendid old gentleman — tall, handsome, genial and affectionate. He left three children by his second wife, who live in Burlington, Iowa.

280 (a) JAMES K. DUKE, b. in Washington, Ky., 1799; d. at Georgetown, Ky., August 2, 1863, = at Georgetown, Ky., February 5, 1822, MARY BUFORD, b. December 2, 1805; yet living in Georgetown, Ky. Mr. Duke was a graduate of Yale College; studied law, but ceased to practice after his marriage; removed to the splendid farm of his wife, near Georgetown. Here he spent his life in literary ease, dispensing generous hospitality to a large circle of gay and sportive friends. He was sorely distressed by the war; opposed secession; worked faithfully for reconciliation, casting his influence for the Union. He did not live to see the close of the war.

Mrs. Duke is now in her 80th year. She still owns the farm inherited from her father. It is one of the largest and most fertile farms in the Bluegrass region of Kentucky. But from the infirmities of age she found it necessary to rent it out, and now lives in Georgetown. I visited her in July, 1884, and was surprised to find one of her age so hale and hearty. She superintends her household, and possesses wonderful intelligence, memory, energy and spirit.

THE BUFORD FAMILY.

(b) Abraham Buford was born in Virginia, July 31, 1749; d. in Kentucky, June 29, 1833, = October 4, 1788, Martha McDowell, (See McDowell family, No. 68 g), b. June 26, 1766; d. July 6, 1835. Issue:

A
1. SAMUEL BUFORD, b. July 19, 1789.
2. COL. JOHN BUFORD, of Rock Island, b, February 29, 1792, = in Woodford Co., Ky., January 4, 1825, Ann B.

(282) CAPT. NATHANIEL WILSON DUKE.

A   Watson, b. September 20, 1785. Her father Dr. John Watson, was b. March 17, 1766; d. April 12, 1821. Issue:
1. Gen. John Buford, = PATTIE DUKE, No. 950.

A   3. CHARLES BUFORD, b. in Woodford Co. Ky., June 30, 1797; d. in St. Louis, January 4, 1866, = 1st, Henrietta Adair, dr. of Gov. John Adair. Issue:

B   1. *Henry Buford*, b. October, 1822; d. 1848, = 1844, BETTIE MARSHALL, No. 814.

Charles Buford = 2d, January 20, 1835, LUCY ANN DUKE, No. 286.

A   4. ABRAHAM BUFORD, b. September 25, 1800.

5. WILLIAM BUFORD, b. March 12, 1803, = Fanny Kirtley, his cousin. Issue: 1. Tom Buford, who killed Judge Elliott. From the Kirtley family came his crazy blood, and the other branches of the Buford family are not infected.

6. MARY BUFORD, b. December 2, 1805, = February 5, 1822, JAMES K. DUKE, No. 280.

282   CAPT. NATHANIEL WILSON DUKE, b. in Washington, Ky., 1806, d. at Paris, Ky., July, 1850, = October 4, 1833, MARY A. P. CURRIE, b. in Richmond, Va., December 17, 1813, d. in Lexington, Ky., February 24, 1847. Wilson Duke was sent to the navy at the age of sixteen; rose to the rank of Captain; was an accomplished gentleman and a gallant officer. I remember his occasional visits to Washington, Ky., and the honor and affection shown him. He left but one child, now the heroic and accomplished Gen. Basil Wilson Duke, of Louisville.

Mary Currie was born and educated at Richmond, Va. Mrs. Rebecca Marshall, No. 160, was her school-mate at the academy of Mrs Browne, in Richmond, and remembers her well. She describes her as a lively, intelligent, accomplished and lovely girl.

THE CURRIES.

James Currie, father of Mrs. Duke, was a native of Scotland, and came to Virginia after having served for some years as an officer in the British Navy. His uncle, Dr. James Currie, had previously settled in North Carolina, and had removed thence to Vir-

THE MARSHALL FAMILY. 181

(286) LUCY ANN DUKE—(*Buford*).

ginia. Having no children, he invited his nephew, James Currie, and his sister, to Virginia, and made them his heirs. This Dr. Currie, of North Carolina, was a nephew of the celebrated James Currie, of Edinburg, well known as the editor of Burns' poems.

The younger James Currie married in Richmond, Va., October 14, 1807, Caroline Rives Pickett. They were the parents of Mary Currie [Duke], and her older sister, who married William Burnett, of Cincinnati. See Pickett's Chart, No. 64.

284 JOHN MARSHALL DUKE, b. in Washington, Ky., October 29, 1811, d. in Maysville, Ky., 1882, = HANNAH MORTON, dr. of John M. Morton and Lucy Baylor. She died about 1864. Dr. J. M. Duke was educated at the private school of his uncle, Louis Marshall; studied medicine with his brother-in-law, Dr. J. F. Henry; attended lectures at Transylvania University, and in 1832 graduated at the Medical College of Ohio. Full of ambition and hope, Dr. Duke started on a career of honor, usefulness and success, in the town of Washington, Ky. I remember his debut well, for I was one of his first patients. In 1832 he physicked me through the severest spell of sickness I ever experienced. After a short time, he settled in Maysville, where his life-work was done. His devotion to his profession and the interest he manifested in the advancement of medical science, placed him at once among the leading physicians of Kentucky. But after the death of his wife, he lost his energy and ambition.

286 LUCY ANN DUKE, b. in Washington, Ky., January 11, 1814, = January 20, 1835, CHARLES BUFORD (his second wife), b. June 30, 1797, d. January 4, 1866, at St. Louis; buried at Rock Island. Mrs. Buford is a charming old lady, and delights to talk and write of the olden times. I have many letters from her which show not only literary taste and culture, but a heart full of tenderness. Reared in the Presbyterian Church, she is distinguished for piety and good works. During the war, her charity manifested itself in sympathy and kindness to hundreds of Confederate soldiers imprisoned at Rock Island.

Charles Buford graduated at Yale College, and studied law. But

(288) CHARLOTTE JANE DUKE—(*Taylor*).

his large inheritance called him away from professional pursuits. His magnificent stock farm demanded his attention, and literary pastimes, conviviality and field sports became his ambition. He was fond of shooting and fishing, and frequent hunting parties were held on his estate. In one of his excursions, he visited Rock Island, Ill., and was delighted with the country and the opportunities for manly sports that it afforded. He therefore sold his Kentucky possessions, and in the fall of 1853, removed to Rock Island, that he might enjoy his favorite amusements. But in 1866, he became affected with some disease of the kidneys, and visited St. Louis, to consult the best physicians as to his case. Here at the house of his nephew, Basil Duke, he was taken with a congestive chill, and died without regaining consciousness. His remains lie in Rock Island cemetery, and his handsome monument contains no other epitaph but his name and the dates of his birth and death. See No. 282.

288 CHARLOTTE JANE DUKE, b. at Washington, Ky., January 20, 1817, = in Scott Co., Ky., January 14, 1840, HARRISON TAYLOR, b. August 10, 1810; d. November 28, 1876. I knew Cousin Jane in her maiden beauty and loveliness. She married my law preceptor, and participated in his civic honors. But when Mr. Taylor died, she was astounded to learn that he had left nothing for his family. She lives in Maysville, Ky., and is made comfortable by the help of her sons.

Harrison Taylor commenced the practice of law in Washington, Ky., about 1835, as the partner of Mr. McClung (272). They removed to Maysville when it became the county seat of Mason County, and were the leading firm when Mr. McClung gave up the practice, in 1849. Mr. Taylor still practiced up to the time of his death. No man ever enjoyed public confidence in a higher degree. His pleasant, engaging manners, his humble and unassuming address, his diffidence and politeness, inspired confidence, and made him an universal favorite. A Whig in early life, a Union man in the war, and a Democrat after its close, he was always with the majority in his county. He was elected to the State Senate, 1857–61; to the House in 1836, 1861, 1865–66–67. The two last sessions he was Speaker of the House. I last saw him in 1872. He had then be-

THE MARSHALL FAMILY. 183

(292) SALLIE TAYLOR.

come corpulent, and bent with disease; yet his cordial greeting was that of old. He died suddenly, while attending court in Bracken County.

290 ANNA KEITH TAYLOR, b. at Petersburg, Va., October 31, 1808; d. at Mt. Ephraim, Fauquier Co., Va., March 7, 1884; = March 17, 1830, REV. JOHN JAMES ROYALL, D. D., of the Presbyterian Church, b. December 2, 1805; d. February 17, 1856. I have many letters from Cousin Anna K. Royall,—most of them written in the last year of her life. She was one of God's chosen spirits, and lived, labored and loved that others might be happy. She wrote me that she was very deaf and nearly blind; yet her letters were long, and she begged me not to break off the correspondence. She longed for companionship, and proposed to support and remunerate any agreeable lady that would become her constant associate. She delighted to have her grand children stay with her, and feared their removal from her. To the last, her delight was to teach the little ones. She possessed a bright temperament, was always happy, and enjoyed good health. She died suddenly, without warning, insomuch that none of her children had an opportunity to be with her.

Rev. John J. Royall, D. D., was an earnest and eloquent preacher. His labors still follow him. His praises are in all the churches to which he ministered. He was supplying the Presbyterian church at Petersburg when he met and married his wife. He removed to Mt. Ephraim, and as an evangelist labored throughout adjacent parts of Virginia. But the two churches in Winchester agreed to unite, on condition that Dr. Royall was called to that city. After remaining there a few years, he returned to Mt. Ephraim. He fell dead on his way to church to preach.

292 SALLIE TAYLOR, b. at Petersburg, Va., June 13, 1812; d. at Staunton, Va., 1881. She never married. I met her at Danville, Ky., in 1837, when, with her mother, she came west. I remember her delight and proficiency in music. A friend who knew the two girls writes: "Sallie and Georgia were quite ac-

(294) GEORGIANA TAYLOR.

complished, especially in music. Sallie particularly, was an adept on the violin, as well as the harp and piano. They lived in Winchester, and were admired and loved." A fall from a horse affected Sallie's brain, and she died in the Lunatic Asylum at Staunton, Va.

294 GEORGIANA TAYLOR, b. at Petersburg, Va., July 9, 1814; d. 1866. She became paralized in 1856, and for ten years lay a living corpse, unable to lift her hand. See No. 292.

296 JOHN J. MARSHALL, jurist, reporter, statesman and politician, was b. in Woodford Co., Ky., August 4, 1785; d. in Louisville, July, 1846; buried at Rosedale Cemetery; = June 14, 1809 ANNA REED BIRNEY; graduated at Princeton College, N. J., in 1806, taking the first honors; represented Franklin County, 1815, 1816 and 1833; State Senator 1820-24; Elector 1833; Judge of the Louisville Circuit Court 1836-1846; published seven volumes of Kentucky law reports; was appointed Judge of the Kentucky Court of Appeals, but was rejected on political grounds; died poor, having lost his large estate by his generous support of failing friends during the financial crash of 1837; was for many years a leading politician in Kentucky, and left the impress of his powerful mind on the jurisprudence of the State.

THE REED AND BIRNEY FAMILY.

A
1. JOHN REED, of Ireland, came to Virginia; = a Wilcox.
2. THOMAS REED, Senator from Mississippi His sister = James Birney, of farmer, of Boyle Co. Issue:

B
1. *James G. Birney*, Abolition candidate for President, b. February 4, 1792; d. in New Jersey, November 25, 1857; = Agatha McDowell, daughter of Judge William McDowell and Margaret Madison, of Bowling Green. No. 68 (*f*).
2. *Anna Reed Birney*, = J. J. MARSHALL. No. 296. See McDowell chart 68 *f*.

(340) DR. WILLIAM MARSHALL.

298 JUDGE THOMAS ALEXANDER MARSHALL, L. L. D., b. in Woodford Co., Ky., January 15, 1794; d. in Louisville, Ky., April 17, 1871; buried in Lexington, = November 26, 1816, ELIZA PRICE, b. May 1, 1795; d. November 17, 1875; buried beside her husband. He graduated at Yale College, 1815, commenced the practice of law in Frankfort, Ky.; removed to Paris, 1819; removed to Lexington, 1835; removed to Frankfort, 1857, and to Louisville, 1859. He was in Congress from the Paris district, from 1831 to 1835; Supreme Judge of Kentucky, 1835 to 1856; and again in 1866; was on the bench of the Court of Appeals twenty-one years, and twice Chief Justice of that Court; represented Bourbon County in the Legislature, 1827 and 1828, and represented the City of Louisville, 1863, 1864 and 1865; was professor of law in Transylvania University, 1836 to 1849; celebrated his golden wedding, 1866, in Louisville; twenty-four volumes of Kentucky Reports attest his legal attainments. I heard a distinguished jurist remark that his decisions on Aquatic rights alone would form a treatise superior to any text book on the subject. His kinsman, Judge James P. Harbeson, was associated with him for years, and remarked to me that "He was a Christian gentleman; a classical scholar; an erudite jurist, and, altogether, the greatest and best man I ever knew."

Mrs. Marshall was said to have been the most lovely woman in Kentucky. She was a grand-daughter of Col. Thomas Hart, and a niece of Henry Clay. In 1883, I visited the family tomb, which stands in the Lexington cemetery, under the shadow of the magnificent monument of Kentucky's favorite son. Names and dates are the epitaphs of the family.

300 ELIZA MARSHALL, a lovely sister of Judge T. A. Marshall, at the age of 14 years, after reading to her mother, stepped out upon a piazza, at Paris, during a storm, and was instantly killed by lightning. The aged mother was so overcome with grief, that she became blind and never recovered her sight.

340 DR. WILLIAM MARSHALL practiced medicine in Louisville, Ky., and removed to Carrollton, Indiana. Had a large family.

(342) JANE MARSHALL — (*Aynes*).

342 JANE MARSHALL, = JOHN AYNES. She died in Franklin Co., Ky. Their daughter Eliza, = Stephen Allen.

344 MARTIN P. MARSHALL, = DORCAS OVERALL. He was educated by Martin Marshall, of Augusta; died at Chaplin, Nelson Co., Ky., leaving a large estate and several children. His son, Humphrey, was a surgeon in the C. S. A.

346 PAULINA MARSHALL, = GEORGE MORRIS. He died in Louisville, Ky., leaving a large family.

348 ELIZABETH MARSHALL, = JOHN NEAL. She died in Anderson Co., Ky., in 1884, aged 82 years.

350 NANCY MARSHALL, = DR. WILLIAM BALLOU. Their son, William T. Ballou, is a merchant of Frankfort, Ky.

360 MARY ANN MARSHALL, b. at Augusta, Ky., July 29, 1804; d. January 19, 1873, = January 23, 1821, GEORGE DONIPHAN, b. in St. George Co., Va., July 4, 1790; d. in Augusta, Ky., February, 1864. They lived in Augusta. He was a prosperous farmer and kept a tanyard.

362 WILLIAM CHAMPE MARSHALL, lawyer, orator and statesman, b. in Augusta, Ky., August 9, 1807; d. May 2, 1873, = October 7, 1834, SUSAN MYERS, who died October, 1876, daughter of Thomas Myers (merchant) and Elizabeth Davidson, of Augusta, Ky. Mr. Marshall was educated at Augusta College; studied law with his father, and practiced in Augusta; represented Bracken County, 1834, 1840, 1841, 1842, 1844 and 1850; was a member of the State Convention in 1849; served as Commonwealth's Attorney, and as Mayor of Augusta. He was a brilliant speaker and a successful lawyer.

(364) DR. NICHOLAS TALIAFERRO MARSHALL.

364 DR. NICHOLAS TALIAFERRO MARSHALL, b. in Augusta, Ky., March 1, 1810, d. June 7, 1858, = April 23, 1846, ELIZABETH SOWARD, b. April 23, 1827, d. December 27, 1859. In 1833, he received the degree of M. D. of the University of Pennsylvania, and practiced in Washington, Ky., in partnership with his uncle Dr. W. Thornton Taliaferro. In 1843 he removed to Cincinnati, and entered on a large practice. In 1846 he was happily married and seven children were born to him, only two of whom survive. In 1853 he was elected to a chair in the Ohio Medical College, at Cincinnati, and for four years found pleasure in the duties of his station. An intense student, he had qualified himself for distinction, not only in his profession, but in other departments of a liberal education. The medical science was his delight, and his lectures were interesting as well as learned. He was wedded to his profession, and he did not marry until he was thirty-six years of age. I knew "Cousin Nic." well, and often took his prescriptions in my boyhood. Every one loved and trusted him. He was one of the finest talkers I ever listened to. His health in 1857 broke down, and he retired with his family to the home of his wife's grandfather, Gen. Soward, in Minerva, Ky., where he died suddenly from apoplexy. The members of the profession in Cincinnati and Covington passed highly complimentary resolutions on the occasion. His will is recorded in Maysville, Ky.; is dated November 14, 1853, probated August 9, 1858, and grants all his property to his widow, whom he appoints guardian of his children.

THE SOWARD FAMILY.

General Richard Soward, b. May 19, 1778, d. January 5, 1872, = September 27, 1799, Nancy Campbell, b. January 17, 1780, d. February 24, 1862. Their son, COL. ALFRED SOWARD, b. September 7, 1800, d. December 22, 1879, = 1st, February 12, 1822, Elizabeth Chiles, who d. April 30, 1827. Issue:

1. Anna Frances Soward, = Samuel Forman.
2. Elizabeth Soward, b. April 23, 1827, d. December 27, 1859, = April 23, 1846, DR. NIC. T. MARSHALL, b. March 1, 1810, d. June 7, 1858. See No. 364 a

ALFRED SOWARD, = 2d, Mrs. Prudence Knight. Issue:

1. Richard L. Soward, = Fanny Tabb.

HE = 3d, Mrs. Mary P. Nelson. Issue:

(366) THOMAS ALEXANDER MARSHALL.

1. Thomas H. Soward, = Elizabeth E. Smith.
2. Alfred V. Soward, = Tucie E. Keith.

HE = 4th, Mrs. Margaret Gorsuch. No issue.

HE = 5th, December 22, 1852, Mat. Ann Taliaferro, b. December 28, 1814; yet living in Augusta, Ky. No issue.

366 THOMAS ALEXANDER MARSHALL, b. in Augusta, Ky., March 29, 1812, = March 5, 1844, LETITIA MILLER, b. February 19, 1844. Both are living in Vicksburg, Miss. He was educated at Augusta College; studied law with his father; settled in early life in Vicksburg, Miss., and enjoyed for many years a large practice; with his relative, W. C. Smedes, he compiled Smedes and Marshall's Mississippi Reports. His wife was a daughter of Capt. Anderson Miller, a celebrated steamboat captain and Marshal of the Southern District of Mississippi. For eleven years he has been afflicted with rheumatism, and for the last five years he has been unable to leave his bed. By paying security debts, and through the disasters of the war, he lost a fortune; but by energy and talent he has regained a competency.

368 THORNTON F. MARSHALL, b. in Augusta, Ky., July 11, 1819, = ANN ELIZA MACKEY. Mr. Marshall was educated at Augusta College; studied law with his father; was in the State Senate 1859–63; a Presidential Elector 1865; is an eminent lawyer, a profound statesman and an active Democratic politician. He has accumulated a good estate, and is still in active and successful practice. He and his wife were both born in Augusta, and still live there.

370 ELIZA J. MARSHALL, b. at 'Augusta, Ky., March 1, 1826; = November 19, 1846, JAMES W. ARMSTRONG, b. February 14, 1822; d. October 13, 1877. She was born at the old Marshall homestead in Augusta, and still lives there. I met her in 1884, and found her a sensible and agreeable lady, much interested in giving her children a good start in the world. Mr. Armstrong

(416) MALINDA BALLOU—(*Hackett*).

was a son of William Armstrong and Sallie Lee; born at West Union, Ohio; educated at Augusta College; studied law with Martin Marshall; graduated at Transylvania Law School; practiced law for a time; opened a store at Augusta, and continued in the mercantile business the rest of his life. He was a stout man of robust health, and died suddenly of a congestive chill. He was highly esteemed for his intelligence, energy and public spirit.

372 GEORGE WILLIS MARSHALL, b. at Augusta, Ky., May 5, 1829; = Sue Handsford. He is a planter, near Vicksburg, Miss. They are both living.

402 EMILY DURRETT, = June 25, 1829, COL. SHADRACK BARNES, b. May 4, 1798; d. June 19, 1880. Mr. Barnes was a lawyer of eminence in Mississippi.

406 WILLIAM BALLOU, b. August 24, 1809: d. August 14, 1874; = NANCY HOWARD, b. December 1, 1815; d. November, 1880.

408 ELIZABETH BALLOU, b. September 20, 1797; d. October 5, 1823; = January 20, 1818, SHADRACK BARNES. See No. 402.

416 MALINDA BALLOU, b. May 10, 1814, d. 1884; = JAMES HACKETT, b. December 31, 1805; d. April 6, 1859. Mr. Hackett, was a farmer of Shelby Co., Ky., remarkable for his superior intelligence, but wanting in energy. He did not prosper. I visited Mrs. Hackett, at her pleasant and neat home in Louisville, in 1884. She was then in her bed from which she never arose again. She was a remarkable woman for sound judgment, and was certainly an accomplished lady in her prime. I acquired much genealogical information from her lips, and was favorably impressed with her family. She died soon after my visit.

(424) GEN. DUFF GREEN.

424 GEN. DUFF GREEN, b. in Virginia, d. in Mobile, Ala., June 10, 1875; = LUCRETIA EDWARDS. He was a distinguished lawyer, statesman, journalist and author. One of his books has already been referred to. He edited the Washington *Telegraph*, and was a member of Jackson's cabinet. See Green chart, No. 180 *j*, and No. 116.

454 ALEXANDER MARSHALL ROBINSON, b. in Greenville, S. C., November 17, 1802; d. in Platte City, Mo., 1884; = 1st, 1822, LOUISA BASYE, b. 1803, daughter of Lisbon Basye, of Bourbon Co., Ky. After her death, he married 2d, CATHERINE A. HUGHES, daughter of William Hughes, of Bourbon Co., Ky., she died in 1884, in Platte Co., Mo. In 1810 Dr. Robinson came with his parents to Bourbon Co., Ky.; in 1825, removed to Howard Co., Mo.; spent the year 1856 in Jefferson City, Mo.; in 1829 went to Columbia, Mo.; in 1842, removed to Clay Co., Mo.; and in 1844, settled in Platte City, Mo. Official business called him successively to Lewis County, to St. Louis and St. Joseph. He was State Senator from Boon Co., Mo., in 1838; was Secretary of the Missouri Senate in 1840, was a Commissioner to select for the State the 500,000 acres of land granted by Congress; was in the State Legislature 1850, and elected speaker; Senator again 1852; was afterwards Superintendent of Indian affairs, at St. Louis and St. Joseph; cast his first vote for Jackson ; a Democrat to the day of his death; a R. A. Mason. In intervals of official duties, Dr. Robinson practiced medicine. His father was John Robinson of Norfolk, Va. His grandfather, Garrard Robinson, came from England to Virginia.

Dr. Robinson read medicine with Dr. Loyd Warfield, at Paris, Ky., and attended a course of lectures at Lexington, Ky., 1825-26. A handsome tomb to his memory stands in the Platte City cemetery.

470 ELIZABETH ELEANOR H. SMITH, b. December 3, 1806; = JAMES C. VASS of Fredericksburg, Va. They left a large family of children. The Marquis of Lafayette met her when he visited us in 1824, and pronounced her the most beautiful woman he had seen in America.

(474) MARY S. SMITH—(*Smith*).

472 FRANCIS LEE SMITH, b. in Warrenton, Va., November 25, 1808; d. in Alexandria, Va., May 10, 1877; = April 13, 1836, SARAH GOSNELLE VOWELL, daughter of John C. Vowell, of Alexandria, Va. She still lives at Alexandria. Mr. Smith received his professional education at the law school of Judge Tucker, at Winchester, Va. After practicing a few years in Virginia, he removed to Louisville, Ky., and by his intelligence, eloquence, energy and spirit, was fast rising to distinction. But in 1842 he determined to return to his native state. He settled at Alexandria, among friends and relatives, and there entered upon a successful practice, and found fame and distinction, as well as fortune. He was in the Legislature; member of the City Council; and City Attorney. He was employed in nearly every important case in the City Courts and was highly esteemed by his associates, for his suavity in private, and his courtesy to bench and bar. An orator and logician by nature, he was well read in classical literature, in philosophy and in law. To these acquirements he added untiring energy and consummate tact. His character was an element of success, and called for love as well as admiration.

Mr. Smith was trained in the christian faith, and became a zealous and efficient member of The Episcopal Church. In his will he leaves this testimony:

"To my beloved children, I urgently recommend the divine precepts, contained in the Holy Scriptures, as the only safe rule for their conduct, to guide and sustain them amidst the cares and trials of time, and to secure to them a blessed immortality."

He was the personal friend and attorney for Gen. R. E. Lee, and brought the suit for the Arlington estate. He opposed secession, but when Virginia went out he joined his fortunes with the State to which he owed allegiance, and went South with his family. On his return, he found his residence had been turned into a hospital, and his property almost destroyed. But with energy he took hold of his professional business and soon retrieved his fortunes. His widow and children have piously published a small memorial volume in his honor.

474 MARY S. SMITH, b. August 7, 1810, d.; = SMITH.

(476) HARRIET E. B. SMITH.

476 HARRIET E. B. SMITH, b. May 4, 1812, d.

478 JULIEN H. SMITH, b. November 4, 1813, d.

480 JOHN THOMAS SMITH, was b. at Warrenton, Va., January 15, 1816; d. January 28, 1872; = at Oakhill, September 25, 1845, MARGARET LEWIS MARSHALL, b. October 29, 1823; living at Theological Seminary, near Alexandria, Va. At the time of his father's death in 1832, he was pursuing his studies at the University of Virginia. But owing to the small estate left for the support of the family, and the need of his help at home, he returned to Warrenton. Through the influence of Gov. Gamble of Florida, he obtained a situation in that territory, and remained there for several years. But his health failing, he joined his brother Robert, (182,) who had gone to Mobile, Ala. Here he found a place in the bank of Mobile, and was able to send a part of his salary to his mother, in Warrenton. After marriage, he removed to his wife's estate in Fauquier. She possessed a part of the Oakhill farm. It was well improved, and she insisted on making it their home. Here they resided for fifteen years. But twelve months prior to the war they sold, and removed to "Ashland," near Richmond. As the purchase money became due, the notes were paid off in confederate money, which proved of little value; and they were left in straitened circumstances. Mr. Smith found employment and good wages in the South during the winter, and spent his summers in Virginia. In 1872, he died at Ashland, and the widow, with the purpose of educating her children, removed to Theological Semenary, Fairfax Co., Va. Three of her daughters have married Episcopal ministers. With the proceeds of her husband's life insurance, she purchased "Ingleside," and is educating her noble sons for usefulness. Her youngest boy will soon complete his studies, and the happy mother proposes to join her sons in forming a household in some city where they will engage in business. When I was in Baltimore in August, 1884, the young men called to see me, and I was highly pleased with their polite address and sensible conversation (1220-2). Mrs. Smith, with the aid of her dutiful children, is able to live comfortably, and to devote her leisure to literature and social correspondence. I have the pleasure to acknowledge many letters from her and find her a lady of sense and culture,—proud of her lineage and of her worthy children. Her postoffice is Theological Seminary, Fairfax Co., Va.

482 ROBERT SMITH was born in Warrenton, Va., November 15, 1817, = in Mobile, SARAH HUNTER. Both live there. About 1834, Mr. Smith established himself in Mobile, Ala., in the mercantile business, and prospered until the war, when he was ruined. But his good name remained, and he resumed business, and was doing well, when the financial crash of 1874 again overthrew him. His health is not good, and his business yields him only a competence. Has several children.

484 ELIZA ADELAIDE SMITH was born in Warrenton, Va., April 10, 1819, = DR. CHARLES D. BOARMAN, of Baltimore. They removed to Boonville, Mo. They had eight children, some of whom reside in Kansas City, and others are in Colorado. Mrs. Boarman died about 1856, and Dr. Boarman married again.

486 STOVER C. SMITH, b. May 7, 1821, d.

488 EMILY S. SMITH, b. January 23, 1823, d.

492 MARSHALL JOSEPH SMITH, was b. in Warrenton, Va., October 19, 1824, = 1849, MARY TAYLOR, of Norfolk, Va.; his father died in 1832, leaving but little property; he dwelt among his relatives, wherever a home was offered; at thirteen, his brothers sent him to school in Baltimore; in 1841, through the influence of Henry A. Wise, he got a position in the U. S. navy; made a cruise to the West Indies,—then to the East Indies and around the world; came home, and was sent to the Naval School at Annapolis; when the

(500) JOHN MARSHALL.

Mexican war broke out, he went to sea, and took part in the siege of Vera Cruz; returned to the Naval School; passed No. 19, in a class of 135; made a cruise to the Baltic, as passed midshipman; and, after his return, married Miss Mary Taylor, to whom he had been attached for seven years, in Norfolk, Va.; made a trip of a few months to the Mediterranean, and, on his return in 1851, resigned to accept a partnership with his brother Robert in the mercantile business in Mobile, Ala.; in 1854, removed to New Orleans, and engaged in the mercantile business on his own account; prospered until the war commenced; raised a regiment for the South; was in the battle of Shiloh; served afterwards in the regular artillery; was taken prisoner at Port Hudson, and continued in captivity for fourteen months; was exchanged in Charleston in 1864; served in front of Richmond; was sent to Halifax on special duty, and was there when the surrender took place; returned home to start anew without a cent left from his fortune; his family had suffered great hardships during his separation from them; made another fortune, which went in the crash of 1872; nothing daunted, started again; tried St. Louis, but neither the climate nor the people suited him; returned to New Orleans and settled down to the insurance business; he now has a comfortable income; is respected and trusted; is an active promoter of all schemes of city improvement, and, by his intelligence and industry, has become a leading citizen of New Orleans. I have many interesting and scholarly letters from Col. Smith, and I have been deeply impressed with his literary attainments, his varied experience, and his solid good sense. Few men have seen more of the world, and still fewer have passed through such trials and discouragements. I owe him much for the valuable assistance he has given me in the present heraldic work.

In 1884, I met Mrs. Smith and one of her daughters at Fauquier, Va., Springs, her usual summer resort, and found her an exceedingly prepossessing lady,—intelligent, agreeable and handsome. She is a daughter of Arthur Taylor, whose grandfather came from London, and settled in Yorktown, Va., before the Revolution. On her mother's side she is of the Saunders family of lower Virginia. Mr. Smith and family spend their summers in Fauquier Co., Va.

500 JOHN MARSHALL, b. at Weyanoke, Charles-City Co., Va., May 7, 1811; d. December 14, 1854, = November 20, 1837,

(502) AGNES HARWOOD MARSHALL — (*Taliaferro*).

ANNE ELIZA BLACKWELL, b. January 5, 1822; d. November 18, 1854. Mr. Marshall was educated at the University of Virginia. One of his letters written to his sister, Agnes, while he was attending the university, has been placed in my hands. It displays literary and epistolary talent beyond his years. It is written in chaste style, and shows not only spirit and vivacity, but sound judgment. If it were not so long, I would publish it as a proof of his intelligence. Being the oldest son, Mr. Marshall took charge of the Oakhill estate, after he had married. Here he lived a life of a scholar and literary gentleman, and by his profuse hospitality, made Oakhill a home of delights. But he was unable to keep up this free and liberal life, and in 1852, sold the estate to his younger brother, Thomas. For a number of years he represented Fauquier County in the State Legislature. He was an ardent Whig, and a zealous and exemplary member of the Episcopal Church. The last two years of his life were spent in Culpeper County. Here his lovely and much beloved wife died in 1854. He survived her less than a month, and with a broken heart followed her to the grave. Their remains lie side by side in the Oakhill cemetery. He left home in the morning of his death, apparently well, but had to stop at the house of his friend, James Bickham, of Culpeper County, and soon died. The parents of Mrs. Marshall were William Blackwell, of Fauquier County, and Anne Sparke Gordon. She was much admired for her beauty and grace, as well as for her amiability.

502 AGNES HARWOOD MARSHALL, b. at "Oakhill," Fauquier Co., Va., November 5, 1813, *l*; = May 4, 1836, GEN. ALEXANDER GALT TALIAFERRO, b. at "Churchill," Gloucester Co., Va., September, 1808; d. at "Ninondale," Culpeper Co., Va., June 29, 1884. Mrs. Taliaferro is a lovely old lady, living at "Ninondale" with her widowed daughter, Agnes Maupin. Her other children have families and homes. Many letters which I have received from Mrs. Taliaferro, show a tender regard and an affectionate sympathy. She is deservedly proud of her home, her lineage, her husband's memory, and her children's reputation.

Gen. Taliaferro graduated at William and Mary College, and after taking the degree of A. B., attended law and other lectures

(502) AGNES HARWOOD MARSHALL—(*Taliaferro*).

during the sessions of 1831 and 1832, graduating in law. He had an ample fortune, and after marrying, he abandoned the practice of law, and spent the remainder of his life on his farm. His father died in 1850, and Gen. Taliaferro purchased a splendid farm in Culpeper County, known as "Ninondale;" and this is still the homestead of the family.

When the civil war broke out in 1861, Alex. G. Taliaferro was Lieutenant Colonel of Cavalry, in the Second Military Division of Virginia. He at once applied to Gov. Letcher for orders, but was told that all militia officers were superceded, and new ones had been appointed. Failing to get an appointment, he hastened to Harper's Ferry, and entered as a private in the company of Culpeper Minute Men. But a few days later he accepted the command of a company of roughs, who had fled from Baltimore on account of being implicated in an attack upon the Massachusetts troops passing through that city. He was assigned to Col. A. P. Hill's regiment, and sent to Romney. Returning to Winchester, he found a commission from Gov. Letcher as Lieutenant Colonel of Infantry, and was assigned to the Twenty-third Regiment, Third Brigade of the Stonewall Division. The command left Winchester, January 1, 1862, and made a bootless expedition through Maryland with the secret purpose of destroying the Baltimore & Ohio railroad, and of occupying Pittsburg. But the design was treacherously communicated to the enemy, and, with the aid of cold weather and bad roads, the purpose was defeated. The brigade returned, by way of Romney, to Winchester. At the battle of Kernstown, Col. Taliaferro's horse was killed under him.

(b) On the reorganization of the army, Col. Taliaferro was, by acclamation, chosen Colonel of the Twenty-third Regiment of Infantry. His nephew, Gen. Wm. B. Taliaferro, was placed in command of the Third Brigade of the Stonewall Division. At the battle of McDowell a second horse was killed under Col. Taliaferro. At the first battle of Winchester, his sword was torn from his side by a grape shot. At Port Republic he was wounded in the shoulder, and from sickness was unable to take part in the fights around Richmond.

While confined to his house at Culpeper Court House, with two sentinels to give him warning, and his horse ready saddled for 'scape, the enemy entered the town and came to his house intent

(502) AGNES HARWOOD MARSHALL — (*Taliaferro*).

on capturing him. The sentinels were asleep, and were killed. He was awakened by the report of guns, and a thundering upon his door. At the Colonel's suggestion, Mrs. Taliaferro looked out of the window, and asked a moment to allow her to dress. The time was used by the Colonel in investing himself with full uniform — cocked hat, sword and pistols. The party of soldiers was admitted at the front door, after the Colonel had escaped by the back window. At that time the dress of an officer of one army did not differ from that of the other; and with a bold front, Col. Taliaferro walked through the ranks of the enemy. Taken for a Federal officer, he escaped unchallenged.

(c) On the death of Gen. Winder, Col. Taliaferro was promoted to the rank of Brigadier General, and succeeded to the command of the Third Brigade through all its campaigns. On the first day of the second battle of Manassas, Gen. Taliaferro lost a third horse. On the second day a minie ball struck the eagle of his sword-belt, and glanced off without damage. On the third day, while leading a charge on a battery, the grip of his sword was struck by a minie ball, and two of his fingers crushed. At Oxhill, he commanded the Stonewall Division, during the sickness of Maj. Gen. Starke, and would have succeeded to the rank of that officer, had he not been required to return home on account of his crippled condition. This promotion he however enjoyed after serving some time as the commander of the military post at Charlottesville. In this position he was found at the time of the surrender.

(d) I hope I will be pardoned for repeating a story that Gen. Taliaferro often told on himself. At the time referred to, he was Colonel of the Twenty-third Regiment. The men of the Thirty-seventh Regiment had found a game cock that was ready to fight any thing from a horse to a kitten. Chanticleer often rode on the shoulders of the men, and was always ready for a fight. He made himself useful: for if the men wanted to catch a turkey or other fowl, the fighting bird was brought forward and an engagement followed. Before the fight had fairly begun, a soldier would wring off the head of Chanticleer's adversary. Of course he was very popular with the men. But he had no name. So a meeting was held to christen Chanticleer. A number of names were suggested; but when the name of "Col. Taliaferro" was proposed, it was carried with uproarious acclamation. Gen. Taliaferro used to say he had

THE MARSHALL FAMILY.

(502) AGNES HARWOOD MARSHALL—(*Taliaferro*).

had many children named after him, but, to have this game cock for his name sake, was the highest compliment he had ever received.

At the return of peace, Gen. Taliaferro was quite old, and he retired to his estate of "Ninondale," and devoted himself to literary pursuits. I have been furnished with his auto-biography, which is well written, and should be published in full.

(e) LINEAGE OF THE TALIAFERROS.

1. John Taliaferro, emigrant from Italy. (?)
2. His son Philip Taliaferro, who married Lucy Baytop.
3. Dr. William Taliaferro, educated abroad, at the medical schools of London and Edinburg. He married Harriet Throckmorton. Issue: 3 sons.
    1. Warner Taliaferro. father of Maj. Gen. William B. Taliaferro.
    2. Dr. William Taliaferro, educated in England and Germany.
    3. Gen. Alex. Galt Taliaferro, who married AGNES H. MARSHALL. See 102 *g*.

APPENDIX TO THE TALIAFERRO FAMILY.

After the Taliaferro Chart, pages 83–86, was in print, I received a letter from J. S. Pitchen, dated Nashville, September 20, 1885, giving me the following list of Deeds, Bonds and Wills, taken from the records of Essex Co., Va., showing that Robert Taliaferro, called "Gentleman," and most likely of English extraction, was born about 1635, and probably was the founder of the family. He had four sons: 1, Francis, who married Elilabeth Catlett; 2, John,= Sarah, dr. of Lawrence Smith; 3, Richard; 4, Charles, and perhaps a fifth, named Robert, who = Sarah, sister of Elizabeth Catlett:

1. Deed, September 28, 1682, from Francis Taliaferro, of the County of Gloucester, *Gent.*, son and heir apparent of Robert Taliaferro, to his bother John, 1,000 acres as an advancement on account of his marriage to Sarah, dr. of Lawrence Smith. The deed recites that said Robert Taliaferro and Lawrence Smith had on the 26th of March, 1666, surveyed and patented 6,300 acres, in what is now Essex Co., Virginia.

2. Deed from said Francis Taliaferro to his brothers Charles and Richard, 1,600 acres of the same tract.

THE MARSHALL FAMILY. 199

(502) AGNES HARWOOD MARSHALL—(*Taliaferro*).

3. Deed, March 30, 1689, from Robert Taliaferro and Sarah, his wife, to John Battaile, for 300 acres, being part of 600 bequeathed by John Catlett to his daughters, Elizabeth and Sarah.

4. Deed, August 15, 1687, from Francis Taliaferro and Elizabeth, his wife, the other half of said land, to John Battaile.

5. Bond, June 19, 1699, of John Taliaferro, as Sheriff of Essex County, Va.

6. Deed, March 11, 1701, from Francis Taliaferro and Elizabeth, his wife, to Augustus Smith, of Gloucester County, for 416 acres, one-half of a patent granted Col. John Catlett, the 10th of September, 1660.

7. Deed, from John Taliaferro and Richard Buckner, to John Lomax and Elizabeth, his wife, who was Elizabeth Wormley, two tracts; dated July 8, 1704.

8. Deed, from Charles Taliaferro to Robert Slaughter, 300 acres, part of a patent for 966, dated November 2, 1705, to said Charles; dated January 7, 1706.

9. Bond, August 10, 1710, of Elizabeth, administratrix of Francis Taliaferro.

10. Deed, May 9, 1711, from Richard Taliaferro, of Richmond Co., and Charles Taliaferro, of Essex, to Wm. Woodford.

11. Deed, August 8, 1711, from Robert Taliaferro to Augusta Smith, 200 acres in Parish of St. Mary, in Essex County.

12. Deed, August 8, 1711, from same to Samuel Short, for 100 acres granted Robert Taliaferro, deceased, father of said Robert.

13. Deed, March 20, 1715, from John Taliaferro to his son, Lawrence, 300 acres.

14. Bond, March 20, 1716, of John Taliaferro, as administrator of Elizabeth Taliaferro.

15. Deed, from Charles Taliaferro to John Brown, 67 acres; dated July 15, 1717.

16. Deed, January 21, 1717, from John Taliaferro to John Taliaferro, jr., land conveyed to John Taliaferro, sr., by Francis Taliaferro.

17. Deed, August 11, 1718, from Robert Taliaferro, only son and heir opparent of Robert, to Thomas Catlett, 200 acres.

18. Deed, November 20, 1721, from Lawrence Taliaferro and John Battaile to Zachariah Taliaferro, in consideration of said Zach-

(502) AGNES HARWOOD MARSHALL—(*Taliaferro*).

ariah resigning his interest in the estate of his father, John Taliaferro, to his brother Lawrence.

19. Deed from Robert Taliaferro to Paul Micon, 300 acres given him by his father, John Taliaferro.

20. Gift of Robt. Taliaferro, sr., January 17, 1724, to his daughters, Ann and Elizabeth.

21. Deed, February 15, 1724, from Charles Taliaferro to his son Charles.

22. Deed, July 19, 1725, from John Taliaferro, of Stafford Co., to Robert Taliaferro, of Essex County.

23. Will of Lawrence Taliaferro, May 7, 1726.

24. Will of Robt. Taliaferro, dated December 3, 1725, probated June 26, 1726.

25. Will of Zachariah Taliaferro, dated February 1, 1721, probated May 21, 1745.

Refering to the number for authority, I present the following chart of the family:

A 1. ROBERT TALIAFERRO, emigrant, b. about 1635; d. about 1700; had 5 sons.

B 1. *Lawrence* (1, 2), eldest son, b. about 1670; d. 1710 (9), = Elizabeth Catlett (6), d. 1716 (14). It is probable they left no children, as John, the second son, seems to have transmitted the property.

2. *John Taliaferro*, Sheriff of Essex Co., Va., (5), b. about 1672; d. 1720, = Sarah Smith, daughter of Lawrence Smith (1). Issue:

C 1. Lawrence Taliaferro (13); d. 1726 (23).
2. John Taliaferro (16).
3. Zachariah Taliaferro (18); d. 1745 (25).
4. Robert Taliaferro (19).

B 3. *Richard Taliaferro* (1).
4. *Charles Taliaferro* (1), had one son, Charles (21).
5. *Robert Taliaferro* (12); d. 1726 (24), = Sarah Catlett, daughter of John Catlett (3). Issue:

C 1. Robert Taliaferro (the only son). (12, 17).
2. Ann Taliaferro (20).
3. Elizabeth (20).

(508) ANNE LEWIS MARSHALL—(Jones).

504 MARY MARSHALL, b. at "Oakhill," Fauquier Co., Va., March 25, 1816, d. January 3, 1878; = January, 1837, WILLIAM ARCHER, of Richmond, Va., b. 1814, d. 1847. Mr. Archer was a promising lawyer of Richmond, but died young.

506 FIELDING LEWIS MARSHALL, b. at "Oakhill," Fauquier Co., Va., March 29, 1819, living at Orange Court House, Va., = 1st, April 10, 1843, REBECCA F. COKE, b. October 26, 1824, d. April 20, 1862; = 2d, July 9, 1867, MARY N. THOMAS, b. August 9, 1842, living. Mr. Marshall was educated at the University of Virginia, and after taking his literary course, graduated in law. He never practiced, but went on his portion of the "Oakhill" estate, and farmed until the war broke out in April, 1861, when he was mustered in the service of the Confederacy, at Dumfries, as Orderly Sergeant of Company H., (Capt. J. A. Adams) of the Wise Dragoons, from Fauquier County, and assigned to the Sixth Regiment of Cavalry, under Col. C. W. Field; received his commission as First Lieutenant of Artillery, June, 1862, and put on ordiance duty at Lynchburg, Va., and continued in the service until the surrender in April, 1865. In 1869-70 and 71, he was a member of the Virginia House of Delegates, from Fauquier Co.; was a Henry Clay Whig from the first, and claims to be a Whig still. Mr. Marshall is a man of fine literary acquirements, superior judgment, unblemished honor, and acknowledged social position. Like his great progenitor, Col. Thomas Marshall, he has presented to his country fifteen worthy children, and the same number of grand children. All of them are industrious, frugal and self reliant. Perhaps it is a blessing that Mr. Marshall has not much to leave to his children but the good education he has given them. They know they must rely on their own efforts. His noble and generous spirit did not allow him to grasp nor to hoard. He is now teaching school for a support. For his first wife's family see the Lewis chart, No. 150 *l*.

508 ANNE LEWIS MARSHALL, b. at "Oakhill," Fauquier Co., Va., August 2, 1823, d. April 26, 1880; = January 2, 1845, JAMES FITZGERALD JONES, b. at "Vaucluse," near Winchester, Va., September 10, 1822; killed October 9, 1866. Mr. Jones was

(510) MARGARET L. MARSHALL.

a farmer and lived on part of the "Oakhill" estate. He served the Confederacy throughout the war, having been assigned to the nitre and mining department at Staunton. He was killed by a man whom he was denouncing for cowardice, in keeping out of danger during the war. He was of slender form; was highly esteemed for honor and probity, and his death was much lamented.

510 MARGARET L. MARSHALL. See No. 480.

512 COL. THOMAS MARSHALL, b. at "Oakhill," Fauquier Co., Va., January 17, 1836, d. in battle, November 12, 1864, = August 24, 1848, MARIA BARTON, b. near Winchester, Va., April 20, 1830, d. February 11, 1861. After receiving rudimentary instruction at various academies in Fauquier County, Thomas entered, 1845, the University of Virginia, and pursued the full course of that institution; studied law under the distinguished D. W. Barton, of Winchester, and married his daughter; settled at "Shady Oak," six miles from Winchester, and engaged in farming; in 1852 bought "Oakhill" of his brother, John, and the following year removed his family to the old homestead. Here he resided with his lovely wife until her death, February 11, 1861. His children were then removed to "Springdale," near Winchester, and placed under the tender care of their maternal grandmother. "Oakhill" from this time ceased to be the homestead of the Marshalls, yet belonged to Col. Thomas until his death, when it was sold, October 26, 1866, publicly by his administrator. Mr. Knight, of Maryland, purchased it. He sold it to Mr. Kefauver, who sold it to Mr. F. W. Maddux, the present gentlemanly proprietor.

Mr. Marshall was an ardent Whig, and a sincere patriot. He opposed secession with all his powers; but when his State seceded and coercion was attempted, he deliberately made up his mind to risk fortune, honor and life in defending the Confederacy, to which he owed allegiance. At the first trump of war he hastened to Harper's Ferry, and became the volunteer aide of Col. [Stonewall] Jackson, with the rank of Captain. At the battle of first Manassas his horse was killed. When Jackson was promoted to the rank of Major General, Captain Marshall deemed it his duty to resign. He

(512) COL. THOMAS MARSHALL.

then raised, in Frederick County, a cavalry company, and was assigned to Col. Ashby's command, and followed his beloved leader through all his heroic career. But when Col. Ashby's overgrown regiment was divided and reorganized into three regiments, Captain Marshall was chosen by the men to command the 12th regiment. But Gen. Jackson was not satisfied with the officers elected, and refused to commission them. He, however, gave Captain Marshall the position of Major of the 7th Cavalry.

At Orange C. H., in August, 1862, Major Marshall was severely wounded, taken prisoner and sent to Washington; was exchanged in September; returned to Winchester, and soon thereafter succeeded to the position of Lieutenant Colonel of the 7th Cavalry, under Col. Dulany. In March, 1863, Gen. Jones' brigade was ordered to make a raid into Western Virginia. This service was gallantly accomplished, and throughout nearly the whole campaign Col. Marshall was in command of the regiment. Early in the march, Col. Dulany had been severely wounded, and had to retire; in the spring of 1863, Jones' brigade participated in the repulse of Hooker on the Rappahannock. On the 9th of June, 1863, at the battle of Brandy Station, Col. Marshall's regiment did good service; at Gettysburg, he was in the thickest of the fray, and he lost another horse; during the fall and winter of 1863-64, Col. Marshall was with his regiment in the Valley of Virginia; Col. Dulany relieved him in the spring of 1864, and Lieut.-Col. Marshall resumed his position. At Trevillians, Col. Marshall lost another horse—the fifth that had fallen under him since the beginning of the war. When Gen. Rosser was wounded, and Col. Dulany took his place, Lieut.-Col. Marshall again succeeded to the command of the 7th regiment. As Grant advanced, the 7th regiment, under Col. Marshall, was sent South of the James River, and placed in front of Petersburg. In August, 1864, Col. Marshall was severely wounded in the shoulder, and was sent home. After spending a month in Winchester, the advance of the enemy required its evacuation, and Col. Marshall joined his regiment, though his wound was far from being healed. On the 12th of November, 1864, in an engagement near Winchester, he with several companions, became separated from the body of the regiment, and the enemy came upon them. Setting spurs to their horses, they dashed away amid a shower of balls. Col. Marshall was observed to sink in his saddle, and immediately his companions on each side sup-

(514) MARY AMBLER MARSHALL — (*Douthat*).

ported him in his position. After a few minutes he faintly said, "Put me down, boys, I am dying; save yourselves." These were his last words. The ball had passed through his heart. He was buried at the University, but after the war, was removed to Winchester, where he lies beside the Ashbys.

Col. Marshall was trained by pious parents and joined the army from religious motives. He served his God in serving his country. He has been compared to Havelock and to Gordon. He was eminently a man of prayer. His strong faith and humble deportment gave him a powerful influence among his men. On the field or in camp he sought opportunities for private devotion. His conversation and his writings showed an ever present trust in God. His children have inherited his piety, and I believe all of them are members of the Episcopal Church. They all venerate their father's memory and adore his God. For Mrs. Marshall's ancestry see No. 802. She was buried at Leeds' Church, and her epitaph reads:

> DIED at Oakhill, the residence of her husband, Thomas Marshall, in the thirty-first year of her age, Annie Maria Marshall, eldest daughter of David W. Barton. Lovely in every attribute of the Christain lady — sweet, gentle and guileless as a child — she was deeply loved by a large circle of relatives and friends. Timid by nature, death had no terrors. Her Savior was near, and right dearly did He answer her prayer.

514 MARY AMBLER MARSHALL, b. in Fauquier Co., Va., January 1, 1820, d. January 25, 1862, = August 1, 1841, ROBERT DOUTHAT, b. at Westover, on the James River, August 5, 1820, yet living. Mary was educated at the best schools in Richmond, making her home for the time with her grandfather, the Chief Justice. Mr. Douthat lost his father when eight years old; his mother had inherited "Weyanoke," ten miles distant, in Charles-City Co., and she removed there with her children. "Weyanoke" had belonged to the Lewis family for more than a hundred years, and here Mr. Douthat lived until 1875, when he sold out and removed to a farm in the same county, eight miles distant. He was a graduate of the Virginia University, and a gentleman of a high order of intelligence. His life has been devoted to farming. When the civil war broke out, he raised a cavalry company for the Confederacy, and was among the first in the field. He rose to the rank of Major in the service; was taken prisoner in 1863, and not exchanged for

(520) ANNA MARIA MARSHALL—(*Braxton*).

eighteen months. He is a man of firmness and determination, and Christian consistency. After his first wife's death, he married Miss B. M. Wade, daughter of Rev. Anderson Wade, of Charles-City Co., by his first wife. For Mr. Douthat's ancestry, see 150 *j*.

516   JACQUELIN AMBLER MARSHALL, b. at Prospect Hill, Fauquier Co., Va., February 9, 1829, = December 17, 1856, REBECCA PEYTON MARSHALL, his cousin, b. July 22, 1833. Mr. Marshall was educated at the Virginia Military Institute, at Lexington, having attended the years 1845 and 1846; was administrator of his fathers estate. In 1870, he removed to "The Crag," a farm of two hundred acres adjoining Markham, where he farms, and, during the summer months, takes city boarders. Mrs. Marshall is large, handsome, intelligent and genial.

518   ELIZA MARSHALL, b. 1827, d. 1868, = 1850, HARRISON ROBERTSON. They lived in Danville, Va. He has married again, and has removed to Baltimore.

520   ANNA MARIA MARSHALL, b. at Prospect Hill, Fauquier Co., Va., July 27, 1833, = November 23, 1854, ELLIOTT M. BRAXTON, b. in Mathews Co., Va., October 8, 1823. I met Mrs. Braxton in 1884, and found her a highly accomplished lady, of agreeable manners and literary taste. Her form is wasted by disease and her countenance indicates suffering; yet when lighted up by excitement, her face beams with intelligence, and her eyes sparkle with humor. Captain Braxton studied law at Richmond, in the office of Judge Daniel; practiced in Fredericksburg, where he now lives; represented King and Queen Co. in the House of Burgesses; was elected to the State Senate in 1851, and re-elected in 1853; was a Captain in the C. S. A., and assigned to the Q. M. department. Served to the close of the war; lost all of his property; resumed the practice of law in Fredericksburg, and recovered his losses; was elected a member of the Common Council of Fredericksburg in 1866; was elected to Congress as a Democrat from the Eighth District of Virginia, and served from March 4, 1871, to March 3, 1873.

(522) CAPT. WILLIAM MARSHALL.

Mrs. Braxton's patrimony, "Kilkenny," a farm of 510 acres in Fauquier, still belongs to her. Captain Braxton's parents were Carter M. Braxton and Maria Meuse.

522 CAPT. WILLIAM C. MARSHALL, b. at Prospect Hill, Fauquier Co., Va., April 17, 1838, = April 25, 1860, KATE EDLOE. At the beginning of the war he raised an artillery company, in Fauquier County, which did good service in Pickett's division. He participated in the battles of Williamsburg, Fredericksburg, Gettysburg, the fights about Richmond, the capture of Plymouth, the second Manassas, and at Petersburg. Near the latter place he was severely wounded by a minie ball striking and breaking his under jaw. He lives at "Cleaveland," his estate, six miles south of Markham, in Fauquier Co., Va. He has a store at "Crossroads," near his residence, and with the assistance of a few friends, he sustains what is called "Cleaveland High School," where a number of young men are prepared for a course in the State University.

Mrs. Marshall is a highly accomplished lady. Her parents were Henry Edloe and Elizabeth Travis, of Williamsburg, Va. She lost her father when she was an infant, and was raised by her mother among her kindred.

Capt. Marshall was a gallant and chivalrous officer, and is highly esteemed for his personal graces, his intellectual attainments and business qualifications. From my short association with him, I think he merits the title of "a splendid fellow," given him by a female admirer.

524 ELLEN H. MARSHALL, b. at Prospect Hill, Fauquier Co., Va., September 21, 1839, = September 27, 1859, Charles M. Barton, b. November 30, 1836; d. May 25, 1862. Mrs. Barton received a classical education under the tutorship of Prof. Armstrong, a graduate of Oxford, England, and her literary course was completed at Fredericksburg. She now lives at Markham. Lieut. Barton was educated at Winchester Academy, and the Episcopal High School near Alexandria; entered the Virginia Military Institute in 1853, and graduated July 4, 1856; settled on his father's farm near Winchester, and the same year united with the Episcopal

(530) ELLEN STROTHER HARVIE—(*Ruffin*).

Church. After marriage, removed to "Springdale," six miles from Winchester, on the road to Staunton. At the first call to arms, in April, 1861, he offered his services to the Confederacy, was appointed First Lieutenant, and duty assigned him as inspector of fortifications around Winchester; aided in the organization of Cutshaw's Battery. In these duties his military education was of great value. While defending Winchester and in pursuit of a retreating battery, he was killed. He was buried in the Winchester cemetery, and two brothers lie at his side. All fell in battle. See 2004.

326 MARY MARSHALL HARVIE, b. March 17, 1815; d. July 27, 1873. At the age of eighteen, she was paralyzed by a stroke of lightning, and her nervous system permanently deranged. Hers was a holy life of patience and suffering.

528 JOHN MARSHALL HARVIE, b. in Richmond, October 9, 1816; d. September 7, 1841. After graduating at West Point, and serving as Professor of Mathematics in the Academy for several months, he was at his own request appointed for active service in the Florida war, and at Cedar Keys fell a victim to the climate. It was a remark of Gen. Worth, his commanding officer, that "he was as brave as his sword."

530 ELLEN STROTHER HARVIE, b. in Richmond, Va., December 10, 1818, = March 27, 1860, COL. FRANK GILDART RUFFIN, b. in Woodville, Miss. He is a son of William Ruffin, son of an emigrant from Liverpool, who settled in Virginia and removed to Mississippi. Here William married Frances Gildart, who was the mother of Col. Ruffin. His parents dying before he was eight years of age, Frank G. came to Virginia, was educated at the State University, served the Confederacy in various departments at Richmond, and is now Second Auditor of the State of Virginia. He lost most of his property by the fall of Richmond, but still evinces his public spirit by taking an interest in and giving support to every laudable enterprise. Mrs. Ruffin's letters to me are charming epistolary compositions, and evince that piety so commendable in the Harvie family. They reside in Richmond and have no children.

(534) VIRGINIA HARVIE—(Patrick).

534 VIRGINIA HARVIE, b. in Richmond, Va., November 1, 1821, = June 15, 1852, DR. SPICER PATRICK, b. 1792, d. 1884. She lives at Forest Hill, near Charleston, W. Va. The letters of Mrs. Patrick lay bare a heart pure and holy. Dr. Spicer was born in New York. After taking his degree of medicine at the University of New York, he settled in Kanawha Co., Va. He served many terms in the Legislature at Richmond, and was a member of the convention that took the State out of the Union. He opposed secession as long as there was hope of defeating the measure. After the organization of the new State of West Virginia, he was chosen a member of the first House and elected speaker. As a statesman and physician he enjoyed the unbounded confidence of his patrons and constituents.

536 SUSAN COLSTON HARVIE, b. in Richmond, Va., October 7, 1824, = March 10, 1853, REV. ANDERSON WADE, d. 1880, in Prince Edwards Co., Va. Studied medicine in Philadelphia; settled in Henry Co., Va.; married a Miss Clarke, who was the mother of the second wife of Robert Douthat (514). Dr. Wade afterwards became a minister in the Episcopal Church. Mrs. Wade and her daughter reside in Richmond, Va.

538 WILLIAM WALLACE HARVIE, after serving in the Confederate army to the close of the war, went to Arkansas, where he died May 29, 1868.

540-42 EMILY H. HARVIE and ANNE FISHER HARVIE are living with their married sisters in Richmond, Va. See No. 600.

544 JOHN MARSHALL, b. at "Mt. Blanc," Fauquier Co., Va., April 7, 1821, d. July 10, 1872.

746 ASHTON ALEXANDER MARSHALL, b. at "Mt. Blanc," Fauquier Co., Va., April 23, 1824, d. February 23, 1861.

THE MARSHALL FAMILY. 209

(552) JOHN MARSHALL.

548 JAMES EDWARD MARSHALL, b. at "Mt. Blanc," Fauquier Co., Va., October 17, 1830, d. October 21, 1872, = March 4, 1856, MARY MORRIS MARSHALL, b. March 6, 1835, living at "Mt. Blanc." Mr. Marshall was educated at the University of Virginia; farmed at "Mt. Blanc," his patrimonial estate, until the war. In the fall of 1861 he entered Ashby's cavalry as adjutant; resigned after Ashby's death, but, after remaining idle for a few months, he joined Mosby's command of scouts, or irregular troops, and did good service until the end of the war. He then returned home and managed his farm successfully until his death. He was at the battles of Kernstown, Winchester, Cedar Mountain, second Manassas, and other bloody fields. I met Mrs. Marshall at "Mt. Blanc," in 1884, and have received several well written letters from her. She is possessed of not only intelligence, but independence, energy and firmness. She rules her household, educates her children, manages her farm and attends to her business affairs with diligence and success. Mr. Marshall was her third cousin. See No. 734.

550 MARY WILLIS MARSHALL, b. at "Mt. Blanc," Fauquier Co., March 30, 1834, = September 21, 1852, FIELDING LEWIS DOUTHAT, b. in Charles-City Co., Va., 1826, d. December 23, 1881. Mrs. Douthat's postoffice is Weyanoke Wharf, Charles-City Co., Va. For Mr. Donthat's ancestry, see No. 150 *j*. During the Mexican war Mr. Douthat was employed as Captain's Clerk on the Steamer "Mary," and cruised on the gulf. He then took charge of his farm in Charles-City County, and engaged in agriculture until the war of 1861, when he joined the cavalry company raised in his county and went to the Peninsula. At a later date he had charge of the Artillery at Mulberry Island. Near the close of the war he was taken prisoner and confined at Point Lookout until the surrender. See 550 *j*.

552 JOHN MARSHALL, b. at "Leeds," Fauquier Co., Va., October 9, 1822; d. at "Glendale," one mile north of Markham, February 1, 1877, = September 17, 1861, MILDRED PICKETT STRIBLING, b. February 22, 1823. Mr. Marshall graduated at Princeton College, studied law and practiced at Alexandria until the close of

(554) DR. NATHANIEL BURWELL MARSHALL.

the war, when he removed to "Glendale," his wife's estate. I visited Mrs. Marshall at "Glendale," in 1884, and found her a pleasant lady, living with her aged mother, and her own blooming daughter. Her two sons have tombstones in Leeds churchyard. See Pickett chart, 64 c.

554 DR. NATHANIEL BURWELL MARSHALL, b. in Fauquier Co., Va., March 16, 1824; d. in Louisville, Ky., May 22, 1861, = August 5, 1852, in Louisville, Ky., SALLIE MOORE EWING, a niece of the distinguished Finis Ewing; he graduated at Trinity College; received his medical education at Jefferson College, Philadelphia; settled in Cumberland, Md.; removed to Cincinnati, and practiced medicine several years; met Miss Ewing, who was a great beauty, in Louisville. After marriage his wife induced him to remove to Louisville; formed a partnerthip with her father, Dr. U. E. Ewing; after several years opened an office for himself; was a devoted member of the Episcopal Church, and Secretary of the Vestry of Christ's Church, Louisville. On his death, a prominent Louisville physician, in the *Medical Journal* wrote: "The list of worthies would be incomplete without the name of Dr. N. B. Marshall. That name, though so distinguished, was never borne more worthily than by this talented physician. Though he died young, he had already established an enviable reputation as a teacher and a practitioner." Dr. Marshall was Dean of the Kentucky School of Medicine, and Professor of Materia Medica and Therapeutics.

556 JAMES K. MARSHALL, b. at "Leeds," Fauquier Co., Va., April 7, 1826, = September 6, 1854, FANNIE AMRLER, b. at "Marven," Fauquier Co., Va., August 8, 1825. Mr. Marshall is a successful farmer, and a worthy citizen. He lives at "Marven," two miles south of Markham, which was the ancestral home of the Amblers. I called at the house in 1884, but the family were absent. See No. 776.

558 MARIA GALT MARSHALL was born at "Leeds," in Fauquier Co., Va., March 31, 1828, and still resides there. She is an intelligent and faithful member of Leeds Church.

(560) MARY AMBLER MARSHALL — (*Coleman*).

560 MARY AMBLER MARSHALL, b. at "Leeds," April 29, 1830; = August 2, 1855, LEWIS MINOR COLEMAN in Hanover Co., Va., February 3, 1827; d. at "Edgehill," Carolina Co., Va., March 21, 1863. In 1884, I spent a day at "Sunnyside," the residence of Mrs. Coleman, and was favorably impressed by the intelligence, courtesy and amiability of the family. Among her relatives she is regarded as a model manager, a lively and agreeable associate, and a sincere christian.

Col. Coleman received from his venerated mother his early moral sentiments and religious impressions. He was first sent to a private school at Beaver Dam, and subsequently he attended the academy of his uncle, Frederick Coleman, at Concord, Caroline Co., Va. In 1844, when Louis was seventeen, he entered the University of Virginia, and at nineteen graduated with the degree of A. M. On the 12th November, 1846, he united with the Baptist church at Richmond, Va. Having determined to devote his life to teaching, he became, by the invitation of his uncle, an assistant in Concord Academy. His wonderful proficiency as a disciplinarian, and his success as an educator, encouraged him to open a school of his own. Accordingly when Concord Academy was closed about 1854, he founded Hanover Academy, at Taylorsville, Va., and by firmness, perseverence and executive ability, as well as on account of his scholarship, the school flourished and his reputation was established. His christian fortitude and pious example had a happy influence on his pupils, and elicited their reverence and affection. In 1859 he was elected Professor of Latin in the University of Virginia, and Hanover Academy passed to his assistant, Professor Jones (568) who is still at its head. In the University, his scholarship and classical erudition added to the reputation of the institution. But in the midst of his useful labors, the tocsin of war aroused the nation to arms. His duty to his native state he regarded as imperative. His allegiance was due to Virginia, and not to the Union. An Artillery Company was in August, 1861, mustered into service of the Confederacy, with Capt. Coleman as its chief officer. With diligence he prepared himself to fill his new position, and drilled his men for service. His religious zeal never forsook him. His men were called morning and evening for religious services, under the leadership of their faithful commander. The effect was, that his men were heroes such as were led by Cromwell and Havelock.

(562) THOMAS MARSHALL.

Capt. Coleman's company was placed in Gen. Pendleton's division, and at Yorktown, the Peninsula, the battles around Richmond and on many other bloody fields in Virginia and Maryland, did valuable service for the South. At the reorganization of the army in 1862, Capt. Coleman was promoted to the rank of Major; and shortly afterward was elected Lieutenant Colonel of the First Virginia Artillery. He was with his regiment at Richmond, but had to retire to recruit his health. A short time before the battle of Fredericksburg, he resumed his place. On that bloody field he was wounded in the leg but not disabled. Yet the wound, which seemed but slight, proved mortal; and after ninety days of intense physical suffering, he found the peace of death at " Edgehill," Caroline Co., Va. Thus died a moral hero and martyr to conscientious duty — a scholar, soldier, patriot and christian. For the Coleman family see 184.

562 THOMAS MARSHALL, b. at "Leeds," Fauquier Co., Va., November 19, 1834, d. at Culpeper Court House, Va., September 1, 1861. He studied medicine and graduated at the Jefferson school at Philadelphia; entered the Confederate army as a Surgeon, and died from overwork. He was buried at Leeds Church. His epitaph states the dates of his birth and death, and concludes with the text: "I would not have you ignorant concerning them which are asleep, that ye sorrow not even as others, which have no hope."

564 ANN (NANNIE) BURWELL MARSHALL, b. at Leeds, Fauquier Co., Va., October 3, 1832, = June 1, 1854, REV. GEORGE HATLEY NORTON, D. D., of Alexandria, b. May 7, 1824. Dr. Norton is at present rector of St. Paul's Church, Alexandria. He was born in Ontario Co., N. Y.; graduated at the Theological Seminary of Virginia in July, 1846; rector of St. James' Church, Warrenton, Va., 1846–58; of Trinity Church, Columbus, Ohio, 1859; and of St. Paul's Church, Alexandria, to the present time. He received the degree of D. D. from William and Mary College. See Ambler family, 50 n.

THE MARSHALL FAMILY. 213

(568) CLAUDIA HAMILTON MARSHALL — (*Jones*).

THE NORTON FAMILY.
1. John Norton, of London, England.
2. John Norton, of Yorktown, Virginia.
3. George Hatley Norton, of Winchester, Va., = Catherine Bush. See Ambler chart, No. 50 *n*. She afterwards married John Ambler, and was mother of eight children. By her first husband she had:
    1. Dr. George Hatley Norton, = ANN B. MARSHALL.
    2. Dr. John Norton, of Louisville, Ky.

566 ALICE MARSHALL, b. at "Leeds," Fauquier Co., Va., May 16, 1837, = December 18, 1856, LIEUT. GRAY CARROLL, son of Gray Carroll, of Isle of Wight Co., Va., and Martha Ball, of Norfolk, Va. I did not meet Cousin Alice when I visited "Leeds." She is in delicate health and sees but little company. She owns the old homestead, "Leeds," seven miles south of Markham. She is highly esteemed for her virtues, and graces of person, mind and heart. Her letters show intelligence, tact and piety. Mr. Carroll taught school until the war, and then entered the Fauquier Artillery Company as a private, and rose to the rank of First Lieutenant. He is a large, handsome and intellectual gentleman, of pleasant address. No children.

568 CLAUDIA HAMILTON MARSHALL, b. at "Leeds," Fauquier Co., Va., February 7, 1839, = at "Leeds," August 5, 1861, COL. HILARY JONES, b. in Fluviana Co., Va., July 13, 1833; both living at Hanover Academy, Taylorsville, Va. Mrs. Jones was well educated and possesses the accomplishments that adorn the literary society in which she moves. She is said to be the best living likeness of her grandfather, Chief Justice John Marshall. Col. Jones was raised in Forestville, Albemarle County; entered the University of Virginia in 1853; graduated with the degree of M. A. in 1856; became assistant to his brother-in-law, Lewis M. Coleman, principal of Hanover Academy; continued in that capacity for three years; when Prof. Coleman was called to the chair of Latin in the University of Virginia, Mr. Jones purchased Hanover Academy;

(570) EDWARD CARRINGTON MARSHALL.

when the war of 1861 commenced, he entered the Confederate army as First Lieutenant of Artillery, and served through all the campaigns of the army of North Virginia; rose successively to the ranks of Major, Lieutenant Colonel and Colonel of Artillery; was appointed Brigadier General, but the war closed before the delivery of his commission; returned, after the surrender, to find his home despoiled by being used as a hospital. His wife remained in Fauquier during the war. His academy was reopened, and has demanded his attention up to this day. I have several letters from him, which give evidence of superior scholarship and profound judgment. Col. Jones is the son of Basil Jones and Lucy Timberlake, of Fluvianna Co., Va. His grandfather was Benj. Jones, of Rockville, Montgomery Co., Md., who was the First Lieutenant of a Maryland Company in the war of 1812. His grandmother was a Miss —— Magruder, of Prince George Co., Md. Col. Jones is a brother of Willie Jones (Marshall). No. 576.

570   EDWARD CARRINGTON MARSHALL, b. at "Leeds," Fauquier Co., Va., March 31, 1842, = February 23, 1865, ISABEL (BELLE) REANEY, b. September 2, 1845. They reside at "Millroy," five miles southeast of Leeds Church, in Fauquier Co., Va.

572   LIZZIE MARSHALL, b. at "Leeds," Fauquier Co., Va., October 9, 1844, and lives there.

574   REBECCA P. MARSHALL, b. at "Leeds," Fauquier Co., Va., November 5, 1847, = June 16, 1869, HENRY CLARKSON STRIBLING, b. October 4, 1836. They live at "Clairmont," five miles southwest of Markham, Fauquier Co., Va. He was a Lieutenant in the Thirty-eighth Battalion Virginia Artillery, and was assigned to Pickett's Division. Among his fellow officers were Capt. William C. Marshall (522), and Lieut. Gray Carroll. He participated in the battles of the Seven Pines, Frazier's Farm, Second Manassas, Fredericksburg, Burmudas Hundred, Cold Harbor, Get-

(580) REBECCA MARSHALL.

tysburg, and around Petersburg. "Clearmont" is a farm of 700 acres. The family, like all the relatives, are Episcopalians. For the genealogy of the Striblings and Clarksons, see Nos. 50 and 152.

576 JOHN MARSHALL, b. at Carrington, four miles south of Markham, Fauquier Co., Va., January 17, 1830, = 1st, February 18, 1854, LUCRETIA FITZHUGH. She died, and he = 2d, at Hanover Academy, Taylorsville, Va., WILLIE T. JONES, b. September 5, 1838. Mr. Marshall was educated at the Episcopal High School, near Alexandria, and at the State University. In 1862, he enlisted in the Confederate army, was assigned to the Nitre and Mining department, and was employed in the manufacture of saltpetre at Staunton, under his cousin, Major J. F. Jones (806). In this service he continued until the end of the war. He is living at "Bergen," a farm of 365 acres, one mile north of Markham. With my daughter, I enjoyed his hospitality in 1884, and have had several letters from him. I admire him for his sound judgment, practical views, liberal sentiments, conservative politics, conscientious deportment and religious convictions. He is a man of general information and fine literary attainments. His first wife was a daughter of Norman Fitzhugh and Miss Vowell. His present wife is a sister of Prof. Hilary Jones, of Hanover Academy, and daughter of Basil Jones and Lucy Timberlake. See No. 568. She was raised in Forestville, Albemarle Co.; educated at Piedmont Female Academy. She is a classical scholar, and an accomplished lady. She attends Leeds Church and leads the choir.

578 MARY LEWIS MARSHALL, b. at "Carrington," Fauquier Co., Va., May 16, 1831; resides at "Innis" with her mother and sister Courtenay. She is an amiable and highly accomplished lady, with those domestic traits that make her useful and beloved. I am indebted to her for personal attentions and much assistance in my heraldic work.

580 REBECCA PEYTON MARSHALL. See No. 516.

(582) EDWARD CARRINGTON MARSHALL.

582 EDWARD CARRINGTON MARSHALL, b. at "Carrington," Fauquier Co., Va., March 26, 1835, = December 16, 1856, VIRGINIA E. TAYLOR, b. 1835, dr. of Samuel Taylor and Eliza Smith. Edward was educated by his learned father, at home, and by tutors. He also attended the school of Benjamin Hallowell, in Alexandria. Having chosen the mercantile business, he served as a clerk for three years in Baltimore, and sold goods three years in Markham. He then removed to Berryville, Va., and continued the mercantile business until 1880, when he removed to Kansas City, Mo., where he is engaged in the produce and commission business with good success. He is an agreeable gentleman, an interesting conversationalist, and a superior business man. Mrs. Marshall is a pleasant and graceful matron, domestic in her habits, and possessed of a gentle and loving spirit. Her father was a physician, and came from Maryland to Clarke Co., Va. He married Eliza Smith, a relative of the Amblers. Mrs. Marshall was raised near Winchester. The family are Episcopalians.

584 COL. JAMES KEITH MARSHALL, b. at "Carrington," Fauquier Co., Va., April 16, 1839, killed at the battle of Gettysburg, July 3, 1863. He graduated with honor at the Lexington Military Institute July 4, 1860; went to North Carolina and taught in the family of Dr. Warren, of Edenton. When the war broke out, he raised a company for the Confederacy, and by his achievements gained quite a reputation. On the reorganization of the army, he was chosen Colonel of the 52d N. C. regiment, and was assigned to Pettigrew's brigade. Here his sagacity and courage were displayed in resisting the advance of the Federal gunboats upon Norfolk. With the Southern army he was at Gettysburg, and in the charge on Cemetery Hill he received two balls in his forehead, causing his immediate death. His body was never recovered. His servant brought home his horse, papers and clothing. Every effort was made to recover his body, but in the heaps of the dead his form was never recognized. He was in his manner quiet and retiring, and yet distinguished for sound judgment in council and intrepidity in battle. He was the senior Colonel under Gen. Pettigrew, and at one time was in command of the brigade.

THE MARSHALL FAMILY. 217

(590) COURTENAY NORTON MARSHALL—(*Marshall*).

586 ELIZABETH (BETTIE) LEWIS MARSHALL, b. at "Carrington," June 10, 1841, = November 10, 1863, WILLOUGHBY NEWTON, b. in Westmoreland Co., Va., about 1836. She was educated at Mr. Powell's Female School in Richmond, Va. Until her beauty was marred by disease, she was much admired. She is still a lovely woman of quiet, calm and dignified demeanor. She is a lively and interesting companion. Mr. Newton is a highly respected citizen of Westmoreland Co., Va. For the Newtons see the Brockenbrough chart No. 162 *e*.

588 DR. JACQUELIN AMBLER MARSHALL. See No, 1322.

590 COURTENAY NORTON MARSHALL, b. at Carrington, Fauquier Co., Va., February 15, 1847, = December 5, 1866, her second cousin, THOMAS MARSHALL, (736), b. at "Fairfield," Fauquier Co., Va., August 29, 1842. Cousin Courtenay is as sweet as her name. It is not beauty that makes her interesting, but her modest and respectful demeanor and her soul speaking eyes. One would select her out of a thousand strangers, and claim her as a long lost sister. When I visited "Innis," in 1884, I felt at home before I was seated. The family knows how to make one feel welcome. Mr. Marshall is a pleasant and sensible gentleman, modest, unassuming and social. He received instruction from tutors at home, and was sent successively to Clifton High School, Mr. Harrison's school, and Charlottesville Military Institute. When a mere youth he entered Ashby's Cavalry, and fought through the war; was wounded in the fight in the Wilderness, by a ball that struck his forehead and glanced off without breaking the skull. It is almost a miracle that he was not killed, and the boys jestingly say that the ball was flattened to the thickness of a knife blade. His duties during the war were assigned him chiefly in the adjutant's office, for which position he was well qualified. Cousin Tom is a genial and generous friend. I owe him for the use of a horse while in Fauquier.

(594) ELIZABETH M. COLSTON — (*Williams*).

594 ELIZABETH M. COLSTON, b. in Richmond, Va., October 24, 1827, = May, 1849, MAJ. ROBT. A. WILLIAMS, b. August, 1823, in Richmond, Va. Mr. Williams is a merchant in Baltimore. He served the confederacy in the war of the States. He is a son of John Williams, an emigrant from London. His mother was a Miss Dandridge, of New Kent Co., Va., a relative of Martha Dandridge (Custis) Washington.

598 MARY W. COLSTON, b. February, 1832, = October 24, 1854, LIEUT. WILLIAM LEIGH. Both are living at "Maidstone," Berkeley Co., Va. Lieut. Leigh was educated for the Navy, and served several years, but resigned, and now lives the life of a farmer. His literary acquirements, and varied experience make him a pleasant companion. He married first Gabriella B. Wickham, who died childless.

600 CAPT. RALEIGH THOMAS COLSTON, b. at Richmond, Va., at the house of his grand mother, Mrs. Brockenbrough, February 18, 1834, d. December 23, 1863, from the effects of a wound received at the battle of Mine Run. He was educated at the Episcopal High School, near Alexandria; entered the Military Institute, at Lexington, Va., in 1850; returned home to assist his mother in the management of his father's estate. When the war broke out he enlisted in Company E., Second Virginia Infantry, under Col. Jackson; fought in the battle of the first Manassas, Kernstown, McDowell, Front Royall, Winchester, Cross Keys, Port Republic, seven days around Richmond, Cedar Mountain, Second Manassas, Fredericksburg, Chancellorsville and Mine Run. On the battlefield of Cold Harbor, Capt. Colston was struck on the thigh by a spent shell, which bruised the flesh and disabled him for some days. In the winter of 1862–63, he was commissioned Lieutenant Colonel, of the Second Virginia Infantry. At Mine Run, November 27, 1863, his left leg was shattered by the parting shot of an opposing battery, and amputation of the limb was necessary. He was conveyed to the house of his relative, Prof. John B. Minor,

(610) DR. JOHN HANSON THOMAS.

and his mother's family summoned. With them came one (542) even more tenderly loved, to whom he was betrothed, and who even yet weeps over his untimely end. He was buried Christmas day, 1863, according to the rites of the Episcopal church.

602 WILLIAM BROCKENBROUGH COLSTON, b. at "Honeywood," Berkeley Co., W. Va., April 25, 1836, = MARIAN SUMMERS, daughter of Dr. R. Summer's of Martinsburg, W. Va., April 18, 1866. Mr. Colston's education was liberal; he was an officer in the C. S. A., and is now a magistrate, commissioner in Chancery, and editor of the Martinsburg *Statesman*.

604 ANNIE COLSTON, b. at "Honeywood," Berkeley Co., W. Va., December 25, 1838. She lives with her mother at Martinsburg, W. Va.

606 LUCY COLSTON, b. at "Honeywood," March 9, 1842, = June 19, 1866, Col. Bennett Taylor, of Albemarle Co., Va.

608 EDWARD COLSTON, b. at "Honeywood," April 22, 1844, = 1875, S. C. STEVENSON, daughter of Hon. J. W. Stevenson, Member of Congress, 1857-61; Governor of Kentucky 1868-1871 and United States Senator 1871-77. Mr. Colston entered the C. S. A., at the age of seventeen, and served in Wickham's Brigade; lost his left arm in a skirmish at the Long Bridge, Appomatox County in 1865; was taken prisoner and confined until the surrender; returned to Berkeley County; studied law at home, and with his uncle, Judge J. W. Brockenbrough, in Lexington, Va.; went to Cincinnati, O., 1869, and is now practicing law as one of the distinguished firm of Hoadly, Johnson & Colston. No living children.

610 DR. JOHN HANSON THOMAS, b. in Frederick, Md., September 23, 1813; d. at the White Sulphur Springs, in Virginia, July 15, 1881, = November 15, 1837, ANNIE CAMPBELL GORDON,

(610) DR. JOHN HANSON THOMAS.

of Falmouth, Va., b. October 29, 1819. Dr. Thomas lost his father in his infancy, and was reared by his excellent mother. He graduated at the University of Virginia, and came to Baltimore to reside, September 23, 1834. Here he pursued the study of medicine under Dr. Ashton Alexander. After receiving his diploma from the University of Maryland, he was appointed resident physician of the Baltimore Infirmary, which afforded peculiar opportunities for the acquisition of surgery. In 1841, he relinquished the practice of medicine to accept the Presidency of the Farmers' & Mechanics' Bank. For thirty years he held this position, with credit to himself and profit to the stockholders. On one occasion, during unusual stress, when disaster overtook many financial institutions, he pledged a large part of his private securities for the benefit of the Bank, thereby placing it in a position of safety. In 1867, he was appointed by the Governor of Maryland as State's Agent for the negotiation of loans, and payment of interest on the public debt. This position he held for twelve years. But in 1879, failing health compelled him to resign his public offices.

Dr. Thomas was an ardent Whig, and in 1852, was Chairman of the State Central Committee of his party. In 1855, he was elected a member of the City Council, and in 1861, was appointed one of the Committee to attend the Peace Conference which met at Richmond. At the election, April 24, 1861, he was chosen to represent the city of Baltimore in the State Legislature, with a view of determining the question of secession. The ordinance was not passed; yet Dr. Thomas, and other leading citizens were arrested by military order, at midnight, and confined at Fortress Monroe, and thence removed to Fort Lafayette. After six months imprisonment, he was released on parole. This outrage only strengthened his sympathy with the South. A local paper in announcing the death of Dr. Thomas, said:

"Yesterday the tidings of Dr. John Hanson Thomas' death were received with great sorrow at the Maryland Club. The members in subdued voices dwelt, with melancholy pleasure, over the merits of the deceased. They spoke of his gentle manners, yet knightly bearing,— of his tender kindness, yet unfaltering firmness and devotion to duty, — of his sterling integrity, his unblemished reputation, his benevolence, and those other traits that distinguished him through life. In commercial circles there was but one general expression of sorrow, and in social circles it was felt that Baltimore had lost one of her first citizens. Few have lived more beloved and respected, and few have died more regretted."

(614) MARY SUSAN LEIGH — (*Robinson*).

Mrs. Thomas is a daughter of Basil Gordon and Annie Campbell Knox, of Falmouth. Her palatial residence on Mt. Vernon Place, Baltimore, is still the scene of continuous generous hospitality. She is possessed of literary accomplishments, as her letters to me attest. When in Baltimore in 1884, my sickness prevented me from forming her personal acquaintance. During the war she evinced great interest in the Confederate prisoners, and the sufferings of hundreds of them were alleviated through her generous liberality.

612 WILLIAM LEIGH. See No. 598.

614 MARY SUSAN LEIGH, b. in Richmond, Va., July 25, 1816, = July 14, 1836, JUDGE CONWAY ROBINSON, b. September 15, 1805, d. January 30, 1884.

Mrs. Robinson was born, reared and married in Richmond, and now lives at her residence, adjoining the "Soldiers' Home," near Washington, D. C. Her children live with her. Though weighted down by cares and bereavements, her letters to me are full of hope and cheerfulness. Two of her darling boys were patriotic offerings on Virginia's bloody fields, and the husband of her youth, with whom she lived for nearly a half century, has gone to his reward, leaving her in widowed loneliness.

Judge Robinson's name is familiar to every Virginian. For many years he was an honored member of the Richmond bar. In 1858, he removed to Washington, and the last twenty-five years of his life were spent in practicing in the Supreme Court, and in writing the numerous books of both English and American law, that bear his name. His life was one of untiring literary labor. When only twenty-one years of age, he published his "Forms Adapted to the Practice in Virginia," in one volume, which was afterwards enlarged to three. In 1842-44, he published two volumes of Virginia Reports. He made some important contributions to the Virginia Historical Society. In 1849, he, with I. M. Patton, revised the Virginia Code. Between the years 1854 and 1874, he wrote his great work, "Robinson's Practice," embracing in seven volumes, the jurisprudence of England and America. It is a whole law library in

(616) RALEIGH COLSTON.

itself. But Mr. Robinson's book making did not end with this great work, for the venerable author, in 1882, issued the first volume of his "History of the High Court of Chancery and other Institutions of England," 1,215 pages. I have not learned whether this work will be completed or not from his notes. In January, 1884, Mr. Robinson visited Philadelphia, and, while there, died of pneumonia, at the house of a brother. Since the death of Marshall, Story and Kent, the world has not produced a jurist superior to Conway Robinson.

616 RALEIGH COLSTON, b. in Fauquier Co., Va., March 13, 1821, = May 25, 1845, GERTRUDE POWELL, daughter of Humphrey B. Powell, of Loudown Co., Va., and a sister of the wife of J. Randolph Tucker. Mr. Colston is now in the department of the State Treasurer at Richmond, Va. He is an exemplary citizen, officer and Christian, and highly esteemed for honor, diligence and faithfulness. His letters indicate a gentleman of superior literary acquirements.

618 ANNIE FISHER COLSTON, b. in Fauquier Co., Va., January 3, 1827, d. at the University of Virginia, September 23, 1883, = March 12, 1859, PROF. JOHN B. MINOR, of the University of Virginia. One who knew Mrs. Minor well writes: "She was one of the purest and most exemplary of wives and mothers." The position of Prof. Minor is sufficient evidence of his literary attainments. As an apology for this short notice, I must state that he and his friends did not reply to my letters.

620 SUSAN L. COLSTON, b. in Fauquier Co., Va., February, 1835, = January, 1856, CHAS. M. BLACKFORD, a prominent lawyer of Lynchburg, Va.

622 MARIE JULIA COLSTON, b. at Glasgow, Scotland, February 10, 1848, = —— RODGERS.

(630) ELIZA COLSTON MARSHALL—(*Grant*).

624 ALICE COLSTON, b. March 27, 1857.

626 EMILY MARSHALL, b. in Lewis Co., Ky., November 8, 1821, d. September 18, 1859, = December 19, 1844, CHARLES M. FLEMING. Cousin Emily and I were children together. She was an amiable, slender and beautiful girl. I never met her after her marriage. She was educated and refined, and was generally beloved. Mr. Fleming lived a few miles from Flemingsburg. Educated for law, he has spent his life on his farm. He has married again.

628 FANNIE ANNE MARSHALL, b. in Lewis Co., Ky., Jan. 9, 1825; d. in Mason Co., Ky., April 29, 1863, = September 9, 1845, DR. ADDISON DIMMITT, of Mason Co., Ky., b. May 4, 1822, d. March 30, 1865. Cousin Fannie was a pure and true little woman, but exceedingly nervous and irritable. Shortly after her marriage she united with the Lewisburg Baptist church, under the preaching of Elder Gilbert Mason; and she continued a zealous and useful member until her death. She was brilliant in conversation, passionate in her temper, and indomitable in her will. Her heart was full of sympathy, and her hand was liberal in alms. Her children almost idolize her memory, and all who enjoyed her friendship praise her. Her feelings were never concealed. In the war she was enthusiastic for the South.

Dr. Dimmitt was a son of James Dimmitt and Elizabeth Ramey. He read medicine with Duke & Shackelford, in Maysville, Ky.; graduated at the University of Pennsylavania; attended for eighteen months the hospital at Philadelphia; settled after marriage, at Lewisburg, Mason Co., Ky., and here as a beloved and honored physician his useful life was spent. In the war he was at first for the union, but his Southern blood soon brought him in sympathy with the Confederacy. His second wife was Mrs. Laura Everett, *nee* Chenoweth. She survives him, and, with her son, Addison Dimmitt, lives in Maysville, Ky.

630 ELIZA COLSTON MARSHALL, b. in Lewis Co., Ky., November 27, 1827, = November 27, 1851, MAJ. NOAH GRANT, b. in Maysville, Ky., April 1, 1824, d. in New Orleans, October 4,

(632) JULIANNA WHETCROFT MARSHALL—(*Bland*).

1867, of yellow fever. He was a farmer until the war broke out; entered the Confederate service and rose to the rank of Major; went to New Orleans when peace returned, and was a member of the house of Jewett Norton & Co. Cousin Eliza now lives at Canton, Mo., and is sorely afflicted with cancer in the breast. I knew her only as a child, but have often heard her praised.

632 JULIANNA WHETCROFT MARSHALL, b. in Lewis Co., Ky., July 14, 1832, d. of cancer in the breast, at Quincy, Ill., June 30, 1884; buried at Maysville, Ky., beside her mother, = November 6, 1855, CAPT. BENJ. BLAND, of New Orleans, b. in Maysville, Ky., October 2, 1821, d. June 24, 1864. Cousin Julianna possessed beauty and intelligence; was firm, resolute and determined; of strong sympathies and aversions. I have several finely written letters from her, from which, in the notice of her father, I have quoted (176). Capt. Bland's grandfather was a Virginian, who married Margaret Jones. His parents were Benj. Bland, sr., and Mary Rolfe. Capt. Bland served the Confederacy under Gen. Kirby Smith. He was a merchant. Six children were born to him, but all died in infancy.

634 FRANCIS MARSHALL, b. in Mason Co., Ky., March 7, 1819, d. February 25, 1840, = 1838, FRANK T. CHAMBERS, 1818—60. Cousin Fannie was a fair and lovely girl. From the age of fifteen she suffered from dyspepsia, which made her form and features angelic. She was only five days younger than I. As I received the fostering care of her mother, so she was cherished by my step-mother. Therefore we were companions throughout our early lives. She died soon after marriage, leaving an only son. Frank Chambers was a lawyer, and was regarded as one of the most promising young men in the State of Kentucky. He was uncommonly handsome, a chaste and eloquent speaker, and an intelligent and interesting companion. His life was short, yet he was married three times. His second wife was ELIZABETH DURRETT, and his third, a MISS FELEGAR. His last years were spent in Cincinnati. He became intemperate before he died. His parents were Gov. John Chambers, 1779—1852, and Hannah Taylor.

(642) LUCY AMBLER MARSHALL—(*Casey*).

636 DR. ALEXANDER KEITH MARSHALL, b. in Mason Co., Ky., January 21, 1822; d. 1882, = 1st, October 30, 1845, ELIZA ADAMS; d. February 9, 1876, = 2d, MARIA LOUISE MARSHALL, b. in Augusta, Ky., September 12, 1842 *l*. Cousin Aleck received a good literary and professional education, but he practiced but little. He was a fine manager, handsome, agreeable and wealthy. Having no children, and nothing to stir his energies, he took the world leisurely, and lived like a gentleman. He was reared in Mason County; after marriage, settled in Fleming; removed to Maysville, and finally went to his farm near Washington, and there died. His large estate went to his brothers and sisters, and to his widow. His first wife was a daughter of Gilbert Adams, by his first wife (216), and his second wife was a daughter of Hon. Thornton Marshall, of Augusta (368). She is now residing with her parents.

638 JOHN MARSHALL, b. in Mason Co., Ky., March 15, 1830. He now lives near Washington, Ky., and is a good, intelligent, social old gentleman, and a confirmed old bachelor. People all like him for his agreeable peculiarities.

640 MOLLIE McDOWELL MARSHALL, b. December 31, 1827, in Mason Co., Ky. She lives with her brother John (638). She is much loved for her gentle and affectionate disposition, and generous and noble heart.

642 LUCY AMBLER MARSHALL, b. in Mason Co., Ky., in 1832, = in April, 1851, COL. JAMES B. CASEY, b. November, 1829. Cousin Lucy is a handsome, intelligent, stately and dignified woman. She was only three years old when her mother died. She found a home with her aunt, Mrs. Green (180), in Danville. She was a haughty little lady, when four years old, and the pet of the family. She would sit up in the parlor and entertain company with her well considered opinions on every topic. I met her at her hospitable home, in Covington, in 1884, and found her still dignified, courteous and kind. Col. Casey is a handsome, lively and cordial gentleman. He served as a Lieutenant of a volunteer company in

(644) JAMES MARSHALL.

the Mexican war; was a dry goods merchant when married. In 1861, he engaged in the manufacture of tobacco in Covington, and prospered until the close of the war. He then opened a large tobacco warehouse in Cincinnati. In 1871 to 1873, he represented Kenton County in the Kentucky Legislature. He is now tobacco inspector of the city of Cincinnati, but lives in Covington.

644 JAMES MARSHALL, b. in Mason Co., Ky., January 17, 1835, = May 15, 1862, SUE ALLEN, b. in Mason Co., August 28, 1842. Cousin James was only a week old when his mother died. He was raised by his aunt, and my sister, Mrs. P. A. Marshall (188). Before marriage he came to Platte Co., Mo., and purchased a farm. After a few years, he returned, and now cultivates a farm near Washington, Ky. Cousin Sue has no children, but is the mother of all the boys and girls she can gather about her. She is a kind-hearted and whole-souled matron, that everybody loves.

648 THOMAS MARSHALL GREEN, b. at "Waveland," near Danville, Ky., March 12, 1837, = April 27, 1860, ANNE E. BUTLER, b. July 20, 1840, d. June 11, 1881; = 2d, April 17, 1883, PATTIE E. CRAIG, b. April 7, 1839, in Lincoln Co., Ky. They now live at "Anchorage," Maysville, Ky., and he edits the Maysville *Eagle*. Col. Green has been hard of hearing since his infancy. His native talents, superior education, sound practical judgment, extensive reading and almost universal information, with fearless independence and sacred regard for truth, give him a wonderful power and influence. His respect for justice and honor, and the calls of friendship and patriotism, have often led him into controversy, and in every contest he has proved himself an intellectual giant. During the war, his fearless denunciation of every wrong, and his intrepid advocacy of what was right, were only equalled by the success with which he was rewarded. He was a decided Union man, and freely expressed his convictions, whether they suited those in power or not. Though a Democrat and an editor, he has always thought for himself. He cares not for the party lash, but sustains the cause and the candidate he approves. Familiar with the history of Kentucky, and

(650) JOHN DUFF GREEN.

with the lives, principles and lineages of the leading men of his State, his positions are generally impregnable, and his facts irresistable. But deafness curbs his ambition—drives him from the stump and the forum—and leaves him his pen as his only weapon. As an essayist, he is equalled by few. His style is chaste, his diction clear and his logic powerful. He masters every subject he touches, and few have the temerity to contradict him.

Mr. Green was educated at Center College, edited the Frankfort *Commonwealth*, 1857-60; has since edited the Maysville *Eagle;* ran as a Union man for Congress in 1866; and in 1868, was chosen an elector for Seymour. See Green Chart, 180 *j*.

THE BUTLER FAMILY.

Thomas Butler, of Ireland, emigrant, = Eleanor Parker. Issue:
1. Maj.-Gen. Richard Butler, killed at St. Clair's defeat.
2. Col. William Butler, of the Revolutionary war.
3. Maj. Thomas Butler, of the Revolutionary war.
4. Capt. Pierce Butler, = Mildred Hawkins. Issue:
    1. Gen. William O. Butler, = Eliza Todd, dr. of Gen. Robert Todd.
    2. Maj. Thomas Butler, = his cousin, Miss Hawkins.
    3. Richard Butler, = 1st, Miss Bullock; = 2d, a dr. of Dr. Blythe, of Hanover College.
    4. Pierce Butler, = Eliza Sarah Allen, dr. of Col. John Allen, who fell at the Raisin; and Jane Logan, dr. of Gen. Ben. Logan. Their daughter
        1. Ann Eliza Butler, = COL. T. M. GREEN. No. 648.
    5. Col. Edward Butler, of U. S. A.

650 JOHN DUFF GREEN, was born near Danville, Ky., March 12, 1839, = in 1862, to ILLA TRIPLETT, dr. of Hon. Philip Triplett, twice a member of Congress from the Owenboro District of Kentucky. Her mother was a dr. of Gen. Samuel Hopkins, of Henderson. She died in Danville, ten weeks after marriage. Mr. Green was educated at Center College, Kentucky, and is now practicing law in St. Louis.

(652) FANNIE MARSHALL—(*Maltby*).

652 FANNIE MARSHALL, b. in Cincinnati, Ohio, July 23, 1820; d. in Northampton, Mass., August 22, 1883, = June 25, 1840, LAFAYETTE MALTBY, b. in Oswego Co., N. Y., August 11, 1819. Both were my associates in early life, but upon their marriage we were separated to meet no more. After Mr. Maltby's literary education, he studied law at Utica, N. Y. About 1827, he came to Fleming Co., Ky., and became a tutor in the family of Martin P. Marshall (234). In 1839, he entered on the practice of law in Vicksburg, Miss., in partnership with N. D. Coleman (184). In 1840, he purchased an interest in the wholesale grocery house of Paxton & Keys. Until 1859, Mr. Maltby continued the traveling and purchasing partner of his Cincinnati house, residing at times in New Orleans and elsewhere. He then sold out, and removed to Northampton, Mass. Here in 1865, he assumed control of a Savings' Bank, whose deposits now amount, under his judicious management, to over $2,000,000. He is a moderate Republican, and voted for Cleveland. He is a man of thought, judgment, spirit and ambition. He belongs to the Congregational Church. His health is failing. His lineage:

1. Timothy Maltby, of Conn., = Mabel Dimmock.
   2. Anson Maltby, of Conn., = Electa Duncan, of Vermont, dr. of Samuel Duncan and Patience Choate, of Mass.
      3. Lafayette Maltby, = FANNIE MARSHALL.

654 CHARLES MARSHALL, b. at "Belle Grove," Fleming Co., Ky., March 1, 1825, = November 22, 1854, JANE TAYLOR, b. March 3, 1823, dr. of ROBERT TAYLOR and Sarah Dewees. Mr. Marshall has spent his life in the house where he was born. When his father left "Belle Grove," Charles purchased the estate, which consists of eleven hundred acres. He started a dairy, and did a large business in cheese, shipping it, in great quantities to the South. The war broke up his business, and he has since been rearing stock. He is a pushing, thriving farmer, rough and boisterous in his manner, and overbearing in his conduct; but his sound judgment and integrity are undoubted. He is growing in wealth and influence yearly. Mrs. Marshall is a worthy matron, of superior education and native grace and purity.

THE MARSHALL FAMILY.   229

(660) ROBERT MORRIS MARSHALL.

656 LUCY PICKETT MARSHALL, b. at "Belle Grove," Fleming Co., Ky., July 20, 1827; d. 1881, at Washington, Ky., = October 19, 1848, LOGAN MCKNIGHT, son of Virgil McKnight, of Louisville, Ky. Mr. McKnight was a young lawyer of fine attainments, but died at an early age. Cousin Lucy was possessed of fine accomplishments, but was more remarkable for her childlike amiability and angelic purity.

658 MARY W. MARSHALL, b. at "Belle Grove," Fleming Co., Ky., July 22, 1829. Her father, by his will, gave her the old Marshall homestead, in Washington, known as "The Hill," and there her pure and generous heart overflows with charity and hospitality.

660 (a) ROBERT MORRIS MARSHALL, b. at "Belle Grove," Fleming Co., Ky., February 10, 1832, = May 21, 1856, ELIZABETH FORMAN. After receiving the instruction of tutors at home, and attending the private school of his uncle, Dr. Louis Marshall, Robert graduated at Yale College. He studied law with Hon. Harrison Taylor, in Maysville, Ky., and was licensed in 1853. After practicing for fifteen months in Maysville, he went to Rock Island, Ill., and practiced for five years successfully. In 1860, he returned to Mason Co., Ky., and settled on his farm of 600 acres, near Sardis, on the line of Mason and Robertson Counties, where he now lives, and where I visited him in 1884. His natural abilities and finished education make him an interesting gentleman. Failing health was the cause of his giving up the practice of law.

(b)   THE FORMAN FAMILY.

The Formans came from Monmouth Co., N. J., where they are still numerous. The Kentucky branch came from two brothers, 1, Ezekiel Forman, and 2, John Forman.

A 1. EZEKIEL FORMAN, = Elizabeth Wyckoff.

B 1. *Thomas Forman*, = Jane Throckmorton, his cousin, (below).

   2. *Mrs. Scudder*, mother of Dr. Chas. Scudder.

230   THE MARSHALL FAMILY.

(660) ROBERT MORRIS MARSHALL.

A 2. JOHN FORMAN, = Jane Seabrooke.

B   1. *Mary Forman,* = Joseph Throckmorton.

C (c)   1. Jane Throckmorton, b. January 22, 1750, d. November 24, 1812, = in New Jersey, Thomas Forman, b. December 18, 1740, d. in Mason Co., Ky., about 1825.

D   1. Ezekiel Forman, b. in New Jersey, September 9, 1770, d. in Mason Co., Ky., April 26, 1836, = in Mason, February 18, 1808, Dolly Wood, b. December 14, 1786, d. May 4, 1872.

2. Mary Forman, b. December 11, 1772, = May 29, 1794, George Lewis, b. December 25, 1763, d. 1800; son of Isaac Lewis, of Delaware.

(d)   3. Joseph Forman, b. in New Jersey, February 7, 1775, d. March 7, 1844, = Mary Dye, b. March 12, 1777, d. August 24, 1835; dr. of Wm. Dye and Phebe Monteer.

4. John Forman (twin), b. February 7, 1775.

5. Samuel Forman, b. August 20, 1778, d. January 4, 1833, = Margaret Smith.

(e) THE FAMILY OF EZEKIEL FORMAN AND DOLLY WOOD, 12 CH.

A 1. THOMAS SEABROOKE FORMAN, b. in Mason Co., Ky., November 9, 1808, d. in Louisville, Ky., June 24, 1849, = October, 1835, Mary Ann Brown, d. July 20, 1850. Issue:

B   1. *Sarah P. Forman,* b. April. 2, 1837, = November 22, 1855, Wm. J. Anderson. Children.

(f)   2. *Ezekiel S. Forman,* b. February 25, 1839, d. April 28, 1867.

3. *Col. Jas. B. Forman,* b. December 12, 1842, d. December 31, 1862.

4. *George,* b. August 7, 1844, = October 13, 1864, Hannah M. Bartley.

5. *Mary Ann Forman,* b. January 11, 1847, d. May 2, 1884, = February 2, 1864, Wm. T. Hamilton.

THE MARSHALL FAMILY. 231

(660) ROBERT MORRIS MARSHALL.

A 2. ELIZABETH FORMAN, b. December 25, 1809, living,= May 7, 1829, Robert Taylor, b. March 4, 1806, d. September 2, 1852.

B
1. *Jennie Taylor*, b. November 15, 1831,= March 1, 1854, Robert Taylor (cousin).
2. *Mary Taylor*, b. April 26, 1833, = April 5, 1866, Rev. Robert Caldwell.
(g) 3. *Sarah Tarlor*, b. July 9, 1838, living.
4. *Nannie Taylor*, b. March 30, 1840, = January 14, 1863,
(c) Richard Durrett.
5. *Robert Taylor*, b. August 6, 1842,= November 12, 1879, Mary A. Wood.
6. *Ezekiel Taylor*, b. July 31, 1844, = November 5, 1879, Amelia S. Metcalfe.
7. *Charles F. Taylor*, b. February 16, 1846, = November 10, 1874, Hattie S. Wood.
8. *George Taylor*, b. August 9, 1847.
9. *Samuel F. Taylor*, b. March 17, 1850, = September 8, 1880, Elizabeth N. Forman (cousin),

A 3. GEORGE FORMAN, b. July 17, 1811, d. March 25, 1854.
4. JOHN SAMUEL FORMAN, b. February 15, 1813, d. March 1, 1879, = March 8, 1838, Jane Chambers, d. August 18, 1853. Issue:

B (h)
1. *Hannah Forman*, b. December 10, 1838, = February 6, 1862, William Forman (cousin), dead.
2. *Throckmorton Forman*, b. March 27, 1842, = May 1, 1866, Azenath Stanton.
3. *Laura Forman*, b. February 2, 1845, = October 13, 1868, J. M. McCarthy.
4. *Lizzie Forman*, b. May 9, 1849, = Rev. Moore.
5. *Daisie Forman*, b. January 29, 1852, = Dr. Wilson.

A 5. THROCKMORTON FORMAN, b. October 3, 1814, d. August 25, 1834.
6. JANE FORMAN, b. July 25, 1816,= September 29, 1836, Joseph Forman, b. January 12, 1812; both living. Issue:

THE MARSHALL FAMILY.

(660) ROBERT MORRIS MARSHALL.

B (*i*)
1. *Mary Forman*, b. November 5, 1837.
2. *Elizabeth*, b. January 5, 1840, = January 21, 1869, Jos. T. Forman; dead.
3. *Thos. S. Forman*, b. July 31, 1843, = October 20, 1868, Mary E. Davenport.
4. *William Forman*, b. January 20, 1848.
5. *Alice*, b. August 7, 1852.
6. *Joseph*, b. March 11, 1856.

A
7. MARY FORMAN, = W. M. PAXTON. See No. 862.
8. REV. EZEKIEL FORMAN, D. D., b. June 20, 1819, = May 25, 1841, Anna S. Rice, d. leaving an only child: 1, Ben. R. Forman, of New Orleans; Dr. Forman = 2d, October 26, 1848, Ellen Russell. Issue:

(*j*)
1. Thos. T. Forman, b. December 29, 1852, = October 11, 1876, Lelia C. Donahoo; 2, Jane Y. Forman, b. August 6, 1849, d. December 28, 1875, = January 5, 1875, G. W. Williams; 3, David R. Forman, b. September 7, 1856, = October 18, 1882, Bettie H. West; 4, Caroline, b. September 10, 1859; 5, Mary E., b. July 31, 1862; 6, George Y. Forman, b. July 23, 1865.

A
9. REV. CHARLES W. FORMAN, D. D., Missionary to India, b. March 3, 1821, = July 3, 1855, Margaret Newton, d. leaving several children. He has married again.
10. ANN FORMAN, b. March 2, 1824, = September 14, 1848, Dr. J. W. Henry, d. One dr., Tillie, = March 11, 1884, Andrew Wood.
11. MATILDA FORMAN, b. December 5, 1828; d. June 9, 1849, = March 10, 1847, Wm. B. Huston *l*. One dr., Clara Huston, b. July 25, 1848, = September 8, 1870, Thos. C. Johnson, b. December 6, 1840.
12. WHITEMAN, b. June 1, 1832, = September 5, 1855, Helen Kelly, b. August 28, 1834. Issue:

(*k*)
1. Kate B. Forman, b. October 8, 1856; 2, Mollie B. Forman, b. July 8, 1858, = October 18, 1883, Heming B. Crooke.

THE MARSHALL FAMILY.   233

(660) ROBERT MORRIS MARSHALL.

THE FAMILY OF JOSEPH FORMAN AND MARY DYE — 7 CH.

A
  1. PHŒBE FORMAN, b. June 3, 1797, = Jos. Broderick.
  2. THOS. W. FORMAN, b. December 8, 1798, = Elizabeth Tebbs. See Tebbs chart, 2168.
  3. JANE FORMAN, b. September 14, 1801, = McDonald, of St. Louis.
  4. WILLIAM FORMAN, b. December 10, 1804, = Phebe Glenn, dr. of Robert Glenn. She d. February 8, 1885. Issue:

(*l*)   1. Elizabeth Forman, = ROBERT M. MARSHALL, No. 660.
  5. HARRIET FORMAN, b. October 21, 1807, = Edward S. Perrie.
  6. HON. GEORGE LEWIS FORMAN, b. February 25, 1810, = February 20, 1834, Alice Ann Tebbs, b. September 13, 1815; d. March 21, 1854.
  7. JOSEPH FORMAN, = Jane Forman (above).
  8. CHARLES FORMAN, b. February 2, 1814; d., = Mary Pickett. See Pickett Chart, No. 64 *h*.
  9. SAMUEL FORMAN, b. December 9, 1818, = Anna Soward.. See Soward Chart.

THE FAMILY OF MARY FORMAN AND GEORGE LEWIS — 3 CH.

A
  1. JANE LEWIS, b. in Mason Co., Ky., February 19, 1795; d., = August 1, 1815, William Greathouse.
  2. ISAAC LEWIS, b. July 10, 1796; d. December 6, 1856, = January 23, 1824, Sarah Bell Brent, b. May 4, 1808, living in Hopkinsville, Ky. See Brent chart, No. 2424. Issue:

B (*m*)   1. *Charles T. Lewis*, b. October 4, 1830, = November 19, 1857, Henrietta M. Gray. 7 ch.
  2. *George Lewis*, b. November 18, 1832.
  3. *Forman*, b. November 18, 1834.
  4. *Mary F. Lewis*, b. March 5, 1836, = Col. Charles.B. Alexander, b. December 25, 1830; d. 1885.

A   3. ELIZABETH LEWIS, b. January 18, 1799; d., = May 18, 1820, Wm. L. McIlvaue, d.; ch.

(662) ELIZABETH COLSTON MARSHALL—(*Durrett*).

662 ELIZABETH COLSTON MARSHALL, b. at "Belle Grove," Fleming Co., Ky., April 25, 1834, = at Washington, Ky., May 22, 1856, WILLIAM DURRETT, b. near Washington Ky., May 12, 1830. Cousin Lizzie is a sensible, amiable and domestic lady, and superintends her large household with diligence and economy. Mr. Durrett was well educated, and is a prominent citizen of Mason Co., Ky. He is a successful farmer, residing one mile west of Washington, Ky. He is a son of the late Paul Durrett, of Mason County. The Durretts are of the lineage of Col. William Marshall, of Mecklinburg Co., Va., grandson of Thomas Marshall, of Westmoreland Co., Va. (No. 11).

664 SUSAN MCCLUNG MARSHALL, b. at "Belle Grove," Fleming Co., Ky., January 5, 1839, = October 6, 1863, NATHANIEL MASSIE, b. August 8, 1837; d. March 14, 1869. Cousin Sue is a handsome, intelligent and spirited lady. She lives at the old homestead in Washington, Ky., with her daughter. By her father's will she has a large part of the home tract of land. Mr. Massie was a son of the late Nathaniel Massie, a pioneer from Virginia, who was born December 28, 1763; Governor of Ohio in 1807. Nathaniel, jr., was born in Chillicothe, Ohio; volunteered as a private in the Union army; was discharged on account of protracted sickness, which finally resulted in death. His widow and daughter draw a pension.

666 PHŒBE A. MARSHALL, b. December 7, 1842, is a tall, handsome, amiable and accomplished woman. Her health is bad, and she is boarding in Maysville, Ky.

668 (*a*) FANNIE MARSHALL COLEMAN, b. in Washington, Ky., June 6, 1830, = in Vicksburg, Miss., December 2, 1851, GOV. THEO. F. RANDOLPH, b. in New Jersey, June 24, 1826, d. November 7, 1883. I never met Cousin Fannie after she removed with her father to Vicksburg. She is highly esteemed and beloved by the family.

(668) FANNIE MARSHALL COLEMAN — (*Randolph*).

Mr. Randolph was born in New Brunswick, N. J., June 24, 1826; educated at Rutger's Grammar School, and entered on mercantile life at the age of sixteen. His early years were improved by the performance of the duties of clerk, accountant, printer, editor and merchant. In 1851, he was married, removed to Eastern Pennsylvania, and was engaged in mining coal and iron. In this business he was sent to Jersey City. In 1859, he was elected to the New Jersey House of Assembly. He was also a member of the Special Assembly of 1861. He favored the prosecution of the war for the Union. In October, 1861, he was elected to the Senate of New Jersey to fill a vacancy. In November, 1862, he was re-elected to a full term, receiving 6,300 of the 6,400 votes cast. In 1868, he was elected Governor of the State. During his three years administration, New Jersey made great advances in material wealth; the laws were improved, reforms were instituted and general prosperity prevailed. The progress made in every department has proved the wisdom of Gov. Randolph's administration, and it has been pronounced the best the State has ever enjoyed. In 1875, Gov. Randolph was elected to the U. S. Senate, and served his full term of six years. He was on the Committees of Commerce, Education and Civil Service Reform, the Military, the Centennial, and to enquire into the political frauds of South Carolina. His career in the Senate and as Governor of New Jersey, established his reputation as a statesman, and his death was considered as a national calamity. On the expiration of his term in the Senate, he retired to his country home at Morristown. Here he displayed in the management of his private estate the energy and liberal views that characterized his public life. Systematic even in the details of his personal expenses, everything he touched prospered. Every year, one-tenth of his income was devoted to charity. The poor looked to him for counsel as well as alms. He died suddenly in his fifty-eighth year.

(b) THE FITZ-RANDOLPH FAMILY.

1. Edward Fitz-Randolph, b. in Nottinghamshire, England, about 1615; landed in Barnstable, Mass., in 1630, = 1637, Elizabeth Blossom, dr. of Thomas Blossom, one of the Pilgrims who sailed in the "Mayflower," 1620. Issue: 1, Nathaniel; 2, Hannah; 3, Mary; 4, Joseph; 5, Elizabeth; 6, Thomas; 7, Hope; 8,

(670) LUCY MARSHALL COLEMAN—(*Smith*).

Benjamin. Edward Fitz-Randolph removed to Middlesex Co., N. J., two miles from New Brunswick.
2. Joseph Fitz-Randolph, = 1687, Hannah Conger. Issue: 1, Hannah; 2, Joseph; 3, Mary; 4, Bertha; 5, Lydia; 6, Moses; 7, Jonathan; 8, Susanna; 9, Ann; 10, Ruth; 11, Prudence; 12, Isaac.
3. Joseph Fitz-Randolph,= ——?. Issue: 1, Jeremiah; 2, Mary; 3, Sarah; 4, Rachael; 5, Joseph; 6, Ephraim; 7, Jacob; 8, Rebecca; 9, John; 10, Grace; 11, Thomas; 12, Paul.
4. Ephraim Fitz-Randolph, = July 22, 1752, Rachael Steele. Issue: 1, Elizabeth; 2, Mercy; 3, Lewis; 4, Steele; 5, Isabel; 6, Rachael.
5. Lewis Fitz-Randolph, = Rachael Snowden. Issue: 1, Eliza-
(d) beth; 2, Stout; 3, Snowden; 4, James; 5, David; 6, Lewis; 7, John; 8, Joseph; 9, Cornelia.
6. James Fitz-Randolph, b. in Piscataway, N. J., June 26, 1791, = February 20, 1812, Sarah K. Carman, dr. of Phineas Carman, of New Brunswick, N. J.; elected to Congress 1824. Issue: 1, Carman; 2, Louise; 3, Julia; 4, Isabel; 5, Sarah; 6, Edgar; 7, Theodore; 8, Elizabeth; 9, James; 10, Emma. Theodore Fitz-Randolph, = MARY FRANCES COLEMAN. Issue: See chart.

670 LUCY MARSHALL COLEMAN, b. in Washington, Ky., February 4, 1832, = in New Orleans, La., May 16, 1859, REV. H. M. SMITH, D. D., b. June 24, 1828. Dr. Smith is editor of the *Southwest Presbyterian* and pastor of the Second Presbyterian Church, of New Orleans. Dr. J. G. Montfort, of Cincinnati, Ohio, thus notices him: "He is far above the average of wise and good men. He has been thirty years in New Orleans, and, as pastor and editor, he has done, and is doing, a laborious and successful work. He is regarded as the representative of the spirit and attitude of the Southern Church towards the Northern." His address is No. 94 Camp Street, New Orleans.

672 COL. JAMES T. COLEMAN, b. in Washington, Mason Co., Ky., March 17, 1834, = August 14, 1863, MARIE LOUISE HAMMOND, b. March 30, 1846. Mr. Coleman's first recollections

(672) COL. JAMES T. COLEMAN.

tell him of the "Old Field School" of David Rannells, Washington, Ky., where he received the first rudiments of education; he removed with his parents to Vicksburg, Miss., about 1844; in 1848, attended the Mississippi Military Institute; in 1850, he was sent to Kenyon College, Ohio; after passing through the Sophomore year, he was sent to Princeton College, and graduated with honor; he then graduated in law, at the University of Louisiana, and was licensed to practice; at this time, Walker, the great filibuster, was enlisting men for his schemes upon Nicaragua, and Mr. Coleman offered his services; was chosen Captain of his company; passed through the tropical beauties of Nicaragua; experienced hardships and encountered dangers; often triumphing in battle over superior numbers, until defeat required a hasty evacuation of the lovely region. Capt. Coleman says that in his flight he showed the speed and endurance of his Kennan ancestry, and that he, on foot, distanced his well-mounted companions. Under President Walker, Capt. Coleman received the appointment of Solicitor of the Treasury of the State of Nicaragua, but his financial operations were light. In 1857, Capt. Coleman returned, and located at St. Louis, to practice law. But his restless nature could not be confined to the duties of a law office. He became a reporter for the *Republican*; and next we find him editor of the *Southeast Democrat*, published at Cape Girardeau, Mo., acquiring the encomiums of even his Republican foes, for the force and spirit of his editorials. Encouraged by his success, he was induced to establish the *Daily Mountaineer*, at Denver, Colorado, in the year 1859. It supported Douglas, and was conservative in its tone. But when the war broke out, his Southern blood could not brook Northern frenzy. So in June, 1861, he hurried South, to offer his services to the Confederacy. At St. Joseph, Mo., he joined a party of forty men, and hastened on to unite with Gen. Price, at Lexington, Mo. Gen. Price gave him the rank of Captain, and he participated in the terrible battle of Elkhorn, and many other actions on the retreat from Missouri. He was next authorized by Gen. Price to recruit a regiment in Arkansas and Louisiana, and was sent to New Orleans. Four companies were raised before the evacuation by Gen. Lovell. After removing supplies to Vicksburg, he joined Gen. Miles, and aided in organizing his "Legion," of which Capt. Coleman was appointed Major. From this time until the surrender of Port Hudson, his daring and chivalrous spirit led him into dan-

(674) SUSAN M'CLUNG COLEMAN—(*Dickinson*).

gers, and gained for him the reputation of a gallant officer. His bravery and discretion at Plain Store, were commended in the dispatches of his commander. He was one of the small band of heroes who so nobly defended Port Hudson, and, when taken by the enemy, July 9, 1863, he was imprisoned at New Orleans. But Major Coleman was engaged to be married to Miss Hammond, and the wedding day had already passed. Inspired by love and gallantry, Maj. Coleman, through the agency of his body servant, and of a disguise, effected his escape from the New Orleans prison, and hastened to meet his waiting bride. He received her carresses on the 13th of August, 1863, and the next day the happy pair were united in marriage. Maj. Coleman, after his honeymoon, rejoined the Confederate army in East Louisiana, and served faithfully to the end. A New Orleans paper thus speaks of him: "We regard the heroic Maj. Coleman as the most brilliant, gifted and brave young officer we have ever met. Possessed of a splendid mind and education, and the most excellent social qualities, he has endeared himself to his companions for life." James is the only survivor of the four Colemans who entered the service of the Confederacy. The three others (560, 676, 678) lie in soldier's graves. Their dauntless courage and chivalrous honor have wreathed the name in festoons of glory. Mr. Coleman, after the war, settled in Vicksburg, and is successfully practicing law. Mrs. Coleman was a Creole of remarkable loveliness, and her lineage is thus recorded:

1. Aneke Jans.
2. William Bogardus Jans.
3. Evorosders Jans, = Satie Hoffman.
4. Peter Jans, = Rebecca Dubois.
5. Jacob Jans, = Patience Henry.
6. Rebecca Jans, = Frederick Schollett.
7. Jane Catherine Schollett, = John T. Hammond.
8. Marie Louise Hammond, = J. T. COLEMAN.

674 SUSAN McCLUNG COLEMAN, b. February 19, 1836, = in New Orleans, May, 1861, COL. A. G. DICKINSON, b. in Virginia, April 15, 1835. Col. Dickinson received a liberal education at the old Rappahannoch Military Institute, in Caroline Co., **Va.**

(676) CHARLES L. COLEMAN.

At the age of eighteen he went to Vicksburg, Miss., and thence to New Orleans. He volunteered for the Southern cause at the first call, but married, in uniform, the day before he started for Pensacola. Here he was rejoined by his bride, who continued close to him in all his campaigns. Going to Virginia he was called to the staff of his relative, Maj. Gen. Magruder, at Yorktown, and became his Adjutant General. He participated in all the battles in which his commanding officer was engaged, and followed him to Texas, New Mexico and Arizona. At the recapture of Galveston, he was severely wounded, losing his left eye. When he had recovered he was placed in command of the Northern division of Texas, with the rank of Colonel. While in this position, the return of peace ended his military career. He then removed to New York city, and engaged in mercantile adventures, with varied success. Engaging in the Insurance business, he was employed to organize the Southern department of the New York Life Insurance Company. Under his skillful management, the department has grown into vast proportions, and is now doing one-fifth of the business of that gigantic institution. His office is 346 Broadway. Col. Dickinson possesses remarkable energy and administrative ability, and has made himself one of the leading men of the city of New York. He is an affable gentleman, a chivalrous officer, and an able financier. I remember Cousin Sue Dickinson only as a child; but I learn that she has all the generous and noble qualities, and the heroic virtues of the Coleman family.

676 CHARLES L. COLEMAN, b. in Vicksburg, Miss., October, 1842, d. May 12, 1864. He was educated at his ancestral home in Virginia, by Thos. B. Coleman, of Concord Academy, and by Prof. Lewis M. Coleman, of Hanover Academy. In 1860-61, he entered the Virginia University, but the war broke in upon the studies of Charley and his brother, Harry W. Coleman. Both returned to Vicksburg, and entered the "Volunteer Southrons." Harry's health soon failed, and he went home. But believing he was able to bear service, he joined his brother, Maj. James Coleman, of "Miles Legion," was made First Lieutenant in the Voorhees Guards, of Louisiana, and after nearly three years service,

(678) HARRY WARFIELD COLEMAN.

was captured at Port Hudson, and sent to Johnson Island. Charles continued in the "Southrons" for a time, and then left them to join the Morris Artillery, under his kinsman, Prof. Lewis M. Coleman. On the reorganization, he was made Captain. After three years arduous service, he fell at Spotsylvania Court House, May 12, 1864. The Union forces held the ground after the engagement and Charles' body was never recovered. He was highly complimented by Gen. R. E. Lee, as a soldier and officer. Harry, still a prisoner, was sent to Point Lookout for exchange in April, 1865; but, Lee's surrender occurring, Harry was sent to Fort Delaware. Here he refused to take the oath, and died in prison, May 25, 1865. His body was taken in charge, by his brother-in-law, Gov. Randolph, and interred at Easton, Penn.

678 HARRY WARFIELD COLEMAN, b. in Vicksburg, Miss., November 8, 1846, d. at Fort Delaware, May 25, 1865. See No. 676.

680 THOMAS MARSHALL, born at "Walnut Grove," Mason Co., Ky., August 25, 1834, = November 27, 1855, SARAH JANE HUGHES, b. August 14, 1837, in Clay Co., Mo. Mr. Marshall studied the ancient languages with his uncle, Dr. Louis Marshall, at "Buckpond," Woodford Co., Ky.; went to Kenyon College, Ohio; left in the junior year; returned to Mason Co., Ky., and wrote in the clerk's office for one year, reading law while there; went to St. Louis and entered the law office of Leslie, Williams & Barrett, as their clerk; returned to Kentucky and continued the study of law with Judge T. A. Marshall (298); returned to St. Louis in 1855, became a member of the law firm of Williams, Barrett & Marshall; engaged in speculation and made and lost a fortune; removed to Utah, 1866; admitted to the bar of the Supreme Court of the United States, 1872; has been in active practice ever since, and is still doing a large and profitable business; has been engaged in all, or nearly all, the heavy litigation of the large mining companies, and the result has generally proved his legal ability. After many years separation, I met my nephew in September, 1883, at the golden wed-

(686) LIZZIE C. MARSHALL—(*Waller*).

ding of his parents (188), and took pains to draw him out upon many legal questions. The result was that I discovered he was one of the finest lawyers of the day. His reading in history, politics, philosophy and law, has been extensive; but his profound judgment and perfect understanding of the fundamental principles of the legal science are equal, if not superior, to those of any man I have ever met. His analytic mind grapples with the deepest mysteries of his profession, and he applies his deductions with irresistible logic. He is six feet two inches tall, his address is genial, and his manners winning. He has been among strangers since his boyhood, and the roughness of his early manners has been polished down to a winning suavity. He is a forcible speaker, a fine conversationalist, and makes a good impression on a stranger. Mrs. Marshall is in bad health. She is a great sufferer. Her husband treats her with that kind and patient attention that characterized the deportment of his great uncle, the Chief Justice, to his afflicted wife. Mrs. Marshall is the daughter of Hon. James M. Hughes and Nannie Dykes. Mr. Hughes was a native of Nicholas Co., Ky.; removed, at an early day, to Liberty, Mo.; represented his district in Congress, 1843–5, removed to St. Louis, engaged in mercantile pursuits, and died about 1865.

682 MARIA MARSHALL, b. October 18, 1836; d. December 24, 1862. She was an angel sent on a mission of love. Devoid of selfishness, her pleasure was to make others happy. Without a particle of guile herself, she believed all around her were good. Too pure and lovely for earth, she was translated, like Enoch, to receive her reward without delay.

684 FANNIE MAITLAND MARSHALL, b. March 5, 1839, wears the mantle of her sister Maria (682).

686 LIZZIE C. MARSHALL, b. at "Walnut Grove," Mason Co., Ky., July 27, 1841, = October 12, 1871, REV. MAURICE WALLER, b. at Maysville, Ky., April 7, 1840. Lizzie is a tall, handsome and accomplished lady. Her letters to me show the ability and style of one highly accomplished. Rev. Mr. Waller had his

(688) CAPT. WILLIAM LOUIS MARSHALL.

literary education at Center College, Kentucky, and was graduated in 1864, at the Theological Seminary of the Northwest, at Chicago. On account of ill health, he did not preach for several years. From 1867 to 1872, he preached to the Presbyterian Church at Hancock, Ind. From 1872 to 1878, he was pastor of the church at Petersburg, Ill. From 1878 to 1880, he preached at Helena, Ark. He became in 1880, pastor of the Presbyterian Church at Manchester, Ohio, where he is now preaching. As an earnest and successful preacher — as a learned theologian, and as an able eclesiastic, he stands high with his brethren. Mr. Waller is a son of Hon. Henry Waller, of Chicago, and Sarah Bell Langhorne, who were married May 3, 1837. Mrs. S. B. Waller died in 1883, in Chicago. See the Langhorne tree, 1012.

THE WALLER FAMILY.

William S. Waller, = Catherine Breckinridge, dr. of James Breckinridge, and grand dr. of Judge Sebastian. Issue:

A   1. HENRY WALLER, b. in Lexington, Ky., = May 3, 1837, Sarah Bell Langhorne, b. November 17, 1821; d. in Chicago, December 13, 1883. He is now a resident of Chicago. Issue:

B   1. *Maurice Waller*, b. April 7, 1840, = October 12, 1871, . LIZZIE MARSHALL, No. 682. See Langhorne Chart, No. 1012.

A   2. JAMES WALLER, b. January 20, 1817 *l*, = Lucy Alexander, b. September 18, 1822 *l*, dr. of William Alexander and —— Weisiger, and sister of the late (Lord) R. A. Alexander and the present A. J. Alexander, of Woodford Co., Ky. Issue:

B   1. *Susanna Lees Waller*, = F. L. MARSHALL, No. 1316.

A   3. SUSANNA P. WALLER, = —— Lees.
A   4. EDWARD WALLER, = Mary Rawson.

688   CAPT. WILLIAM LOUIS MARSHALL, b. at "Walnut Grove," Mason Co., Ky., June 11, 1846; entered Kenyon College, Ohio, September 1, 1860, left on the breaking out of the war in 1861, enlisted in the Tenth Kentucky Volunteer Cavalry, August 16,

(690) JAMES PAXTON MARSHALL.

1862; served in Eastern Kentucky, until September 17, 1863; entered as cadet in United States Military Academy at West Point, July 1, 1864; graduated No. 7, in a class of fifty-four members, June 15, 1868; commissioned Brevet Second Lieutenant of Engineers, same date; First Lieutenant, June 21, 1871; Captain, June 15, 1882; served at Willets Point, N. Y., from October 1, 1868, to August 28, 1870; as Acting Assistant Professor of Natural and Experimental Philosophy, in the United States Military Academy, at West Point, from August 28, 1870 to August 28, 1871; at Willets Point again from August 28, 1871 to July 5, 1872; in charge of the Colorado Section of the United States Geographical and Geological Explorations and Surveys west of the 100th meridian, from 1872 to 1875, making extensive topographical surveys in Colorado, New Mexico, Arizona and Utah; discovered the "Marshall Pass," across the main ridge of the Rocky Mountains, now used by the Denver and Rio Grande Railroad, and also the gold placers in "Marshall Basin," in Southwestern Colorado, on the San Miguel river; served as Assistant Engineer on the improvement of the Tennessee river at the Mussel Shoals, and other works in Georgia and Alabama, from 1876 to 1881; and as Engineer in charge of the improvement of the Mississippi river from 1881 to 1884; and has charge at this time, of the improvements at Milwaukee, and other lake harbors. Capt. Marshall's professional education and experience have made him one of the best officers in the Engineer Service. His practical knowledge has enabled him to present to the government some excellent inventions to facilitate the work in his department. ·

690 JAMES PAXTON MARSHALL, b. at "Walnut Grove," Mason Co., Ky., December 30, 1848, = October 28, 1875, his second cousin HESTER MARSHALL (730), b. at "Edgeworth," Fauquier Co., Va., July 26, 1852. Mr. Marshall was educated for a farmer. After marriage he spent several years on his wife's native farm in Virginia; and about 1881, returned to Kentucky, and purchased a farm adjoining his father's, where he now resides. Mr. Marshall is an amiable gentleman, and an industrious and successful farmer. His wife is accomplished, and is greatly beloved. They have no children.

(692) LUCY COLEMAN MARSHALL—(*Bentley*).

692 LUCY COLEMAN MARSHALL, b. at "Walnut Grove," Mason Co., Ky., September 22, 1851, = November 29, 1877, JOHN BAYN BENTLEY, b. in Essex Co., Va., May 16, 1843. Lucy is tall, stately, dignified and uncommonly handsome and intelligent. Mr. Bentley is the oldest son of Mr. John G. Bentley of Essex Co., Va., and a Miss Parker. They were wealthy, but the adversities of war greatly reduced their income. Mr. John Bentley, Jr., was preparing for college when the war broke out; entered the Confederate army, and served to the close; entered Roanoke College; graduated the first in his class, and received the degree of A. M., the highest honor conferred by the college; the Greek oration delivered by him on the occasion is still preserved; came to Kentucky and opened a High School at Washington, Ky. After marriage he started a grocery house, in Maysville, Ky., and is doing well.

694 SALLIE HUGHES MARSHALL, b. at "Walnut Grove," near Washington, Ky., November 24, 1858, = June 17, 1885, EDMOND WILKES, Jr. Sallie is tall, handsome, lively and accomplished. She has been the life and soul of the family. But ah! This 17th of June, 1885, as I write, she kneels at the altar of Hymen, garlanded in myrtle and orange-blossoms, a willing victim to Cupid. I pray that their journey may be through Beulah's land, and may end in the New Jerusalem.

696 BENJAMIN HARBESON MARSHALL, b. at "Walnut Grove," Mason Co., Ky., August 28, 1861. Ben has been helping his father on the farm, and is now waiting for some lassie to volunteer to attend to his wardrobe. Ben. is modest, but he is handsome and sensible.

704 HESTER MORRIS MARSHALL, b. at "Mt. Morris," Fauquier Co., Va., November 27, 1819. She was finely educated at Warrenton, Va., and still lives at "Happy Creek," renting out her share of her ancestral estate, laboring to make others happy and dis-

(708) CHARLES MARSHALL.

pensing lavish hospitality. I incurred her condemnation by spending so short a time at "Happy Creek." She enjoys company,
  And like the palm tree stands,
  In modest grace, mid burning sands,
  With fruit and water in her hands,
  The famishing to cheer.

706 CAPT. JAMES MARSHALL, b. at "Mt. Morris," Fauquier Co., Va., March 9, 1823, = March 18, 1846, his cousin, LUCY S. MARSHALL, b. at "Belle Grove," Fleming Co., Ky., March 12, 1824. Cousin James was taught in his father's house by tutors; attended the Virginia Military Institute, and graduated in 1842; studied law, but found farming more to his taste; opened an academy at Front Royal, Va., in 1861; enlisted as First Lieutenant in Capt. Bowen's company, 7th Virginia cavalry; served under McDonald and Ashby; in 1862, raised for himself Company E, 12th Cavalry, and served under Jones and Rosser until the end of the war; after farming a few years, resumed his school at Front Royal; removed in 1876 to Florida; health failing, returned after two years, and has farmed and taught school up to this time. I spent a day in 1884, at "Horseshoe," on the Shenandoah, seven miles from Front Royal. The family are devoted Episcopalians, and nearly all the children reside with their parents. They seem to be the best people I ever met. The father is a patriarchal old gentleman, and, notwithstanding the vicissitudes of his life, possesses the meekness and earnestness of a disciple of the Prince of Peace. The mother is a large, lively, whole-souled and generous matron—genial and hospitable. Altogether they form a household where love to each other rules, where friends find kindness and attention, and the stranger receives a hearty welcome. See No. 810.

708 CHARLES MARSHALL, b. at "Happy Creek," Warren Co., Va., February 5, 1826; unmarried; educated by tutors at home, at the Episcopal High School, and at the University of Virginia; studied law; settled in Wheeling, W. Va., and did well until the war broke out; enlisted in the Confederate army, and was de-

(710) LUCY PICKETT MARSHALL—(*Morris*).

tailed for the business of manufacturing gunpowder; after the close of the war, engaged in surveying; was surveyor of Warren County; is now farming at "Happy Creek." He is a modest and retiring gentleman, handsome and intelligent.

710 LUCY PICKETT MARSHALL, b. at "Happy Creek," Warren Co., Va., October 26, 1829, = June 1, 1854, her cousin, DR. ROBERT MORRIS, b. 1815. They live in Philadelphia, and spend their summers at "Happy Creek." Dr. Morris is a son of Robert Morris, of Philadelphia, and a grandson of the great financier of the same name. After graduating in medicine, he spent a year in Paris. His first wife was a cousin, a Miss Nixon, who died, leaving a son. Dr. Morris is an eminent physician and a highly respected gentleman, but has ceased to practice.

712 LIEUT. THOMAS MARSHALL, b. at "Happy Creek," April 15, 1831, killed at Brandy Station, October 12, 1863, = October 17, 1860, BETTIE WILLIAMS, b. November 25, 1837. He was educated at Front Royal; farmed for his father; was an engineer on the Manassas Gap R. R., and on other railroads, until his marriage. In 1862, enlisted in his brother's (706) company in the Confederate army, and was elected First Lieutenant; killed at Brandy Station. He was a gallant officer and much beloved. His widow and two children reside in Richmond, Va. They are Presbyterians.

714 ROBERT MORRIS MARSHALL, b. September 7, 1832; educated at Front Royal; was assistant engineer on the Manassas Gap R. R.; went to Missouri and served as engineer on the Hannibal & St. Joe R. R.; went to Brazil, and afterwards to India, as an engineer; failing health required him to return in 1866; he is still delicate; lives at "Happy Creek."

716 MARTIN P. MARSHALL, born at Happy Creek, Warren Co., Va., September 9, 1833; educated at Front Royal; was an engineer on the Manassas Gap railroad; was engaged as engineer on

(722) JAMES M. MARSHALL.

several roads up to the time of the war; enlisted as a private in Stribling's Battery; was captured at Malvern Hill, and again at Richmond; was in prison much of the time up to the surrender. He lives at Happy Creek, spends most of his time in reading, and is a general favorite.

718 MARY MORRIS MARSHALL, b. at Happy Creek, September 21, 1834. She lives with the Happy Creek family.

720 ANNA M. MARSHALL, b. at Happy Creek, November 7, 1835. She lives at Happy Creek.

722 JAMES M. MARSHALL, b. at "Edgeworth," Fauquier Co., Va., March 17, 1838, = February 19, 1879, MARY ALEXANDER WELLFORD, b. in Fredericksburg, Va., August 14, 1846. Mr. Marshall is a highly cultivated gentleman; was educated at the University of Virginia; served as a Confederate soldier throughout the war; was a Lieutenant in his Cousin James Marshall's Co. "E," Twelfth Regiment Virginia Volunteers, and proved himself a gallant soldier and splendid officer; was dangerously wounded, June 9, 1863, at Brandy Station, and was confined to the hospital until peace enabled him to return to his patrimonial estate, "Priestly," situated seven miles south of Markham, in Fauquier Co., Va. He has not yet entirely recovered of his severe wound. He is a vestryman of Leeds' Church, and all his family are in the Episcopal Church. His wife is a beautiful and charming lady, and I was much pleased by the hearty reception she gave me, when I visited her in 1884; and her letters show high literary acquirements. She was educated at the Southern Female Institute, at Richmond, Va.

(b)   THE WELLFORD LINEAGE.
1. Dr. Robert Wellford, of England, settled in Fredericksburg, Va., = a Mrs. Thornton, a dr. of Rev. Robt. Yates, and his wife, who was a dr. of William Randolph, of Turkey Island. See Randolph chart (16).
2. Dr. Beverley Wellford, President of the National Medical Association, of Richmond, Va., = Mary Alexander, of Fredericksburg, Va. Issue:

(724) WILLIAM MARSHALL.

1. Mary Alexander Wellford, = JAMES M. MARSHALL.

(c) THE ALEXANDER LINEAGE.

1. Sir William Alexander, b. in Scotland, 1580; d. in London, 1640; Knighted, 1613; created Earl of Stirling, 1633.
2. John Alexander, of Scotland, came to Stafford Co., Va., 1659; d. 1677.
3. Robert Alexander; d. June 1, 1704.
4. Robert Alexander, b. 1688; d. 1735, = —— Foushee.
5. William Alexander, 1758–1803, = Sarah B. Casson, of Stafford Co., dr. of Thomas Casson and Sarah Bruce, 1760–1814. See 1428.
6. Mary Alexander, 1802–1869, = 1824, Dr. Beverley Randolph Wellford. Issue:

(d) 1. Dr. Armstead N. Wellford, = Elizabeth Landon.
2. Dr. John S. Wellford, = 1858, Emeline M. Tabb.
3. Judge Beverley R. Wellford, b. May 10, 1828, = March 3, 1858, Susanna S. Taliaferro, b. 1829.
4. Major Philip Wellford, 1833–78, = Mary Bell Street.
5. Charles E. Wellford.
6. Mary Alexander Wellford, = J. M. MARSHALL (722).

724 WILLIAM MARSHALL, b. at "Edgeworth," August 1, 1840. He was educated by tutors at home, and at Winchester Academy. When the war broke out, he entered the Confederate army; served part of the time in the Engineers Corps, and part in the Fauquier Battery, commanded by Capt. W. C. Marshall (522). After serving until the surrender, he returned, and is farming in Fauquier Co., Va. He lives with his brother James.

726 CHARLES SHACKELFORD MARSHALL, b. at "Edgeworth," Fauquier Co., Va., March 16, 1843, = December 13, 1866, his relative, CARY RANDOLPH JONES (1292), b. at "Woodside," October 21, 1845. He received a good English, classical and scientific education; entered the Southern army as a common Infantry

soldier, in 1861, and served until the end, in 1865; was wounded at Mechanicsville, by the explosion of a bomb; lost his right eye ; was first under Henry A. Wise, then in Hill's division and lastly with Ashby's Cavalry; was in the principal battles in Virginia, throughout the war; on restoration of peace, returned to his estate, the "Evergreens," a farm of 510 acres, seven miles south of Markham, where he now resides. His wife is the bright and lovely daughter of J. F. Jones (508).

728 ROBERT MORRIS MARSHALL, b. at "Edgeworth," Fauquier Co., Va., July 12, 1845; d. October 13, 1863. At the age of seventeen he entered as a private, Company E, Twelfth Virginia Cavalry, C. S. A., at the beginning of the war. His spirit and galantry placed him ever in front, and before twelve months of the strife were past he was a veteran. He participated in many battles, and his eagerness for the fray caused his death. He had been detailed for the duty of conveying to the grave the remains of Lieut. Thos. Marshall (712), his former leader, when he learned that his companions expected to go into action. He joined them and was killed. His body was brought home and buried at Leeds church, where a handsome shaft is a testimonial of the love of friends.

730 HESTER MARSHALL; see 690.

732 JOHN AUGUSTINE MARSHALL, b. at "Edgeworth," Fauquier Co., Va., September 5, 1854. After receiving a liberal education and studying law, he went to Salt Lake City, Utah. A friend writes me: "He is a member of the rapidly rising lawfirm of Hall & Marshall, and is a lawyer of great promise, and most marked ability."

734 MARY MORRIS MARSHALL; see No. 548.

(736) THOMAS MARSHALL.

736 THOMAS MARSHALL; see No. 590.

738 JAMES MARSHALL, b. at "Fairfield," Fauquier Co., Va., October 7, 1845, = December 18, 1872, Alice Poindexer, b. in Tennessee, January 29, 1850. Mr. Marshall is engaged in grazing cattle on a farm of 1,700 acres, known as "Texas," situated six miles southeast of Markham. He is a pushing, energetic man, and has prospered financially. He was educated at Clifton High School, but left in 1861, at the age of sixteen, to take his place in the Confederate army. He entered Ashby's Cavalry, and as a private served to the end. His sound judgment and business talent are admitted and respected. His wife's lineage may be thus expressed:

1. John Poindexter, = Elizabeth Graves.
2. John Poindexter, = Adelaide Jacobs.
3. Alice Poindexter, = JAMES MARSHALL.

Her letters to me indicate intelligence and amiability.

740 ELIZABETH BROOKE MARSHALL, b. at "Fairfield," Fauquier Co., Va., April 1846, = 1871 CAPT. BOWLES ARMISTEAD, b. at Upperville, Fauquier Co. He is a son of Gen. Walker Armistead, U. S. A.; was educated at Armstrong's Military School, at Upperville; enlisted as a private in Gen. Payne's division, but was promoted for gallantry on the field, to the rank of Captain; was wounded four times; both legs and one arm were broken; but he is now strong and healthy; is a fine business man; Assessor of Fauquier County; growing in reputation and fortune; lives near Delaplane. See 1270.

742 HESTER M. MARSHALL, b. January, 1848; lives with her parents, near Linden Station, Warren Co., Va.

744 WILLIAM MARSHALL, b. February 1851; lives with his parents, near Linden Station, Va.; farmer.

(750) DR. JAMES M. AMBLER.

746 HENRY M. MARSHALL, b. July, 1853; lives with his parents, near Linden Station, Va.; farmer.

748 JOHN MARSHALL, b, at "Fairfield," Warren Co., Va., December 1855. He was named after his uncle, "Navy" John Marshall, and his widow (196), Cousin Rebecca, is his godmother. She says he is a noble youth, full of energy and ambition, and is bound to succeed. He is a lawyer of fine promise at Detroit, Mich.

750 DR. JAMES M. AMBLER, b. at the "Dell," in Fauquier Co., Va., December 30, 1848, d. 1881. He graduated at at the University of Maryland, in March, 1869; studied medicine; entered the naval service as assistant surgeon, April 1, 1874. While serving in the naval hospital at Norfolk, Va., he received a dispatch from the Navy Department asking him to volunteer for duty on the "Jeannette," to be sent to the Northern Seas. He accepted the duty and started on the ill-fated expedition, from which he was never to return. He might have saved himself by leaving his companions, but this he would not do. He died in the cause of science and humanity, but his heroism will live in history. His frozen body was recovered, and, in February, 1884, at Leeds Church, was committed to the grave. His casket was covered with floral wreaths, which had accumulated all the way from Siberia. His fellow surgeons of the U. S. Navy have placed in Leeds church a brass tablet, thus inscribed: "James Markham Ambler, Past Assistant Surgeon, U. S. Navy, died on the banks of the Lena River, during the memorable retreat of the ship's company of the U. S. Arctic Steamer Jeannette, in the year 1881. His sense of duty was stronger than his love of life. In memory of his noble example and heroic death, this tablet is erected by the medical officers of the U. S. Navy."

At the June, 1885, commencement of Washington and Lee University, Lexington, Va., a tablet, the contribution of officers, students and friends, was unveiled, bearing the following legend:

(752) RICHARD CARY AMBLER.

IN MEMORY OF
JAMES MARKHAM MARSHALL AMBLER,
PAST ASSISTANT SURGEON U. S. NAVY.

Born in Fauquier County, Virginia, December 30, 1848. A student of Washington College 1865–1867. He perished on the banks of the Lena River, Siberia, in the retreat of Capt. DeLong's company from the U. S. Steamer Jeannette, in October, 1881. He declined the last chance of life, that he might help his comrades. His last written words were the confident expression of his Christian faith. To him "Duty was the noblest word in the English language."

ERECTED BY HIS COLLEGE FRIENDS AND CLASSMATES.

752 RICHARD CARY AMBLER, b. at the "Dell," Fauquier Co., Va., June 10, 1850, = November 15, 1877, LIZZIE MARSHALL (1710), b. April 12, 1857. They live on a farm a few miles from Flemingsburg, Ky.

754 MARY MORRIS AMBLER, b. at the "Dell," Fauquier Co., Va., October 28, 1852; was educated at Mrs. Witherspoon's school in Baltimore; is highly accomplished, visits and travels much and is greatly admired and beloved. I met her at her mother's, in 1884, and was pleased with her good sense and her polite attentions.

756 EDWARD AMBLER, b. at the "Dell," Fauquier Co., Va., July 6, 1854; is farming for his mother; graduated at the University of Virginia; studied law and practiced for a time in Washington, but gave it up to help his mother.

768 LUCIE MARSHALL BURWELL, b. at "Glen Owen," Clarke Co., Va., 1814?, = September 17, 1835, JOHN JOLLIFFE, b. 1812?; d. September 15, 1860. Lucie lost her parents in her infancy, and lived with her grandmother, Mrs. Lucy Burwell, of

THE MARSHALL FAMILY. 253

(778) JAMES M. TAYLOR.

Winchester, Va.; and here she was married. Her husband was intemperate. She now lives at Millwood, Clarke Co., Va. I have letters from her, and, from their style and execution, I find her possessed of superior literary attainments.

770 ELIZA BURWELL, b. at "Glen Owen," Clarke Co., Va.; d. May 30, 1856, = August 4, 1835, at the residence of her grandmother, in Winchester, DAVID H. McGUIRE, a lawyer of Romney, W. Va. He died at Berryville, Va., February 11, 1882, aged 71 years.

772 ANN C. T. BURWELL, b. at "Glen Owen," Clarke Co., Va., = May 2, 1837, at "Saratoga," the residence of her uncle, Nathaniel Burwell, to PHILIP COOKE, b. 1811, a lawyer of Winchester, Va., and a chaste and forcible writer. He died January 20, 1850, and she now lives at Millwood, Clarke Co., Va.

774 NATHANIEL BURWELL, b. August 17, 1819, at "Glen Owen," Clarke Co., Va., = December 8, 1842, DORA W. PAGE, b. June 1, 1823. He graduated at the University of Virginia, in 1836; was a Major in the C. S. A. He now resides with his wife, at Millwood, Clarke Co., Va. I have had some correspondence with him, and find him a man of intelligence.

776 FANNIE MAITLAND ADAMS, b. April 11, 1840, = April 17, 1866, DR. WILLIAM HAYS, b. January 21, 1835; d. February 8, 1869. She is now living at Millersburg, Ky., where her son is attending college. I met Cousin Fannie at "The Hill," in Washington, Ky., in 1884, and was much pleased with her handsome person and well cultivated mind.

778 JAMES M. TAYLOR, b. at Taylorsville, Va., April 26, 1822, = February 14, 1844, ISABELLA D. JACOBS. Mr. Taylor lives in Richmond, Va. For many years he was employed in the State Treasury department, but some years ago he had to retire on account of failing eyesight.

(780) JOHN R. TAYLOR.

780 JOHN R. TAYLOR, = May 23, 1850, SALLIE E. WINSTON.

782 GEORGE K. TAYLOR, = 1st, REBECCA L. COLEMAN, and, after her death, he married her sister, ANNE COLEMAN. They live at Richmond, Va. Issue: Four children by first, and five by the second. See chart. Mr. Taylor is Clerk of the Court of Appeals of Virginia.

784 GEORGE W. MARSHALL, b. September 9, 1828, = November 14, 1847, Mary E. Anderson, b. November 15, 1827. Her parents were Eli and Nancy Anderson.

786 MARIA L. MARSHALL, b. in Fauquier Co., Va., August 27, 1830; d. July 24, 1872, = May 26, 1870, BARNES KERRICK, b. November 11, 1824. No children. A marble shaft at Leeds' Church preserves her memory. Epitaph: "SACRED to the memory of Maria Louisa, daughter of Thomas G. and Ann E. Marshall, and wife of Barnes Kerrick, born August 27, 1830, died July 24, 1872." I met Mr. Kerrick at Markham, Va., in 1884, and found him a dignified, sensible and polite gentleman.

788 JOHN R. MARSHALL, b. in Fauquier Co., Va., June 17, 1832, = December 14, 1852, ANGELINE W. NOEL, b. November 27, 1830. Mr. Marshall was a graduate of the Lexington, Va., Military Institute. He is now farming and teaching in Fauquier Co., Va. His letters to me prove his liberal education, and recommend his moral and religious integrity. Mrs. Marshall is a daughter of Thos. G. and Caro. Noel.

790 ROBERT A. MARSHALL, b. in Fauquier Co., Va., February 6, 1834, = November 26, 1872, LAURA HERNDON, b. November 27, 1848. Mr. Marshall was educated at the University of Virginia. He is now farming and teaching.

THE MARSHALL FAMILY.

(800) CHARLES MARSHALL JONES.

792 LUCY B. MARSHALL, b. in Fauquier Co., Va., July 19, 1836.

794 JANE MARSHALL, b. in Fauquier Co., Va., October 26, 1841.

796 DR. HARDIN BURNLEY, b. in Virginia, February 4, 1827, = September 24, 1862, BLANCHE D. WILLIAMS, of Hancock Co., Miss. They now live at Hazlehurst, Miss. Dr. Burnley is a graduate of Jefferson. Medical College of Philadelphia. After practicing medicine in Mississippi for twenty-five years, his health gave way, and he now keeps a drug store. His wife is the eldest daughter of Dr. John H. Williams, of Rockcastle Co., Ky., and Cornelia Dupree, of Hinds Co., Miss. She was born at Clinton, Miss., March 4, 1847.

798 WILLIAM MARSHALL BURNLEY, b. February 1, 1829, d. December 7, 1872, = March, 1861, MARY MILLER, of Madison Parish, La. She died July, 1871.

800 CHARLES MARSHALL JONES, known among his friends as "Marshall" Jones, b. at "Vaucluse," near Winchester, Va., December 26, 1806, d. January 2, 1847, = 1841, THERESA STRINGER. Mr. Jones was well educated and thoroughly read in the law. After practicing for some years in Virginia, he removed, for the reason hereinafter stated, to New Orleans. There he married Theresa Stringer, who survived him. He attained quite a reputation as a lawyer, but died early. The following letter from Chief Justice John Marshall to Henry Clay will interest those who cherish his memory. It is dated Washington, March 13, 1833:

DEAR SIR:—My nephew, Marshall Jones, purposes to remove to New Orleans, with a view to the practice of law, and is, I believe, now in that place. The circumstances under which he left Virginia increase my solicitude for his success. A personal rencounter with a young gentleman who had abused him wantonly and grossly, terminated very unfortunately in the death of his adversary. This compelled him to fly from Virginia, and from very flattering professional prospects. After

(802) FRANCES L. A. M. JONES—(*Barton*).

visiting Canada and Texas, he has at length, I am told, determined on trying his fortune in New Orleans, I am extremely desirous of promoting his object, but with the exception of Mr. Johnston, I am not acquainted with a single gentleman in that place. May I ask the favor of you to mention him to some of your friends, not as a person known to yourself, but as my friend and relative, whom I strongly recommend. I have entire confidence in his honor, integrity and amiable qualities, and shall feel myself greatly obliged to you if you will bestow on him so much of your countenance as may favor his introduction into society. For the rest, he must depend on himself. With the greatest respect and esteem, I am your obedient servant,

J. MARSHALL.

Mr. Marshall's widow married a Mr. Bradford, who was intemperate. She died, and one of her daughters resides in Baltimore.

802 FRANCES L. A. M. JONES, b. at "Vaucluse," near Winchester, Va., October 15, 1808, = December 18, 1828, DAVID WALKER BARTON, b. 1801, d. July 5, 1863. Mrs. Barton still lives with her children, sometimes at Baltimore, and at other times at Staunton or Winchester. She is revered by her descendants, and highly esteemed by all. Mr. Barton was educated at Yale College; was a scholar of decided attainments, and highly cultivated literary taste; though diffident, he was a fine speaker; he was a chaste and forcible writer, and contributed largely to the political papers and literary journals of his day. As a lawyer, he was successful; accumulated a fortune, and lost it by indorsing for friends and by the disasters of the war. He was a brilliant conversationalist and fine company for young and old. His reading was general and his information varied. He had a happy faculty of making himself interesting to all, so that his society was much sought. His professional life was spent at Winchester. His partner was Philip Williams.

THE BARTON FAMILY.

1. Rev. Thomas Barton was a native of Ireland, descended from an English family; was educated at Dublin University; emigrated to Philadelphia and opened a school, which ultimately grew into the University of Pennsylvania. In 1754, he went to England, received ordination and returned to Pennsylvania; married Esther, sister of David Rittenhouse, L. L. D., F. R. S., President of the American Philosophical Society, etc.

(808) MARY PIERCE MARSHALL—(Foree).

2. Their son, William Barton, in delicate health, sought a warmer climate, and came to Petersburg, Va., where he married a Miss Walker, of "Kingston."
3. DAVID WALKER BARTON was one of their sons.

804 WILLIAM STROTHER JONES, b. at "Vaucluse," Frederick Co., Va., December 20, 1817, = 1st, 1842, FLORINDA TAYLOR, she d. April 1, 1846; = 2d, May 22, 1850, MARY E. BARTON, who d. January 10, 1868. Cousin Strother, as everybody called him, is a genial, kind hearted soul, full of jest and jollity. He was reared at "Vaucluse," and as his mother died in his infancy, he became the protege of his father. He was educated at Bristol College, an Episcopal Institution, and is strongly attached to the ancient faith in which he was reared. He was to have studied medicine; but bad health demanded exercise and pure air; so he was put to work on his father's farm, and there he continued until his father's death in 1845. His usual home is now at "Happy Creek," Warren Co., Va. There, I spent a pleasant hour with him in 1884. His cordial greeting, his graceful attention, and his charming courtesy won my heart and secured my esteem. He has taken a great interest in my heraldic work, and has given me aid and encouragement. In one of his letters he calls himself a "social crank," and asks my charity for his "syntax and prosody, cabolistic writing and Pickett orthography." Mary E. Barton, was daughter of a distinguished lawyer, of Fredericksburg, Va., and was not related to D. W. Barton (802). Florinda Taylor was a daughter of William Taylor, of Clarke Co., Va. She was the niece of Bushod Taylor, of Winchester, Va., and of Griffin Taylor, merchant of Cincinnati, Ohio. She was related to the Kennans (56 *h*) and to Katherine Taylor (176), but not to W. D. Taylor (218).

806 JAMES FITZGERALD JONES; see 508.

808 MARY PIERCE MARSHALL, b. in Virginia, September 27, 1822, d. in Shelbyville, Ky., October 6, 1882, = July 8, 1846, in Lewis Co., Ky., JUDGE JOS. P. FOREE, b. March 26, 1820.

258   THE MARSHALL FAMILY.

(810) LUCY STEPTOE MARSHALL.

Mrs. Force was much beloved and highly esteemed for her graces and virtues. Her photograph attests her remarkable beauty, and those who knew her pronounce her name with veneration. I visited Judge Force in 1884. He is a patriarchal old gentleman, with that benignity of countenance and cordiality of manner that inspires love as well as confidence. He was a second son of William P. Force and Elizabeth J. Major, of Shelby Co., Ky. After receiving his literary education at Transylvania University, and graduating in the law department of that Institution in March, 1843, he settled at Charleston, Miss., and engaged in the practice of law. He represented Tallahatchie Co., Miss., in 1848, and was Probate Judge for a term; returned to Shelbyville, Ky., 1852; represented Shelby County in 1871–72; has been elected County Judge three times, and is now presiding Judge of the Court of Magistrates. A Democrat, he is one of the active and influential politicians of Kentucky.

810   LUCY STEPTOE MARSHALL; see No. 706.

812   SUSAN M. MARSHALL, b. at "Bentley," Lancaster Co., Va., the Ball family homestead, d. at Charleston, Miss., January 1, 1883, = in Mississippi, July 20, 1847, ABEL B. BETTS. Mrs. Betts was beloved and admired. Her husband was a successful merchant, and had retired from business before his wife's death. He is now assisting his son-in-law Mr. Crow, in his store. He often visits his wife's relatives in Virginia, and by his kind spirit and social turn, makes many friends.

814   MARIA JANE MARSHALL, b. in Virginia, April 1, 1828, = 1st, July 5, 1849, in Mississippi, M. W. Watkins, who d. October 20, 1851, leaving an only daughter, Laura; = 2d, September 19, 1853, Rev. R. L. Andrews, who died in 1865. Mr. Andrews was a Methodist Episcopal preacher of Florence, Ala., and had a number of children by a former wife, one of whom married her daughter, Laura (2052). Mr. Watkins was a planter. Mrs. Andrews now lives with a step-son in Florence.

(824) ELIZA COLSTON MARSHALL.—(*Stewart*).

816 MARTIN PICKET MARSHALL, b. in Virginia, March 8, 1830, d. 1876, = 1st, ANNA SHELTON, who d. 1867. He afterwards married a MISS JAMESON. Mr. Marshall seems to have had but little intercourse with his relatives. A niece writes me: "Martin P's children are scattered and we know little of his family. He was not living with his first wife at the time of her death. He had six children. Susan and Roberta married Lollas, brothers, and died childless. James S. Marshall married Bettie Quarles, of Tallahatchie Co., Miss., and left a son, who is a worthy young man. Maria, married a Jameson, and lives near Sardis, Miss. Mary died, and Lucy is yet living. The two children by his second wife are named William L. and Martin P."

818 JUDITH BALL MARSHALL, b. in Kentucky, September 26, 1832, d. in Mississippi, July 8, 1858, = 1853, GEORGE G. HARVEY, a farmer, of Tallahatchie Co., Miss. He is dead.

820 CHARLES C. MARSHALL, b. in Lewis Co., Ky., August 6, 1836, d. in Mississippi, March, 1868, = June 20, 1865, MATTIE HILL, who d. September, 1868. He was twin brother of William (822). He practiced law in Charleston, Miss.

822 WILLIAM BALL MARSHALL, twin brother of the last (820), was b. in Lewis Co., Ky., August 6, 1836, removed with his parents to Tallahatchie Co., Miss., in 1847, = January 21, 1868, IDA A. MANLY. He is a lawyer, and is County Attorney of Tallahatchie County.

824 ELIZA COLSTON MARSHALL, b. in Lewis Co., Ky., September 25, 1839, = 1st, September 24, 1870, in Mississippi, WILLIAM H. STEWART, who died 1872; = 2d, November 27, 1883, D. L. YOUNG. Stewart was a small farmer of Tallahatchie Co., Miss. Young is postmaster at Winona, Miss.

A tenth child of C. C. Marshall was Roberta, b. in Ky., January 2, 1842; d. of consumption in Mississippi, April 4, 1868.

826 COL. CHARLES MARSHALL, b. at Warrenton, Va., October 3, 1830, = 1st, December 18, 1856, EMILY ROSALIE ANDREWS, who died April 25, 1858; = 2d, December 12, 1866, SARAH R. SNOWDEN. Col. Marshall, after receiving a finished education at Warrenton was appointed, in 1850, Professor of Mathematics in the Indiana University. In 1853, he settled in Baltimore, and engaged in the practice of law. When the war broke out he was appointed on Gen. R. E. Lee's staff, and served until the Surrender. When peace was restored, he resumed practice in Baltimore, and now stands at the very head of the profession. A lady well known in the literary society of Virginia, remarked to me, in 1884, that Charles Marshall, of Baltimore, was generally admitted to be the most talented man in the Marshall family. Mr. Marshall's first wife was a daughter of Gen. T. P. Andrews, U. S. A., at one time Paymaster General, and Emily Snowden. His second wife was a daughter of Thomas and Ann Rebecca Snowden, of Maryland.

828 CATHERINE TAYLOR MARSHALL, b. in Warrenton, Va., December 18, 1832; d. in Maryland, March 27, 1866, = October 6, 1857, FENDALL MARBURY, b. April 23, 1830, at "Wyoming," the family homestead, in Prince George Co., Md. Catherine was said to have been a lovely girl, well educated and highly accomplished. Fendall Marbury was a son of William L. Marbury, Judge of the Orphans' Court of Prince George County, and Susan Fitzhugh Fendall, of a good old Maryland family. Her grandfather and great-grandfather were distinguished civil and military officers of their day. His grandmother, Marbury, was a sister of Judge Alex. C. Magruder, of the Maryland Court of Appeals. Fendall Marbury graduated at Princeton College in 1850; read law with his uncle, Philip R. Fendall, of Washington, D. C., for two years; attended the law department of the University of Virginia; commenced practice in Alexandria, Va. But his widowed mother needing his assistance to manage her large estate, he returned to "Wyoming;" married, and after a few years lost his wife. Some years later, he married Miss Sallie C. Berry, who proved a good stepmother; continued to practice law, and to take an active part in politics; represented his county in the State Legislature, and in

THE MARSHALL FAMILY.

(832) LILY T. MARSHALL—(*Green*).

two Constitutional Conventions; and three times has been the standard bearer of the Democracy in his own county, in contests for the nomination for Congress; was an elector in the Tilden campaign; he took no part in the war, waiting on the action of his State, whose fortunes he would have followed. Mr. Marbury is now quietly living at his farm, taking no part, yet feeling a great interest in public affairs.

830 ROBERT TAYLOR MARSHALL, b. July 15, 1835; killed at the battle of Beverly's Ford, Culpeper Co., Va., August 23, 1862. He entered the Confederate service in the Washington Artillery, of Virginia; was an intrepid soldier, and on the occasion of his death, his cannon exploded at its seventy-eighth discharge, killing him instantly. The report of his commander records his gallantry, and suggests that the broken gun be cast into a tablet to his memory. He was buried at Warrenton, and a white shaft marks his grave.

832 LILY T. MARSHALL, b. in Warrenton, Va., March 12, 1838, = December 17, 1878, MOSES M. GREEN, b. July 1, 1837. She lost her parents in her infancy, and Mrs. Martin P. Brooke adopted her and her younger brother, and became a mother to them. Mrs. Brooke died a year ago, and Mrs. Green mourned the loss of a parent. Her only child she has named for Mr. Brooke. I dined with her in 1884, and was much interested in the family. Mr. Green was born in Northumberland Co., Va., but his father, soon after his son's birth, returned to Culpeper, his ancestral home. He was educated at William and Mary, and Emory and Henry Colleges; served throughout the war as a private in the Thirteenth Infantry, C. S. A., and the Black Horse Cavalry. He was in the principal battles of the war on Virginia soil. Mr Green is now in charge of the Warrenton Depot, and his energies are taxed with manifold duties. He is a large, handsome and very prepossessing gentleman, with fine social qualities and executive ability. See the chart of the Greens, No. 180.

(834) JAMES MARKHAM MARSHALL.

834 JAMES MARKHAM MARSHALL, b. at Warrenton, Va., September 14, 1842 d. When the war broke out he was a student at the University of Virginia; enlisted in the Black Horse Cavalry, C. S. A.; fought through the war until the battle of Second Manassas, where a horse was killed under him; and being unwell, was sent home to Warrenton, where he died, September 6, 1862. Like his sister (832), he was adopted and raised by Mrs. Martin P. Brooke.

836 LUCIE P. MARSHALL, b. at Warrenton, Va., August 31, 1852.

838 AGNES R. MARSHALL, b. at Warrenton, Va., November 8, 1858.

840 LUCY AMBLER, b. at "Morven," Fauquier Co., Va., January 29, 1820; d. August 22, 1852.

842 REV. JOHN AMBLER, b. at "Morven," April 3, 1821, = August 5, 1847, ANNA MASON, b. 1826; d. 1863. He is rector of Bloomfield Parish, Rappahannock Co., Va., and has charge of three churches — St. Paul's, Trinity and St. James'. His post-office is Washington. He is highly esteemed for piety, zeal and intelligence. His wife was the daughter of the Hon. James M. Mason, the distinguished embassador to France from the Confederacy, who, with Slidell, was captured and restored by England. Her mother was Eliza Chew. Mr. Ambler has not married again.

844 ELIZABETH AMBLER, b. at "Morven," in Fauquier Co., Va., January 20, 1823. She is a lady of literary culture and sincere piety — fond of religious reading, a pleasant correspondent, and an agreeable companion. She lives with her mother at "Church Hill," Markham. Her letters to me attest superior abilities.

(850) THOMAS MARSHALL AMBLER.

846 FANNIE AMBLER. See No. 556.

848 REV. CHARLES EDWARD AMBLER, b. at "Morven," Fauquier Co., Va., June 6, 1827, d. at Charlestown, W. Va., January 21, 1876, = 1st, July 29, 1851, BETTIE BURNETT McGUIRE, b. April 23, 1827, d. April 29, 1856; = 2d, September 5, 1860, SUSAN WOOD KEYS, b. January 29, 1837. She still lives at Charlestown, W. Va. Mr. Ambler was educated at the Episcopal Theological Seminary, near Alexandria, Va.; was ordained by Bishop Meade in 1838; ministered to several churches in Albemarle Co., Va.; was called to Charlestown, W. Va., in 1853, and was for nearly fourteen years rector of the parish, which prospered spiritually under his affectionate ministry; resigned in 1866, on account of ill-health; afterward served for a few months, the church at Front Royal, but disease required him to quit preaching. He died at Charlestown, at the residence of his father-in-law, the late Humphrey Keys. His labors in Charlestown were greatly blessed, and all denominations mourned his loss. A tablet to his honor was placed in the church by his affectionate parishioners. His first wife was a daughter of Rev. Edward C. McGuire, rector of St. George Church, Fredericksburg, Va., whose mother was Judith Lewis, a grand niece of Washington. See Lewis chart, 150 *i*. His second wife was a daughter of Humphrey Keys, a merchant, of Charlestown, b. April 20, 1797, d. September 12, 1875, and his wife, Jane Hammond Brown, b. October 7, 1803, d. March 14, 1879. I have an excellent letter from Mrs. Ambler, which testifies to her finished education and literary acquirements, as well as her pious appreciation of her husband's memory. For the McGuires, see the Lewis chart, No. 150 *h*.

850 THOMAS MARSHALL AMBLER, b. at "Morven," Fauquier Co., Va., May 21, 1829, = 1st, May 20, 1856, ANNA BLAND BOLLING, dr. of Robert Bolling, and —— Blackwell. She was born 1835, d. March 10, 1859; = 2d, October 18, 1860, VIRGINIA MARGARETTA SHARP, b. December, 1836, d. February 11, 1871. She was a dr. of William Sharp and Marianna Schoolfield, of Norfolk. = 3d, October 16, 1873, ELIZABETH FISHER CUSTIS, b. June 12, 1845, in

(852) RICHARD JACQUELIN AMBLER.

Accomac Co., Va. Mr. Ambler was educated at the Episcopal High School, near Alexandria; graduated, 1849, at the University of Virginia, and finished his theological course at the Episcopal Seminary, near Alexandria, in 1853; preached successively in Dinwiddie, Powhatan and Botetourt Counties, and at Williamsburg, Va., and now officiates at St. Paul's, Wilmington, N. C. As a minister, he is much esteemed and beloved. The Custis family, of Virginia, are descended, from the Hon. John Custis, of Arlington, Northampton Co., Va., who was a member of the Colonial Council, and April 17, 1692, petitioned to be relieved from his several official positions, on account of old age and infirmity. The Council, in granting his request, referred in complimentary terms to the valuable services he had rendered the Colony, and especially during Bacon's rebellion. His daughter,

1. Tabitha Custis, grand-daughter of John, of Arlington, = Edmund Custis, nephew of the same. Edmund died in 1700.
2. Their son, Thomas Custis, d. 1721.
3. John Custis, d. 1809.
4. John Custis, d. 1847.
5. James W. Custis, d. 1878, = Margaret P. Bayly.
6. Elizabeth F. Custis, = T. M. AMBLER.

852 RICHARD JACQUELIN AMBLER, b at "Morven," three miles south of Markham, Fauquier Co., Va., April 13, 1831; d. at Clifton, in the same county, February 17, 1876, = August 12, 1857, ANNA MADISON WILLIS, b. October 16, 1836; lives at Clifton, near Markham, Mr. Ambler was educated at the University of Virginia, receiving the degree of A. M. In 1858, he built a fine house at Clifton, and opened a High School for boys,— fitting them for college. Here he labored with success until the war broke out. He enlisted in the Twelfth Virginia Cavalry, and experienced all the dangers and hardships of a common soldier. He was captured April 11, 1865, and imprisoned at Point Lookout, until the surrender. He came home in bad health and dejected spirits, but his wife rejoicing in his return, urged a resumption of his school, which flourished until his death. In his closing years he engaged the assistance

THE MARSHALL FAMILY. 265

(854) MARY CARY AMBLER—(*Stribling*).

of his venerable relative, Edward C. Marshall (160). He was buried at Leeds' Church, where a monument marks his grave. Mrs. Ambler lives with her younger children at Clifton, and her house is the summer resort of city boarders. I have never met her, but her letters to me prove she is a good, pure and intelligent lady. Mr. Ambler was honored and beloved.

THE WILLIS FAMILY.

1. Thos. C. Willis, = Fanny Madison Hite, cousin of President Madison.
2. Thos. Hite Willis, b. 1800; d. January 14, 1884, = Elizbeth Ryland.
3. Anna M. Willis, = RICHARD JACQUELIN AMBLER.

854 MARY CARY AMBLER, b. at "Morven," Fauquier Co., Va., September 9, 1835, d. February 9, 1868, = August, 1857, COL. ROBERT M. STRIBLING, b. December 3, 1833. She is said to have been a lovely character. She was buried at Leeds' church, and her epitaph reads: " Mary Cary, wife of Robert Stribling, and daughter of Thomas M. and Lucy Ambler, born September 9, 1835, died February 9, 1868. Rejoice in the Lord, O, ye righteous, 33 Ps. 4." Col. Stribling is a soldier, a statesman and a scientist. He was born at Mountain View, in the town of Markham, and still resides there. He received his literary course at the University of Virginia; graduated in medicine at Philadelphia, and spent four years at the Dispensary of that city; practiced both before and after the war; raised a regiment of Artillery, which he commanded throughout the war. He was at the first and second battles of Manassas; the nine days fight around Richmond; Fraizier's farm; Fair Oaks; Malvern Hill; Gettysburg, and at nearly every bloody field on the soil of Virginia. After the war, he served three successive terms in the Virginia Legislature, and is now a member of that body. He married for his second wife, AGNES A. DOUTHAT, No. 1324, who still lives. The first Mrs. Stribling, attended her husband in many of his campaigns, and witnessed the terrible carnage of the red fiend of war. She attended school in Winchester and Alexandria, and like the other members of the Ambler family,

(856) MARY PAXTON — (*Harbeson*).

she was a zealous and much beloved member of the Episcopal Church. Col. Stribling is descended from the Lewis family. See chart, No. 150 c 152 d.

856 MARY PAXTON, b. in Washington, Ky., October 22, 1813; d. in Flemingsburg, Ky., March 5, 1868, = December 5, 1831, in Mason Co., Ky., BENJ. HARBESON, b. in Pennsylvania, July 18, 1810; d. in Flemingsburg, Ky., October 25, 1860. Sister Mary, after the death of our parents, was reared by our Aunt Lucy Marshall (178), in Mason Co., Ky., and by our stepmother (180). Her finishing education was at a female school at Cincinnati, where she met Mr. Harbeson, then in the leather trade. She was married by Dr. Wm. L. Breckenridge, at our uncle, John Marshall's house, four miles west of Washington, Ky. After living a year in Cincinnati, Mr. Harbeson spent some years in, and near, Washington, when he purchased the Humphrey farm, two miles northwest of Washington. In 1844, he purchased the Cox farm, adjacent to Flemingsburg, and here he lived until his death. Sister Mary was tall and slender, with dark eyes and smiling face, cordial in her greetings and constant in her affections,—artless as a child, guileless as a lamb, and pure as the dews of heaven   (See 244 j). She united with the Presbyterian Church when young, and was seldom absent from the weekly prayer meeting, and the stated services of her church. Her pastor, Dr. J. P. Hendrick, thus notices her:

"It was my pleasure to know your sister well, during the latter years of her life, and there are but few persons whose memory I cherish with more sincere veneration and affection than hers. She was brought up in the neighborhood of Washington, Ky., and carefully instructed both in secular knowledge and divine truth. Early in life she yielded herself to the claims of the blessed Master, and became a communicant in the Presbyterian Church of Washington, Ky., then under the pastorate of John H. Conditt. I knew her best after her removal to Flemingsburg. She possessed great force of character. Her mind was quick in its operations, and well stored with useful knowledge. She was an observer of current events, read the periodical literature of her day, and in bible truth and ecclesiastical matters was well informed. Her religious convictions were clear, deep and controlling. Duties to her Master were paramount to all other duties, or rather permeated and entered into every other. Her piety was intelligent, uniform and consistent; and though her temperament was ardent, and at times enthusiastic, her religion was of the even and thorough type. In her personal attachments she was singularly earnest. Her friendships were warm and lasting. In early and middle life, she was a woman of remarkable

(858) ALEX. MARSHALL PAXTON.

beauty. In later years ill health effaced some of her earlier personal attractions,—though to the day of her death she was beautiful. She was deeply loved and greatly bemoaned."

Mr. Harbeson was born in Philadelphia, Penn., of Scotch-Irish parents. His father died when Benjamin was three years old, and he was reared by his maternal grandfather, Mathew Lawler, who was a sea captain, and afterwards in the leather trade. The boy was taught the currier and tanner's trade. Before his majority, Benjamin, by the death of his grandfather, inherited $33,000. With his mother, he and his two brothers came to Cincinnati, and engaged in the leather business. After removing to Fleming County, he was elected to the Leglislature in 1849. His person was handsome and impressive, with black curling hair and sparkling black eyes. He was five feet ten inches high, and weighed 230 pounds. Until his strength and agility were reduced by rheumatism, he was an athlete. Intelligent, lively, convivial, generous and hospitable, he made many friends, and never lost one. The most remarkable trait of his character was his stern regard for truth. He was an over-indulgent father, and the tenderest of husbands. He was a remarkable judge of character, and seemed to know men by intuition. It was said that he was never mistaken in his opinion of persons. In religion he possessed the predilictions of his Scotch ancestry for Presbyterianism. He lies buried in the Flemingsburg cemetery, where his fine monument is inscribed with only his name and the dates of his death and birth.

858 (a) ALEX. MARSHALL PAXTON, b. in Washington, Ky., February 4, 1816, d. in Covington, Ky., February 12, 1851, = in Covington, Ky., October 22, 1840, SALLIE BUSH, b. April 2, 1823, d. June 24, 1854, in Covington, Ky. My brother was called Marshall or "Mat." From his infancy he stuttered, and the mercantile business was selected for him. After receiving a good English education at Augusta College, and a smattering of Latin, from his cousin, Dr. J. A. McClung (272), he went to Cincinnati as a clerk in the wholesale grocery house of Kilgour, Taylor & Co. Here he remained until his majority, when he, with another clerk, started the wholesale house of Paxton & Keys, on Main street. Keys was a splendid salesman, and Marshall an excellent bookkeeper and cor-

(858) ALEX. MARSHALL PAXTON.

respondent. The young men met with favor, and did a large business. After a few years, Lafayette Maltby (652) became a partner, and stationed himself at New Orleans; and branches were established at Rio and Havana. His marriage was extremely fortunate. Sister Sallie was one of the most amiable young ladies that I ever met. She made my brother's home an Eden of delight. She was a favorite among her husband's relatives. He was supremely blest in his lovely wife and blooming daughter (2164). They were beautiful in their lives, and in death they were not divided. At the age of thirty-five, he died of disease of the kidneys; and a few years later his widow followed him. They are buried at Covington. On the death of my brother, our sister Mary (856) wrote me a long letter, which is now mislaid. Sister Phœbe (188), in a letter dated April 16, 1851, writes: "Sister wrote you immediately on the death of our dear brother, and told you about his last days. It will be gratifying to you to know that Marshall, though delirious, mentioned you three times in the last day of his life. He appeared conscious that you were not near him, and was, I think, very anxious to see you. Brother, I think we will all be short lived. Our parents were so before us, and one of our number being taken, should warn us to prepare for death. God in his mercy grant that this effect may be produced on all of us. I send you a small lock of Marshall's hair." [Now before me.]

(b) I copy a letter from sister Sallie, dated Covington, Ky., May 4, 1851: "DEAR Brother—I send you by mail a likeness of your dear deceased brother. I would have sent it sooner, knowing it would have been a gratification to you to even see his likeness, but I have been entirely unfitted for anything. It is a copy of one I had, and therefore not so good a likeness. When Marshall received your letter desiring him to send you his likeness, he said it was just what he had been thinking of doing, and that he wanted yours. It would give me much satisfaction to have your likeness, and also to receive letters from you. The happiness and prosperity of your family will always be a subject of great interest to me. Lydia is in fine health. She feels more and more, every day, the loss of her dear father. My health is not good, but I have a great desire to live for the sake of my child. There are none who can supply the place of parents. I was much in hopes we would see you this spring. Lydia will write to you soon. I heard from sister Mary (856) and

(858) ALEX. MARSHALL PAXTON.

Phœbe (188) a short time ago. They were all well. Love to your wife. Ever your sister, Sallie P. Paxton." My brother lived most of his married life with his father-in-law, Philip Bush, one of the best men I ever knew. In 1870, I called at his house in Covington to see him. He was not at home, but I was told he could be found in the cemetery. All his family, except one daughter, were there, and he desired to be near them. He therefore had had himself appointed superintendent of the grounds, and he busied himself in making green the graves of those he loved. I went to the cemetery to meet him, and to drop a tear on my brother's grave. I found him there with several hands improving the grounds. But Oh, how he was changed! He was now unconcerned about this life. His dear ones and his home were beyond the skies. Instead of the genial, hearty salutation of his early life, he met me with a tear. Not long afterwards he was gathered to his own. While his dear ones lived, he was one of the most cordial and agreeable men I ever met. It was sunshine to the heart to be in his company. His unbounded love for "Marshall," and his perfect confidence in him, were his favorite themes. On the occasion referred to, he spoke of him so feelingly that my own grief was lost in his superior sorrow. When I look back to the dark and cheerless years of my brother's orphanage, I rejoice that he had ten years of married bliss, while surrounded by intelligent Christian friends, who loved and almost adored him. I will add the inscriptions on their tombs:

"MARSHALL PAXTON, born February 4, 1819; died February 12, 1851. And God shall wipe away all tears from their eyes, and there shall be no more death. Rev. 21: 4."

"SALLY PENDLETON, daughter of PHILIP S. and V. BUSH, and wife of A. M. PAXTON, born April 2, 1823; died June 24, 1854. Looking unto Jesus. These all died in faith."

(c) THE BUSH FAMILY.

Philip Bush, the eldest son of John Bush and Sally Craig, was b. at North Bend, Ky., March 27, 1795, d. at Covington, Ky., October 4, 1871, = March 27, 1817, Vicy Tonsey, dr. of Thomas Tousey and Lydia Percival, of Harpersfield, N. Y., b. July 25, 1799, d. July 28, 1868.

THEIR CHILDREN.

(d) 1, Victor T. Bush, b. March 6, 1818; 2, John Smith Bush, b. September 11, 1819, d. November 16, 1850, = 1st, July 10, 1843,

(860) PHŒBE ANN PAXTON — (*Marshall*).

Mary J. Riddell; = 2d, October 2, 1845, Elizabeth Smith Bush; 3, Lydia Ann. Bush, b. June 20, 1821, = April 23, 1849, William Ernst, son of John C. Ernst, b. December 9, 1813; 4, SALLY PENDLETON BUSH, = A. M. PAXTON; 5, Mary Gaines Bush, b. March 17, 1825, d. April 7, 1855, = February 20, 1843, Joseph Chambers, son of Robert; 6, Elvira P. Bush, b. July 9, 1827; 7, Eliza Smith Bush, b. April 23, 1829, d. August 7, 1852; 8, Julien C. Bush, b. May 8, 1831, d. October 30, 1862, = October 15, 1850, Robert R. Lynd, son of Samuel; 9, Matilda T. Bush, b. August 7, 1834; 10, Catherine A. Bush, b. May 27, 1837; 11, Ella Bush, b. August 7, 1840.

860 PHŒBE ANN PAXTON. See No. 188.

862 WILLIAM MCCLUNG PAXTON, b. in Washington, Ky., March 2, 1819, = October 1, 1840, MARY FORMAN, b. September 25, 1819. My father, when I was four years old removed to Columbus, O., to continue the practice of law; here my mother died. My father married again, the cousin of my mother, and we continued to reside in Columbus. In 1825 my father died, while on a visit to Kentucky, and his four children were left in charge of their step-mother. Though a faithful and pious woman, she had no love for children, and was over zealous in training, but wanting in affection. Perhaps it was for our good. She was a woman of uncommon intellectual accomplishments, but she had no patience with her wayward charges. Yet I owe so much to her instructions, that I shall never cease to thank her while she lives, and to honor her name when her gray hairs shall descend to the grave. (See No. 180.) We were sent to live with our Aunt, Lucy Marshall (178), whose indulgence was a veil of charity, that covered our many sins. But it was a severe change from parental love to the rule of a step-mother. After my mother's death, I had been my father's pet. I had inherited from the McDowells a flaming red head, and had derived from some unknown source a magnificent cowlick, which left my forehead large and prominent. These peculiar features called forth many remarks that were generally flatter-

THE MARSHALL FAMILY. 271

(862) WILLIAM M'CLUNG PAXTON.

ing. Our step-mother soon grew tired of us, and sent us to school, The nest was broken up, and the brood scattered. My sisters were sent to boarding schools, and my brother Marshall and I went two years to Augusta College. In 1832 we were at Cousin John A. McClung's, studying Latin under his tuition. There he left me, and became a clerk in a wholesale house in Cincinnati (858). Left alone, friendless, homeless and companionless, how I longed for affection and fellowship. In the "Orr Mansion," on the Ohio Cliffs, with its wide corridors, high ceilings, haunted halls, and clattering shutters, I had to sleep upstairs at the extreme end of the house, and out of hearing of the family, all alone. I was just at the ghost-seeing age of thirteen. How happy I was when Aunt McClung would come, and allow me to make my pallet in her room. I next went to Cincinnati and spent two years at the Catholic "Athenæum"—now St. Zavier's College. In December, 1834, my step-mother took me to Danville, Ky., and entered me in the Freshman Class of Center College. A month later she married Judge John Green (180), and I took up my home for four years at "Waveland," his hospitable dwelling a mile from Danville. Here the happiest years of my unmarried life were spent. In 1838 I returned to Washington, Ky., and entered on the study of law with McClung & Taylor, living with my sister Phœbe. In 1849, I was licensed, and after practicing a few months, removed to Platte Co., Mo., where I still reside. In 1840 I returned and married Miss Mary Forman, whose beauty charmed my youth, whose love inspired my manhood, and whose faithfulness drives back the clouds of age. After our return to Missouri, I purchased a large body of unimproved land, and foolishly left my practice, to live on it. After nine years of unsuccessful farming, I returned to Platte City, and in 1850, opened a general store in partnership with Dr. H. B. Callahan. In 1853 we purchased the Platte City Water Mills. I was active in business, and had accumulated a small fortune. But when the war broke out, and all my friends went South, I found that my security debts exceeded my property, and I saw nothing but ruin before me. I therefore determined to resume the practice of law. I succeeded and all my debts were paid and a competency left. I paid $25,000 of other people's debts, without a suit being instituted against me. In 1870, finding myself free of debt and every liability, I divided what I had into five parcels, giving one share

(864) DR. SAMUEL MARSHALL.

to my wife, three shares to my three daughters, and kept one for myself. But in 1875, I became hard of hearing, and my practice was ruined. My deafness has increased from year to year, until now I can converse only by using a trumpet. I still keep an office and make a few hundred dollars annually by conveyancing and examining titles. To employ the intervals of business, I commenced in 1878 to write poetry, and occasionally published a piece. In 1881, I issued a volume of 135 pages of my fugitive pieces, and gave six hundred copies to my friends. I had long been gathering genealogical data, and in 1884 I formed a chart of the Marshall family, and had it engraved. Two hundred copies were printed and sent to the principal members of the family. In July, 1884, I started on a visit to all my mother's relatives in Kentucky, Virginia and Maryland. My daughter, Phœbe, went with me. We spent two months going from house to house, during which I gathered the materials for this work. I have since been corresponding with friends all over the Union to get the facts to be embodied in my chart and book. If God spares me, I propose in a year or two, to issue another volume of poems, some of which have appeared in our county papers. I inherited Presbyterianism; have long been a member, and an elder in that church; have for thirty-five years superintended a Sabbath School, though deafness is a great disqualification. I was a Whig before the war, and a mighty poor party-Democrat since. I opposed secession with all my powers; sympathized deeply with friends at the South, but knew their cause was hopeless; never left my home for an hour; both parties seemed to think I was harmless, and let me alone. My decided stand against secession in the outstart, gave me influence with Federal officers, and I did much to soften the asperities of war in my county. I have only Southern blood in my veins—my friends and kindred are all in the South, and it was to save them that I raised my voice for the Union, and bowed to the stars and stripes. For the Forman family, see No. 660.

864 DR. SAMUEL MARSHALL, b. at Northfork, Mason Co., Ky., October 9, 1828, = May 10, 1854, to MARY C. STEVENSON, who died September 17, 1867. Dr. Marshall is well read in medi-

THE MARSHALL FAMILY. 273

(870) ELIZA LEWIS MARSHALL—(*Anderson*).

cine, an agreeable gentleman, and a successful physician, but lacks energy. He is doing an irregular practice at Northfork, and lives by himself. His wife was a daughter of Thomas B. Stevenson, so well known as an editor, and Sarah Combs.

866 EDWARD MARSHALL, b. at Northfork, Mason Co., Ky., October 5, 1830; is a confirmed old bachelor, intelligent and agreeable. He lives with his brother James (872) and makes himself useful.

868 ALEXANDER K. MARSHALL, b. at Northfork, Mason Co., Ky., July 7, 1832, = July 12, 1859, ELIZA DUDLEY, b. in Flemingsburg, Ky., June 20, 1843. Cousin Aleck's father left him a handsome estate, which he has increased by prudent management. In early life he turned his attention to rearing fine stock; and, with a view of selecting the best breeds that the world afforded, he paid a visit to Europe, and after a thorough investigation, returned with a choice herd. He possesses untiring energy, sound judgment, and enlightened enterprise. A railroad depot is on his place, and he has fostered a little town at Marshall's station. He is growing wealthy, and is beginning to manifest some political aspirations. He often speculates successfully in tobacco and other produce. Everything about him indicates prosperity. I have often enjoyed his hospitality. Cousin Eliza has a heart full of kindness. She is a daughter of James Dudley and Eliza Shumate, of Flemingsburg, Ky.

870 ELIZA LEWIS MARSHALL, b. September 8, 1834, = March 28, 1859, GEORGE W. ANDERSON, b. in Jefferson Co., Tenn., May 22, 1832. Cousin Eliza was born and reared at Northfork, Mason Co., Ky., and received a good education. She visited her maternal uncle, John Luke, at Louisiana, Mo., and there met her cousin, Mr. Anderson. They were married, and he arose to distinction, but his prodigality and their incompatibility of temper, caused a separtion in 1876, and Eliza is now living with her children, upon her brother A. K. Marshall's farm. I met her in 1884,

(872) JAMES MARSHALL.

and was much pleased with her and her noble children. Mr. Anderson graduated at Franklin College, Tenn.; went to Missouri in 1853; was in the House in 1859, and the Senate, 1862; was a Colonel of Militia from 1862 to 1864, in active service; was twice elected, as a Republican, to Congress. He is now practicing law in St. Louis. He is a gentleman of cordiality, sprightliness and humor, and a fine lawyer. He is a first cousin of his wife, his mother being a Luke, sister of Eliza's mother (248).

872 JAMES MARSHALL, b. March 7, 1841, = February 11, 1864, AMELIA EVANS, b. February 3, 1844. Cousin James is a prosperous farmer, and lives on a part of the ancestral farm, at Northfork, Mason Co., Ky. Amelia's parents were John Evans and Lucinda Parker, of Mason Co., Ky.

874 BETTIE MARSHALL, b. in Bourbon Co., Ky., July 18, 1828, = November 14, 1844, HENRY BUFORD, b. October, 1822, d. 1848. I have not met Cousin Bettie since she was a little girl, but I have lately received a kind letter from her. She is a widow, staying chiefly at Lexington, Ky. Mr. Buford was the only child of Charles Buford, then of Scott Co., Ky., but afterwards of Rock Island, Ill. (286), and his first wife, Henrietta, daughter of Gov. John Adair. He died young, just as he was rising to distinction.

876 JOHN L. MARSHALL, b. in Paris, Ky., October 28, 1831, = November 2, 1852, MARY E. TURNER, dr. of Judge Fielding Turner, of Lexington, Ky., b. June —, 1834; they were divorced in 1859; and he = 2d, August 10, 1871, KATE F. WALKER, *nee* ANDREWS. Cousin John is a handsome and accomplished gentleman. He was educated for the law, but never entered into the regular practice, further than required in the discharge of his duties of Commissioner in Chancery and Abstractor of land titles — the former in Louisville, and the latter in Milwaukee. He served four years in the Confederate army as a private in the First Kentucky, or "Orphan Brigade," which was to the Western army what the famous "Stonewall Brigade" was to the army of Virginia. He is an

THE MARSHALL FAMILY. 275

(882) KATE CALLOWAY MARSHALL.

accountant, and is employed at a good salary in Louisville, Ky. He is a gentleman of fine literary attainments, solid judgment, and enlightened views on the social and political questions of the day. His children have all found employment away from home, and with his wife he keeps house. She is in delicate health, and is a great sufferer. I visited them in 1884, and was much pleased with them. Cousin Kate is a charming lady, and her efforts to be agreeable in spite of the irritations of disease, call for sympathy as well as love. She was an Andrews, of Fleming Co., Ky., and widow of William Walker.

878 ALEXANDER KEITH MARSHALL, b. at Paris, Ky., September 25, 1839, = November 8, 1877, MARY GREATHOUSE, dr. of Dr. —— Greathouse and Mary E. Hancock, b. September 8, 1841, d. June 1, 1878. He went at the age of thirteen, with the family to Milwaukee; attended the University of Wisconsin, and passed through the junior year; entered on the study of medicine with McDowell & Marshall, at Chillicothe, Mo.; when the war commenced, entered the irregular service of the Confederacy; afterwards lived successively in Cincinnati, Chicago, San Francisco, Louisville and St. Louis. He was, in 1884, clerk of a granite and marble company in the latter city.

880 MARY McDOWELL MARSHALL, b. in Paris, Ky., 1843, = 1862, CHARLES W. MITCHELL, oldest son of the late Thomas M. Mitchell, cashier of the Bank of Kentucky, at Danville, Ky. They are now living, in reduced circumstances, in Louisville, Ky. Mary was at one time said to be the loveliest woman in the State of Kentucky. I have not met her since her infancy, but have seen her likeness, which testifies to her beauty. Mr. Mitchell is a traveling agent for a publishing house.

882 KATE CALLOWAY MARSHALL, b. March 2, 1846; is a handsome and accomplished lady. She now enjoys a good salary as a clerk in the money order department of the Louisville, Ky., postoffice. She is a noble and heroic young woman, devoting all her time and means to the support and consolation of her aged and bed-ridden mother.

(884) JANE MARSHALL SULLIVANT — (*Neil*).

884 (*a*) JANE MARSHALL SULLIVANT, b. in Franklinton, Ohio, December 11, 1824, = May 30, 1843, ROBERT ELKIN NEIL, of Columbus, Ohio, b. May 12, 1819. Cousin Jane lost her mother a few days after her birth. But the feeble child survived, and when four years of age, she was sent with me and my orphan brother and sisters to live with Aunt Lucy Marshall (178) in that kindergarten she kept at her home. Cousin Jane grew in beauty and loveliness, and when I last saw her, at sweet seventeen, she possessed queenly beauty. For some years we have kept up an occasional correspondence. Though now upwards of sixty, she has not lost her dove-like innocence, purity and affection. I am vain enough to quote from one of her letters the following passage: " I assure you I appreciate the kind motive that prompted you to wish to keep up a correspondence with a cousin who never can forget how, as a mere child she loved you devotedly. I can see myself running to meet you and greet you in the evening, when returning from school to Uncle John's (178) — how you would take me in your arms, caress me and show me a thousand little kindnesses that won my heart's love and devotion. Those days of innocent childhood! How I look back upon them with fond remembrance — upon my innocence and faith in every one who was kind and tender to me. You, dear Cousin William, I believe, was my *beau ideal* of all manliness. I have often regretted that we had never met since those early days." Cousin Jane's home is in Columbus, Ohio, but she is often with her daughters in Washington or Brooklin, Mass. I have made two efforts to meet her in late years, but on both occasions she was with her daughter in New England. Mr. Neil is a gentleman of sound and practical judgment, a sagacious business man and a successful manager of his large patrimony. His father was wealthy, and his wife brought him a large estate. His father appointed him trustee of the large hotel in Columbus, known as the "Neil House." He has a large landed property in the city, which he is improving. His wealth enables him to give a generous aid to every local enterprise, whether of improvement, charity or religion. He leads in every business project for the advancement of the city, and he has done much to make Columbus a beautiful place.

THE NEIL FAMILY.

(*b*) 1. Allen Neil, b. near Glasgow, Scotland, August 8, 1765,

THE MARSHALL FAMILY. 277

(896) LOUIS CHRISMAN MARSHALL.

d. near Winchester, Ky., June 5, 1806, = in Scotland, Nancy ——, b. June 2, 1770. Their son:

2. William Neil, b. near Winchester, Ky., December 4, 1788, d. in Columbus, May 18, 1870. Came to Columbus, Ohio, in 1818; was cashier of the old Franklin bank; after engaging in enterprises that took him to New Orleans and Liverpool, he formed the great stage company of the West, known as "Neil, Moore & Co.;" through energy and enterprise he accumulated wealth, and was known as the "Stage King." He built the "Neil House," and his wife, Hannah, was distinguished for her beneficence. She was a Methodist of zeal and piety; established what is known as the "Hannah Neil Mission," and liberally endowed it; and her name and deeds of love are recorded on a marble tablet in "Wesley Chapel," which was a large recipient of her bounty.

3. Their son, Robert Elkin Neil, = JANE SULLIVANT.

894 COL. LOUIS HENRY MARSHALL, b. in Baltimore, Md., about 1827; educated at West Point; = 1st, June 25, 1854, FLORENCE BURKE; she d. 1882; = 2d, June, 1884, ELVIRA C. WHITE. They now live at Los Angeles, Cal. Mr. Marshall graduated at West Point; was brevetted Second Lieutenant 3d U. S. Infantry July 1, 1849; Second Lieutenant, 5th of March, 1851; First Lieutenant 10th Infantry, March 3, 1855; Captain, December 29, 1860; Major, 14th Infantry, October 16, 1863; transferred to 23d Infantry, September 21, 1866; resigned, November 23, 1868; brevetted Colonel March 13, 1865, for gallant and meritorious services during the war of the rebellion. After resigning, Col. Marshall went to California, whither his father had preceded him, and engaged unsuccessfully in business. He and his second wife and four daughters of his first marriage are leading an humble life in Los Angeles. I received a kind letter from him, dated April 15, 1885.

896 LOUIS CHRISMAN MARSHALL, b. in Nicholasville, Ky., February 17, 1835, = 1st, October, 1866, LUCY HART, of Fayette Co., Ky. She d. August 1, 1867; = 2d, December 1, 1875, AGATHA LOGAN, his cousin, b. October 11, 1844, at "Sher-

(898) AGATHA LOGAN—(*Marshall*).

wood," Woodford Co., Ky. He received his education from his grand-father, Dr. Marshall, and at Frankfort Military Institute. He and his second wife live on a farm near East Hickman, Fayette Co., Ky. The letters of Cousin Agatha indicate superior mind and education.

898 AGATHA LOGAN; see No. 896.

900 ANNIE PRISCILLA LOGAN, b. at "Sherwood," Woodford Co., Ky., April 26, 1847, = COL. THOMAS WALKER BULLITT, b. at Oxmoor, Jefferson Co., Ky., May 17, 1838. Mrs. Bullitt's letters testify to her literary attainments, sound judgment and business ability. My high opinion of her good sense was strengthened by meeting her at her own hospitable board in 1884. But she is a daughter of my old class-mate at Center College, and I was prepared to see only excellencies. Mr. Bullitt is an eminent lawyer, and has fine practice at the Louisville bar. He was in Morgan's Cavalry in the war. He spent the last two years of the war, a prisoner at Fort Delaware. Mr. Bullitt's family are from Virginia. He is a grand nephew of Patrick Henry. His father was William Christian Bullitt, and his mother Mildred Ann Fry. His great-grand-father, William Christian, was killed by the Indians in 1786. See Fry chart No. 180 *l*.

902 MIRA MADISON LOGAN, b. in Louisville, Ky., April 18, 1849. Lives in Louisville.

904 MARY KEITH LOGAN, b. in Louisville, Ky., November 22, 1851, = August 8, 1880. DR. DAVID CUMMINS, a merchant, who is now dead. She lives in Louisville. Her only child died in infancy.

(914) WILLIAM M'CLUNG WOOLFOLK.

912 REV. LUCIEN B. WOOLFOLK, D. D., b. in Woodford Co., Ky., July 21, 1829, = April 17, 1855, ELIZABETH CUNNINGHAM, of Davidson Co., Tenn. Educated at Yale College and Brown University; entered the Baptist ministry early in life; edited the *Baptist Standard* at Nashville, Tenn., for two years, until the war began; was pastor two years at Knoxville, Tenn.; after the war ,preached in Kentucky six years, and in the midst of ministerial duties, wrote voluminously for the religious press; wrote and published the "World's Crises," a volume of political philosophy o, six hundred pages; was compelled, by failing health, to go to the Rocky Mountains; preached two years at Helena, Montana, as a missionary, under appointment of the Board at New York; returned to the States in 1873, on acceptance of a call from the First Baptist Church of Lexington, Ky.; preached by appointment the Centennial sermon before the General Association at Louisville, Ky., which was published and much admired; delivered two addresses by invitation before the Legislature of Kentucky, one on Meteorological Science, and the other on Penal Reform; this honor was never shared by any other minister except Dr. R. J. Breckenridge; received the doctorate of divinity from Georgetown College; was disabled by a railway accident in 1877, which rendered him an invalid for two years; health restored, he engaged in evangelical work; and he is now pastor of the Baptist Church, at Nevada, Mo. If spared, his remaining days will be devoted to literary labors, for which the materials are already prepared.

914 WILLIAM McCLUNG WOOLFOLK, b. in Woodford Co., Ky., April 28, 1831; d. December 6, 1858, = September 11, 1855, MARY ANNIE HIGGASON, b. in Henry Co., Ky., January 1, 1830. He was educated at home under the tuition of Dr. Newton. At the age of eighteen he became a local Methodist preacher, and subsequently joined the Conference; became dissatisfied with the policy of the church, and retired from the ministry, and joined the Baptist Church; after marriage he lived a retired life in Trimble Co., Ky. His widow yet lives in Westport, Oldham Co., Ky. Her parents were Thos. C. Higgason, of Henry Co., Ky., but originally from Virginia, and Helen Stone, whose father was from Maryland. She was a niece of the celebrated Barton Stone, and was related to Wade Hampton.

(916) COL. ALEXANDER M'CLUNG WOOLFOLK.

916 COL. ALEXANDER McCLUNG WOOLFOLK, b. in Woodford Co., Ky., September 1, 1835,= 1868, ANNA SWALLOW, b. in Missouri, June 26, 1848. He graduated at Georgetown College; was chosen valedictorian in a class of twenty-five; after studying law, settled at Chillicothe, Mo., in 1858; two years later was elected a member of the State Convention; went into the Missouri E. Militia as Lieutenant Colonel of Cavalry; published a tract advocating a Southern alliance, which gave offense to the Federal officers; resigned in 1863; was Democratic candidate for Attorney General of Missouri in 1864; removed in 1865, to Helena, Montana; practiced law successfully for several years, until failing health demanded rest; afterwards edited the Helena *Independent*; has declined two Democratic nominations for Congress; has of late years been greatly interested in mining speculations, and was, when last heard from, getting up an invention of some kind. Col. Woolfolk is a noble and chivalrous gentleman, full of energy and enthusiasm in every cause in which he is enlisted, and is much honored for his intelligence, energy and integrity. His wife is the only child of the celebrated geologist, Prof. G. C. Swallow, of Missouri. Col. Woolfolk first married Lizzie Ware, daughter of John H. Ware, of Lynn Co., Mo. She lived only about a year, and died childless.

918 CHARLES E. WOOLFOLK, b. in Woodford Co., Ky., February —, 1838; removed to Illinois in 1860; = a Miss RICHARDSON, and died in 1868, leaving an only daughter.

920 JOHN WILLIAM McCLUNG, b. in Mason Co., Ky., November 21, 1826, = June 5, 1851, MARY R. ALLEN, b. July 16, 1830. After acquiring the rudiments of an English, Latin and Greek education, Mr. McClung entered Center College, Danville, Ky. Here he passed through the junior year, and returned to Washington, Ky., where, for two years he read law with McClung & Taylor; graduated in law at Transylvania University; practiced in Mason County, during the years 1848–50; went to Cincinnati and embarked all his means in the wholesale grocery business, and after two years found he had lost nearly all he had invested; tried

(920) JOHN WILLIAM M'CLUNG.

the commission business with no better success; in July 1854, removed to St. Paul, Minn.; resumed the practice of law, and after one year's experience, was tempted to invest in real estate; succeeded for a time, — was burned out, and reduced to financial extremities; took courage, borrowed money at exorbitant interest, and built several houses; lost all during the war, but at its close profited by the advance of property, and at length found himself possessed of a sufficient sum to pay all his old debts. During all his financial embarassments, Mr. McClung preserved his credit for promptness, and could raise the money for his various speculations. As Assessor of the city and subsequently of the county, he enjoyed a good salary, and acquired much honor for his ability. In 1868, he was chief editor of the St. Paul *Pioneer*, and gained from his Democratic friends the reputation of the best writer in the West. In 1870, he published a volume entitled "Minnesota as it is in 1870," which still remains a book of standard authority. It brought him $2,500 over expenses. In 1872 he was Secretary of the St. Paul board of Public Works, with a salary of $1,000, and at the same time was Assessor. For many years he has been an influential member of the Chamber of Commerce, and by his intelligence and enterprise, has done much for the city and county of St. Paul. He has been active in impressing on the people and city authorities the importance of securing parks and roads, and in procuring from Congress appropriations for the improvement of the Mississippi. But in nothing, has his energy and public spirit appeared to greater advantage, than in the organization and management of Building Associations. Starting without capital, he has proved himself a successful financier, and yet he has paid for most of his capital from fifteen to twenty-five per cent per annum. His real estate and loan office, dates from 1856, and the firm of "McClung, McMurran & Curry," is doing an extensive business, and enjoys an enviable reputation. I knew William well in his boyhood, but for forty years all our communion has been through the mails. His likeness is a fine picture of his father (272), and like him, in middle life, he has more regard for the subtle deductions of logic, than for the demonstrations of faith. He is a chaste and impressive speaker, and a clear, forcible and epigrammatic writer. But the calls of business leave him but little time for literary pursuits. His

(922) ELIZABETH M'CLUNG—(*Browning*).

sketch of the life of his grandfather, Judge William McClung, displays talent, as well as filial veneration.

Mrs. McClung, was a daughter of Wm. S. Allen, of Mayslick, Ky., and Fanny Pepper. She received her education at the Steubenville, Ohio, Female School. She is a woman of sound good sense, and much devoted to her family.

922 ELIZABETH McCLUNG, b. in Mason Co., Ky., November 15, 1829; d. at St. Paul, Minn., April 14, 1874, = at Indianapolis, Ind., November 2, 1852, MAJ. GEORGE THOMAS BROWNING, b. at West Union, Ohio, December 5, 1820; d. at St. Paul, Minn., July 19, 1882. I remember Cousin Lizzie only in her sweet, prattling childhood. I have always heard her spoken of with affection. Mr. Browning was a wholesale grocer at Cincinnati, and Indianapolis, before the war; entered the Federal army, and served until the end of the war; was brevetted Lieutenant Colonel; was commander at the great cavalry depot at Giesboro, D. C.; in 1866, he removed to St. Paul. His father was Edward Browning, b. in Culpeper Co., Va., October 16, 1794, = Eliza Gordon, of Cincinnati, but born in Virginia. From Virginia, Mr. Edward Browning removed to Mason Co., Ky., and successively to Columbus, to Dayton, Ohio, and to Indianapolis, Ind., where he died in 1877.

924 SUSAN McCLUNG, b. in Washington, Ky., November 25, 1838. Lives with her brother, J. W. McClung, in St. Paul, Minn.

926 ANNA M. McCLUNG, b. September 8, 1842; lives in St. Paul, Minn.

940 DR. ABRAM B. DUKE, b. November 25, 1822; d. 1873, = 1st, CHARLOTTE PAYNE, dr. of Romulus Payne. After her death he married a daughter of John Armstrong. Mr. Duke went to Dr. Louis Marshall's private school, at "Buckpond," Woodford

(944) WILLIAM DUKE.

Co., Ky.; graduated in medicine at Philadelphia; commenced practice in Cincinnati; removed to St. Louis; after two years there, went to California and staid two years; returned to Georgetown; married Miss Payne; after her death, went to Covington; married Miss Armstrong.

942 BASIL DUKE, b. at Georgetown, Ky., February 28, 1824; d. in St. Louis, June 20, 1885, = April 10, 1851, in Louisville, Ky., ADELAIDE ANDERSON. He was a student of Transylvania University while his grand uncle, Dr. Louis Marshall, was president; afterwards entered Yale College, and graduated in 1845; attended the law department of Transylvania, and received a diploma in 1847; removed to St. Louis and entered the office of Geyer & Dayton, at that time one of the most noted law firms of the State; in 1849, opened a law office for himself, and was successful; was land attorney for the Iron Mountain railroad, and secured their right of way from St. Louis to Pilot Knob; was appointed Metropolitan Police Commissioner in St. Louis, by Gov. Jackson, in 1861, but retired on the change of State administration the same year; was again appointed Police Commissioner by Gov. Phelps in 1877, and served four years; was a Whig until the disorganization of that party, and afterwards was a Democrat. He was from his youth passionately addicted to manly field sports, and his dog, gun and fishing tackle engaged his leisure hours. He was six feet tall, and, prior to 1883, weighed 180 pounds; but in March of that year some disease of the heart prostrated him on his couch, which he never left. I visited him in 1884, and spent an hour by his bedside, enjoying his genial conversation. His wife is tall and stately, intelligent and agreeable, writes an excellent letter, and was tenderly attentive to her husband. She is the daughter of James Anderson, a wholesale merchant of Louisville, Ky., and Mary Anderson, an English lady of intelligence and remarkable beauty. Though of like name, they were not related.

944 WILLIAM DUKE, b. at Georgetown, Ky., April 17, 1825, = January 27, 1848, CARRIE P. HICKMAN, of Bourbon Co., Ky., b. November 21, 1829; d. September 23, 1866; = 2d, July

(946) CHARLOTTE DUKE—(Strahan).

22, 1868, ELLA DUERSON, of Louisville, b. May 1, 1842. He was educated by his great uncle, Dr. Louis Marshall; assisted his father on his farm until his first marriage; in a duel with the Confederate General Roger Hanson, brought on by a controversy about Miss Hickman's hand, Mr. Duke was slightly wounded on the second round, and on the fourth, Hanson's thigh was broken. Mr. Duke is now cultivating his farm adjacent to Danville, Ky. I met him in 1884, and was much pleased with his fine person and social disposition. I have several letters from him, which prove his superior literary attainments. Carrie P. Hickman was the mother of all Mr. Duke's children. She was the lovely daughter of John L. Hickman, Representative and Senator from Bourbon Co., Ky. His present wife is the daughter of Col. William Duerson, of Louisville, and Nancy Tate, of Pennsylvania. When last heard from, Mr. Duke's health was failing.

946 CHARLOTTE DUKE, b. at Georgetown, Ky., December 17, 1826, d. 1876, = REV. F. G. STRAHAN, b. in Mercer Co., Ky., of Scotch parentage; became a Presbyterian minister; preached at Hopkinsville and Danville, Ky., Nashville and Clarksville, Tenn., and New Orleans, La.; raised $70,000 for Danville College, and finally settled at Georgetown, Ky., and preached for several churches in Scott County, and died in 1874.

948 MARY B. DUKE, b. at Georgetown, Ky., September 27, 1828, d. at Georgetown, 1878.

950 PATTIE DUKE, b. at Georgetown, Ky., January 25, 1830, = 1st, May 9, 1854, GEN. JOHN BUFORD, b. in Woodford Co., Ky., 1828, d. December 16, 1863; = 2d, September 11, 1873, REV. BURR H. MCCOWN, D. D., b. October 29, 1806, d. August 29, 1881. I met Cousin Pattie in Louisville, Ky., in 1884, and was much interested in her conversation, as well as I have since been in her sensible letters. She is a pleasant lady, proud of the three names she has borne, and anxious to preserve the memory of her illustrious hus-

(950) PATTIE DUKE—(*McCown*).

bands. She is now with relatives in Florida. In 1837, John Buford went as a boy in his father's family to Rock Island, Ill. Here he was appointed a cadet of West Point, where he graduated with distinction in 1849, and was brevetted Second Lieutenant in the 2d Dragoons, then commanded by Col. Twiggs. But, unlike his commander, Buford remained true to the Union. In 1853, he was made First Lieutenant, and in 1859 reached the rank of Captain; was in the Utah expedition; in 1861, was made Inspector General, with the rank of Major; in 1862, was on Gen. Pope's staff; July 27, 1862, was appointed Brigadier General of volunteers, and assigned to Banks' command; was Chief of Cavalry under Burnside, and was prominent in all the cavalry operations of the Army of the Potomac. On his death-bed he was appointed Major General by President Lincoln. Gen. Buford was a soldier by nature, and his military education and experience made him one of the best commanders in the service. He enjoyed the confidence of his superiors, and was a favorite with the rank and file. His fearlessness in the hour of danger, and his coolness and discretion when others were in dismay, fitted him for hazardous enterprises. He was wounded near the Rappahannock River, in August, 1862; was reported killed at Manassas, and on the bloody field of Gettysburg his intrepidity saved the day. In November, 1863, his labors and exposure brought on disease. He was removed to Washington, where, after lingering several weeks, he died. His wife, then at Rock Island, was sent for, but did not arrive until after his death. When President Lincoln learned that the hero was dying, with characteristic promptness he wrote on a card: "I am informed that Gen. Buford will not survive the day. It suggests itself to me that he be made a Major General, for distinguished and meritorious services at the battle of Gettysburg." Two hours before his death he received with a smile of gratitude, the hastily made out commission. After services at the New York Avenue Presbyterian Church, by Dr. Gurley, the remains of the soldier were removed to West Point for burial. The officers and men of his command have erected at his grave a monument twenty-five feet high, to the honor of their brave commander. The following is one stanza of a poetic tribute to his memory, which has been extensively published:

(950) PATTIE DUKE—(*McCown*).

BUFORD.

Buford is dead!
His men no more shall see that form
Dash fearless through the battle's storm ;
They'll charge no more with him the foe,
That falls beneath his crushing blow:
For tears and voiceless sorrow tell
In tones as sad as tolling bell,
That Buford's dead.

Mrs. Buford lost all her children. A lovely daughter went to the skies, repeating the nursery prayer: "Now I lay me down to sleep;" and a son, aged seventeen, was snatched from his school-fellows and from a fond mother's heart, to join the cherubs that had gone before. It was said of Gen. Buford that he was the handsomest man in Rock Island County. Col. John Buford (father of Gen. Buford) of Rock Island, Ill., was a brother of William Buford, of Woodford Co., Ky. The latter married Fanny Kirtley, and from her their sons, Tom and Abe, get their insanity. There is no crazy blood in the descendants of Col. John Buford and of Charles Buford, and these branches alone married into the Marshall family. See Buford chart, 280 *b*.

Dr. McCown was educated at St. Joseph's College, Bardstown, Ky. He first became a Methodist preacher, and was a professor in Augusta College. When Transylvania University passed into the control of the Methodists, Profs. McCown and Bascom went there. But Prof. McCown witnessed so much crookedness in Bascom's conduct, that he left the University. In a short time Prof. McCown united with the Presbyterian Church, and preached at Walnut Hill. He next went to Hopkinsville, and finally settled in Jefferson Co., Ky., and established "Forest Academy," near Louisville. For twenty-five years, he taught and preached, without receiving compensation for the latter. But three years before his death, he found the two Presbyterian Churches to which he had been so long preaching were supplied with pastors, and that several Methodist Churches in his vicinity were vacant. So he applied to Presbytery and obtained permission to join the Methodist Conference, that he might, without compensation, preach to the vacant Methodist Churches. He fully explained to the Presbytery that his theological views were unchanged, and to the honor of all concerned, consent was given. Dr. McCown was not only a profound scholar, but was a meek, conscientious and prayerful man. He retired three times every day with his wife for prayer.

(954) CAROLINE DUKE—(Smith).

952 HENRIETTA DUKE, b. at Georgetown, Ky., July 20, 1835, = May 1, 1856, EDGAR KEENON, b. in Frankfort, Ky., August 6, 1833; d. December 4, 1882. Mr. Keenon was educated at the school of Mr. B. B. Sayer; was in the boot and shoe trade, but was broken up by the war. For the last fifteen years of his life he was U. S. Military Storekeeper at Newport, Ky.; was a Republican, and in religion leaned to the Presbyterian Church. Mrs. Keenon is now living in Covington, Ky., and my correspondence with her convinces me that she is a kind, good and sensible woman. I have never met her, though I visited her house in her absence in 1884.

954 CAROLINE (LENA) DUKE, b. at Georgetown, Ky., January 10, 1838, = October, 1856, GEN. GREEN CLAY SMITH, b. at Richmond, Ky., July 2, 1830. Mrs. Smith is a gay, lively and handsome woman,—sprightly and spirited,—fond of fashionable society and proud of her family. I visited her in 1884, having the impression on my mind that Gen. Smith was dead, and when I alluded to the *late* Gen. Smith, she frantically exclaimed: "What! do you think I am a widow! I'll let you know Gen. Smith is as live as a cricket." "Cousin Lena," I replied, "you think I am a widower, in search of a wife." "Yes," she exclaimed, "that is just what I suppose." She was mollified and became very complaisant, when I told her that I had a wife just as spry as Gen. Smith. I have since received several very pleasant letters from her. Gen. Smith is the son of the distinguished John Speed Smith, aide of Gen. Harrison. His mother was a sister of the noted Cassius M. Clay. At the age of fifteen he served in the Mexican war, and rose to First Lieutenant in the First Kentucky Cavalry, under Humphrey Marshall, whom he afterwards met as a foe in the war for the Union. He graduated at Transylvania University; read law in the office of Chief Justice T. A. Marshall, and has practiced his profession when not under arms. He was in the Kentucky Legislature at the outbreak of the war, and signalized himself by his ardent opposition to secession and the neutrality of his State. He made a memorable speech against J. C. Breckinridge and L. W. Powell on the resolution requesting them to resign as Senators from Kentucky. He enlisted as a private in the Union cause; was with Gen. Baker at the

(956) JAMES K. DUKE.

battle of Ball's Bluff; returned to Kentucky and assisted in organizing the Third Kentucky Cavalry; was appointed, February, 1862, Colonel of the Fourth Kentucky Cavalry; after serving in several minor engagements, and defeating Morgan at Lebanon, Tenn., he was promoted to the rank of Brigadier General; was highly complimented by Gen. Rosecrans, for defeating Gen. Forrest at Ruthford; was promoted as a Major General in 1863; was elected to Congress while yet in the field, from the Covington district; was re-elected in 1865, as a war Democrat; before the close of his second term, he was appointed Governor of Montana Territory; resigned in 1869, and returned to Kentucky. Gen. Smith, in 1876, was the candidate for President on the Prohibition ticket. He is now an evangelist of the Baptist Church of Kentucky, and a warm advocate of an U. S. Constitutional amendment prohibiting the manufacture, importation and sale of spiritous liquors. He is now lecturing in the Eastern States in favor of Prohibition, and prophesies the speedy success of the cause. See Green chart, 180 *k*, and Jones and Strother charts, No. 228.

956 JAMES K. DUKE, b. at Georgetown, Ky., September 2, 1839, = PAULINE BRUCE. Studied law; spent the years 1866 and 1867, in Montana, where his brother-in-law, Gen. Smith, was Governor; was appointed Clerk of the Territorial House, and discharged his duties with credit. Much of his time in the west was spent in wild sports and adventures. His marriage was unfortunate, and a separation ensued; his wife resides with her father at the St. James Hotel, in Kansas City; one of the boys is with his father in Georgetown, where he is a clerk in the postoffice; the other children are with their mother. Mr. Duke is true to the instinct of his ancestors, and follows shooting squirrels, snipes and turtles. From my short acquaintance, he seems to be a polished gentleman, and an agreeable companion.

958 LUCY DUKE, b. at Georgetown, Ky., July 13, 1842, d. 1872, = JOHN A. STEELE, of Woodford Co., Ky. She was greatly admired for her beauty and loveliness. In her mother's parlor I saw a life-size portrait of Mrs. Steele, which attests the splendor of

(960) GEN. BASIL DUKE.

her beauty. Mr. Steele was educated as a physician; was an officer in the C. S. A.; captured and imprisoned at Rock Island for two years; afterwards married and settled on a farm in Woodford Co., where his wife died. He was a son of Theophilus Steele, of Woodford County.

960 (a) GEN. BASIL DUKE, b. in Scott Co., Ky., May 28, 1837, =June 18, 1861, HENRIETTA H. MORGAN, b. April 2, 1838. He studied law in Lexington, Ky.; went to St. Louis and practiced law for three years; at the first trump of war, hastened to Lexington, Ky.; joined J. H. Morgan's militia company; in September, 1861, when the Federal troops took possession of the State, Morgan and Duke went South, and were mounted, and their followers reorganized into a cavalry company; Morgan was made Captain and Duke First Lieutenant; this company and two others formed what was known as "Morgan's Squadron;" the fall of 1861 was passed in the vicinity of Bowling Green, in various military operations, under Gen. Hindman; in February, 1862, the Confederates evacuated Kentucky; went to Nashville; Fort Donaldson surrenders; Nashville evacuated; the army of Gen. A. S. Johnston march South; Morgan and Duke continue to harass the Federals in the vicinity of Nashville; they go to Huntsville; thence to Corinth; April 4, 1862, Morgan is commissioned as Colonel, and is authorized to continue his independent operations; his "Squadron" is attached to Breckinridge's division; after the battle of Corinth, Morgan and Duke make an excursion into Tennessee, starting late in April, 1862; in May, 1862, Morgan proceeds North towards Bowling Green, Ky., leaving Duke behind on account of a severe wound received at Shiloh; Duke, having sufficiently recovered, collects some scattered men of the "Squadron," and goes to Chattanooga; meets Morgan there, and their force is increased to four hundred men; Duke is made Lieutenant Colonel; starts from Knoxville, July 4, 1862, on the first raid into Kentucky; Duke commands the 2d Kentucky Cavalry; the raid lasted until July 28, 1862; Duke goes to Sparta; thence in August, 1862, to Gallatin, Tenn., to destroy the railroad, and cut off Gen. Buell, at Nashville, from his supplies; Duke leaves Gallatin; returns to Hartsville, and remains until August 19, 1862; second raid into Kentucky commences August 29, 1862; at Lexing-

(960) GEN. BASIL DUKE.

ton, September 4, 1862; after operating in Northern Kentucky, Morgan's command reaches Lexington, October 4, 1862; he returns South; reaches Gallatin, Tenn., November 4, 1862. In December, 1862, Duke is commissioned a Colonel; the third raid into Kentucky starts December 22, 1862; in retreat, they leave Bardstown, December 30, 1862; Duke is wounded December 29, 1862, at Rolling Fork; spends the winter of 1862–63 in Tennessee; the Ohio raid starts June 10, 1863; cross the Ohio July 9, 1863; pass Cincinnati July 16, 1863; battle at Bluffington, July 19, 1863; Duke is captured and taken to Johnson's Island, and thence to the Ohio penitentiary; Morgan escapes; in February, 1864, Duke is removed to Camp Chase; he is transferred to Fort Delaware; June 26, 1864, he is exposed with other prisoners, in retaliation, to the dangers of battle; taken to Charleston and exchanged; raid into Kentucky; at Mt. Sterling, June 9, 1864; Morgan's death, September 4, 1864; Duke commissioned Brigadier General, September 15, 1864; the fall of Richmond; Duke flies South with President Davis and surrenders.

(b) Gen. Duke, after the war, settled in Louisville, engaged in the practice of law, and met with flattering success. In 1867, he published his "History of Morgan's Cavalry," a volume of 578 octavo pages. It displays great military genius, and superior literary acquirements. The author modestly veils himself in shadows, while he paints his hero in effulgent light, and secures to him merited honors, which his adversaries are disposed to withhold.

In July, 1884, I visited him, his charming wife and lovely children, at their hospitable mansion in Louisville. Though a stranger, I met with most cordial reception and flattering consideration. He is a small man with a great soul. Mrs. Duke is a beautiful woman, sprightly, intelligent and spirited. She is a sister of Gen. John H. Morgan, and cherishes his memory with affection and pride. Her children are patterns of beauty, sweetness, modesty and intelligence.

Gen. Duke was elected a representative of the City of Louisville in the State Legislature in 1869.

THE MORGANS.

(c) Calvin C. Morgan was a native of Augusta Co., Va., and a relative of Daniel Morgan of Revolutionary fame. He emigrated to Alabama, and commenced life as a merchant. In 1823,

THE MARSHALL FAMILY.

(972) BASIL D. BUFORD.

he married a daughter of John W. Hunt, of Lexington, Ky. Calvin C. removed from Alabama, and settled on a farm near Lexington, Ky. Issue:
1. Gen. John Hunt Morgan, b. June 1, 1825, d. September 4, 1864.
2. HENRIETTA MORGAN, b. April 2, 1838.

962 JOHN DUKE, = SARAH DEWEES, and died leaving no children. His widow is keeping boarding house in Washington City.

964 HARRISON TAYLOR DUKE, b. in Maysville, Ky., = NELLIE TAFT; removed to Salt Lake City, and is the cashier in the Banking House of Wells, Fargo & Co., the largest monetary institution in the West.

966 CHARLES B. DUKE, = NANNIE LEWIS. He is a merchant in Maysville, Ky. For the Lewis pedigree see 180 k, and 228.

968 LOUIS MARSHALL DUKE; unmarried; lives at Salt Lake City.

970 BASIL DUKE, b. in Maysville, Ky., = SARAH P. PHISTER. He is a merchant of Maysville.

971 MARY C. DUKE; unmarried; lives with her brothers at Salt Lake City.

972 BASIL D. BUFORD, b. in Scott Co., Ky., December 11, 1835; unmarried; he is noted for his enterprise and business qualifications. He is the principal stockholder in the manufacturing house of D. B. Buford & Co., and the manager of their immense " Plow Works," at Rock Island, Ill.

(973) CHARLES BUFORD.

973 CHARLES BUFORD, b. in Scott Co., Ky., November 18, 1837, d. June 7, 1870, = December 12, 1866, MARY POSTELWAITE, b. 1846. Mrs. Buford is in Munich, Bavaria, educating her children. The children's funds are invested in the Plow Works (972). She is not a member of the church.

974 LOUIS MARSHALL BUFORD, b. in Scott Co., Ky., November 6, 1839, = June 22, 1873, MARY SLEVIN, of Cincinnati, b. 1842. He is interested in the Rock Island "Plow Works."

976 CHARLOTTE BUFORD, b. Scott Co., Ky., November 6, 1841, lives with her mother at Rock Island (286). She is a member of the Episcopal Church.

978 SUSAN McCLUNG BUFORD, b. in Scott Co., Ky., July 20, 1844, = at Rock Island, June 17, 1869, MAJ. THEODORE EDSON, b. March 23, 1837; d. at Rock Island, November 17, 1870. Maj. Edson was a professor in West Point, and died when on a visit to his family, at Rock Island. She is an Episcopalian; lives with her mother at Rock Island.

980 HENRIETTA BUFORD, b. in Scott Co., Ky., June 27, 1847, = August 17, 1876, THOS. FRY BARBEE, b. March 29, 1846. They have no children. Mr. Barbee is a lawyer, and is also engaged in banking, in Carroll, Iowa, and was lately the Mayor of the city. He is the son of Thomas Barbee and Nancy Fry, of Boyle Co., Ky. His mother, Nancy, was a niece of Judge John Green's (180) first wife, and a sister of Mary Fry, wife of Dr. Lewis Green. They are Presbyterians. See Fry Chart 180 n.

982 LUCY BUFORD, b. in Scott Co., Ky., June 22, 1849; lives with her mother at Rock Island, is fond of reading; has visited Europe; is a member of the Presbyterian Church.

(998) JOHN J. ROYALL.

984 BLANCHE BUFORD, b. in Scott Co., Ky., December 15, 1851. She lives with her mother, at Rock Island; is a Presbyterian; is of a literary turn; fond of music; has visited Europe; and that she is clever, is demonstrated by the good letters she wrote to me.

986 GEORGE BUFORD, b. at Rock Island, Ills., October 1, 1856; removed to Kansas City about 1880, and established the house of Buford & George, in the Agricultural Implement business. He is a member of the Episcopal Church, and a young man of good literary and business acquirements.

988 MARY TAYLOR, b. in Washington, Ky., November 9, 1840, = June 8, 1871, HENRY PELHAM, b. October 8, 1840; d. October 30, 1871.

990 BESSIE H. TAYLOR, b. February 28, 1843; d. 1881, = May 30, 1867, GEORGE GILL, a lawyer of Maysville, Ky. No issue.

992 CHARLOTTE TAYLOR, b. in Maysville, Ky., November 27, 1845; lives with her mother in Maysville, Ky.

994 HARRISON TAYLOR, JR., b. February 15, 1851, in Maysville, Ky., where he now lives.

996 JOHN D. TAYLOR, b. January 16, 1856, in Maysville, Ky., where he now lives.

998 JOHN J. ROYALL, b. at Petersburg, Va., October 3, 1832; d. December —, 1880. He was precocious, and at the age of seven, was a good Latin and French scholar. He became imbecile but harmless.

(1000) GEORGE KEITH ROYALL.

1000 GEORGE KEITH ROYALL, b. in Winchester, Va., February 4, 1837. Killed August 30, 1862, at the battle of Second Manassas. He was educated at Mr. Pope's school, near "Mt. Ephraim," his father's residence; entered Princeton College in 1855; his father died in 1856, and he returned home to attend to his mother's business. In October, 1857, he entered the University of Virginia, and graduated with the degree of A. B., in 1859. Having taken his diploma in the law department of the University, he settled in Richmond and practiced until the war broke out; enlisted as a private in Company G, Eleventh Virginia Infantry; he passed through the battles of Williamsburg, the Seven Pines, the fights around Richmond, and the second battle of Manassas. At the last his head was pierced by a musket ball. His brother William saw his lifeless body, but in the heat of battle, could not give it attention. It was therefore buried on the field.

1002 MARY ARCHER ROYALL, b. November 28, 1839, = June 7, 1859, REV. R. L. McMURRAN, of the Southern Presbyterian Church. They live at Mt. Washington, Baltimore, Md. Mr. McMurran is highly esteemed as a minister. His wife's letters to me show intelligence and piety, and are full of concern for her children.

1004 HELEN MATILDA ROYALL, b. at Petersburg, Va., December 22, 1842, = January 24, 1866, DR. JOHN G. COOKE, b. May 25, 1825. I met Cousin Helen, and in 1884, spent a day with her at "Edgeworth," Fauquier Co., Va. She has since sold "Edgeworth" to her brother William, and has removed to her parental home, "Mt. Ephraim," near Pine View, Va. She is of medium height, of portly person, with brilliant eyes, and independence, nerve and resolution printed on every feature. She is a fine talker, and her address is cordial and impressive. She has inherited Presbyterianism, and makes it her religion. Dr. Cooke is a tall and agreeable gentleman, and stands well as a physician. He is a son of Henry S. Cooke, and a grandson of John Cooke, an emigrant from London.

THE MARSHALL FAMILY. 295

(1010) GEN. HUMPHREY MARSHALL.

1006 WILLIAM LAWRENCE ROYALL, b. at Winchester, November 17, 1844; unmarried; entered the Confederate service, when a mere boy, as a private in Company A., Ninth Virginia Cavalry; displayed bravery tempered with discretion; was captured and endured a long and severe imprisonment; studied law, acquired reputation, wrote and ,published several law tracts; first settled in New York City, and is now of Richmond, Va.; practices in the United States Supreme Court, where his talents have secured him distinction. He is now pressing with marked ability some foreign claims on the State of Virginia. In 1884 he purchased "Edgeworth," of his brother-in-law, Dr. Cooke (1004).

1008 JAMES BIRNEY MARSHALL, b. in Frankfort, Ky., May 25, 1810, d. in Memphis, Tenn., September 3, 1870, = October 6, 1829, MARY ANN MOORE, b. June 14, 1809. I met Mr. Marshall once in Covington, Ky., and remember him as a handsome gentleman and a brilliant talker. In Collins, Ky., he is ranked among the poets of that State. He was the principal, or the assistant editor of literary or political papers at different periods in Louisville, Frankfort, Columbus, Cincinnati and Memphis. He was an erratic genius, and his life was tarnished by extravagancies, dissipations and gallantries. Mrs. Marshall yet lives in Covington, Ky. I received a letter from her in 1884, written with her own hand, and I visited her the same year. She has lost the sight of one eye, and her hand trembles with age, but she is still agreeable, and takes a lively part in conversation. She does not refer with pride to her married life.

1010 GEN. HUMPHREY MARSHALL, b. in Frankfort, Ky., January 13, 1812, d. in Louisville, March 28, 1872, = at Franklin, Tenn., January 23, 1833, FRANCES E. McALISTER, b. December 15, 1814; he graduated from the United States Military Academy at West Point; was brevetted Second Lieutenant Mounted Rangers, July 1, 1832; transferred to First Dragoons, March 4, 1833, resigned April 30, 1833; studied law and was admitted to the bar in 1833; settled in Louisville in 1834. When the

THE MARSHALL FAMILY.

(1012) CHARLES EDWARD MARSHALL.

Mexican war broke out in 1846, he raised the First Kentucky Cavalry regiment, and at its head marched to the front; and did good service at the battle of Buena Vista. After a year's service he returned to Louisville; in 1847, removed to Henry Co., Ky.; was elected to Congress in 1849, as a Whig; was re-elected in 1851; in 1852, he declined the offered appointment of Minister to Central America; in August 1852, he accepted the position of Commissioner Plenipotentiary to China; resided at Shanghai until 1854; returned to Louisville; elected to Congress in 1855, and re-elected in 1857, as an American; made strenuous efforts to preserve peace in the early part of 1861, but finding war inevitable, went to Nashville and accepted the position of Brigadier General in the Southern army; he was engaged in all the principal operations of the army in Kentucky, throughout 1862, and the early part of 1863; resigned and settled in Richmond, Va., to practice law, was elected as a delegate from Kentucky to the Second Confederate Congress; after the surrender opened a law office in New Orleans. He was pardoned by President Johnson, December 18, 1867, and he returned to Louisville and continued the practice of law until his death. Mrs. Marshall still lives with her children. She is a daughter of Dr. Charles McAlister, of Franklin, Tenn. She is highly respected by all her acquaintances. I was shown a letter written by her in 1873, to the late Martin P. Marshall (182) which I pronounced, at the time, as of surpassing excellence of both matter and style.

1012 (*a*) CHARLES EDWARD MARSHALL, b. at Frankfort, Ky., April 17, 1821; d. at New Orleans, March 31, 1868, = at Maysville, Ky., January 18, 1847, JUDITH FRY LANGHORNE, b. in Mason Co., Ky., June 15, 1826. Mr. Marshall represented Henry County in the Kentucky Legislature, in 1846, entered the Confederate army, and became Adjutant to his brother, Gen. Humphrey Marshall (1010); died of Bright's disease. Mrs. Marshall, a highly accomplished lady, lives with her daughter (2444), in Chicago. Her ancestry is thus shown:

THE LANGHORNE FAMILY.

(*b*) John Cary, of Bristol, England, ancestor, b. 1620, came to Virginia, 1640, and d. 1677, = Ann, dr. of Capt. Thos. Taylor, and

(1012) CHARLES EDWARD MARSHALL.

had four sons. His second son was Henry Cary, who was father of 1, Archibald Cary; 2, Judith Cary; 3, Mrs. Spear. The latter lived in Edinburg, Scotland.

Judith, dr. of Henry Cary, = David Bell, of Scotland. They lived and died near Lynchburg, Va. The late Montgomery Blair owned a beautiful oil painting of her, which he had photographed, and Mrs. M. F. Alexander, of Hopkinsville, Ky., has a copy. Issue:

A 1. HARRY BELL, = Miss Harrison. Lived in Virginia. They had an only child, Rebecca Bell, who = a ——— Branch. Their son, Harrison Branch, moved to Missouri about 1855.

2. JUDITH BELL, = Col. Gist, of Va., a revolutionary officer. He had large grants of land for military service, and came to Kentucky. Issue:

B (c) 1. *Sarah Howard Gist*, b. 1780, = Jesse Bledsoe.
2. *Henry Gist*.
3. *Ann Gist*, = Capt. Nathaniel Hart, captured at the River Raisin, and massacred by the Indians.
4. *Thomas Gist*, = Miss Barbour.
5. *Judith Gist*, = Dr. Joseph Boswell, of Lexington, Ky.
6. *Eliza Gist*, = Francis Preston Blair, of Frankfort.
7. *Maria Cecil Gist*, = Benj. Gratz, of Philadelphia. They came to Kentucky.
8. *Dandella Gist*, d. single.

After the death of Col. Gist, his widow married Gov. Charles Scott, of Kentucky.

A 3. SARAH BELL, b. August 24, 1754, = April 30, 1774, John Langhorne, b. October 8, 1751; d. March 14, 1784. Issue:

B 1. *Maurice Langhorne*, b. February 10, 1775, = 1st, Nancy Johnson, = 2d, ——— Brooks. They lived in Maysville, Ky. Issue: 1, Jack H. Langhorne; 2, Robert Langhorne.

(d) 2. *David Bell Langhorne*, b. December 14, 1776. He was a soldier of the war of 1812.

3. *John Trotter Langhorne*, b. January 4, 1779, = Elizabeth Baxter Payne, b. November 20, 1798, dr. of Col. Duval Payne and Hannah Brent, sister of Hugh Brent, sr. See Brent Chart, No. 2424. Issue:

(1014) JOHN J. MARSHALL.

C
    1. Elizabeth Langhorne, b. October 23, 1816 (living at Great Crossings, Ky.), = November 11, 1840, William Green d.
    2. Maurice Langhorne, b. August 6, 1819, = Eve A. Grieffe (living).
    3. Sarah Bell Langhorne, b. November 17, 1821; d. December 13, 1883, = Henry Waller, yet living in Chicago. Issue:
        1. Maurice Waller, b. April 7, 1840, = October 12, 1871, LIZZIE MARSHALL, No. 686.
    4. John D. Langhorne, b. January 1, 1824, = Tayloe.

(c)   5. Judith Fry Langhorne, b. June 15, 1826, = 1847, CHAS. E. MARSHALL, No. 1012.

B
    4. *Elizabeth Trotter Langhorne*, b. July 11, 1782, = Hugh Brent, sr., b. January 18, 1773. See Brent Chart, No. 2424.

A
    3. SARAH BELL, after the death of John Langhorne, = 2d, Cary Harrison. Issue:

B
    1. *Judith Cary Harrison*, b. July 25, 1790, = Dr. John Fry, son of the celebrated teacher, Joshua Fry. Issue:

C
    1. Peachy Fry, = Robert Montgomery.
    2. Maj. Cary Fry, U. S. A., = Ellen Gwathney.
    3. John Fry, = a dr. of Robert Tilford. See Fry Chart, No. 180 *l*.

A   4. ELIZA BELL, = Bates.

1014 JOHN J. MARSHALL, b. at Frankfort, Ky., 1826, = 1st, LUCY C. BARRY, who died December, 1861; = 2d, SALLIE HUGLEY, who lived only eighteen months after marriage. Mr. Marshall lives in Louisville, and, if I may judge from the few minutes interview I had with him in 1884, he is a highly cultivated gentleman.

(1020) ANNA MARIA MARSHALL—(Smedes).

1016 ANNA MARIA MARSHALL, b. in Frankfort, Ky., May 5, 1830, d. in 1857, = 1855, JULES C. DENNIS, of New Orleans. She left no children.

1018 THOMAS ALEXANDER MARSHALL, b. in Frankfort, Ky., November 4, 1817, d. in Charleston, Ill., November 11, 1873, = September 4, 1838, ELLEN J. MILES, dr. of Dr. Jas. Miles and Isabella Tarleton, of Frankfort, Ky. Mr. Marshall was educated at Kenyon College, Ohio; graduated in law at Transylvania, in 1837; practiced law two years in Vicksburg, Miss; removed to a farm near Charleston, Ill.; resumed the practice of law in Charleston; engaged in banking, in partnership with James Marston, of New York, in 1853. In 1856, was associated with Abraham Lincoln, Lyman Trumbull, David Davis and others, in the organization of the Republican party; served two terms in the Senate of Illinois, being President pro tem., the latter term; was a member of the Constitutional Convention of Illinois in 1847. In 1861, became Colonel of 1st Illinois Cavalry, and served until the regiment was mustered out in the fall of 1862. In 1863, he was appointed postmaster at Vicksburg, Miss., and served two years. In 1869, organized the private bank of T. A. Marshall & Co., of Charleston, Ill. In 1872, on account of failing health, he retired to his farm, and in 1873 died. His bank was reorganized into the Second National Bank of Charleston. His widow and some of the younger members of the family reside on the farm near Charleston. They are Episcopalians.

1020 ANNA MARIA MARSHALL, b. August 15, 1819, living at Vicksburg, Miss.,=November 9, 1837, WILLIAM CROSBY SMEDES, b. March 24, 1818, died at Vicksburg, February 22, 1863. Mr. Smedes was educated at the Eclectic Institute, at Transylvania University, Lexington, Ky., and at Kenyon College, Ohio. He was a lawyer of distinction at Vicksburg, Miss.; President of the V. & M. R. R. Co.; one of the authors of Smedes and Marshall's Mississippi Reports; author of Smedes' Digest; member of both branches of Mississippi Legislature, and a leading member of the Episcopal Church of the U. S.

(1022) JUDGE CHARLES SIMS MARSHALL.

1022 JUDGE CHARLES SIMS MARSHALL, b. at Paris, Ky., January 19, 1821, living at Paducah, Ky.,== August 30, 1848, EMILY V. CORBETT, b. in Ballard Co., Ky., February 12, 1832. Mr. Marshall was educated at the Bourbon Academy, Paris, and Transylvania University, Lexington; he graduated at Transylvania Law School, in 1842; settled at Paducah; removed to Ballard County and practiced law until 1867; County Attorney of Ballard County 1854–58; presiding Judge of the Ballard County Court; elected, in 1862, Judge of the Circuit Court for the First Judicial District; resigned, in 1867, to accept the office of Register in Bankruptcy; returned to Paducah in 1867; a Whig before the war, and a Republican since; was a strong Union man, but did not go into the army. He is a member of the Christian Church. His wife's father is Jacob Corbett, who yet lives in Ballard County. He has held the offices of both County and Circuit Clerk.

1024 JOHN HART MARSHALL, b. in Paris, Ky., November 20, 1822, d. at sea, November 9, 1856. This is his epitaph, as I copied it from his tomb in the Lexington, Ky., cemetery.

1026 HUMPHREY MARSHALL, b. in Paris, Ky., May 12, 1824. He removed with his parents to Lexington, in 1836; graduated at Morrison College, and in law at Transylvania University; a schoolmate of J. C. Breckinridge, F. P. Blair and Senator Beck; went to California, and stayed ten years; was a Whig in early life, and afterwards a Republican; opposed secession, but went with his friends South, during the war; in 1866, went West, and has spent his latter years, up to this time, in wandering among the mountains of Colorado, Wyoming and New Mexico. He is now a farmer near Taos, N. M., and he expects to die there. In religion, he is an agnostic, and his profession is a "wanderer." I received a long letter from him at Taos, N. M., February 1, 1885.

1028 ELIZA NANNETTE MARSHALL, b. in Lexington, Ky., May 4, 1837, living a widow with one child, in Louisville, Ky., in Paducah, Ky., January 12, 1876, WILLIAM TURNER, b.

(1057) MARGARET DONIPHAN --(Powers).

June 12, 1818, d. June 5, 1882, in Louisville, Ky. Cousin Nannette is leading a very retired life in Louisville. She writes me long and interesting letters. I met her at her home in 1884, and liked her very much. She is an Episcopalian, as most of her father's family are. Mr. Turner was born in Loudon Co., Va., and spen his life in Louisville, as a merchant.

1054 JOSEPH DONIPHAN, b. in Augusta, Ky., August 19, 1823, d. May 2, 1873, = December 16, 1856, ELIZABTEH A. WARD, daughter of Washington Ward and Maria Reynolds. He was a graduate of Augusta College; studied law with his grandfather, Martin Marshall; practiced law in Augusta; elected to the State Legislature in 1849; when the war broke out, he espoused the Union side; chosen Lieutenant Colonel of Col. C. A. Marshall's Sixteenth Regiment of Infantry; resigned in 1862, and the same year was elected Circuit Judge of his District, and served out his full term of six years. He then declined re-election and resumed the practice of law. In 1871, he was chosen Chancellor of the Covington District, and held office until his death. During the war, some new and interesting points of law were discussed before him, and his decisions were regarded as conclusive and of vast importance. In 1867, he united with the Baptist Church, and became a zealous worker in the Church and Sabbath School. He died suddenly, and was buried by the order of Odd Fellows. Three hundred members joined in the procession. His wife possessed great personal beauty, and her family were noted for loveliness. I met her at her home in 1884, and found her a handsome and interesting matron.

1057 MARGARET DONIPHAN, b. in Augusta, Ky., September 3, 1832, = August 21, 1855, SILAS L. POWERS, b. June 27, 1833. They have been residing at the old Doniphan homestead in Augusta, but I have learned that they have removed to Tennessee. Mr. Powers has been a merchant, but for some years has been speculating in tobacco.

(1058) MARY T. MARSHALL—(*Middleton*).

1058 MARY T. MARSHALL, b. in Augusta, Ky., August 19, 1836, = November 23, 1860, WM. C. MIDDLETON, who died in 1879. They lived in Cincinnati.

1060 ELIZABETH MARSHALL, b. in Augusta, Ky., July 28, 1839, = September 5, 1867, JOHN EWING.

1062 MARTIN P. MARSHALL, b. February 3, 1843, in Augusta, Ky. Lives in Kansas, on a ranche.

1064 WILLIAM T. MARSHALL, b. in Augusta, Ky., March 30, 1844. Lives in Cincinnati.

1066 GEORGE C. MARSHALL, b. in Augusta, Ky., November 17, 1845, = MARIA BRADFORD, daughter of Dr. Johnson Bradford and Maria Stuart, of Augusta, Ky. They live in Uniontown, Pa. No children. See 1072.

1068 MATILDA B. MARSHALL, b. in Augusta, Ky., January 12, 1846, = June 4, 1868, SAMUEL BLAINE, cousin of Hon. James Blaine, late Republican candidate for President. He lives on a farm near Washington, Pa.

1070 ROBERT P. MARSHALL, b. at Augusta, Ky., April 7, 1848, = 1882, MRS. LAUGHLIN. They live at Mahoning, Pa. and have one child.

1072 MARGARET P. MARSHALL, b. in Augusta, Ky., March 5, 1851, = December 29, 1876, DR. THOMAS BRADFORD, son of Dr. Johnson Bradford and Maria Stuart. See 1066.

1074 CHARLES L. MARSHALL, b. in Augusta, Ky., December 14, 1852.

(1086) MATILDA MARSHALL—(*Young*).

1076 MATTIE MOORE MARSHALL, b. October 9, 1852; living with her uncle T. H. Soward, Register of Deeds at Winfield, Kan., and she is supporting herself by writing for her uncle. Her letters show heart, soul and truth.

1078 ANNA CAMPBELL (CAMIE) MARSHALL, b. in Cincinnati, Ohio, June 26, 1856, = in Augusta, Ky., November 18, 1880, ROBT. L. COCHRANE, b. in Natchez, Miss., October 23, 1854, son of William M. Cochrane, b. 1820, d. November 11, 1859, and Eliza A. Ogden. Mr. Cochrane started as a banker in Colorado, but his health failing he has settled in Pitkin, Col., and is a mail contractor.

1080 ELIZABETH MARSHALL, b. in Vicksburg, Miss., February 7, 1845, = DANIEL L. HEBRON. They live in Vicksburg, Miss. No children.

1082 MARTIN MARSHALL, b. June 27, 1846, = ELLA BUSH. They live in Vicksburg.

1084 WILLIAM CHAMPE MARSHALL, b. in Vicksburg, Miss., November 13, 1848, = December 5, 1876, KATE M. READING, of Vicksburg. He graduated at the University of Mississippi, in 1869; commenced the practice of law in St. Louis, in 1870; in 1873 entered into partnership with S. Bradley; the latter was elected Circuit Judge in 1882, and Mr. Marshall has since been alone. He is possessed of the qualities that ensure success, and is fast rising to eminence. He is short of stature, but a profound lawyer, and an agreeable gentleman. I met him only once, and have received only one letter from him; but both his epistle and his conversation recommended him as a young man of promise.

1086 MATILDA MARSHALL, b. in Vicksburg, Miss., October 16, 1850, = in Vicksburg, JUDGE UPTON YOUNG. He was reared in Northwest Missouri; removed to Vicksburg and thence to St. Louis, Mo., where, as a lawyer, he is doing a prosperous business.

(1088) LETITIA MARSHALL—(Booth).

1088 LETITIA MARSHALL, b. in Vicksburg, Miss., August 28, 1852, = R. V. BOOTH. They reside in Vicksburg.

1090 HORACE MARSHALL, b. in Vicksburg, Miss., August 18, 1854, = LIZZIE HENRY. They reside in Vicksburg.

1092 MARY B. MARSHALL, b. in Vicksburg, Miss., November 8, 1856, = July 15, 1884, H. ST. L. COPPEE.

1094 THOMAS A. MARSHALL, b. in Vicksburg, Miss., October 9, 1858, = April 12, 1884, BESSIE RUSSELL, of Delhi, La., and they reside there.

1096 ANNIE MARSHALL, b. September 1, 1860.

1098 HELEN MARSHALL, b. March 24, 1864.

1100 MARIA L. MARSHALL. See No. 636.

1102 GEORGE M. ARMSTRONG, b. October 1, 1847. A physician of St. Louis, Mo.

1104 MATILDA T. ARMSTRONG, b. July 29, 1849, = C. S. WALKER. They reside in Cincinnati.

1106 SALLIE LEE ARMSTRONG, b. in West Union, Ohio, May 5, 1851, = C. R. McCORMICK, merchant of Augusta, Ky.

1108 LOUISA ARMSTRONG, b. November 6, 1853, = ED. E. PORTER, of Cincinnati.

(1134) JANE BALLOU — (Hope).

1110 THOMAS H. ARMSTRONG, b. November 19, 1858.

1112 THORNTON T. ARMSTRONG, b. May 6, 1861.

1114 DARLING ARMSTRONG, b. in Augusta, Ky., May 13, 1863.

1116 ROBERT E. L. ARMSTRONG, b. February 10, 1865.

1120 T. DABNEY MARSHALL, b. in Vicksburg, Miss., about 1863. He is a brilliant youth, and has already made his mark as an orator, jurist and poet.

1122 FRANCIS J. BARNES, b. March 26, 1833, = April 24, 1855, E. M. SAYLE.

1124 SHADRACK C. BARNES, b. October 26, 1835, d. February 28, 1873, = December 30, 1858, S. N. E. GARNER.

1126 F. D. BARNES, b. March 4, 1838, d. August 9, 1869.

1128 LUCY A. BARNES, b. October 24, 1843, = December 24, 1869, D. L. SAYLE, d.

1132 MARY E. BALLOU, b. November 3, 1832, = GORDON LOGAN. Mr. Logan is President of the Shelbyville Bank, and a man of wealth and influence. I enjoyed his hospitality in 1884, and was highly pleased with his family. His country mansion is just beyond the limits of Shelbyville, Ky.

1134 JANE BALLOU, b. April 3, 1837, d. 1872, = NICHOLAS HOPE, of Owensboro, Ky. 3 children.

1136 AMERICA BALLOU, b. July 30, 1839, d. 1872.

1138 HARRISON BALLOU, b. November 4, 1841, = ADDIE DUNN. They live in Shelby Co., Ky.

1140 FANNIE BALLOU, b. December 11, 1843, = JOHN SMITH. They live in Cedar Co., Mo.

1142 GEORGE S. BALLOU, b. November 17, 1847, I met him in 1884, and am grateful for his polite attentions. He is an intelligent and worthy young gentleman. Lives near Shelbyville, on his farm.

1144 SUSAN BALLOU, b. August 29, 1849, = SAMUEL VANCE. They live in Cedar Co., Mo.

1146 EMILY BALLOU, b. May 15, 1852, = W. T. KELSO. He is a farmer of Oldham Co., Ky.

1148 HETTIE BALLOU, b. October 17, 1855. Lives in Shelby Co., Ky.

1150 EDWARD BALLOU, b. June 6, 1858, = JENNIE GLENN. He is a farmer of Shelby Co., Ky.

1152 MARTIN BARNES, b. September 24, 1819, d. 1878. He was a lawyer of Granada, Miss.

1154 EMILY BARNES, b. January 9, 1821, = July 20 1837, GEO. A. DURRETT, b. November 8, 1817. Frank Durrett, No. 110; after the death of his first wife, married James Masterson,

(1200) L. JACQUELIN SMITH.

of Kentucky, and Geo. A. Durrett was their son. They live at Air Mount, Miss. I have several long and interesting letters from Mrs. Durrett, who seems to be a lady of fine sense and good literary acquirements.

1156   RUSSELL READING, b. October 10, 1831; d. 1879.

1158   BENJAMIN HACKETT, b. November 17, 1843, = MOLLIE BASKET.

1160   ELIZA HACKETT, b. May 17, 1845.

1162   PRESTON HACKETT, b. January 22, 1848. He stayed with and helped to support his aged mother, until her death in 1884. He taught school, and is now a commercial traveler for Louisville houses. I have many letters from him, and feel greatly indebted to him for polite attentions.

1164   FRANK HACKETT, b. January 19, 1850. He lives in Louisville, Ky.

1166   RICHARD HACKETT, b. September 6, 1854, = ANNIE THOMAS. They live in Louisville.

1168   SUSAN HACKETT, b. March 14, 1856, = F. G. DURR.

1170   MATTIE B. HACKETT, b. January 28, 1859, = W. C. McKEE.

1200   L. JACQUELIN SMITH, b. October 2, 1837, = MARY CAMPBELL, of New York City; graduated with distinction at the Virginia Military Institute; served four years in the Confederate army, and reached the rank of Lieutenant Colonel of Artillery; is now a merchant in New York. Issue: 1, John Campbell Smith; 2, Augustine; 3, Sarah P.; 4, Gladys.

1202 MARGARET VOWELL SMITH, b. March 2, 1839. Her letters to me display rare intelligence and great purity of heart.

1204 CLIFTON H. SMITH, b. August 19, 1841; served four years in the Confederate army; Captain and A. A. General on Gen. Beauregard's staff; member of the New Stock Exchange.

1206 MARY JACQUELIN SMITH, b. October 4, 1843; d. September 7, 1884, much beloved and sincerely lamented.

1208 FRANCIS LEE SMITH, b. October 6, 1845, = JANE S. SUTHERLIN. He graduated at the Virginia Military Institute; wounded twice in the battle of New Market, May 15, 1864, being then a member of the corps of Confederate Cadets; elected to the Virginia State Senate, 1879–83; declined re-election; is now an attorney at law in Alexandria, Va. He was Lieutenant Colonel of the Third Regiment Virginia Volunteers. Issue: Jane S. Smith.

1210 ALICE CORBIN SMITH, b. June 15, 1848, = WILLIAM E. STRONG, of New York City. Issue: 1, Francis Lee Strong; 2, Anne Massie Strong; 3, Alice E. Strong.

1212 COURTLAND HAWKINS SMITH, b. August 29, 1850, = CHARLOTTE E. ROSSITER d. He was in the Confederate service; Mayor of Alexandria, Va., 1879–81; declined re-election; is now a prominent attorney at the Alexandria bar. Issue: 1, Courtland H. Smith.

(1218) MARIA LOVE SMITH — (*Goodwin*).

1214 SARAH VOWELL SMITH, b. March 23, 1853, = ALEX. DANGERFIELD, of Alexandria, Va. Issue: 1, Sarah V. Dangerfield; 2, Mary H.; 3, Francis L.

1216 MARY SMITH, b. at "Ashleigh," Fauquier Co., Va., July 26, 1846, = July 26, 1866, DR. DAVID B. SMITH, of Richmond, Va., b. 1841; d. 1871. He was a graduate of the University of Virginia; was a son of E. Harvie Smith, who was descended from the Amblers and Strothers; his short married life was spent in Richmond. Mrs. Smith, since the death of her husband, has resided with her mother at "Ingleside," near Alexandria. Issue: Harrie Smith, b. August 22, 1867.

1218 MARIA LOVE SMITH, b. at "Ashleigh," Fauquier Co., Va., April 18, 1847, = January 11, 1881, REV. EDWIN LOUIS GOODWIN, b. in Nelson Co., Va., January 23, 1855. When two years old, Edward removed with his parents to Wytheville Va., and there grew up to manhood. He was educated at the University of Virginia, and took his theological course at the seminary near Alexandria, where he graduated in June, 1880. He at once took Holy Orders in the Episcopal Church, following the footsteps of his father, three uncles and a brother. His first charge was in Franklin Co., Va. In 1885, he became rector of Grace Church, in Albemarle County, and St. John's Church, in Louisa County. He resides at Bowlesville. Issue: 1, Margaret L. Goodwin, b. October 15, 1881; 2, Mary Frances Goodwin, b. June 27, 1883; 3, Maria Lee [Lelia] Goodwin, b. August 9, 1884.

Mr. Goodwin's father was the Rev. Frederick D. Goodwin, a native of Massachusetts; descended from old and prominent families of that State; educated at Amherst College; came to Virginia and served as a tutor in the family of Strother Jones (228), at "Vaucluse," Frederick Co., Va.; studied at the Theological Seminary of Virginia, and served for a half century in the Episcopal ministry. He married Mary Frances, daughter of Dr. Robert Archer, of Norfolk and Richmond, and for many years Post Surgeon at Fortress Monroe; had nine children, of whom Edward L. was the youngest. His widowed mother still resides at Wytheville.

(1220) ROBERT W. SMITH.

1220 ROBERT W. SMITH, b. at "Ashleigh," Fauquier Co., Va., March 3, 1849. He is now cashier of John S. Gitting's bank, Baltimore, Md.

1222 THOMAS MARSHALL SMITH, b. at "Ashleigh," Fauquier Co., Va., September 5, 1851. He is in the chemical and phosphate business in Baltimore, Md.

1224 MARGARET LEWIS SMITH, b. at "Ashleigh," Fauquier Co., Va., March 24, 1853, = December 12, 1883, REV. R. W. FORSYTH, b. in Baltimore, Md., October 7, 1857. He graduated at the Baltimore City College, in July, 1874; spent four years in the wholesale mercantile business; entered the Theological Seminary of Virginia, September, 1878; ordained deacon in Baltimore, February 15, 1883, by Rt. Rev. Wm. Pinkney, D. D., late Bishop of Maryland; assisted Rev. Dr. Williams, rector of Christ Church, Baltimore; July, 1883, was transferred to the diocese of Virginia, and assumed regular charge of St. John's Church, Liberty, Va.; ordained Presbyter, June, 1884. Mr. Forsyth was a son of Edward Forsyth and Charlotte E. Baron. The latter still lives in Baltimore. Issue: Charlotte E. Forsyth, b. March 6, 1885.

1226 CLAUDIA W. SMITH, b. at "Ashleigh," Fauquier Co., Va., May 26, 1856, = July 10, 1878, REV. JOHN HARRY CHESLEY, b. in Westmoreland Co., Va., December 10, 1856. Mr. Chesley graduated, 1878, at the Virginia Theological Seminary; ordained deacon, June 20, 1878, in All Faith Church, St. Mary's Co., Md.; ordained priest, December 19, 1880, in Trinity Church, Upper Marlboro, Md., and is now rector of St. Thomas Parish, Prince George Co., Md., having assumed charge October 1, 1883. His postoffice is Croome. Issue: 1, Margaret L. Chesley, b. January 16, 1880; 2, Claudia L. Chesley, b. June 15, 1881; 3, Bessie B. Chesley, b. August 17, 1884.

THE CHESLEY FAMILY.

A 1. WILLIAM CHESLEY, = Mary Ascom Parran, of Point Patience, Calvert Co., Md. Their son:

(1240) ANN GORDON MARSHALL—(*Byrd*).

B   1. Rev. *William Fitzhugh Chesley*, = Jane Dare, of Calvert Co., Md. Issue:

C
1. Nathaniel Dare Chesley, M. D.
2. Jane Gray Chesley,= Rev. Joshua Morsell, D.D.
3. Mary Ann Chesley.
4. Rev. John William Chesley, = Harriet Beall Harry, of Georgetown, D. C. Issue:

D
1. Capt. Wm. F. Chesley, = Mary A. Lyon.
2. Eliza Chesley, = Thos. A. Reeder.
3. Emily Chesley, = Rev. Charles E. Buck, rector of St. Peter's Parish, Easton, Md.
4. Rev. John Harry Chesley,= CLAUDIA WALTON LEVERT SMITH (1226).

THE BEALL FAMILY.

A   1. BROOKE BEALL, who owned Beall's Addition to Georgetown; had a daughter, who married Capt. Williams, of the Revolutionary army. Their dr.:

B   1. Harriet Eliza Williams, = John Harry, son of Jacob Harry, one of the early settlers of Hagerstown, Md. Their dr.:

C   1. Harriet B. Harry, = Rev. John William Chesley, present rector of Miles River Parish, Talbot Co., Md. (above.)

1228   AGNES T. SMITH, b. at "Ashleigh," Fauquier Co., Va., March 1, 1860. She lives with her mother at "Ingleside," near Alexandria, Va.

1230   HARRY B. SMITH, b. at "Ashleigh," Fauquier Co., Va., March 23, 1868. He will complete his academic studies in 1885, and select some pursuit.

1240   ANN GORDON MARSHALL, b. in Fauquier Co., Va., January 21, 1842, = November 20, 1860, RICHARD C. BYRD, b. in Gloucester Co., Va., September 9, 1837. Both live at "White

(1242) FANNIE L. MARSHALL.

Hall," Gloucester Co., Va. Mrs. Byrd is a pious and highly cultivated lady, as her letters to me attest. Her husband is a worthy farmer, well educated, and much esteemed in his county. For his descent from the Lewis family, see chart, No. 150. His lineage may be thus traced:

1. Warner Lewis, = Eleanor Bowles.
2. Addison Lewis, = Sue Fleming, descendant of Pocahontas.
3. Susan Lewis, b. March 7, 1782; d. November 12, 1865, = William Byrd, son of Col. William Byrd.
4. Samuel P. Byrd, = Catherine C. Corbin.
5. Richard C. Byrd, = Ann G. Marshall.

THEIR CHILDREN.

1. Samuel P. Byrd, b. in Gloucester Co., Va., January 23, 1861.
2. Richard C. Byrd, b. July 29, 1862; 3, Lewis W. Byrd, b. March 11, 1866; 4, Mary B. Byrd, b. January 22, 1868; 5, Fannie M. Byrd, b. October 15, 1869; 6, Ann G. Byrd, b. April 4, 1873.

1242 Fannie L. Marshall, b. January 16, 1847. She lives at City Point, Va., and has written me a letter which shows fine literary attainments. She is teaching in the family of Dr. Richard Eppes. Like all other orphans, she has known the want of a parent's love, and feels a tender regard for the memory of father and mother.

1244 John Marshall, b. at "Oakhill," Fauquier Co., Va., August 15, 1852; left an orphan at two years of age, he went to live with his uncle, F. L. Marshall, at "Ivanhoe." During his boyhood he stayed with his uncle's family at Richmond, and with his aunt, Mrs. Taliaferro; spent three years at the University of Virginia; then attended the school of Richard C. Marshall, at Upperville, Fauquier County. His only patrimony was a portrait of Chief Justice John Marshall. This he sold for $2,000, and with it finished his education at Washington College. In July, 1872, he

THE MARSHALL FAMILY. 313

(1252) MARGARET LEWIS TALIAFERRO—(*Maupin*).

went to New York, and, after serving several houses as clerk, finally entered the large tea importing house of Ramsay & Co. Here he remained until June, 1883, when he established himself in the tea and coffee business, at 119 Water street, New York. He resides in Brooklyn. His letters show the man of business, and exhibit his pious reverence for the memory of his sainted parents.

1246 WILLIAM C. MARSHALL, b. in Culpeper Co., Va., October 31, 1854, = November 11, 1884, SADIE ROBB TYLER, dr. of Col. Nat. Tyler, of Washington, D. C. He lost his mother a few days after his birth, and ere he was three months old, he was parentless; was reared by his aunt, Mrs. H. E. Moxley; was educated as a lawyer, but soon after coming to the bar, established the Warrenton *Virginian*, of which he is editor and owner. Mrs. Marshall's mother was Sarah Robb, a niece of Ann E. Robb, second wife of Alex. J. Marshall (238).

1248 MARY ARCHER TALIAFERRO, b. January 15, 1841; d. March 30, 1864, = March 18, 1863, DR. CHARLES W. CHANCELLOR, b. 1831. Dr. Chancellor served in the Southern army as a Surgeon throughout the war, and has since been a professor in the Medical College at Baltimore. He is now Secretary of the Board of Health of the State of Maryland. Mrs. Chancellor left an only child, Leah Seddon Chancellor, b. March 24, 1864.

1250 LEAH S. TALIAFERRO, b. January 17, 1843; d. October 8, 1862.

1252 MARGARET LEWIS TALIAFERRO, b. November 10, 1844, = December 21, 1870, CHAPMAN MAUPIN, b. April, 1844. Professor Maupin has a successful High School at Ellicott City, Md. He is a son of Prof. S. Maupin and Sallie Washington. Their children are: 1, Agnes Marshall Maupin, b. October 8, 1871; 2, Sallie Washington Maupin, b. August 14, 1874; 3, Margaret Lewis Maupin, b. October 24, 1877.

(1254) ELEANOR WARNER TALIAFERRO—(*Nelson*).

1254 ELEANOR WARNER TALIAFERRO, b. March 15, 1847, = December 7, 1871, GEORGE E. NELSON, b. September 8, 1849. He is a son of Arthur B. Nelson and Mildred Eggborn, of Culpeper Co., Va., and is now practicing law at Baltimore. Their children are: 1, Alex. Taliaferro Nelson, b. October 8, 1872; 2, Mildred Braxton Nelson, b. November 8, 1873; 3, Agnes H. Nelson, b. May 8, 1876; 4, George E. Nelson, b. August 8, 1879.

1256 AGNES MARSHALL TALIAFERRO, b. August 12, 1849, in Culpeper Co., Va., = December 16, 1874, ROBERT W. MAUPIN, b. August, 1847, d. at "Annandale," Culpeper Co., October 4, 1876. Mrs. Maupin is living with her mother (502) at "Annandale," and mourns her early widowhood, and drops tears over the fresh grave of her honored father. Her letters to me breathe sadness, and she complains that her life is blighted. Mr. Maupin was the third son of the late Prof. S. Maupin, of the University of Virginia, and Sallie Washington. In 1863, at the age of sixteen, he entered the naval service of the Confederacy, and was attached to the ship "Patrick Henry," stationed in James River for the defence of Richmond. When the city was evacuated, in 1865, he undertook to join Kirby Smith, west of the Mississippi. At New Orleans he was confined in a loathsome prison, and subjected to treatment which brought him to death's door. When released, he returned to Virginia, and through the influence of his uncle, Col. Peter G. Washington, then residing in New York, he got a position on a ship engaged in the China trade, and made two voyages to that country. His father died in 1871, and he returned to his home, united with the Episcopal Church, became a vestryman of Emmanuel Church, Rapidan Station, and the remainder of his life was devoted to his Master's cause. His thrilling adventures, his varied experience and his humble Christian spirit made a lovely character. His life is an interesting episode, and his memory is a fragrant boquet of flowers.

1258 WILLIAM ALEXANDER TALIAFERRO, b. October 13, 1851, at "Annandale," = November 13, 1879, CHARLOTTE FRANKLIN, dr. of Rev. Benj. Franklin, D. D., of Shrewsbury, N. J.,

THE MARSHALL FAMILY. 315

(1266) MARGARET LEWIS MARSHALL—(*Hite*).

and Emma Windsor. She was b. December, 1854. Their children are: 1, Windsor L. Taliaferro, b. March 7, 1881; 2, Agnes Marshall Taliaferro, b. July 10, 1883.

1260 WILLIAM S. ARCHER, b. March 23, 1840. Lives in Fauquier County., Va.

1262 LIZZIE ARCHER, b. September 16, 1843. She is handsome, lively and spirited. I met her at the "Dell," in Fauquier Co., Va., in 1884, and found her very intelligent.

1264 RICHARD COKE MARSHALL, b. July 5, 1844, = November 21, 1865, CATHERINE WILSON, b. September 2, 1843. At eighteen, Mr. Marshall took up his sword for the Confederacy, and surrendered it at. Appomattox; was desperately wounded in Hampton's fight with Sheridan, at Trevillians, Louisa Co., Va., in 1864; after the war, taught school at Upperville, Fauquier Co., Va.: studied law and settled at Portsmouth, Va.; has been twice the nominee of the Democrats for Congress, but his party is in the minority; has been twice elected County Attorney. He stands among the foremost in his State, politically, socially and intellectually. His wife is a daughter of a Mr. Wilson, of South Carolina, and a Miss Barrand, of Norfolk, Va. Their children: 1, Rebecca C., b. February 12, 1868; 2, Susan L., b. April 26, 1870; 3, Samuel W., b. July 3, 1872; 4, Fielding L., b. January 8, 1877; 5, Richard C., b. March 13, 1879; 6, St. Julien, b. November 23, 1881, and 7, Myron B. Marshall, b. September 12, 1883.

1266 MARGARET LEWIS MARSHALL, b. at "Oakhill," Fauquier Co., Va., May 17, 1846,= November 29, 1871, CORNELIUS B. HITE, b. August 6, 1842, at "Belle Grove," Frederick Co., Va. Mrs. Hite's letters to me prove she is a sweet, pure and lovely woman, and in intelligence she has few superiors. She married a "clever fellow," well educated and highly esteemed. He entered the C. S. A. as a private, and was placed in the Topographical Engineers'

(1268) MARY WILLING BYRD MARSHALL—(*Yates*).

Corps. He was at various times under Generals Stuart, Hampton, Rosser, Lee and Payne, and was brevetted First Lieutenant. Since the war he has been sometimes teaching and at other times farming. They have no children. Lieut. Hite's grandfather was:
1. Major Isaac Hite, a distinguished officer in the Revolutionary war,= Ann T. Maury, a cousin of Commodore Mathew Maury, of Observatory fame.
2. Cornelius Baldwin Hite, 1818–1843, = Elizabeth Augusta Smith.
3. Cornelius B. Hite, jr., = MARGARET L. MARSHALL.

For Mr. Hite's descent from the Smiths, see No. 196 *g*.

Dr. Cornelius E. Baldwin, a brother of the distinguished surgeon, Dr. Archibald S. Baldwin, married Nelly Hite, only daughter of Maj. Isaac Hite, of "Belle Grove," by his first wife, who was the only sister of President James Madison. Maj. Hite named one of his sons, by his second wife, after his son-in-law, Dr. Cornelius Baldwin. See No. 2000.

1268 MARY WILLING BYRD MARSHALL, b. at "Oakhill," Fauquier Co., Va., June 26, 1847, = April 10, 1872, JOHN R. YATES, b. 1842, d. 1882. Mr. Yates was a good business man, but much addicted to drink. When under the influence of liquor, he was almost crazy At such times his wife and child were in danger. She separated from him after eighteen months, and obtained a divorce. He went to Baltimore and died. She supports herself by a situation in the Pension Bureau, at Washington. Her child, Margaret Marshall Yates was b. April 17, 1873.

1270 SUSAN LEWIS MARSHALL, b. in Fauquier Co., Va., December 11, 1848, d. July 8, 1868, = October 15, 1867, BOWLES E. ARMISTEAD, b. 1841, living near Delaplane, Fauquier Co., Va. (See No. 740.) He was a son of Gen. Walker Armistead, U. S. A. She, with her infant, was buried at Emmanuel Church, near "Oakhill." For Mr. Armistead's see No. 740.

(1282) GEORGE T. MARSHALL.

1272 THOMAS MARSHALL, b. in Fauquier Co., Va., November 14, 1850, = November 3, 1880, MAUD GRISWOLD BARHYDT, b. May 12, 1857, in New York City. He now lives in New York, and is a broker in mining and oil stocks. His wife is a great grand niece of Oliver Walcott, a signer of the Declaration of Independence. His letters indicate a man of fine business capacity.

1274 FIELDING LEWIS MARSHALL, b. at "Ivanhoe," Fauquier Co., Va., September 19, 1854, = February 21, 1877, CAROLINE (LENA) BLACKFORD GWATKIN, b. in Richmond, Va., October 13, 1858. He is a clerk in the Internal Revenue Office, at Washington City, and is at the same time preparing himself for the practice of law. Their children; 1, Sophia G. Marshall, b. June 9, 1881; 2, David Parish Barhydt Marshall, b. September 14, 1882.

1276 REBECCA FRANCES MARSHALL, b. at "Ivanhoe," Fauquier Co., Va., August 14, 1856, = November 20, 1878, CHARLES REID NASH, b. in Portsmouth, Va., June 29, 1849. He is an enterprising young man, and is now a member of the City Council of Portsmouth. Their children: 1, Rebecca Coke Nash, b. in Portsmouth, Va., January 23, 1880. From her letters I ascertain that she is a lady of some literary attainments.

1278 AGNES HARWOOD MARSHALL, b. at "Ivanhoe," Fauquier Co., Va., April 26, 1858, = October 26, 1881, WILLIAM P. HELM, b. in Warrenton, Va., May 26, 1831. Mr. Helm is an extensive merchant in New York City, and now, without dissolving his connection with his business house, resides in Warrenton, Va. Their only child is William P. Helm, b. May 4, 1883.

1280 MARIA N. MARSHALL, b. January 3, 1869.

1282 GEORGE T. MARSHALL, b. July 4, 1871.

1283 ELEANOR WARNER MARSHALL, b. October 2, 1873.

1284 ANN LEWIS MARSHALL, b. October 6, 1875.

1286 WALTON H. MARSHALL, b. May 16, 1877.

1288 JOHN N. MARSHALL, b. September 18, 1879.

1290 ALICE H. MARSHALL, b. January 30, 1882.

1292 CARY R. JONES. (See No. 726.)

1294 DR. THOMAS MARSHALL JONES, of Alexandria, Va., b. at "Woodside," Fauquier Co., Va., September 15, 1848, = June 23, 1880, BESSIE W. PAYNE of Warrenton, Va. He was educated at Winchester Academy, and the University of Virginia, and graduated at the Medical College of Baltimore. He stands at the head of his profession in Alexandria. His wife is a daughter of the late Rice W. Payne, of Warrenton. Her mother was a Semms.

1296 FANNIE B. JONES, b. at "Woodside," Fauquier Co., Va., September 25, 1850, = April 30, 1884, HUGH McILHANY, son of Hugh McIlhany and Ann Rogers. She is his second wife. He was a merchant in Warrenton, and is now Secretary of an Insurance Company in Warrenton.

1298 REV. WILLIAM STROTHER JONES, b. at "Woodside," Fauquier Co., Va., April 10, 1852, = at Alexandria, Va., December 18, 1876, KATIE USHER SMOOT, b. June 27, 1854, daughter of J. H. D. Smoot and —— French, of Alexandria. Mr. Jones was educated at Washington and Lee College, Lexington, Va., and

THE MARSHALL FAMILY. 319

(1306) DAVID BARTON MARSHALL.

took his theological course at the Episcopal Seminary near Alexandria. He is now rector of St. Thomas Church, Baltimore. His postoffice is Owings Mill, Baltimore Co., Md. They have one child, Josiah S. Jones, b. May 21, 1878.

1300 JAMES FITZGERALD JONES, b. at " Woodside," Fauquier Co., Va., July 27, 1853, = August 13, 1879, JANE SELDEN McGUIRE, b. in Fauquier Co., Va., June 3, 1855. He is a farmer, a Republican, and lives near Delaplane, Fauquier Co., Va. His wife is a daughter of Dr. R. L. McGuire and Agnes Douthat. Their children: 1, Robert L. Jones, b. December 21, 1881; 2, William S. Jones, b. October 13, 1883. See Lewis chart 150 *j* and 152 *d*.

1302 FIELDING LEWIS JONES, b. at "Woodside," Fauquier Co., Va., March 16, 1855, = August 17, 1881, NELLIE C. STANLEY. He was educated at the Episcopal High School of Virginia, entered the United States Signal Corps, and went West; resigned in 1882, and is now a farmer and school teacher. His postoffice is Elbert, Col. Mrs. Jones' father was an Englishman, who came to the United States before the war. He now resides in Florida. They have two children; 1, Cary Jones, b. in Colorado, December 17, 1882; 2, Mable F. Jones, b. April 2, 1884.

1304 AGNES ALEXANDER JONES, b. at "Woodside," Fauquier Co., Va., August 3, 1859, = November 22, 1882, DR. WILLIAM S. BUTLER, Professor in the Lunatic Asylum, at Staunton, Va. He is a son of Dr. Samuel Butler, of Norfolk, Va., and grandson of Rev. Samuel Butler, Rector during the Revolutionary War, of the old Brick Church in the Isle of Wight Co., Va. The Butlers are descendants from the Scotch Duke of Ormond.

1306 DAVID BARTON MARSHALL, b. at Winchester, Va., June 25, 1849, = October 14, 1875, THERESA ROBERTS, b. November 9, 1851. He is a merchant of Baltimore, Md., in the Coach

(1308) MARGARET LEWIS MARSHALL — (Duer).

and Saddlery Supplies business. Mrs. Marshall is a daughter of Dr. Roberts, of Cecil Co., Md., and grand daughter of Col. Hartley, of the Revolutionary war. Their children are: 1, Lily Marshall, b. July 14, 1876; 2, T. Hartley Marshall, b. August 15, 1879; and 3, Helen Marshall, b. June 10, 1883.

1308 MARGARET LEWIS MARSHALL, b. at Winchester, Va., December 25, 1850, = October 31, 1872, ANDREW ADGATE DUER, b. December 3, 1846. I met Cousin Maggie several times in 1884, and found her a lovely, brilliant and interesting woman. Mr. Duer is a son of John Duer and Henrietta D. Adgate. He is a merchant in Baltimore, and his country seat is a delightful forest mansion, ten miles from the city. Their children: 1, Henrietta Adgate Duer, b. July 9, 1874; 2, Frances B. Duer, b. February 27, 1876; 3, John Duer, b. July 24, 1877; 4, Isabel Duer, b. September 17, 1878; 5, Thomas Marshall Duer, b. April 2, 1880; 6, Agnes B. Duer, b. March 8, 1882, and 7, Margaret Lewis Duer, b. March 23, 1883.

1310 THOMAS MARSHALL, b. in Winchester, Va., March 31, 1852. He resides in San Francisco, California.

1312 FANNIE JONES MARSHALL, b. at "Oakhill," Fauquier Co., Va., June 18, 1854, = October 7, 1875, REV. CHARLES JOHN HOLT, b. in Ripley Co., W. Va., February 18, 1850. He is now rector of Trinity parish, Portsmouth, Va. Their children: 1, Susan Lees Holt, b. October 2, 1876; 2, Margaret Lewis Holt, b. January 22, 1878; 3, James Lees Holt, b. October 3, 1879; 4, Francis A. Holt, b. January 29, 1883.

1316 FIELDING LEWIS MARSHALL, b. at "Oakhill," Fauquier Co., Va., January 21, 1858, = October 19, 1882, SUSANNA LEES WALLER, b. January 10, 1859. Fielding was left an orphan at the age of six. In Mrs. Susanna Lees he found a foster mother, and married her niece. He yet lives with Mrs. Lees, and regards

(1324) AGNES A. DOUTHAT—(Stribling).

her with the tenderness due to a mother. He prepared himself for the practice of law by taking diplomas in both the literary and legal departments of Columbia College, N. Y., and has opened an office No. 48 Wall street, N. Y. His letters to me recommend him for intelligence and cordiality. For the genealogy of his charming wife, refer to the Waller chart, under No. 686.

1318 LIZZIE DOUTHAT, b. at "Weyanoke," Charles City Co., Va., 1842; d. September 17, 1880.

1320 ELEANOR DOUTHAT, b. at " Weyanoke," Charles City Co., Va., November 19, 1844. I met her at "Mountain View," the residence of her sister, Agnes A. Stribling, in 1884, and found her a sprightly and intelligent lady.

1322 MARY DOUTHAT, b. at "Weyanoke," Charles City Co., Va., December 7, 1845, = December 1, 1869, her cousin, JACQUELIN A. MARSHALL, b. at "Carrington," Fauquier Co., Va., April 5, 1844. He was educated at Clifton, Fauquier Co., Va.; took his degree in medicine at the Baltimore School; practiced at Markham; went to Baltimore and opened a drug store; removed to Florida about 1878, and practiced there for four years; returned to Markham in 1882; opened a dry goods store, which he still superintends, while at the same time he performs the duties of railroad agent at Markham. He still owns an orange orchard in Florida. Mr. Marshall entered the Confederate army as Surgeon in Stribling's Battery, and received a wound in the lungs which nearly cost him his life, and from which he still suffers. Issue: 1, R. Stribling Marshall, b. December 7, 1870; 2, Robert D., b. December 28, 1871; 3, Edward C., b. December 7, 1877; 4, Mary, b. February 14, 1880; 5, Eleanor L., b. May 6, 1882. See No. 588.

1324 AGNES A. DOUTHAT, b. at "Weyanoke," Charles City Co., Va., December 28, 1849, = 1870, COL. ROBERT M. STRIBLING. See No. 854. They live at "Mountain View," in Markham, Va. Their only child is Mary Douthat Stribling, b. August 20, 1871.

(1326) JACQUELIN M. DOUTHAT.

1326 JACQUELIN M. DOUTHAT, b. at "Weyanoke," Charles City Co., Va., January 11, 1852; d. October 2, 1881, = October 16, 1879, CAROLINE HARRISON, dr. of Wm. M. Harrison, a distant relative of President W. H. Harrison.

1328 ROBERT DOUTHAT, b. at "Weyanoke," Charles City Co., Va., June 1, 1854, = December 23, 1883, REBECCA P. MARSHALL, b. September 10, 1857 (1330). Mr. Douthat is farming near Markham, Va. His letters to me prove him to be a man of business, and of superior education.

1330 REBECCA PEYTON MARSHALL. (See No. 1328). I met her at "The Crag," the residence of her parents, in Markham, Va., in 1884. She is a handsome and very interesting lady.

1332 JACQUELIN AMBLER MARSHALL, b. October 22, 1858, = October 22, 1879, ELIZA TURNER. They have one child, Charles T. Marshall, b. July, 1883.

1334 EDWARD C. MARSHALL, b. September 16, 1860.

1336 WILLIAM C. MARSHALL, b. March 12, 1863.

1338 YELVERTON P. MARSHALL, b. January 31, 1866.

1340 MARION L. MARSHALL, b. September 9, 1867.

1342 ELIZA C. MARSHALL, b. July 2, 1871.

1344 MILDRED P. MARSHALL, b. November 8, 1875.

1346 RANDOLPH MARSHALL, b. November, 1878.

THE MARSHALL FAMILY. 323

(1374) ANN CARTER MARSHALL.

1354 ELIZA BRAXTON, b. at "Prospect Hill," Fauquier Co., Va., October 22, 1855, = February 10, 1880, JOHN BROCKENBROUGH, b. November 23, 1855. He was educated at Charlotte Hall, Md.; is a member of the Episcopal Church, and is now in the tobacco business in Baltimore. My acquaintance with Mr. B. is through our correspondence only, and that indicates a gentleman of superior education and fine business qualifications. For his lineage and relationship to other branches of the Marshall family, see the Brockenbrough chart (162 m). Children: 1, Carter Brockenbrough, b. March 6, 1882; 2, Lucy C. Brockenbrough, b. March 17, 1884. See Brockenbrough chart, 152 m

1356 SALLIE M. BRAXTON, b. at "Prospect Hill," September 21, 1857.

1358 MARY A. BRAXTON, b. at "Prospect Hill," August 31, 1859.

1360 ANNA M. BRAXTON, b. at Danville, Va., March 7, 1864.

1362 ELLIOTT M. BRAXTON, b. at Fredericksburg, Va., February 6, 1867.

1364 JACQUELIN M. BRAXTON, b. at Fredericksburg, Va., October 24, 1869.

1366 WESTAR WALLACE BRAXTON, b. at Fredericksburg, Va., January 12, 1874.

1368 WILLIAM C. MARSHALL, b. at "Cleveland," Fauquier Co., Va., June 7, 1864.

1370 FRANCIS B. MARSHALL, b. at "Cleveland," Fauquier Co., Va., July 11, 1867.

1372 KATE TRAVIS MARSHALL, b. at "Cleveland," Fauquier Co., Va., May 10, 1874.

1374 ANN CARTER MARSHALL, b. at "Cleveland," Fauquier Co., Va., July 29, 1880.

(1378) MARY D. BARTON—(Smith).

1378 MARY D. BARTON, b. at "Prospect Hill," Fauquier Co., Va., August 26, 1860, = at "Center Hill," October 18, 1882, RICHARD H. SMITH, b. in Richmond, Va., July 27, 1859. She was educated at Mrs. Jones school in Baltimore. Her winters were spent at Richmond, Fredericksburg, Alexandria or Baltimore, at all of which cities she had relatives. Thus introduced into society, she has become a lady of grace and intelligence. I met her at Markham in 1884, and have received several well written letters from her. Though now living in Richmond, her summers are spent in Fauquier. Mr. Smith is a merchant in Richmond, and his character and credit are among the best. His father was S. B. Smith, Cashier of the First National Bank of Richmond; and his mother was Margaret, daughter of William Strother, of the old Exchange Bank of Richmond. Address 824 Grace street, Richmond, Va. Issue: 1, Richard Smith, b. at "Center Hill," August 29, 1883.

1380 SUSAN HARVIE PATRICK, = HENRY POINDEXTER, d. Issue: 1, Spicer P. Poindexter; 2, Mary M. Poindexter.

1388 ELLEN HARVIE WADE. She is living with her widowed mother in Richmond, Va.

1390 DR. CARTER WADE. After receiving a superior literary and medical education, he settled in Lynchburg, Va., where he is practicing his profession.

1392 WILLIAM HARVIE WADE, is now attending the Engineering College in Hoboken, N. J.

1394 ELIZABETH M. MARSHALL, b. at "Mount Blanc," Fauquier Co., Va., January 25, 1857, = October 10, 1878, JOSEPH READING. Children: 1, William M. Reading, b. August 9, 1879; 2, Charles L. Reading, b. September 20, 1881; 3, Sarah Reading, b. November 25, 1882.

THE MARSHALL FAMILY.

(1424) CAROLINE S. MARSHALL.

1396   CHARLES L. MARSHALL, b. at "Mount Blanc," March 20, 1861.

1398   JAMES EDWARD MARSHALL, b. at "Mount Blanc," December 5, 1863.

1400   JOHN H. MARSHALL, b. January 10, 1866.

1402   ASHTON H. MARSHALL, b. November 20, 1867.

1404   PHILIP T. MARSHALL, b. at "Mount Blanc," December 25, 1869.

1406   MARY M. MARSHALL, b. January 29, 1872.

1408   ELIZABETH ALEX. DOUTHAT, b. in Charles City Co., Va., July 2, 1853.

1410   FIELDING LOUIS DOUTHAT, b. in Charles City Co., Va., February 26, 1857.

1412   REBECCA PEYTON DOUTHAT, b. in Charles City Co., Va., February 27, 1859.

1414   MARY WILLIS DOUTHAT, b. in Charles City Co., Va., January 29, 1864.

1416   AGNES HARWOOD DOUTHAT, b. in Charles City Co., Va., August 6, 1865.

1418   SUSAN HARVIE DOUTHAT, b. in Charles City Co., Va., December 18, 1868.

1420   JOHN MARSHALL DOUTHAT, b. in Charles City Co., Va., August 22, 1872.

1422   CATHERINE THOMAS DOUTHAT, b. in Charles City Co., Va., December 1, 1874.

1424   CAROLINE [*Cannie*] S. MARSHALL, b. at "Glendale," Fauquier Co., Va., July 30, 1866. I met this charming lassie at "Glendale," in 1884, and pronounced her the sweetest girl I had met on my excursion.

(1426) SALLIE E. MARSHALL.

1426 SALLIE E. MARSHALL, b. in Louisville, Ky., July 25, 1853. Cousin Sallie is possessed of rare beauty, uncommon intelligence and every womanly grace and virtue. She often writes for the periodical press, and her essays are much admired. She has the courage to submit her compositions to the reading public, and they have met with favorable notice in many quarters. It is even said that she has a volume of sketches now nearly ready for the press. Should the volume appear, I claim the privilege of recommending it in advance. Though a brilliant conversationalist and an ornament to society, she finds her pleasure in her private study, her home duties and her Christian enterprises. My correspondence with her has convinced me of her literary acquirements; and her personal favors and attentions have secured my gratitude. She lives with her mother, Mrs. Pope (554), N.-W. cor Seventh and Chestnut streets, Louisville, Ky.

1428 CLAUDIA H. MARSHALL, b. in Louisville, Ky., June 10, 1855, = August 19, 1873, J. BRUCE MORSON, a sugar and rice planter of St. Martinsville, La. Children: 1, Sallie Marshall Morson; 2, Claudia H. Morson, and 3, Thomas Seddon Morson.

    (b)   THE MORSON LINEAGE

1. Alexander Morson, of Stafford Co., Va., = Ann Casson Alexander, 1780—1883, dr. of William Alexander and Sarah Casson. See Alexander lineage, No. 722 c.
2. James Marion Morson, = Ellen Bruce, dr. of James Bruce and Elvira Cabell, of Halifax Co., Va. Issue:
    1. James B. Morson, = CLAUDIA MARSHALL.
    2. Alice Morson, = LEIGH ROBINSON, No. 1600.

1430 BURWELL KEITH MARSHALL, b. in Louisville, Ky., March 9, 1857, = June 21, 1883, LIZZIE VEECH, b. in Danville, Ky., October 13, 1856. Mr. Marshall was educated at the University of Virginia, and took his diploma from the law department of the University of Louisville. He graduated with the first honor of the institution, February 28, 1878. He is now practicing law in

THE MARSHALL FAMILY. 327

(1448) CLAUDIA NORTON—(*Mason*).

Louisville, and is fast rising to eminence. His wife is the daughter of Richard S. Veech and Mary L. Nichols, of Danville, Ky. Children: 1, Richard Veech Marshall, b. at Louisville, Ky., September 12, 1884.

1432 EWING MARSHALL, b. in Louisville, Ky., September 16, 1858. Educated at the Louisville High School; received the second honor February 27, 1883, on his first years course, at the medical department of the University of Louisville, Ky. Graduated 1884, and is practicing medicine in Louisville.

1434 MARIE LLOYD MARSHALL, b. January 1, 1860, in Louisville, Ky., = June 3, 1884, PHILIP T. ALLIN, of Louisville. Cousin Lloyd is a charming woman, a tall, handsome blonde, affectionate, pure and true. Mr. Allin is a young man of education, and is descended from a distinguished family.

1436 LUCY MARSHALL, b. 1859, = REV. H. B. LEE, b. 1849; at this time rector of Leeds Parish, Fauquier Co., Va. Children: 1, Harry B. Lee; 2, Claude Lee; 3, Rebecca Lee. Mr. Lee was educated at the Episcopal Theological Seminary of Virginia. His father was Edmund J. Lee, of Shepherdstown, W. Va.

1442 CLAUDIA BURWELL COLEMAN, b. in Hanover Co., Va., December 24, 1858. She is living with her mother (560) at "Sunnyside," near Markham, Va. I met her at her home in 1884, and unite with her friends in pronouncing her a handsome, intelligent, amiable and pious lady.

1448 CLAUDIA NORTON, b. at Warrenton, Va., June 2, 1856, = November 19, 1879, REV. JOHN K. MASON. He graduated at Hampden Sidney College, Va., and the Theological Seminary of Virginia; is rector of St. George's Church, Fredericksburg, Va. He is a son of Dr. George Mason, and a nephew of John Y. Mason, Confederate Secretary of the Navy and Minister to France. Children: 1, Hatley N. Mason, b. September 3, 1880; 2, Lucy Jones Mason; 3, Claudia Mason.

(1450) MARIA G. NORTON.

1450   MARIA G. NORTON, b. at Warrenton, Va., August 26, 1858.

1452   JAMES K. M. NORTON, b. at Alexandria, Va., May 30, 1860.

1454   THOMAS MARSHALL NORTON, b. at Alexandria, Va., November 21, 1863.

1456   NANNIE B. NORTON, b. at Alexandria, Va., August 29, 1867.

1458   GEO. HATLEY NORTON, b. at Alexandria, Va., November 7, 1869.

1460   COURTENAY F. NORTON, b. at Alexandria, Va., January 2, 1876.

1462   HILARY P. JONES, b. November 14, 1863; entered the Naval Academy by appointment of GEN. JOSEPH E. JOHNSTON, in September 1880, and is now serving as a Naval Cadet.

1464   ALICE JONES, b. August 25, 1866, at "Ashleigh," Fauquier Co., Va.

1466   LUCY M. JONES, b. at Hanover Academy Va., November 15, 1867.

1468   CLAUDIA JONES, b. at Hanover Academy, Va., July 19, 1872.

1470   JAMES K. JONES, b. at Hanover Academy, Va., March 21, 1878.

1472   BASIL MAGRUDER JONES, b. at Hanover Academy, Va., September 10, 1880.

1474   MARIA W. MARSHALL, b. in Fauquier Co., Va., April 10, 1867.

1476   DAVID M. MARSHALL, b. in Fauquier Co., Va., November 17, 1869.

(1502) EDWARD C. MARSHALL.

1478 LELIA P. MARSHALL, b. in Fauquier Co., May 27, 1872.

1480 CLAUDIA B. MARSHALL, b. in Fauquier Co., Va., November 17, 1874.

1482 J. REAMEY MARSHALL, b. in Fauquier Co., Va., February 18, 1877.

1484 BELL B. MARSHALL, b. in Fauquier Co., Va., April 19, 1880.

1486 EDWARD P. MARSHALL, b. in Fauquier Co., Va., April 19, 1880.

1488 JAMES K. MARSHALL, b. in Fauquier Co., Va., November 15, 1882.

1490 CLAUDIA B. STRIBLING, b. at Clairmont, Fauquier Co., Va., June 11, 1870.

1492 ROBERT M. STRIBLING, b. at Clairmont, Fauquier Co., Va., January 1, 1872.

1494 HENRY C. STRIBLING, b. at Clairmont, Fauquier Co., Va., August 26, 1874.

1496 JAMES K. M. STRIBLING, b. at Clairmont, Fauquier Co., Va., March 15, 1876.

1498 GRAY CARROLL STRIBLING, b. at Clairmont, Fauquier Co., Va., May 20, 1878.

1500 ELIZA J. STRIBLING, b. at Clairmont, Fauquier Co., Va., January 1, 1882.

1502 EDWARD C. MARSHALL, b. in Fauquier Co., Va., April 25, 1856; educated Clifton High School; clerked in stores in Berryville, Va., and Washington, D. C.; went to Florida; entered the United States Army, and after serving a time, went to Salt Lake City, where he is sustaining himself and making his start in the world.

(1504) NORMAN FITZHUGH MARSHALL.

1504 NORMAN FITZHUGH MARSHALL, b. in Fauquier Co., Va., February 9, 1858; educated at Clifton High School and Hanover Academy; graduated at the Theological Seminary of the Episcopal Church, at Alexandria, Va., and is now rector of a church in Notaway Co., Va.

1506 REBECCA C. MARSHALL, b. November 30, 1859, in Fauquier Co., Va. She is a tall, handsome and refined lady. My daughter (2170) spent a week in 1884, as her guest and recommends her as an agreeable associate, and an educated and pious young woman.

1508 JOHN MARSHALL, b. in Fauquier Co., Va., June 10, 1861; educated at Clifton High School; graduated at the Lexington, Va., Military Institute; studied under his grandfather, E. C. Marshall, (160) and is now in the service of a large mercantile house in Detroit, Mich.

1510 MARY C. MARSHALL, b. at "Bergen," near Markham, Va., April 30, 1874.

1512 BASIL MAGRUDER MARSHALL, b. at "Bergen," near Markham, Va., March 22, 1876.

1514 JAMES D. J. MARSHALL, b. at "Bergen," near Markham, Va., April 9, 1879.

1516 SAMUEL TAYLOR MARSHALL, b. in Berryville, Va., January 7, 1860; is in business with his father in Kansas City, Missouri.

1518 EDMUND PEYTON MARSHALL, b. in Berryville, Va., December 2, 1866.

1520 VIRGINIA CARY MARSHALL, b. in Berryville, Clarke Co. Va., July 8, 1869. She is a sweet and well behaved girl.

THE MARSHALL FAMILY. 331

(1548) ALFRED B. WILLIAMS.

1522   ELIZA BRUCE MARSHALL, b. in Berryville, Va., April 30, 1872.

1524   JAMES KEITH NEWTON, b. in Westmoreland Co., Va., April 3, 1865.

1526   MARY W. NEWTON, b. in Westmoreland Co., Va., November 6, 1866.

1528   REBECCA PEYTON NEWTON, b. in Westmoreland Co., Va., March 7, 1868.

1530   EDWARD MARSHALL NEWTON, b. in Westmoreland Co., October 19, 1870.

1532   BESSIE L. NEWTON, b. in Westmoreland Co., Va., November 8, 1875.

1534   JACQUELIN A. NEWTON, b. in Westmoreland Co., Va., January 2, 1881.

1536   SUSAN A. MARSHALL, b. at "Innis," Fauquier Co., Va., August 27, 1867.

1538   EDWARD C. MARSHALL, b. at "Innis," Fauquier Co., Va., February 28, 1869.

1540   HENRY MORRIS MARSHALL, b. at "Innis," Fauquier Co., Va., December 25, 1870.

1542   THOMAS MARSHALL, b. at "Innis," Fauquier Co., Va., November 15, 1874.

1544   RICHARD C. MARSHALL, b. at "Innis," Fauquier Co., Va., May 25, 1879.

1546   ALICE B. MARSHALL, b. at "Innis," Fauquier Co., Va., February 1, 1881.

1548   ALFRED B. WILLIAMS, b. January, 1856. = MAMIE BRYCE, dr. of Campbell Bryce, of Columbia, S. C. They live in Greenville, S. C., and he is editor of the Greenville *Daily News*. Children: 1, Ethel V. Williams, b. January 6, 1883.

(1550) EDWARD DANDRIDGE WILLIAMS.

1550 EDWARD DANDRIDGE WILLIAMS, b. in Baltimore, Md., November, 1858. He is joint editor with his brother (1548), of the Greenville, S. C., *Daily News*.

1552 ROSALIE B. WILLIAMS, b. in Baltimore, Md., December 17, 1864. Lives with her parents (594).

1554 BENJAMIN WATKINS LEIGH, b. at "Maidstone," Berkeley Co., W. Va., August 26, 1855.

1556 EDWARD C. LEIGH, b. at "Maidstone," Berkeley Co., W. Va., March 26, 1858.

1558 RALEIGH T. C. LEIGH, b. in Powhattan Co., Va., October 31, 1863.

1560 WILLIAM R. LEIGH, b. at "Maidstone," Berkeley Co., W. Va., September 23, 1866. He is a student at the Academy of Fine Arts, Munich, Germany.

1562 THOMAS W. LEIGH, b. at "Maidstone," Berkeley Co., W. Va., July 25, 1869.

1564 ELIZABETH K. M. LEIGH, b. at "Maidstone," Berkeley Co., W. Va., February 17, 1873.

1574 PATTIE JEFFERSON TAYLOR, b. March 24, 1867.

1676 RALEIGH COLSTON TAYLOR, b. June, 1869.

1578 LEWIS RANDOLPH TAYLOR, b. September, 1871.

1580 JOHN RANDOLPH TAYLOR, b. August, 1874.

1582 EDWARD COLSTON TAYLOR, b. February 22, 1877.

1584 JANE BROCKENBROUGH TAYLOR, b. January, 1881.

THE MARSHALL FAMILY. 333

(1594) ANNIE GORDON THOMAS—(*Duval*).

1586 BASIL GORDON THOMAS, b. in Baltimore, April 14, 1839. He is unmarried, and lives in Baltimore.

1588 CAPT. JOHN HANSON THOMAS, b. in Baltimore, September 21, 1841, = MARY HOWARD BEIRNE, dr. of George P. Beirne, of Huntsville, Ala. She died October 9, 1866. Mr. Thomas served in the Confederate army throughout the war; the first year in the 1st Maryland Regiment, and the last three years on Gen. Loring's staff, as Captain. Issue: Howard Beirne Thomas, b. September 26, 1866.

1590 RALEIGH COLSTON THOMAS, b. October 8, 1844, = March 25, 1868, MARY MCDONALD, dr. of William McDonald, of "Guilford," Baltimore Co., Md. He served in the Confederate army for two years as aide to Gen. Lomax, with the rank of Lieutenant. Issue: 1, Mary McDonald Thomas, b. January 30, 1872; 2, Raleigh Colston Thomas, b. August 5, 1875; 3, Reginald Contee Thomas, b. September 11, 1879; 4. Annie Campbell Gordon Thomas, b. May 11, 1883.

1592 DOUGLAS HAMILTON THOMAS, b. in Baltimore, January 1, 1847, = January 25, 1870, ALICE LEE WHITRIDGE, dr. of Dr. John Whitridge, of Baltimore. Mr. Thomas is now cashier of the Merchants' National Bank of Baltimore, and is one of the leading financiers of that city. His handsome figure, dignified bearing, native talents, finished education and cordial manners combine to make him a pleasant gentleman in society and a man of affairs in the walks of finance and commerce. Our correspondence has convinced me of his executive abilities, and his eminent qualification for the place he now fills. Issue: 1, Douglas Hamilton Thomas, b. March 5, 1872; 2, John Hanson Thomas, b. March 1, 1876; 3, Alice Lee Whitridge Thomas, b. August 5, 1883.

1594 ANNIE GORDON THOMAS, b. in Baltimore, May 20, 1849, = February 17, 1878, HENRY RIEMAN DUVAL. Issue: 1, Hanson Rieman Duval, b. April 10, 1881; 2, Rieman Gordon Duval, b. November 5, 1883.

(1596) MARY RANDOLPH THOMAS—(*Carroll*).

1596 MARY RANDOLPH THOMAS, b. October 10, 1851, = April 21, 1870, JOHN CARROLL, of the "Caves," Baltimore Co., Md. Issue: 1, John Carroll, b. March 4, 1871; 2, Charles Carroll, b. July 17, 1872; 3, Douglas Gordon Carroll, b. July 14, 1882.

1598 JOHN MARSHALL THOMAS, b. December 5, 1853, = June 12, 1882, ANNIE GREGG, dr. of John Gregg of Baltimore. Issue: 1, John Gregg Thomas, b. October 3, 1883.

1600 LEIGH ROBINSON, b. in Richmond, Va., February 26, 1840, = January 10, 1883, ALICE MORSON. See Morson chart, No. 1428.

1602 ELIZABETH M. ROBINSON, b. in Richmond, Va., January 25, 1842.

1604 CARY ROBINSON, b. in Richmond, Va., November 9, 1843; enlisted in Confederate service, and was killed in battle, October 22, 1864.

1606 WILLIAM C. ROBINSON, b. in Richmond, Va., March 3, 1845; enlisted in the Confederate service, and was killed in battle, October 14, 1863.

1608 CONWAY ROBINSON, b. in Richmond, Va., December 14, 1852; is now a lawyer of brilliant talents, residing at Washington, D. C.

1610 SUSAN ROBINSON, b. August 9, 1854, at Richmond, Va.

1612 AGNES C. ROBINSON, b. May 28, 1857, at Richmond, Va. She lives with her widowed mother, at Washington, D. C.

1614 ELIZA FISHER COLSTON, b. April 19, 1846, = PROF. B. L. GILDERSLEEVE, of the John Hopkins University, at Baltimore, Md. Issue: 1, Raleigh C. Gildersleeve, b. June, 1869; 2, Emma Gildersleeve, b. June, 1872.

THE MARSHALL FAMILY. 335

(1034) NANNIE COLSTON BLACKFORD—(*Withers*).

1616 ANNE B. COLSTON, b. March 19, 1848,= ROBERT CAMM. Issue: 1, Robert Camm, b. June, 1868; 2, Gertrude Camm, b. March, 1870; 3, Annie L. Camm. They live in Richmond, Va.

1618 JANE COLSTON, b. June 27, 1849,= CONWAY R. HOWARD. Issue: 1, Mary Howard, b. July 4, 1872; 2, Gertrude Howard, b. May 7, 1874; 3, Jane Howard, and 4, Conway Howard, b. March 27, 1881. Mr. Howard is a civil engineer.

1620 THOMAS M. COLSTON, b. July 4, 1851. He is teaching school in Texas.

1622 LAURA H. COLSTON, b. December 3, 1856.

1624 MATTIE MINOR, b. at the University of Virginia, June 1861. I am told she is a remarkably intelligent young lady; but she failed to reply to a kind letter I wrote to her.

1626 SUSAN MINOR, b. at the University of Virginia, August, 1864.

1628 JOHN B. MINOR, b. at the University of Virginia, in 1866.

1630 RALEIGH COLSTON MINOR, b. at the University of Virginia, 1868.

1632 NANNIE C. MINOR, b. at the University of Virginia, June, 1872.

1634 NANNIE COLSTON BLACKFORD, b. at "Diamond Hill," in the city of Lynchburg, Va., April 20, 1857; d. February 8, 1884, = February 6, 1883, LIEUT. SAMUEL T. WITHERS, teller of the Commercial Bank of Lynchburg, b. about 1853 *l*. Nannie was the oldest of three children of Mr. Blackford, when, in 1861, duty to his State called him to arms. But ere a year had passed, Nannie was the only child left, and the yearning wife and mother

(1636) CHARLES M. BLACKFORD.

took her now, only darling, to its father, to endure with him the dangers and exposures of camp life. The little one became the "daughter of the regiment." Her father was a Captain of a company in the Second Virginia Cavalry, and afterwards a member of Gen. Longstreet's staff, and Judge Advocate of his corps. The bright little maiden was a favorite with rank and file, and many a rugged soldier took her to his loving arms, and shed tears on her bright ringlets as she prattled tenderly of the little ones he had left at his distant home. When peace returned her father sought his former residence, on "Diamond Hill," at Lynchburg. Here Nannie was sent to St. Mary's School, and by her affectionate spirit and heartfelt kindness endeared herself to her companions. Her purity and intelligence, her cordial greeting, and her sympathetic heart, as well as the alms she contributed to the poor, introduced her to all classes, and made her a favorite throughout the city. Mr. Withers from a boy had been her schoolmate. He was in all respects worthy of the flower he plucked. The marriage was solemnized with pomp and gayety. The number and value of the wedding presents attested the strong hold Nannie had on the affections of hundreds. As she had been the child of her father's regiment, she was now the idol of the whole city. But ere one year of married bliss was passed, she was called to join the choir of seraphs above. The whole city united in mourning for one they regarded as their own lovely daughter. Four hundred letters of condolence poured in on the stricken parents, and unnumbered evidences of sympathy were bestowed. A memorial volume, with a handsome portrait as a frontispiece, has been published and sent to her friends; and her lovely countenance smiles upon me from the printed page as I write. Mr. Withers is teller in the Commercial Bank of Lynchburg, Va., and is highly respected and greatly beloved.

1636 CHARLES M. BLACKFORD, b. 1865, at Lynchburg, Va.

1638 RALEIGH COLSTON BLACKFORD, b. at Lynchburg, Va., May, 1870.

(1650) ADDISON DIMMITT FLEMING.

1640 ELIZA MARSHALL FLEMING, b. in Fleming Co., Ky., September 18, 1845, = October 11, 1866, JOSHUA DEBELL, b. January 23, 1841. Mr. DeBell is a small farmer in Fleming Co., Ky. He is an industrious, thriving and highly esteemed citizen. Issue: 1, Catherine W. DeBell, b. April 2, 1868; 2, Clarence DeBell, b. December 23, 1869.

1642 THOMAS MARSHALL FLEMING, b. in Fleming Co., Ky., February 3, 1847, = July 29, 1869, PATTIE L. HENDRICK, b. January 19, 1851. Marshall Fleming is in the livery stable business in Flemingsburg, Ky. He is a thorough-going business man, of fine judgment and agreeable manners. Mrs. Fleming was a daughter of William H. Hendrick, b. June 26, 1822, living, and Elizabeth Howe, b. August 15, 1831; d. July 12, 1860. Issue: 1, Fannie H. Fleming, b. February 18, 1878; 2, Addison D. Fleming, b. August 17, 1879; and 3, William H. Fleming, b. October 8, 1882.

1644 JULIANNA MARSHALL FLEMING, b. in Fleming Co., Ky., June 15, 1849, = 1871, ELIAS CARPENTER. They live on a small farm a few miles east of Flemingsburg. I have never met either of them. Issue: 1, Emily M. Carpenter; 2, Benjamin B. Carpenter; 3, Bessie B. Carpenter; 4, Eliza D. Carpenter, and 5, unnamed, b. 1884.

1646 FANNIE MARSHALL FLEMING, b. in Fleming Co., Ky., February 8, 1850, = 1876, BALDWIN DEBELL, b. May 15, 1842. They live on a farm near Flemingsburg, Ky. Mr. DeBell is a brother of (No. 1640). I visited the family in 1884, and found them agreeable, sensible and thriving. No issue.

1648 WILLIAM P. FLEMING, b. in Fleming Co., Ky., June 15, 1852.

1650 ADDISON DIMMITT FLEMING, b. in Fleming Co., Ky., December 27, 1854.

(1652) EMILY MARSHALL FLEMING.

1652 EMILY MARSHALL FLEMING, b. August 24, 1857. I met Cousin Emily in 1884, in Washington, Ky., and found her a lively and intelligent young lady.

1654 JULIANNA (JULIA) WHETCROFT DIMMITT, b. in Lewisburg, Mason Co., Ky., June 29, 1846, December 17, 1862, JOHN C. HERNDON, b. September 23, 1841. In all my excursions among my relatives, I have never met one that possessed in greater perfection the higher and nobler traits of female character. She is a Juno among women! She is large and handsome, dignified and generous, spirited and gracious, and fearless and conscientious. I spent a week with her in Louisville, Ky., in July, 1884. The moment I entered her door I felt at home. As a daughter she met me, and as a father I was treated. She hallows the memory of her parents, and rejoices in the mutual love and reciprocal confidence of her sisters. Her parents and her grandparents had no sons, and I have often noticed that where the children were all girls, they were good and lovely. At the time of his marriage, Mr. Herndon was teller of the Bank of Kentucky, at Henderson. He is now secretary and treasurer of the Gilbert & Mallory Publishing Co., of Louisville, Ky. He is cordial in manners and a splendid talker. He is a son of the Hon. John C. Herndon, of Frankfort, who was a Circuit Judge, an author of several law books. Issue: 1, Leonard L. Herndon, b. March 25, 1867, and 2, Fannie Herndon, b. July 9, 1872.

1656 KATE BUFORD DIMMITT, b. in Lewisburg, Mason Co., Ky., October 25, 1852, = June 3, 1874, DARLINGTON E. FEE, son of Jesse Fee and Maria Knowles, of Clermont Co., Ohio. Mrs. Fee is a large, handsome, dignified lady, very cordial in her address, and possessed of the spirit and independence of her ancestors. Mr. Fee is a banker in New Richmond, Ohio, and is one of the leading politicians of his section of the State. Issue: 1, Jesse D. Fee, b. March 20, 1875; 2, Darlington E. Fee, b. July 21, 1876; 3, Fannie Marshall Fee, b. June 20, 1878; 4, Kate Dimmitt Fee, b. November 23, 1882.

THE MARSHALL FAMILY. 339

(1672) SALLIE F. CASEY — (*Thayer*).

1658 FRANCES MARSHALL DIMMITT, b. in Lewisburg, Mason Co., Ky., April 21, 1857, = February 24, 1881, ROBERT A. DAVIS, b. 1856. Mrs. Davis is possessed of all the virtues of her sisters (1654–6). Mr. Davis is a lawyer, and a son of Hon. M. H. Davis, of New Richmond, Ohio. They reside in the latter place. Issue: Addison Dimmitt Davis, b. January 23, 1883.

1660 CLARISSIE H. GRANT, b. in Fleming Co., Ky., September 28, 1852, d. March 9, 1884, = January 4, 1875, RICHARD H. BENNETT. Issue: Two boys and one girl.

1662 JULIA BLAND GRANT, b. in Fleming Co., Ky., August 18, 1859, = at Canton, Mo., November 20, 1883, EBBEN STEPHENSON, of Kentucky. I have a good letter from Mrs. Stephenson. Her postoffice is Canton, Mo.

1668 JOHN CHAMBERS, b. January 31, 1840, = August 29, 1867, ANN WOOD, b. March, 1845. She was a daughter of William H. Wood and Jane Lashbrooke. Jane was a daughter of William Lashbrooke and a Miss Preston. W. H. Wood was a son of Andrew Wood and Matilda Fox. Mr. Chambers is a wealthy and prosperous farmer, living near Maysville, Ky. He is a man of fine judgment, full of enterprise, and often speculates in tobacco and live stock. They have no children.

1670 FANNIE C. CASEY, b. in Covington, Ky., July 26, 1853, = October 18, 1876, JOHN C. TATE. Cousin Fannie is pretty; her greetings cordial and she was born to be loved. Mr. Tate is farming near Maysville, Ky. He is a son of John H. Tate and Margaret Chenoweth. Issue: 1, James Casey Tate, b. September 1, 1877; 2, Margaret Chenoweth, b. May 11, 1880; 3, John H. Tate, b. August 12, 1882.

1672 SALLIE F. CASEY, b. in Covington, Ky., February 14, 1856, = November 30, 1880, WILLIAM B. THAYER, b. in Kentucky, September 11, 1853. Cousin Sallie is a pure, sweet and

340   THE MARSHALL FAMILY.

(1674) MARY M. CASEY —(*Powell*).

artless kinswoman. She was educated at Dr. Louis Barbour's School, in Danville, Ky., and there she first met Mr. Thayer. Mr. Thayer is a great-grand-son of Gov. John Adair, of Kentucky; was educated at Center College, Danville, Ky.; entered as a clerk the great mercantile house of Bullene, Moores & Emery, of Kansas City, Mo., and in 1883, became a partner in the establishment. He lives in Kansas City, highly honored for his business qualifications. He is a sprightly and a remarkably agreeable gentleman. Issue: William B. Thayer, Jr., b. September 5, 1881. He rules supreme in the household.

1674   MARY M. CASEY, b. in Covington, Ky., 1860, = LOUIS POWELL. He died, and the child inherited a large fortune, chiefly in Covington property. Issue: Marie Louise Powell.

1678   JOHN B. CASEY, b. in Covington, Ky., is now a resident of Dakota.

1680   ILLA L. CASEY, b. in Covington Ky.

1682   ALEXANDER MARSHALL CASEY, b. in Covington, Ky.

1684   JOHN ALLEN GREEN, b. in Maysville, Ky., May 12, 1861. He is the publisher and one of the editors of the *Maysville Eagle*. He is said to be a young man of remarkable industry and high promise.

1686   BESSIE L. GREEN, b. in Maysville, Ky., June 20, 1862, = December 11, 1884, THOMAS E. TRACY. She invited me to her wedding, and I replied with my congratulations, asking for a sketch of her husband. Perhaps she will answer when her long honeymoon ends.

1688   PIERCE BUTLER GREEN, b. August 12, 1863.

(1704) ANSON MALTBY.

1690 LILLIE C. GREEN, b. July 30, 1865.

1692 WILLIAM O. B. GREEN, b. January 20, 1868.

1694 MARY R. GREEN, b. April 12, 1870.

1696 PATTIE C. GREEN, b. November 25, 1873.

1698 NANNIE T. GREEN, b. October 6, 1877.

1700 LEWIS W. GREEN, b. July 19, 1880.

1702 Dr. MARTIN MARSHALL MALTBY, b. at "Belle Grove," Fleming Co., Ky., July 3, 1845, = October 16, 1873, LOUISE BOGARDUS, b. in New York City, September 3, 1853. Dr. Marshall is a skillful dentist of New York City. Mrs. Marshall is a daughter of Abram Bogardus, son of Cornelius and Eleanor Bogardus. Her mother was Emmeline Doremus, daughter of John and Margaret Doremus. She is a descendant of Ameke J. Bogardus, whose farm is now held by Trinity Church, and is worth many millions. The Church has no moral right to the ground, but adverse possession makes its claim indefeasible. Issue: 1, Edith Frances Maltby, b. October 15, 1874; 2, Martin Marshall Maltby, b. July 1, 1879; 3, Louise B. Maltby, b. June 14, 1880; 4, Elizabeth M. Maltby, b. August 18, 1884. Dr. Marshall was educated at Amherst and Yale Colleges, and he graduated at the New York Dental College. He lives at 128 W. Forty-seventh street, New York.

1704 ANSON MALTBY, b. at "Belle Grove," Fleming Co., Ky., September 8, 1848, = in New York City, December 20, 1877, MARY DESHA BRECKINRIDGE, b. near Lexington, Ky., March 31, 1854. Anson received the rudiments of his education from private tutors, in Northampton, Mass. At the age of sixteen he made a year's tour through Europe, Asia and Africa; on his return, taught school in Kentucky and Ohio; took a two years course in Columbia College Law School, New York City, graduating in 1869, and is now

(1706) ELIZABETH MALTBY.

a successful practicing attorney at 48 Wall street, New York City. He stands at the front of his profession, and has been the chief counsel in some very important cases. His wife I greet as the daughter of my classmate, Vice-President John C. Breckenridge. Her pedigree may be thus expressed:
1. John Breckinridge, of Jefferson's Cabinet, = Mary Cabell, of Albemarle Co., Va.
  2. Joseph Cabell Breckinridge, = Mary Stanhope Smith.
    3. John C. Breckinridge, = Mary C. Burch, daughter of Clifton Rhodes Burch and Aletha Viley.
      4. Mary D. Breckinridge, = ANSON MALTBY. Issue: 1, Marion Maltby, b. November 2, 1878; 2, Frances M. Maltby, b. in Essex Co., N. J., May 3, 1880; 3, Mary B. Maltby, b. in Essex Co., N. J., August 20, 1883.

1706 ELIZABETH MALTBY, b. in Covington, Ky., March 30, 1850. She lives with her father in Northampton, Mass.

1708 ROBERT TAYLOR MARSHALL, b. at "Belle Grove," Fleming Co., Ky., September, 1855,= September 15, 1880, his distant relative, REBECCA L. TAYLOR (1944). He is farming in Fleming Co., Ky., and is rising to wealth and influence.

1710 LIZZIE MARSHALL. See No. 752.

1712 SARAH D. MARSHALL, b. at "Belle Grove," Fleming Co., Ky., February 3, 1859. She lives with her parents. (654)

1718 ELIZABETH FORMAN MARSHALL, b. February 2, 1859.

1720 MARTIN P. MARSHALL, b. April 7, 1859.

1722 CHARLES MARSHALL, b. September 18, 1863.

(1748) JAMES RANDOLPH.

1724 LOGAN McKNIGHT MARSHALL, b. December 23, 1866.

1426 ROBERT MORRIS MARSHALL, b. January 27, 1869.

1728 LOUIS MARSHALL, b. October 7, 1873.

1730 JOHN MARSHALL, b. February 7, 1877.

1732 MARTIN M. DURRETT, b. February 1, 1857, = September, 1881, ANNA MONTGOMERY, dr. of Alex. and Agnes Montgomery, of Covington, Ky.

1734 RICHARD C. DURRETT, b. February 1, 1861.

1736 ELIZA M. DURRETT, b. January 1, 1863.

1738 LUCY M. DURRETT, b. August 16, 1866.

1740 MARY P. DURRETT, b. October 15, 1870.

1742 CHARLES M. DURRETT, b. November 17, 1872.

1744 WILLIAM DURRETT, b. December 16, 1874.

1746 ALICE MASSIE, b. October 12, 1868, in Washington, Ky. I have a letter or two from this sweet little girl. She is living with her widowed mother on "The Hill," where she was born.

1748 JAMES RANDOLPH, b. September 30, 1852, at Easton, Penn., = October 15, 1879, JENNIE WESTON SAYRE. He graduated at Rutger's College, and at the School of Mines, Columbia; practiced engineering and the construction and operation of blast furnaces, at Bethlehem, Penn. He then took up railroading, and was made Superintendent of the Long Branch Division of the New Jersey Central railroad. He is now a coal merchant at 211 Broadway, New York City. Issue: 1, Theo. F. Randolph, b. August 9, 1880; 2, Elizabeth F. Randolph, b. November 9, 1883.

(1750) THOMAS MARSHALL F. RANDOLPH.

1750 THOMAS MARSHALL F. RANDOLPH, b. January 4, 1857. He graduated at Rutger's College, New Jersey, and Columbia Law School. He is now practicing law in New York City. His letters to me recommend him not only as a gentleman of literary and legal attainments, but as a scholar of lofty principles, honor and ambition.

1752 LUCY AMBLER F. RANDOLPH, b. January 17, 1859, is living with her mother at Morristown, N. J.

1754 EDGAR F. RANDOLPH, b. at Uniontown, N. J., April 29, 1861; graduated at Rutger's College, N. J., and is now studying law.

1756 LUCY MARSHALL SMITH, b. in New Orleans, August 30, 1862.

1758 MARY R. SMITH, b. in New Orleans, March 17, 1866.

1760 CHARLES F. COLEMAN, b. in Vicksburg, September 4, 1865.

1762 MARIE ESTELLE COLEMAN, b. in Vicksburg, January 2, 1867.

1764 HARRY H. COLEMAN, b. in Vicksburg, April 29, 1872.

1766 HARRY M. DICKINSON, b. March 18, 1862.

1768 CHARLIANNA (NANNIE) DICKINSON, b. June 4, 1865.

1770 ANDREW G. DICKINSON, b. November 14, 1866.

1772 FANNIE RANDOLPH DICKINSON, b. October, 1870.

1774 NANNIE MARSHALL, b. December 21, 1869.

1776 HENRY WALLER, b. July 30, 1874.

(1798) ROBERT MORRIS MARSHALL.

1778 PHŒBE F. WALLER, b. June 2, 1876.

1780 SARAH BELL WALLER, b. December 29, 1878.

1782 CHARLES MARSHALL BENTLEY, b. in Va., July 30, 1881.

1784 FRANK M. BENTLEY, b. in Ky., April 10, 1883.

1790 LUCY MARSHALL, b. in Warren Co., Va., February 16, 1847. Cousin Lucy is a tall, blackeyed and thoughtful young lady, who finds her pleasure in flowers and literature. I have scores of letters from her, and am proud to admit she is the most prompt and faithful correspondent I have. Though I have barely seen her, yet I am always glad to get her warm and gushing letter, each accompanied by an appendix of heraldic lore. She lives with her parents at " Horseshoe," Warren Co., Va.

1792 JUDITH BALL MARSHALL, b. in Warren Co., Va., April 28, 1849. She is living with her parents at "Horseshoe," Warren Co., Va.; Some times teaches.

1794 HESTER MARSHALL, b. in Warren Co., Va., August 5, 1851, = October 17, 1876, A. J. DAVISON, son of J. Smith Davison and Mary Hite, b. July, 1850. Mr. Davison is a farmer near Front Royal, Va. Issue: 1, Marshall Davison, b. July 25, 1877; 2, Fontaine Davison, b. March 8, 1879; 3, William R. Davison, b. July 2, 1881; 4, Cary A. Davison, b. September 8, 1883.

1796 CHARLES C. MARSHALL, b. in Warren Co., Va., June 25, 1853, = December 27, 1878, LUCY E. TURNER, daughter of R. H. Turner, of Front Royal. Mr. Marshall is farming near "Happy Creek," Warren Co., Va. They are Episcopalians.

1798 ROBERT MORRIS MARSHALL, b. in Warren Co., Va., March 29, 1885. Lives with his father.

(1800) JAMES M. MARSHALL.

1800   JAMES M. MARSHALL, b January 23, 1857, in Warren Co., Va. Has a Steam Saw Mill in Warren Co., Va.

1802   MARY M. MARSHALL, b. in Warren Co., Va., May 24, 1859. Well educated and occasionally teaches.

1804   SUSAN B. MARSHALL, b. October 9, 1863, in Warren Co., Va.

1806   ANNA M. MARSHALL, b. in Warren Co , Va , August 11, 1865.

1808   DR. HENRY MORRIS, b. June 6, 1855, = October 12, 1880, BESSIE ELLIOTT. Dr Morris is practicing medicine at Philadelphia, Penn. Issue: 1, Robert Morris b in Philadelphia, July 21, 1881; 2, Grace Morris, b. May 30, 1884.

1810   ANNA MORRIS, b. in Philadelphia, Penn , November 11, 1859.

1812   SUSAN M. MORRIS, b. in Philadelphia, Penn., November 26, 1860.

1814   LUCY MORRIS, b. March 24, 1866, in Phildelphia, Penn.

1816   SAMUEL W. MARSHALL, b. in Warren Co., Va., September 8, 1861. Lives with his mother in Richmond, Va.

1817   LUCY M. MARSHALL, b. December 14, 1863. She lives with her mother in Richmond, Va.

1818   EMMELINE W. MARSHALL, b. at Priestly, Fauquier Co., Va., February 9, 1880.

1820   BEVERLY ALEX. MARSHALL, b. at Priestly, Fauquier Co., Va., June 19, 1882.

1822   JAMES J. MARSHALL, b. at the "Evergreens," Fauquier Co., Va., May 12, 1869.

(1864) HOMES M'GUIRE.

1824   JOHN MARSHALL, b. January 9, 1871.

1830   ADELAIDE TAYLOR MARSHALL, b. April 13, 1877.

1832   HENRY MORRIS MARSHALL, b. February 29, 1880.

1834   ALICE B. MARSHALL, b. January 25, 1883.

1836   MARY M. ARMSTEAD, b. January 2, 1873.

1840   LOUIS B. ARMSTEAD, b. January 2, 1875.

1856   WILLIAM B. JOLLIFFE, b. January 24, 1837, = October 10, 1858 KATE HEMPHILL. Issue: 1, Samuel H. Jolliffe, b. July 21, 1860; 2, William H., b. July 21, 1870; Ella M., b. July 3, 1876; 4, David M. Jolliffe, b. April 14, 1880.

1858   JOHN MARSHALL JOLLIFFE, b. in Clark Co., Va , May 13, 1843, = KATE MCCORMICK. Mr. Jolliffe entered the Confederate Army and was fearfully wounded, in both his legs, at Chancellorsville, May 3, 1863. He stills suffers from his wounds. He lives in Clarke County. Issue: 1, Fannie M. Jolliffe, b. September 30, 1870; 2, Lucy B., b. November 12, 1873; 3, Alexander, b. October 20, 1876; 4. Joseph J., b. November 10, 1879; 5, Thomas P., b. May 4, 1882.

1860   LUCY MCGUIRE, b. July 4, 1838, d. March 17, 1884, = November 8, 1859, TREADWELL SMITH. He was killed in the battle of "Five Forks," April 5, 1865. Issue: 1, Horace Smith; 2, Lela Smith. LUCY = 2d, February 18, 1868, JOHN W. MCCORMICK. Issue: 1, William McCormick; 2, Homes McCormick.

1862   AGNES B. MCGUIRE, b. November 1, 1840.

1864   HOMES MCGUIRE, b. 1843, d. 1874. He was a lawyer of distinction.

(1866) BURWELL M'GUIRE.

1866 BURWELL McGUIRE, b. August 6, 1845.

1868 REBECCA M. McGUIRE, b. November, 1848. Living in Clarke Co., Va.

1870 MARY MARSHALL McGUIRE, b. May 4, 1850, = June 25, 1883, JOHN STEVENS, of Hoboken, N. J.; millionaire.

1872 LIZZIE COOKE, born July, 1838. Lives in Clarke Co., Va.

1874 MARIA PENDLETON McGUIRE, b. April 15, 1840, = October 11, 1859, ANDREW E. KENNEDY, b. July 10, 1824, d. A lawyer of Charleston, W. Va. Her letters to me show a writer of skill and taste, and I learn that she has the reputation of a scholar. Issue: Philip Cooke Kennedy, b. September 20, 1860; 2, Agnes Esten Kennedy, b. December 19, 1866; 3, Lizzie Pendleton Kennedy, b. October 17, 1869; 4, Rebecca Willoughby Kennedy, b. August 27, 1872; 5, Andrew Eskridge Kennedy, b. March 9, 1875; 6, Marjorie Hughes Kennedy, b. June 23, 1878.

1876 NANNIE B. COOKE, b. March 15, 1843. Lives in Clarke Co., Va., and possesses fine literary acquirements.

1878 NATHANIEL B. COOKE, b. May, 1845, = October, 1867, JENNIE WINSTON, of Hanover Co., Va. Issue: One son and two daughters.

1880 ALETHIA COOKE, = PHILIP MEADE, a grandson of Bishop Meade. Issue: Two sons and two daughters.

1882 SUSIE RANDOLPH BURWELL, b. at the "Briers," August 5, 1845, = October 25, 1874, MAJ. M. W. HENRY, of Kentucky. After her first husband's death, in New York, November 28, 1877, she = DR. A. C. RANDOLPH, of Millwood, Va. By her first husband she had two daughters.

(1896) EVELINE CARTER BURWELL.

1884 GEORGE HARRISON BURWELL, b. March 14, 1847. He served in the Confederate army throughout the war; went to Mexico, entered Maximillian's army, and was killed in battle. His body was not recovered.

1886 DR. PHILIP BURWELL, b. in Clarke Co., Va., January 17, 1849, = MARIA B. HARRISON, dr. of Henry Harrison and Fannie Burwell. They live in Parkersburg, W. Va. Issue: Four children.

1888 MARY WILLING FRANCES BURWELL, b. in Clarke Co., February 13, 1851. Living with her parents.

1890 DR. JOHN PAGE BURWELL, b. in Clarke Co., Va., November 8, 1852, = September 24, 1872, ELIZABETH M. WAINWRIGHT (his cousin), eldest dr. of Com. Jonathan M. Wainwright, U. S. Navy. She died childless, July 28, 1883, and he = February 20, 1884, MARY WARRINGTON, eldest dr. of William Warrington, real estate agent of Berlin, Md. Her grandfather was Hon. L. D. Powell, of Berlin, Md. Dr. Burwell's first wife's mother was Maria Page, dr. of Dr. R. P. Page, of Clarke Co., Va., and Mary Willing Francis, of Philadelphia, Pa. Dr. Burwell is practicing medicine in Wilmington, Del., and stands high in his profession. I have an excellent letter from him.

1892 DR. WILLIAM NELSON BURWELL, b. in Clarke Co., Va., June 12, 1858. Single.

1894 THOMAS H. BURWELL, b. in Clarke Co., Va., February 19, 1861 = JENNIE SHARP, of Wilmington, Del. He is a farmer and lives at "Carter Hall," Va.

1896 EVELINE CARTER BURWELL, b. October 19, 1864. Living with her parents at Millwood, Va.

1898 WILLIAM F. HAYS, b. in Fayette Co., Ky., May 5, 1867. In 1884, was attending the Academy in Millersburg, Ky.

1900 CHARLES TAYLOR, b. February 22, 1847, — October 22, 1874, VIRGINIA CRENSHAW. They live in Richmond, Va. Issue: 1, Joseph C. Taylor, b. Septembrr 1, 1875; Isabella D. Taylor, b. Februrry 2, 1877; 3, Walter M. Taylor, b. February 6, 1882. Mr. Taylor is agent for the Richmond, P. & P. R. R.

1902 ELIZA A. TAYLOR, b. January 1, 1854, = BENJAMIN N. ROBINSON, of King William County. They live in Richmond, Va. Issue: 1, James T. Robinson, b. January 2, 1880; 2, Benjamin N. Robinson, b. August 1, 1882.

1904 ALFRED TAYLOR, b. August 31, 1856. Lives in Richmond, Va., and is agent for the R. P. & P. R. R.

1906 WIRT E. TAYLOR, b. April 4, 1858, = KATE E. CHAMBERLAIN, of Philadelphia. Live in Richmond. He is a merchant.

1908 RICHARD ASHBY TAYLOR, b. March 27, 1860. Lives in Richmond, Va. He is a bookkeeper.

1910 HATTIE A. TAYLOR, b. September 25, 1863.

1912 ALICE M. TAYLOR, b. March 5, 1866, in Richmond, Va.

1914 WARREN P. TAYLOR, b. September 11, 1868, in Richmond, Va. He is a railroad clerk.

1916 WILLIAM M. MARSHALL TAYLOR, b. 1853, LEILA MADISON DABNEY, in October, 1882.

1918 JAMES WINSTON TAYLOR, b. 1855, 1878, EMILY MORRIS TAYLOR. Issue: 1, Maud E. Taylor, b. 1879; 2, Virginia, b. 1881; 3, John Robert Taylor, b. 1883.

THE MARSHALL FAMILY. 351

(1966) ELIZA C. MARSHALL.

1922 ROBERTA BARNARD TAYLOR, b. 1860, =January 31,1883, BENJAMIN R. COWHERD. Issue: 1, Eliza G. Cowherd, b. 1884.

1956 BETTIE MARSHALL, b. October 8, 1848, = January 12, 1869, W. A. HOFFMAN, b. July 18, 1844. Issue: 1, Essex M. Hoffman, b. November 1, 1870; 2, Mary K. Hoffman, b. May 14, 1872; 3, Maria L. Hoffman, b. August 25, 1874; 4, Robert T. Hoffman, b. August 11, 1877; 5, Sarah E. Hoffman, b. November 10, 1879; 6, Ruthanna Hoffman, b. July 10, 1882. Mr. Hoffman's parents were Charles Hoffman and Sarah Ann Taylor, of Pennsylvania. His grand parents were Francis W. Hoffman and Anna Barbara Essex, of Germany. They live near Linden Station, Warren Co., Va.

1958 CATHERINE MARSHALL, b. December 15, 1850.

1960 ANGELINA MARSHALL, b. June 11, 1853.

1962 JOHN THOMAS MARSHALL, b. January 8, 1855, =December, 20, 1876, ELLA M. HOFFMAN, b. January 27, 1855. They live near Markham Station, Va. Issue: 1, Alban Hoffman Marshall, b. October 27, 1877; 2, Mary L. Marshall, b. June 22, 1880; 3, John T. Marshall, b. April 2, 1883. Mrs. Marshall is a sister of No. 1956.

1964 JOHN T. MARSHALL, b. in Fauquier Co., Va., February 12, 1854. By the labor of his hands he earned the means of attaining a good education; has studied law, and has started the practice, alone in Kansas City. I have letters from him and in reply, I have commended his ambition, and have encouraged him to press forward.

1966 ELIZA C. MARSHALL, b. in Fauquier Co., Va., July 6, 1856.

(1968) WILLIAM F. MARSHALL.

1968 WILLIAM F. MARSHALL, b. December 13, 1859.

1970 A. ELOISE MARSHALL, b. April 27, 1862.

1972 GEORGE H. MARSHALL, b. January 29, 1867.

1974 LINSAY MARSHALL, b. November 16, 1870.

1980 MARTIN D. BURNLEY, b. at Hazlehurst, Miss., July 20, 1863, = December 6, 1883, KATE L. BIRDSONG. Issue: 1, Furline Burnley, b. August 30, 1884.

1982 EDWIN BURNLEY, b. November 10, 1865.

1984 ROBERT M. BURNLEY, b. October 29, 1867.

1986 WILLIAM G. BURNLEY, b. August 13, 1870.

1988 NANNIE O. BURNLEY, b. February 16, 1872.

1990 BLANCHE BURNLEY, b. March 10, 1881.

1992 WILLIAM BURNLEY, b. October 9, 1864.

1994 MAY E. BURNLEY, b. December 29, 1866.

1996 JOSEPH H. BURNLEY, b. May 31, 1871.

1998 CHARLES MARSHALL JONES, b. in New Orleans, 1843. He is a Public School teacher in his native city, and stands high in his profession.

THE MARSHALL FAMILY. 353

(2010) LIEUT. DAVID RITTENHOUSE BARTON.

2000 ANNA M. JONES, b. in New Orleans, 1845, d. 1867, = April, 1866, DR. CORNELIUS BALDWIN, who survives her and resides in Winchester, Va. Dr. Baldwin was a son of Dr. Arch. S. Baldwin, who was a son of Dr. Cornelius Baldwin, a Surgeon in the Revolutionary Army, an alumnus of Princeton College, and one of the most eminent physicians of his day. His wife was Kitty Mackey. Issue: Charles Marshall Baldwin, b. 1873.

2002 ANNA MARIA BARTON. See No. 512.

2004 CHARLES MARSHALL BARTON. See 524.

2006 JANE CARY BARTON, b. at "Vaucluse," near Winchester, Va., March 23, 1832, d. March 25, 1878, = Rev. C. H. Shield, D. D., of Staunton, Va. She lived but a short time after marriage. Dr. Shield is in bad health, and is leading a quiet life in Staunton. Issue: Charles H. Shield, b. November 4, 1867. I met this handsome youth in 1884, in the office of Col. T. W. Bullett, Louisville, Ky., where he is studying law. See 2008.

2008 MARTHA W. BARTON, b. at "Vaucluse," near Winchester, Va., February 1834, = October 23, 1856, DR. J. M. BALDWIN, brother of Dr. C. Baldwin, No. 2000. He died 1862, leaving issue: 1, Maria Baldwin; and 2, A. Stewart Baldwin. She married 2d, October 1869, REV. C. H. SHEILD (2006). Issue: 1, George N. Sheild, b. July 22, 1870. The family live in Staunton, Va. Maria Baldwin lives with them. A. Stewart Baldwin is in San Francisco.

2010 LIEUT. DAVID RITTENHOUSE BARTON, b. at "Vaucluse," near Winchester, Va., September 27, 1837; d. December 18, 1862. He was educated at Winchester Academy, the Episcopal High School, near Alexandria, Va., and at the University. Before he had finished his education the war called him to the field, and he

(2012) LIEUT. WILLIAM STROTHER BARTON.

entered the Rockbridge Artillery. After participating in the battles of Falling Waters and Manassas, he was given the place of his brother, who had been killed in battle (2004), as First Lieutenant, and was himself killed at the battle of Fredericksburg, by a ball striking him in the head. His brother, Lieut. W. S. Barton (2012), assisted in bearing his body from the field, and in giving it hasty burial. That brother received his death wound at Mine Run; so that three brothers fill soldiers' graves.

2012 LIEUT. WILLIAM STROTHER BARTON, b. near Winchester, Va., November 24, 1838; d. July 28, 1868, from the effects of a wound received at the battle of Mine Run. He was educated at the Episcopal High School, near Alexandria, Va.; entered in 1861, the Second Virginia Infantry, of the "Stonewall Brigade;" was wounded at the first battle of Manassas; lost a leg at the battle of Mine Run, and died at "Springdale," near Winchester, from ill health induced by the wound.

2014 FANNIE JONES BARTON, b. near Winchester, Va., November 20, 1840; d. May 28, 1864, at "Vaucluse," of consumption.

2016 CAPT. ROBERT T. BARTON, b. near Winchester, Va., November 24, 1842, = February 19, 1867, CATHERINE KNIGHT, of Cecil Co., Md., b. March 22, 1845. He was educated at Winchester, and at Bloomfield Academy, near Charlottesville, Va.; served in the Rockbridge Battery until his discharge on account of failing health. He attained the rank of Captain. After the war he studied law at Winchester; entered on the practice there; is now in the Virginia Legislature, and Chairman of the Committee on Courts of Justice. He is author of "Barton's Law Practice," and of "Barton's Chancery Practice." His law books are standard authority in Virginia; his practice is large and lucrative, and as a lawyer and statesman, he enjoys an enviable reputation. No issue.

(2018) CAPT. RANDOLPH BARTON.

2018 CAPT. RANDOLPH BARTON, b. near Winchester, Va., April 24, 1844, = December 28, 1869, AGNES R. KIRKLAND, of Baltimore, b. June 14, 1849. Capt. Barton was reared by his step-grandmother, Ann Cary Randolph, at "Vaucluse," near Winchester, Va. After receiving a primary education at Winchester, Academy, he went to the Virginia Military Institute, and was interrupted by the breaking out of the war, yet he was afterwards granted a diploma. At the age of seventeen, he entered the Confederate army as Sergeant-Major of the 33d Virginia Infantry, Stonewall Brigade; was slightly wounded in the side at the battle of first Manassas; was taken prisoner at the battle of Kernstown, and confined at Fort Delaware until August, 1862; exchanged, and resumed his place in the army; was made Lieutenant of infantry, and appointed on the staff of Gen. Elisha Frank Paxton, of the Stonewall Brigade, with the rank of Captain; was made Assistant Adjutant-General; was severely wounded at the battle of Chancellorsville, May 3, 1863, by a minie ball, which entered his right shoulder and lodged under the left shoulder; it was removed and is still preserved; rejoined the army in September, 1863; was wounded at the battle of Spottsylvania C. H.; May 12, 1864, by a ball penetrating the fleshy part of the arm, above the elbow; rejoined the army after six weeks, and was slightly wounded at the battle of Monocacy, in August, 1864, and in the same battle his horse was killed under him; was severely wounded at the battle of Winchester, September 19, 1864; after two months, returned, and was wounded February 6, 1865, at Hatchers' Run, near Petersburg, and his horse was also wounded; was slightly wounded at Hare's Hill, near Petersburg, March 23, 1865, and at last surrendered with Gen. Lee at Appomattox C. H. His commission as Major was made out, but was not delivered before the war ended. Capt. Barton was at the side of his commander, Gen. Elisha Franklin Paxton, when, at Chancellorsville, May 3, 1862, the latter fell; he heard the thud of the ball that pierced his breast, received the falling hero in his arms, and heard his dying words, "Bind up my arm." He testifies that Gen. Paxton, whose early life was disgraced by profanity and violence, was so wrought upon by the dangers and vicissitudes of war, as to offer daily prayer, to read daily from his bible and to bear it constantly on his heart. He united with the Church, and, like Gordon and Havelock, was a Christian soldier. I spent a few days with Capt. Barton, in 1884,

(2020) DR. BOLLING WALKER BARTON.

and saw the soldier, not only in his erect form and abrupt bearing, but in the mathematical precision that characterized his words and actions. He is a successful lawyer in Baltimore; and on one of the railroads, ten miles from the city, he has erected a family mansion, and has his own gas factory and water works. Everything about him is reduced to military discipline. The courage and spirit that made him a soldier in war, will make him a nabob in peace. I gratefully remember the hospitality and appreciative attentions shown me during the days I spent with him in 1884. Issue: 1, Robert K. Barton, b. October 17, 1870; 2, Randolph Barton, b. December 12, 1871; 3, Charles Marshall Barton, b. October 26, 1875; 4, Agnes Barton, b. August 31, 1877; 5, Bolling W. Barton, b. April 21, 1881. Mrs. Barton was a daughter of Robert R. Kirkland, a distinguished citizen of Baltimore.

2020. DR. BOLLING WALKER BARTON, b. near Winchester, Va., November 24, 1845, = November 26, 1872, ELLA J. GIBSON, who died October, 1879. After taking his academic course at Winchester, Dr. Barton graduated at the Virginia Military Institute. In 1861, at the age of sixteen, he entered the Confederate army, and served to the end, having reached the rank of Lieutenant; went to Switzerland, and after studying there, finished his medical education at Paris, France; returned and practiced several years in Baltimore; abandoned his profession to devote himself to Botany and other scientific pursuits. He is now teaching a private class in Baltimore, making his home with his brother Randolph. I met him in 1884, and was much pleased, not only with his scientific erudition, but with his gentle and agreeable manners. No issue.

2022. THOMAS BARTON JONES, b. March 3, 1851, = February 14, 1882, MARIAN DUSHANE. He is a civil engineer in Baltimore. The Dushanes are a wealthy and influential family of Maryland. Issue: Marian E. Jones.

2024. ANNIE C. R. JONES, b. in Winchester, November 29, 1854, = June, 1880, J. T. ATTERBURY, b. October 17, 1847. They live in Patterson, New Jersey, and are wealthy. Issue: 1, Josephine Atterbury; 2, Mary B. Atterbury; 3, Ellen M. Atterbury, b. January 3, 1885.

(2038) SALLIE J. FOREE.

2026 FRANK H. JONES, b. September 1, 1856.

2028 WILLIAM STROTHER JONES, b. November 7, 1857, = September 25, 1884, MARY GRACE RUSSELL, b. July 25, 1858. She is a daughter of Charles H. Russell and Caroline Howland. He is a banker in New York City. His address is 13, S. William Street.

2030 FREDERICK B. JONES, b. January 3, 1859. He is a cotton merchant in New Orleans. I met him in Warren Co., Va., in 1884, and found him a "merry and wise" young gentleman.

2032 SUSAN C. JONES, b. March 23, 1861. Lives in Baltimore.

2034 CHARLES MARSHALL JONES, b. September 11, 1863. A civil engineer; his home was in Warren Co., Va., but visiting California, he died on ship, July, 1884, and was buried at sea. His sad and early death, and his tearless burial, by strangers, beneath the great waters, have moistened the eyes and mellowed the heart of a fondly affectionate father.

2036 SUSAN B. FOREE, b. October 18, 1851, = October 11, 1879, D. S. CROCKETT, b. March 26, 1853. Mr. Crockett is a farmer, and lives in Shelby Co., Ky. I met Mrs. Crockett at her father's, in Shelbyville, Ky., in 1884, and she has frequently written to me. Like all the rest of the Foree family, her heart overflows with kindness. Issue: 1, Willie V. Crockett, b. September 12, 1880; 2, Prior F. Crockett, b. August 5, 1882.

2038 SALLIE J. FOREE, b. May 30, 1855. She is an agreeable and intelligent young lady. She lives with her father in Shelbyville, Ky.

(2040) PRIOR J. FOREE.

2040 PRIOR J. FOREE, b. November 6, 1857. He and his younger brother are practicing law in partnership in Shelbyville, Ky. They are well educated, and my short intercourse with them convinced me that they possessed all the qualifications necessary to success.

2042 CHARLES MARSHALL FOREE, b. July 26, 1859. See No. 2040.

2044 MARY FOREE BETTS, b. April 23, 1851, = January 19, 1871, ASA L. CROW. He is a merchant in Charleston, Miss. I have had some pleasant correspondence with Mrs. Crow, which assures me of her goodness of heart, as well as her brightness of intellect. Issue: 1, Abel B. Crow, b. March 1, 1872; 2, D. R. Crow, b. February 15, 1874; 3, Mary F. Crow, b. August 10, 1876; 4, Lucy A. Crow, b. May 29, 1880; 5, Asa L. Crow, b. October 6, 1882.

2048 LUCY S. BETTS, b. March 1, 1858, = February 24, 1878, O. D. ANDREWS. He is a merchant of Memphis, Tenn. Issue: Lucy B. Andrews, b. 1882.

2050 KATIE MAJORS BETTS, b. January 1, 1871. She lives with her father in Charleston, Miss.

2052 LAURA W. WATKINS, b. April 29, 1851, = November 13, 1868, JAMES A. ADREWS, son of her step-father by his first wife, (814). Mr. Andrew's is a farmer, residing near Florence, Ala. Issue: 1, Robert L. Andrews, b. September, 1869; 2, Charles E. Andrews; 3, Laura H. Andrews; 4, James Andrews.

2054 CHARLES MARSHALL ANDREWS, b. July 8, 1854, = 1st, LAURA THOMPSON, who d. June 1877, leaving one child, Marshall L. Andrews. = 2d, April 16, 1879, MARY T. PHILIPS, who died August 17, 1883. Issue: 1, Mattie P. Andrews, b. April 25, 1880; 2, Daisy F. Andrews, b. May 16, 1881. See 814. I presume Florence, Ala., is their home.

(2084) MARGARET MARSHALL.

2056 MARY DRUSILLA ANDREWS, b. July 8, 1855, = October 14, 1875, CHARLES T. PHILIPS, d. October 1883. No issue. She left her husband before his death, and now lives at Jackson, Tenn.

2058 FANNIE E. ANDREWS, b. September 25, 1857, = December 23, 1882, M. F. SLOAN. He is a lawyer by profession, but is now a merchant in Imboden, Ark. Issue: William T. Sloan.

2060 LUCIEN TAYLOR ANDREWS, b. April 29, 1860. He is a farmer near Imboden, Tenn.

2062 GEORGE YOUNG ANDREWS, b. July 8, 1862. He is a clerk at Memphis, Tenn., earning a good salary in the cotton business.

2064 MATTIE J. ANDREWS, b. October 26, 1864. I presume she lives at Florence, Ala.

2076 JUDITH M. HARVEY, b. January 18, 1854, = February 4, 1875, EUGENE E. EVANS. They reside at Crystal Springs, Copiah Co., Miss. He is a traveling dry goods Salesman. Issue: Maggie E. Evans, b. May 8, 1879; 2, Cecilie Evans, b. July 26, 1884.

2078 CHARLES COATSWORTH MARSHALL, b. May 26, 1868. He is now living with Judge Foree, (808) in Shelbyville, Tenn.

2080 WILLIAM THEO. MARSHALL, b. March 23, 1873.

2082 CHARLES M. MARSHALL, b. November 26, 1875.

2084 MARGARET MARSHALL, b. August 14, 1881.

(2086) MARY R. MARSHALL.

2086 MARY R. MARSHALL, b. August 20, 1884.

2088 JENNIE S. STEWART, b. January 1, 1871.

2090 ABEL B. YOUNG, b. September 24, 1884.

2094 HUDSON S. MARSHALL, b. July 15, 1870.

2096 JAMES M. MARSHALL, b. August 1, 1871.

2098 ROBERT L. MARSHALL, b. August 11, 1873.

2100 HARRY T. MARSHALL, b. May 19, 1875.

2102 CHARLES A. MARSHALL, b. February 14, 1883.

2104 WILLIAM L. MARBURY, a lawyer of Baltimore, Md., b. at "Wyoming," Prince George Co., Md., December 26, 1858; graduated at John Hopkins University; studied law with his uncle, Col. Charles Marshall; graduated at the Baltimore Law School, and is practicing law in that city, where his talents and ambition assure him success.

2106 FENDALL MARBURY, a law student, Baltimore, Md.; b. at "Wyoming," Prince George Co., Md., October 27, 1860, = September 12, 1883, LUCY BERRY, of Prince George Co., Md.; was educated at St. John's College, and in 1858, was attending law-lectures at Baltimore, where he expected to open a law office. He is starting life with cheering hopes.

2108 ALEX. MARSHALL MARBURY, b. at "Wyoming," Prince George Co., Md., May 24, 1863; educated at the Maryland Agricultural College, and is now engaged in farming.

THE MARSHALL FAMILY. 361

2110 MARTIN P. BROOKE GREEN, b. at Warrenton, Va., October 6, 1880. A fond mother's romping pet.

2112 LUCY AMBLER, b. May 17, 1848, = 1875, REV. LANDON MASON, b. 1844, near Alexander, Va.; was educated at the University of Virginia; took his theological course at the Episcopal Seminary, near Alexandria, and is now rector of the Parish at Shepherdstown, W. Va. Issue: 1, Randolph Mason, b. 1877; 2, John Mason, b. 1879; 3, Lucy Mason, b. 1881; 4, Landon R. Mason, b. 1884 See 842 and 1448.

2114 BENJAMIN MASON AMBLER, a lawyer of Parkersburg, W. Va., b. January 14, 1850, = November, 1875, NANNIE BAKER. Issue: 1, Mason Ambler; 2. Nannie Ambler; 3, James Ambler; 4, Eliza Ambler: 5, John Cary Ambler.

2116 JAMES M. AMBLER, a lawyer of Baltimore, Md., b. August 21, 1854. I met Mr. Ambler in Baltimore, in 1884, and found him a courteous and promising young attorney.

2118 ELIZA C. AMBLER, b. December 7, 1856, = August 5, 1884, L. M. BLACKFORD, a Professor in the Episcopal High School, near Alexander, Va.

2120 JOHN C. AMBLER, a student at the Episcopal Theological Seminary, near Alexandria, Va.; b. June 25, 1859.

2122 JENNIE K. AMBLER, b. February 8, 1862.

2124 HUMPHREY AMBLER, b. April 11, 1866.

2126 LETTIE C. AMBLER, b. January 21, 1870.

2128 EDWARD CHARLES AMBLER, b. May 9, 1872.

(2130) MARY CARY AMBLER.

2130 MARY CARY AMBLER, b. September 22, 1861. I met my sweet cousin at Markham, in 1884, and found her as merry as her name is euphonious. But from indications I saw, I supposed she was about to change it.

2134 THOMAS MARSHALL AMBLER, a coal merchant of Chicago, Ill.; b. at "Clifton," Fauquier Co., Va., June 25, 1858, = May 21, 1884, CARRIE HAWTHORNE, the lovely daughter of Willis H. Hawthorne, of Chicago.

2136 RICHARD GAGE AMBLER, a teacher and civil engineer of Oregon; b. at "Clifton," Fauquier Co., Va., October 7, 1861.

2138 CATHERINE P. AMBLER, b. at "Clifton," Fauquier Co., Va., March 25, 1864; lives there with her widowed mother.

2140 ARTHUR L. AMBLER, b. March 13, 1866.

2142 FRANK W. AMBLER, b. October 13, 1867.

2144 ANNIE J. AMBLER, b. June 6, 1870.

2146 ROBERT R. AMBLER, b. July 4, 1872.

2148 EMMA E. AMBLER, b. at "Clifton," Fauquier Co., Va., June 10, 1874, is her mother's pet. She is a child of nature, and delights in flowers and in the woods and meadows. She gathers the lambs to her bosom, and feeds the birds and squirrels.

2150 CAROLINE M. STRIBLING, b. June 17, 1863; lives with her father at "Mountain View," Markham, Va. God bless her for her sweet letter to me.

2152 ROBERT C. STRIBLING, b. October 5, 1867; lives with his father at "Mountain View," Markham, Va.

(2158) JUDGE JAMES PAXTON HARBESON.

2156 JOHN MARSHALL HARBESON, a banker at Augusta, Ky.; b. in Mason Co., Ky., February 11, 1834, = August 28, 1856, in Fleming Co., Ky., FANNIE METCALFE, b. January 25, 1836. John removed in 1844, with his parents, to Flemingsburg, Ky.; after receiving an English education, he wrote in the clerk's office; was elected Circuit Clerk in 1850, re-elected 1856, and again in 1862; was licensed as an attorney at law, January 23, 1864; after practicing for a time at the Flemingsburg bar, removed to Augusta, Ky., and engaged in banking. His house possesses unbounded credit, and, in the business world, no man possesses a better name, nor more of public confidence. His wife is the daughter of Hiram Metcalfe, of Fleming Co., Ky., and Ann, daughter of Thomas Summers. She is a pure, sweet and affectionate woman, a member of the Christian Church, and beloved by all who know her. Issue: 1, Mary Lawler Harbeson, b. September 8, 1860; 2, Benjamin Harbeson, b. August 6, 1863; 3, Anna B. Harbeson, b. August 28, 1866; 4, Mathew Lawler Harbeson, b. February 9, 1869; 5, George B. Harbeson, b. April 4, 1874. See the Pickett Chart, No. 64.

2158 JUDGE JAMES PAXTON HARBESON, attorney-at-law, Flemingsburg, Ky., b. in Mason Co., Ky., January 4, 1838, = 1st, in Louisville, Ky., June 31, 1866, MARY E. SHREVE, (nee SHEPARD), b. December 7, 1828; d. December 27, 1870, leaving an only child, James P. Harbeson, b. in Louisville, December 17, 1870; after his first wife's death, Mr. Harbeson married 2d, December 12, 1876, ALICE ANDREWS, b. in Flemingsburg, Ky., October 10, 1855. James removed, in 1844, with his parents, to Flemingsburg; came in 1855, to Platte City, Mo., and pretended to read law with me; took part in the Kansas imbroglio in 1856; graduated at the Louisville, Ky., law school; returned to Flemingsburg, and commenced the practice of law; in 1861, as Captain of the Fleming County Company, he entered the regiment of United States Volunteers recruited by his uncle, Col. C. A. Marshall (188): served in the expedition of Gen. Nelson through Eastern Kentucky; was promoted to the rank of Major of the Sixteenth Kentucky Infantry; resigned and entered into the practice of law with his relative, Judge Thos. A. Marshall (298) in Louisville, Ky.; was appointed by Governor Bramlette, Judge of the Louisville Police Court, and gained great

(2160) MARY HARBESON — (Wilson).

reputation by the able and impartial manner in which he discharged the duties of his office; in 1874, he returned to Flemingsburg, and resumed the practice of law; here he still lives, and his Democratic friends are pressing his name for Congress. He is frank, bold, hospitable and liberal. His generous and unselfish life has surrounded him with friends, who are anxious to do him honor. His liberal habits have cost him two fortúnes, and yet he has led a sober and abstemious life. He never fails to respond to the calls of charity, religion and public enterprise. I am proud of my nephew, and rejoice in his honors. Issue of 2d marriage: 1, Amy Andrews Harbeson, b. November 16, 1877; 2, Mary Harbeson, b. March 30, 1879. Mrs. Alice Harbeson is a daughter of Robert Andrews and Amy Thompson.

2160   MARY HARBESON, b. in Fleming Co., Ky., October 28, 1848, = September 27, 1865, DANIEL M. WILSON, b. March 27, 1844. Mary was reared in Flemingsburg. Here she was married. Mr. Wilson first engaged in the banking business with bad success. They afterwards removed to Goliad Co., Texas, and on an immense ranche are rearing horses and cattle. Mr. Wilson sometimes brings his stock to market in Kentucky. Mary is in person tall, handsome, noble and commanding, and in spirit is as free, joyous and independent as the wild winds of Texas. She mounts her mustang and rides where she listeth. She is as fearless and active as the tiger. And yet she is conscientious, even to piety, fascinating in conversation, diligent in domestic duties, and agreeable in society. Mr. Wilson is a son of John C. Wilson and Elizabeth Morgan. Issue: 1, Mamie Wilson, b. July 14, 1866; 2, Benjamin Harbeson Wilson, b. April 22, 1872.

2162   WILLIAM PAXTON HARBESON, b. in Fleming Co., Ky., May 31, 1854, = 1873, FREDERIKA B. HARRIS, of Bracken Co., Ky. William spent some years in mercantile pursuits, in Augusta, and in Flemingsburg, Ky.; went to Goliad Co., Texas, and has lately returned to Augusta. His wife is an exceedingly sweet and captivating lady. Issue: 1, Mary P. Harbeson; 2, John M. Harbeson; 3, Rosanna Harbeson; 4, Joseph H. Harbeson; 5, Lida Gertrude Harbeson.

2164 Lydia Paxton, b. in Covington, Ky., July 23, 1841, = August 10, 1859, Frank A. Blackburn, b. in Woodford Co., Ky., December 26, 1836; d. in Saline Co., Mo., November 11, 1879. At the age of ten, Lydia had lost her parents, and she was reared in the happy family of her grandfather, Philip Bush (858). At the age of thirteen, Mr. Blackburn removed with his parents to Covington. On attaining his majority, he engaged in the business of a wholesale grocer in Cincinnati, until the war. He then purchased a mill in Covington; in 1863, he purchased a farm in Woodford Co., Ky., and engaged in stock raising; in 1868, he sold out and removed west, settling in the western part of Saline Co., Mo. He was the first Master of the Saline County Grange; through his instrumentality the Chicago & Alton railroad was run through his farm, and a depot established to suit him; he laid off a small town, which was called for him, Blackburn ; while preparing for a hunting expedition, and while exhibiting a new pistol to a friend, it was accidentally discharged, and the ball entering his left side, killed him instantly.' He was a social, refined and agreeable gentleman, but in business he was too generous and lenient to be successful. Lydia possesses remarkable executive abilities, and is a prosperous farmer, a discreet manager, an admirable gardener, and a votary to flowers. I visited her July 4, 1884, and found her crops more promising than I had elsewhere seen. Her table was supplied with nine kinds of vegetables, and among them were cucumbers two inches in diameter, and large, full grown roasting ears. She has three grown sons: 1, Marshall Paxton Blackburn, L. L. B., b. June 9, 1860. He was married August 12, 1884, to Mary E. Logsdon, b. January 19, 1870, and only fourteen and a half years of age. He is a graduate of the law department of the University of Missouri; 2, Churchill J. Blackburn, M. D., b. July 10, 1862. He has also the diploma of the Hospital College, of New York City. He is now practicing medicine in Springfield, Mo.; 3, John Daubrey Blackburn, b. July 1, 1866.

THE BLACKBURN FAMILY.

George Blackburn, of Virginia, = October 12, 1771, Prudence Berry, b. November 5, 1754. They removed to Woodford Co., Ky. Issue:
1. George Blackburn.
2. Luke Blackburn.

(2166) ANNA MARIA PAXTON.

3. Jonathan Blackburn, father of Captain William Blackburn, and progenitor of the St. Louis Blackburns.
4. William Blackburn, father of Henry Churchill Blackburn, who was a candidate for Governor of Illinois.
5. Edward Blackburn (known as Uncle Ned), father of Dr. Luke P. Blackburn, late Governor of Kentucky; of Joe C. Blackburn, present Senator from Kentucky, and of James Blackburn, late Secretary of State of Kentucky.
6. Mrs. White.
7. Mrs. Holloway.
8. Dr. Churchill J. Blackburn, father of Frank A. Blackburn, who married LYDIA PAXTON.

2166 ANNA MARIA PAXTON, b. in Platte Co., Mo., February 12, 1847; named after my mother. They tell me that she is like me in disposition, and that I am partial to her. Well, I shall not deny the charge. Justice as well as natural affection, demands of me some return for her obedience, attention and veneration. She knows instinctively, my tastes, supplies my wants, and suits herself to my whims and caprices. In sickness or affliction, no other nurse could be so faithful, and no other friend so sympathetic. Anna has cultivated her heart as well as her mind. She neither knows nor cares for the ordinary gossip and frivolity of the town. She engages in none of the wordly schemes for mirth or pass-time. The affairs of the church, the labors of the Sunday School, and the works of charity and benevolence call forth her energies. She visits the scholars at their homes, and her zeal, her prayers and her faith are daily at work for the spiritual good of her charges. She seeks out the destitute and afflicted, and carries joy to many hearts by her sympathy and alms. She is a splendid scribe, and the recorder so values her services, that he pays her liberal wages, and will permit no one else to touch his records. Her earnings are all bestowed in charity. She reads much, but is interested only in moral and religious topics. The bible is her daily delight. She is well grounded in theology, and is a thorough Presbyterian.

(2168) TILLIE F. PAXTON — (*Tebbs*).

2168 TILLIE F. PAXTON, named after her mother's lovely sister, b. in Platte Co., Mo., June 11, 1849, = May 7, 1868, DR. ALGERNON SIDNEY TEBBS. Tillie is the fairest of my daughters, and one of the most lovely of women. Cheerful and happy by nature, the troubles of life fall gently upon her. Her amiable disposition and agreeable manners with gentleness, intelligence and truth, make her a general favorite. Her reading is more discursive than Anna's, yet the bible, religious books and papers occupy chief places in her studies. She is admired and beloved for the virtues of her heart, as well as for the excellencies of her person. For years she has had the infant class in her Sunday school. Like her sister she is a solid Presbyterian. She is enthusiastically fond of shrubs and flowers, and claims the yard and garden as her own. Her marriage was not fortunate, and she returned to the parental roof, with two daughters: 1, Laura G. Tebbs, b. in Platte Co., Mo., May 20, 1870. She is now attending Daughters College, Platte City, Mo.; 2, Mamie Paxton Tebbs, b. August 23, 1872, the merry and golden haired pet of the family.

THE TEBBS FAMILY.

(*b*) Daniel Tebbs, (*Gent*) came from England in 1740, and settled in Westmoreland Co., Va. He married a Miss Foushe, from France, of the family of Marshal Foushe. Their son Foushe Tebbs, married a Miss Bowers, of Innisfall, Scotland, and had two sons:

A 1. FOUSHE TEBBS, = Mary Baxter, sister of the wife of Hugh Brent, Sr. No. 2424, b. Issue:

B   1. *Col. Willoughby Tebbs*, = Elizabeth Carr, of Virginia.

     2. *Judge Samuel Tebbs*, of Mason Co., Ky., = a Miss Tebbs and was father of three daughters, who married Formans. No. 660 *k l*.

A 2. WILLIAM TEBBS, = 1st, Mrs. Pope, *nee* Conway, and had two sons: 1, Daniel, and 2, George; both of whom died unmarried. William's second wife was a Mrs. Johnsson, of Maryland, by whom he had two children.

B   1. *Victoria Tebbs*, b. 1782, = Charles Meng.

C'   1. Sarah B. Meng, = Joseph Kennedy, nephew of Lydia Kennedy (below).

(2170) PHŒBE MARSHALL PAXTON.

B

C   2, *William H. Tebbs*, = Lydia Kennedy. Issue:

  (c) 1. Adelaide Tebbs, = W. S. Parker.
    2. Catherine M. Tebbs, = Dr. J. M. Davis.
    3. Algernon S. Tebbs, = Julia Coleman.
      1. Dr. Algernon S. Tebbs, = TILLIE PAXTON, No. 2168.
    4. Elizabeth Tebbs, = Col. John H. Winston.
    5. Dr. William H. Tebbs, = Martha E. Anderson.
    6. O. B. Tebbs, = Susan Anderson.
    7. Daniel Tebbs, = Sue E. Burnes.

2170   PHŒBE MARSHALL PAXTON, named for my sister, (188) b. in Platte City, Mo., January 16, 1853. She is more a woman of fashion and society than my other daughters. She has traveled extensively, and has seen much of the world. Her reading is more in the walks of belleletters and poetry, and her associations more with the gay and wordly. She finds pleasure in reading, contemplation and correspondence. She has strong good common sense, self-reliance, practical judgment and decision. Her literary taste and general information make her a spirited writer. Her letters sparkle with wit, and her conversation ripples with humor. She keeps the house in order, and in matters of taste is supreme.

A FATHER'S DYING BLESSING ON HIS DAUGHTERS.

My daughters, draw near and receive my last blessing;
 For soon shall my spirit be free.
This parting to you will be sad and distressing:
 But death has no terrors for me.

My daughters, I leave you in charge of your mother;
 Be dutiful, loving and true.
In trouble and sorrow you'll comfort each other,
 And life will have pleasures for you.

Dear Anna, this cross I commit to your keeping —
 A type of the faith you've possessed;
From childhood you've borne it, mid gladness and weeping,
 And still on thy heart let it rest.

(2184) GEORGE W. ANDERSON.

  Receive my child my dying blessing,
   I give it from a tender heart,
  You'll need no longer my carressing,
   Since you have chosen Mary's part.

Dear Tillie I give thee this glittering anchor—
The symbol of hope that is thine;
Thy soul is like gold that for ages won't canker;
And pure as the gem from the mine.

Thy children surpass, in their sweetness and beauty,
The roses with which they are decked.
To rear them for God, is a mother's first duty,
And one that she dare not neglect.

  Thy children, Tillie, yet shall bless thee—
   Those idols of thy loving heart—
  Their waywardness shall not distress thee;
   From wisdom's ways they'll not depart.

Dear Phœbe, receive this white mantle my daughter;
'Tis charity's veil that I give;
The faults of thy neighbor, like writing on water,
Should never in memory live.

Dear Phœbe, my darling, I tenderly love thee
With yearnings that death can't destroy;
My spirit, believe me, shall hover above thee,
That nothing thy path may annoy.

  I give thee, Phœbe, my last blessing,
   And may thy heart be filled with love,—
  Good-will to all mankind expressing,
   And fellowship with God above.

2174 CHARLES T. MARSHALL, b. October 2, 1863.

2176 MAE MARSHALL, b. January 20, 1872.

2178 EDWARD ANDERSON, b. in Louisiana, Mo., March 17, 1862, = in Covington, Ky., November 8, 1883, Lulie M. Reynolds.

2180 ANNA M. ANDERSON, b. January 24, 1865.

2182 LIZZIE L. ANDERSON, b. July 10, 1869.

2184 GEORGE W. ANDERSON, b. May 19, 1872.

(2186) CHARLES A. ANDERSON.

2186 CHARLES A. ANDERSON, b. November 26, 1874.

2202 HARRY M. BUFORD, b. November 20, 1845, he is entering on the practice of law at Lexington, Ky., with flattering prospects of success.

2204 JOHN LEWIS MARSHALL, b. at Madison, Ind., September 18, 1853. He is a man of general business qualificatious, and is now running a flouring mill in Henderson, Ky.

2206 IDA MARSHALL, b. at Milwaukee, Wis., December 15, 1854, and is living with her sister (2008), at Mansfield, Illinois.

2208 MINNIE MARSHALL, b. February 8, 1855, = December 16, 1880, in Louisville, Ky., EUGENE ALEXANDER, b. in Hardy Co., W. Va., March 18, 1843. He joined the Rockbridge Artillery, and was assigned to Stonewall Jackson's command. At the second battle of Manassas, he was severely wounded. In 1868, he came to Illinois, and engaged in the grain business in Mansfield, where he is doing well. Issue: 1, Samuel Hamilton Alexander, b. March 1, 1882; 2, Eugene Marshall Alexander, b. April 9, 1883; 3, Paul Alexander, b. February 10, 1885.

THE ALEXANDERS.

1. The grandfather of Eugene Alexander was William Alexander, a native of Belfast, and a descendant of one of that noble band of heroes who barred the gates of Derry against the encroachments of a tyrant. Of course he was a Presbyterian. He settled in Berkeley Co., W. Va., and there married Jane Sherrard, also a native of Ireland. His son:

2. Samuel Hamilton Alexander, was b. in Berkeley Co., W. Va., September 4, 1798; d. in Moorefield, W. Va., April 13, 1882. At the age of sixteen, Samuel left his parents in Berkeley County, and settled in Moorefield, W. Va., and entered the mercantile business. In 1832, he joined the Presbyterian Church, and in 1846,

(2238) AGATHA MARSHALL BULLITT.

was ordained an elder. For forty years he was superintendent of the Moorefield Sabbath School, and endeared himself to old and young by his affectionate disposition, his social virtues, and his business integrity. This family is of the same origin as another branch of the Alexanders, noticed No. 72.

2210   Eugene Marshall, b. March 8, 1858.

2222   Jane Marshall Neil, b. at Columbus, O., March 3, 1844, d. at Cambridge, Mass., May 24, 1881, = December 19, 1865, Col. Theo. A. Dodge, U. S. A., b. May 22, 1842, in Massachusetts. As a young lady, she is remembered as a belle in Washington society, and was even more beautiful in her maturity of womanhood. Her husband was a man of culture and attainments, having spent five years in France, Germany and England, pursuing his studies, and at last graduated at the University of London. When the war at home broke out, he returned, entered the army, and rose by his merits to the rank of Colonel. He was twice wounded, and lost a limb at Gettysburg. Issue: 1, Robert Elkin Dodge, b. January 24, 1867; 2, Theodora Dodge, b. September 14, 1871; 3, Jane Marshall Dodge, b. April 27, 1873.

2224   Lucy Neil, b. in Columbus, O., August 21, 1846, = December 20, 1871, Col. William Wilberforce Williams, U. S. Navy, b. October 9, 1842. Mrs. Williams is in delicate health, and remains in Massachusetts, while her husband is with his squadron on the California Coast. I met Col. Williams at Washington, D. C., in 1876, and he has my lasting gratitude for the polite and continued attention he bestowed on me and my daughter. His education and his experience during the late civil war, make him one of the finest naval officers in the service. Issue; 1, Robert E. N. Williams, b. February 9, 1873.

2234   William Marshall Bullitt, b. March 4, 1873.

2238   Agatha Marshall Bullitt, b. November 24, 1875.

(2250) JULIA WOOLFOLK—(*Larabie*).

2250   JULIA WOOLFOLK, b. January, 1856, = February, 1875, S. A. LARABIE. They reside at Deer Lodge, Mont. Issue: 1, Donnell Larabie; 2, Mary Larabie; 3, Elizabeth Larabie.

2252   ALEXANDER McCLUNG WOOLFOLK, b. October 26, 1858.

2254   HORACE WOOLFOLK, b. June 5, 1860.

2256   LUCIEN B. WOOLFOLK, b. June 7, 1862.

2258   LIZZIE WOOLFOLK, b. September 18, 1866.

2260   EVA WOOLFOLK, b. August 1, 1868.

2262   MAY WOOLFOLK, b. May 19, 1873.

2264   LUCIEN M. WOOLFOLK, b. January 24, 1859; educated at the Louisville Male High School, and in 1881 graduated in law. He is now a traveling salesman for a Louisville house. He has written to me several times and his letters indicate a gentleman of culture.

2266   ADA S. WOOLFOLK, b. December 17, 1869.

2268   CLINTON S. WOOLFOLK, b. May 16, 1874.

2270   SUSAN M. WOOLFOLK, b. July 3, 1876.

2272   ANNA S. WOOLFOLK, b. January 22, 1878.

2274   ALEX. M. WOOLFOLK, b. February 3, 1881.

2276   CARRIE M. WOOLFOLK, b. February 14, 1884.

THE MARSHALL FAMILY. 373

(2296) JAMES K. DUKE.

2278 JULIET WOOLFOLK, d. 1883, = 1883, —— ROBERTS. No issue:

2280 MARY ELIZA McCLUNG, b. May 3, 1852, = December 24, 1873, CHARLES A. BIEGLER, b. 1850. They live in St. Paul, Minn. Issue: 1, Cameron A. Biegler, b. November, 1874; 2, Susan M. Biegler, b. April 1876; 3, John W. Biegler; 4, Philip Biegler; 5, Martin Biegler. Mr. Biegler was b. in Rochester, N. Y.; was for years an insurance agent in Chicago and St. Paul. He is now in the Commissary Department at St. Paul.

2282 HARRISON T. McCLUNG, b. October 29, 1864.

2284 NELLIE M. McCLUNG, b. May 25, 1867.

2286 JULIA L. McCLUNG, b. November 23, 1872.

2288 ELIZA M. BROWNING, b. at Indianapolis, Ind., June 9, 1854, = at St. Paul, Minn., October 6, 1875, NICHOLAS D. COLEMAN, b. August 10, 1851, in New Orleans, La. They live in New Orleans. Issue: 1, Lloyd R. Coleman, b. November 26, 1876; 2, Browning Coleman, b. October 3, 1883.

2290 GRANVILLE W. BROWNING, a lawyer of Chicago, b. in Indianapolis, Ind., March 14, 1856; reared in St. Paul, Minn.; of fine literary and professional acquirements; was a partner of Judge Samuel M. Moore, formerly of the Circuit Court of the Covington District, and afterwards of the Cook County Illinois Superior Court. His spirited and well written letters announce his honor, as well as his talents.

2296 JAMES K. DUKE, = MRS. MARY FERNANDES, a widow. They live at Orlando, Fla., and are highly delighted with their tropical life.

THE MARSHALL FAMILY.

(2298) KATE DUKE — (*Chenoweth*).

2298 KATE DUKE, = HENRY P. CHENOWETH. They live in Mason Co., Ky. Issue: Buford D. Chenoweth, b. March 29, 1884.

2300 HENRY B. DUKE, b. in St. Louis, December 5, 1854, = November 9, 1881, SUSIE WADDELL, dr. of John W. Waddell, banker of Lexington, Mo. She died July 23, 1884. He is in the Agricultural Implement business, at Kansas City. Issue: William W. Duke, b. October 18, 1882.

2302 JAMES CLAY DUKE, b. in St. Louis, Mo., April 26, 1857, = October 26, 1881, MILLIE MORGAN FARRAR, dr. of Dr. John O'Fallen Farrar, and grand daughter of Dr. Barnard Farrar. They are in the Agricultural Implement business in St. Louis. Issue: Sallie F. Duke, b. at St. Louis, August 18, 1882.

2304 1. MARY DUKE, b. July 5, 1850, living with her father at Danville, Ky.

2306 2. CHARLOTTE (LOTTIE) S. DUKE, b. January 23, 1854, = November 26, 1872, G. L. Chrisman, a farmer living near Independence, Mo. No issue.

2308 CARRIE DUKE, b. October 17, 1855, = June 12, 1879, WILLIAM M. KENNY, a farmer, educated at Center College, Kentucky.

2310 JAMES K. DUKE, b. in Boyle Co., Ky., August 4, 1857.

2312 MARGARET (MADGE) DUKE, b. September 27, 1859, = May 19, 1880, EDWIN C. ROBERTS, a grocer, living in El Paso, Texas.

2314 WILLIAM DUKE, b. September 15, 1861.

2316 MATTIE DUKE, b. September 11, 1864.

(2346) JAMES D. SMITH.

2318 LUCY S. DUKE, b. August 27, 1866.

2322 MARY STRAHAN, = SAMUEL WARREN, of Danville, Ky. No issue.

2324 DAVID STRAHAN, lives in Texas.

2326 CAROLINE (LENA) STRAHAN, = ISAAC S. WARREN. Live in Summerset, Ky.

2330 MARY DUKE KEENON, b. in Covington, Ky., July 30, 1857, = March 25, 1880, ROBT. A. SHOEMAKER, b. in Covington, K., March 27, 1854; was educated in Ohio and Michigan; a Democrat; an Episcopalian. They live in Atlanta, Ga. Issue: 1, Sarah A. Shoemaker, b. February 11, 1885.

2332 JAMES D. KEENON, b. January 22, 1859.

2334 JENNIE KEENON, b. in Covington, Ky., April 13, 1861, = January 1, 1884, JOHN W. PENN, b. April 17, 1839, in Scott Co., Ky.; was educated at Georgetown College. He is a farmer of Scott Co., Ky.; a Democrat and a Methodist. Issue: John B. Penn, b. February 1, 1885.

2336 ADAM C. KEENON, b. in Covington, Ky., July 19, 1862.

2338 EDGAR KEENON, b. in Covington, Ky., June 24, 1864.

2340 BESSIE C. KEENON, b. in Covington, Ky., June 2, 1871.

2342 ELIZA C. SMITH, = June, 1881, JAMES HAWKINS, of Frankfort, Ky. At the age of sixteen, Mr. Hawkins left school to join the Southern army; was taken prisoner and spent two years in confinement at Camp Chase. He is now the assistant of James B. Tate, Treasurer of Kentucky.

2346 JAMES D. SMITH, is in the Marine service at Washington City.

(2362) BASIL DUKE.

2362 BASIL DUKE, b. March 30, 1862.

2364 THOMAS MORGAN DUKE, b. August 18, 1863.

2366 MARY CURRIE DUKE, b. July 29, 1866.

2368 CALVIN MORGAN DUKE, b. January 22, 1869.

2370 HENRY HUNT DUKE, b. January 16, 1871.

2372 JULIA BLACKBURN DUKE, b. July 23, 1875.

2374 FRANCES KEY DUKE, b. October 9, 1881.

2380 HATTIE BUFORD, b. October, 1867.

2382 CHARLES BUFORD, b. August, 1869.

2384 ANNIE BUFORD, b. November 27, 1873.

2386 CHARLES BUFORD, b. September 30, 1876.

2388 LOUIS BUFORD, b. May 20, 1878.

2390 BASIL D. BUFORD, b. May 6, 1881.

2392 JOHN S. BUFORD, b. March 27, 1883.

2394 AGATHA B. EDSON, b. June 4, 1870.

2400 JOHN R. MCMURRAN, b. May 26, 1860. He now lives in St. Paul, Minn., one of the real estate firm of McClung, McMurran & Curry. He is said to be a very promising young man.

2402 SAMUEL MCMURRAN, b. May 26, 1860.

(2424) JOHN B. MARSHALL.

2404 ROBERT McMURRAN, b. May 29, 1866.

2406 GEORGE K. McMURRAN, b. January 16, 1871.

2407 MARY A. McMURRAN, b. July 25, 1875.

2408 GERTRUDE V. McMURRAN, b. November 22, 1878.

2410 WILLIAM R. McMURRAN, b. January 7, 1883.

2412 THOS. T. COOKE, b. December 15, 1866.

2414 ANNA K. COOKE, b. December 9, 1867. She is in school in Nelson Co., Va.

2416 JOHN R. COOKE, b. January 14, 1870.

2418 MARY H. COOKE, b. January 1, 1873.

2420 WILLIAM L. COOKE, b. October 20, 1879.

2422 GEORGE K. COOKE, b. February 26, 1883.

2424 (a) JOHN B. MARSHALL, b. March 29, 1831; d. April 10, 1875, = December 10, 1862, LIZZIE BRENT, b. December 14, 1837. Mr. Marshall was a man of fine business qualifications. He lived in Covington, Ky., and there, in 1884, I met his widow, a lovely woman, rearing her children for usefulness, and proud of their proficiency. Issue: 1, Brent Marshall, b. November 27, 1864; 2, Symmes Marshall, b. December 29, 1866; 3, Wallace, b. September 12, 1868; 4, Charleton, b. June 12, 1871; 5, Elizabeth, b. June 23, 1873.

(b) THE BRENT FAMILY.

Hugh Brent, sr., = Elizabeth Baxter, sister of Mary Baxter, mother of Judge Samuel Tebbs, and had issue:

1. Mary Brent, = Hugh McIlvane, of Virginia.

(2426) LOUIS J. MARSHALL.

2. Margaret Brent, = Capt. Thomas Young, a Revolutionary officer.
3. Innes Brent, = Miss Thomas, of Frankfort, Ky.
4. Hannah Brent, = Col. Duval Payne. See Langhorne Chart, No. 1012.
5. Hugh Brent, b. January 18, 1773, = Elizabeth Trotter Langhorne. See 1012.

B
   1. *Hugh J. Brent*, = 1st, Armstrong; 2d, Chambers.
   2. *Thomas J. Brent*.
   3. *Charles S. Brent*, = 1st, Sue Taylor. Issue:

C (c) 1. Hugh Brent, of Covington, Ky.

Charles = 2d Matilda Chambers, dr. of Gov. John Chambers. Issue:
   1. John Brent; 2, Sprigg C. Brent; 3, Lizzie Brent, = JOHN B. MARSHALL, No. 2424; 4, Bell Hart Brent, = Alexander; 5, James Brent; 6, Matilda Brent, = Goodale; 7, Henry; 8, Kelly; 9, Charles; 10, Thomas; 11, Hannah Brent.

B
   4. *Sarah Bell Brent*, = Isaac Lewis, No. 660 n.
   5. *Elizabeth Langhorne Brent*, = Henry C. Hart.

2426 LOUIS J. MARSHALL, b. in Covington, Ky., February 8, 1836. He is unmarried and is wandering in the Western Territories. The last letter I have from him is dated at Hachita, N. M. He writes well.

2428 KATE MARSHALL, b. in Covington, Ky., May 6, 1840, = April 2, 1872, JOHN SANFORD, of Covington, Ky. Issue: J. C. Marshall Sanford, b. August 4, 1875; 2, Julia Breckinridge Sanford, b. November 27, 1877.

2430 JULIA S. MARSHALL, b. October 20, 1843, = October 7, 1868 CABELL BRECKINRIDGE, son of Dr. Wm. L. Breckinridge, b. November 22, 1846. I met Mrs. Breckinridge, in Covington, in August, 1884. She is a handsome, intelligent and spir-

THE MARSHALL FAMILY. 379

(2438) NELLIE NICHOL MARSHALL—(McAfee).

ited lady, and quite an artist. Issue: 1, Mary S. Breckinridge, b. August 14, 1869; 2, Frank P. Breckinridge, b. December 3, 1874. See Breckinridge Chart, No. 70.

2432 CHARLES MCALISTER MARSHALL, b. January 1, 1838, = January 1, 1860, FANNIE PERRY. Issue: 1, Charles Marshall, b. September 18, 1861; 2, William H. Marshall, b. March 29, 1864; 3, Frances E. Marshall, b. September 12, 1867; 4, Nellie Marshall, b. February 1, 1869.

2434 COL. JOHN P. MARSHALL, b. January 7, 1840, d. February 5, 1865. He entered the Confederate service and was killed in battle.

2436 FANNIE E. MARSHALL, b. April 19, 1842, = 1st February, 1864, J. B. STRADER. He died with issue; 1, Humphrey Strader, b. December 1, 1864, = March 1884, Fanny English; 2, Jessie, b. August 7, 1867. Mrs. Strader, = 2d, November 14, 1877, PROF. HENRY A. CECIL, of Henry Co., Ky. He is now President of Cecillian College, Hardin Co., Ky.

2438 NELLIE NICHOL MARSHALL, b. May 8, 1844, = February, 1871, HON. JOHN J. MCAFEE, of Mercer Co., Ky. He represented his County in the State Legislature from 1871 to 1873. Cousin Nellie is one of the most gifted authors of the day, and before her marriage was the acknowledged belle of Louisville and Frankfort, and was the pet and pride of the State. Her beauty, intelligence, vivacity and spirit gave her the first place in Frankfort society. Mr. McAfee was serving his first term in the lower House of the Legislature, and was regarded as one of the most brilliant and promising young men of Kentucky. They were married and received the congratulations of the whole state. She attended her husband, when called to Frankfort for legislative duties; and on one occasion was occupying his seat in his absence, when a vote was taken. She voted in her husband's place, and amidst general hil-

(2440) HUMPHREY MARSHALL.

arity, her vote was, without objection, recorded. She claims that she is the only lady who has ever enjoyed this privilege. She commenced writing for the press at the age of eighteen, and still continues to add to the library she has already published. In Collin's History of Kentucky her name appears high in the list of native poets and novelists, and the periodical press pay liberally for her contributions. Among her published volumes the following are named: "A Bunch of violets," "Leaves from the Book of my Heart," "Eleanor Morton, or Life in Dixie, 1865; "Sodom Apples," 1866; "Dead Under the Roses," 1867; "Wearing the Cross," 1868; "As by Fire," 1869; "Passion, or Bartered and Sold." Her last novel is, "Criminal Through Love." As she is yet young, we may expect continued fruit from her fertile pen. Her style is the result of inspiration rather than study. She writes with great rapidity. It is her habit to rise several hours before day and write uninterruptedly until breakfast. There is neither plot or moral in her stories; but her fascinating style, her bold, lofty, thrilling and sublime flights through the realms of rhetoric, fill the reader with admiration; and the soft, sweet and plaintiff voice of pity and love, move and melt him to tears. In July, 1884 I enjoyed the hospitality of Cousin Nellie, and met for a few minutes her husband. Like her father she is fleshy, and she possesses all his spirit and brilliance. She lives in Louisville. Issue: 1, Julia S. McAfee, b. May 1, 1879. Since the above was writing I have read her "As by Fire," and was delighted with it. Her style is more ornate than any author of the present or past.

2440 HUMPHREY MARSHALL, b. April 10, 1848, = 1st, April 13, 1871, CLARA CRUTCHFIELD, b. in Louisville, Ky., May 16, 1852, d. December 16, 1876, leaving one child, Susie Marshall, b. April 14, 1872; = 2d, August 22, 1878, VIRGINIA CRUTCHFIELD, sister of his first wife, b. May 5, 1858. Mr. Marshall is large like his father and possesses his eminent talents. He is handsome with remarkably winning face. I saw him for a few minutes in 1884, and have been in correspondence with him, and pronounce him, though not in name, yet in mind and reality, one of the most talented men of the west. Issue by second marriage: 1, Clara Marshall, b. December 2, 1879; 2, Mary Marshall, b. February 19,

(2452) WILLIAM SMEDES MARSHALL.

1880; 3, Edith Marshall, b. July 29, 1882. Maj. Edward and Susan Crutchfield, of Louisville, Ky., are the parents of Clara and Virginia Marshall.

2442 ANNIE BIRNEY MARSHALL, b. January 10, 1851, = October 10, 1873, JACKSON TAYLOR BERRY. Issue: 1, William Berry, b. February 23, 1875; 2, Henry Cecil Berry, b. October 10, 1877; 3, Jessie Strader Berry, b. August 27, 1880.

2444 SARAH BELL MARSHALL, b. May 20, 1853, = February 24, 1881, ROBERT W. ROLOSON, merchant of Chicago.

2446 CHARLES EDWARD MARSHALL, b. June 10, 1859. Lives in Louisville, Ky.

2448 HENRY WALLER MARSHALL, b. January 29, 1862. Lives in Cincinnati, Ohio.

2450 ANNA MARIA MARSHALL, = GEO. P. WILSHIRE, an iron manufacturer of Newport, Ky. Issue: Lucy B. Wiltshire, b. October 18, 1882.

2452 WILLIAM SMEDES MARSHALL, b. June 29, 1839, = May 2, 1866, HELEN PARCELS. He graduated at Kenyon College, Ohio; read law with his grandfather, Judge Thos. A. Marshall, in Louisville, Ky., and practiced a short time in Charlestown, Ill. In the war, was a Captain in the First Regiment Illinois Cavalry. He was a member of the firm of Bain & Co., manufacturers of stoves, &c., in Charlestown, Ill. Removed in 1874 to Denver, Col., where, up to 1882, he was in the stove and tinware business. On account of ill-health, he accepted the less active position of Secretary of the Board of Health of Denver. His wife is a daughter of John F. Parcels and Harriet Miller. Issue: 1, Kate Marshall; 2, Edward; 3, Helen, b. September, 1881. Their address: 465 Welton Street, Denver, Col.

(2454) ELIZA MARSHALL — (*True*).

2454 ELIZA MARSHALL, b. in Charleston, Ill., December 2, 1841, = January 8, 1862, JOHN W. TRUE, then living in Charleston, son of Frederick True and Cynthia Wigington. He was a banker at Charleston until 1879, when he removed to Eureka Springs, Ark., and is now Postmaster there. During the war he served as Major of the Fifty-fourth Illinois Regiment, Infantry. Issue: 1, Ellen True, b. September 3, 1863; 2, Eliza N. True, b. August 6, 1865; 3, John William True, b. March, 1869; 4, John True, b. May, 1879; 5, Marshall True, b. February 2, 1883.

2456 CAPTAIN JAMES MILLER MARSHALL, b. in Charleston, Ill., May 31, 1844, = July 2, 1867, KITTY FISHER, dr. of Judge Robert Fisher, of York, Pa. He was educated at West Point; Second Lieutenant Thirteenth Infantry, June 23, 1865; First Lieutenant, June 23, 1865; transferred to Thirty-first Infantry, September 21, 1866; transferred to Twenty-second Infantry, May 15, 1869; transferred to Fourth Artillery, December 15, 1870; appointed Captain and Assistant Quartermaster, April 24, 1875. He is now stationed at St. Paul, Minn. Issue: 1, Kitty Marshall; 2, Ellen; 3, Nannette.

2458 THOMAS A. MARSHALL, b. April 20, 1849, in Charleston, Ill., = December 29, 1870, JULIA ANNA KNOWLTON, dr. of C. M. and E. M. Knowlton, of Michigan. He graduated at the Michigan University Law School in 1870; practiced law in Charleston, Ill., for a few years; then engaged in the clothing business in Iowa, and is now clerking in the Quartermaster's office at Denver, Col. Issue: 1, Benjie Marshall, b. August, 1873.

2460 CHARLES T. MARSHALL, b. at Charleston, Ill., December 17, 1859, = September 14, 1880, HENRIETTA MONROE, dr. of John Monroe and Hannah A. Chambers, b. January 29, 1865. Mr. Marshall is farming near Charleston, Ill., and from his letters I regard him as a man of fine sense. Issue: 1, Lewis Marshall, b. June 26, 1881; 2, Hannah, b. February 11, 1883; 3, Thomas A., b. August 11, 1884.

(2474) JOHN MARSHALL SMEDES.

2462 JOHN HART MARSHALL, b. in Charleston, Ill., January 13, 1864. He attended the Illinois University, 1880–83, and is now engaged in the railway mail service at Charleston, Ill.

2464 THOMAS MARSHALL SMEDES, b. December 2, 1843, = June 13, 1872, OLIVE RAWORTH, dr. of E. P. Raworth, of Vicksburg. Mr. Marshall was educated at St. James' College, Md. He is a planter near Vicksburg, Miss. Issue: 1, Olive Smedes, b. May 22, 1873; 2, Thomas M. Smedes, b. March, 1875; 3, William C. Smedes, b. December 23, 1877; 4, Edward Smedes, b. January, 1882. Mr. Smedes is a business man and is interested in railroads.

2466 SUSIE SMEDES, b. July 16, 1846, = December, 1870, JAMES R. BARNETT, b. 1832; d. May, 1879; surgeon on Gen. Chalmers' staff in the Confederate army, and surgeon after the war in the United States army. No issue. They lived at Vicksburg, Miss.

2468 ANNA SMEDES, b. September 24, 1847, = August 18, 1878, CAPT. WILLIAM VOSBURG, civil engineer and land agent for several of the Vicksburg railroads. He was educated in New York. See next No. No issue living.

2470 ELLEN SMEDES, b. September 14, 1849; d. June 15, 1873, = May, 1870, CAPT. WILLIAM VOSBURG (2468). Issue: William S. Vosburg, b. May 13, 1872.

2472 ALICE MARSHALL SMEDES, b. October 22, 1851; resides with her mother in Vicksburg, Miss. She was educated at Raleigh, North Carolina.

2474 JOHN MARSHALL SMEDES, b. in Vicksburg, Miss., February 10, 1858; educated at Vanderbilt University, Nashville, Tennessee. Now a lawyer of Cincinnatti, O.

(2476) WILLIE CHRISTINE SMEDES.

2476 WILLIE CHRISTINE SMEDES, b. October 21, 1861; educated at Raleigh, N. C. Lives at Vicksburg, Miss.

2478 SUSAN ALICE MARSHALL, b. in Blandville, Ky., July 6, 1849, = 1867, A. P. HALL, b. August 1846, d. January 26, 1880, in Florida, of consumption. Mrs. Hall lives now in Paducah, Ky. Issue: 1, Charles H. Hall, b. September, 1869; 2, Mary E. Hall, b. 1871.

2480 MARY E. MARSHALL, b. July 15, 1850, in Blandville, Ky.,= December, 1870, GEO. W. REEVES, b. in Ballard Co., Ky., 1849. They live at Missoula, Montanna Territory, and he is practicing law. Issue: 1, Emily M. Reeves, b. September 11, 1871; 2, Susan Alice Reeves, b. June 22, 1874; 3, Katie, b. October 15, 1882.

2482 THOMAS C. MARSHALL, b. in Blandville, Ky., December 14, 1851, = 1879, MILLIE JENKINS, b. 1855, in Ballard Co., Ky. Mr. Marshall is a lawyer living at Missoula, Montana. He has just been elected Probate Judge. Issue: Anna Maria Marshall, b. June 15, 1880; 2, Emily Marshall, b. May 22, 1882; 3, Charles Marshall, b. May 22, 1883.

2484 LUCY E. MARSHALL, b. in Blandville, Ky., May 17, 1854, = 1879, DR. WM. W. RICHMOND, b. in Hickman Co., Ky., 1846. They live in Clinton, Hickman Co., Ky. Issue: 1, Fannie D. Richmond, b. July 27, 1880; 2, Hallie Richmond, b. May 22, 1883; 3, William Richmond, b. November 29, 1884.

2486 JACOB C. MARSHALL, b. in Blandville, Ky., April 30, 1856, = October, 1882, ADDIE UTTERBACK, b. April 27, 1862. He completed his education in law at Ann Harbor, Mich., after studying with his father. He is now living on a farm in Ballard Co., Ky., and is in the Internal Revenue service. Issue: 1, Thos. J. Marshall, b. August 9, 1883; 2, Charles S. Marshall, b. December 17, 1884.

(2650) ANNIE COLSTON — (*Michie*).

2488 EMILY CATHERINE MARSHALL, b. at Blandville, Ky., July 15, 1863. Lives with her father in Paducah.

2490 MARSHALL TURNER, b. in Louisville, Ky., January 11, 1878. Mama's only pet.

APPENDIX.

2650 (*a*) No. 604, ANNIE COLSTON was married October 15, 1884, to DR. THEODORE A. MICHIE, of Charlottesville, Va., and they now reside there.

THE BLACKFORDS.

(*b*) Several brothers, Blackford, came to America and settled in New Jersey. The son of one of them went to Indiana, and, when the State was formed, became a Judge of the Supreme Court and Reporter. (Vide Blackford's Indiana Reports). Subsequently he became one of the first Judges of the Supreme Court of Claims of the United States. The son of another brother settled in Maryland, and has descendants there. The son of a third brother, when twenty-one years of age, came to Virginia, about the close of the last century, and established the "Isabella" furnace, in Page County. He amassed a large fortune, lived to a great age, and attained distinction. His son, William M. Blackford, was born in 1801, and died in 1864 of over-anxiety about the war, in which his five sons were actively engaged, and for whose safety and welfare he was deeply solicitous. His wife, who still lives, was Mary Berkeley Minor, the only daughter of Gen. John Minor, of Fredericksburg, Va., and Lucy Landon Carter, of King George County. One of his sons was:

(*c*) 1. Charles Minor Blackford (620), who was born October 17, 1833; was educated at the University of Virginia, where he was a student, academic and legal, from 1850 to 1855. After graduating in both departments, he commenced the practice of law in the

(2650) ANNIE COLSTON — (*Michie*).

city of Lynchburg. He entered the C. S. Army, rose to the rank of Captain, ahd became a member of Gen. Longstreet's staff, and Judge Advocate of his corps. After the surrender he resumed practice in Lynchburg, where he has the honor of being the President of the People's National Bank, and Attorney for the Midland railroad. His wife is the charming daughter of the late Thomas Colston. She still possesses beauty and vivacity. See Nos. 620 and 1634.

(*d*) 2. Another son of William M. and Lucy L. Blackford, is Prof. L. M. Blackford, of the Episcopal High School, near Alexandria, Va. He married Eliza C. Ambler. See No. 2118.

INDEX.

Refer to the numbers which are the same in the chart and volume. Names in Roman are found on the chart, and, if noticed at all in the sketches, it will be under the same number. Females are indexed by their maiden names. Husbands names are in parentheses. Names in Italics are found in the volume and not on the chart. The smaller letters A. b. c., etc., following the numbers, indicate the paragraph in which the name is found. When the word *of* follows a name, supply *son* or *daughter*.

Adair, Henrietta...................*280 b*
Adams, Alice (Marshall)............62
  Ann.....................................*32*
  Eliza (Marshall)....................636
  Elizabeth (Smith)..................32
  Family.................................32
  Fannie M.............................776
  George................................32
  Gilbert................................216
  James..................................32
  John....................................32
  Josias.................................32
  Littleton..............................32
  Sarah (Fry).......................180 l
  Susanna..........................32, 56
  Thomas...............................32
Adgate, H. D. (Duer).............1308
Adkins, Mary A. (Smith)...........14
Alexander, And. and family...244 r
  Anne (Caruthers)................72 e
  Ann C. (Morson)..............1428 b
  Appoline (Blair)..................228 e
  Arch'd................................68 p
  Arch'd of Scotland..............72 c
  Arch'd (1708)......................72 c
  Dr. Arch'd..........................72 e
  Chas. B.............................660 m
  Elizabeth (McClung).....68 d, 72 e
  Eugine.............................2208
  E. M. (Marshall).................156
  Evilyn (Moore)....................68 o
  Family............72 c, 722 c, 2208
  Hannah (Lyle)....................72 e
  John (1659) and family......722 c
  Maj. John and family..........68 p
  Joseph (1742)....................72 e
  Lucy (Waller)......................682
  Mary (Wellford).................722 c
  Paul................................2208
  Peter.................................72 c

Alexander, Phœbe (Paxton)......*244 k*
  Robt.\..................................72 c
  Robt (1704).......................722 c
  Sam'l H...........................2208
  Sam'l H.............................2208
  William (of Scotland)..........72 c
  William........72 c d, 722 c, 2208
Allen, Elizabeth (Armstead)...50 m
  Eliza S...............................648
  Mary R. (McClung)............920
  Sue (Marshall)..................644
Allin, Philip T...................1434
Ambler, Ann (*1772*)...............*50 q*
  Annie J............................2144
  Arthur L..........................2140
  Benj. M..........................2114
  Cath. C...........................*50 n.*
  Rev. Charles E.................848
  Edward............................756
  Edward C........................2128
  Edward C..........................50 m
  Edward, of John................50 m
  Eliza..............................2114
  Eliza C. (Blackford).........2118
  Elizabeth.........................844
  Elizabeth B......................50 m o
  Elizabeth J. (1765)......50 p. 160 c
  Emma E.........................2148
  Fanny (Marshall)........556, 846
  Frank W.........................2142
  Gabriella, B......................*50 o*
  Humphrey......................2124
  Jacquelin (1742).........50 p. 158 d
  Dr. James..........................750
  James M........................2116
  James............................2114
  Jennie K........................2122
  John................................66
  John, of T. M..................842
  John C...........................2120

THE MARSHALL FAMILY.

INDEX.

Ambler, John Cary 2114
   John ....*50 m, n p*
   Kate P.........................2138
   Lettie C........................2126
   Lucy............... 840
   Lucy (Mason)............ 2112
   Lucy J..........................2130
   Lucy N. (*1776*)................*50 q*
   Martha ....*50 p*
   Mary C..........................2132
   Mary C. (Stribling)....*152 d*, 854
   Mary M...........................754
   Mary W. (Marshall)...*158 d*, 50
   Mary........................ *50 p, 152 d*
   Mason 2114
   Nannie............................2114
   Philips St. G......................*50 o*
   Dr. Richard C 202
   Richard C...............752, 1710
   Richard J................852, 2136
   Richard, of England...........*50 l*
   Richard (*1736*)........ ....*50 p*
   Richard..........................*50 m*
   Robert C.........................2146
   Sarah ....*50 m*
   Sarah J........................ *50 o*
   Thomas M.................*50 n*, 242
   Rev. T. M......................850
   Thos. M...................... 2134
   William M........................*50 p*
Anderson, Addie (Duke)........942
   Anna M........................2180
   Edward 2178
   Geo. W..........................2184
   Hon. G. W......................870
   Lizzie L........................2182
   Martha (*Tebbs*).................*2168 b*
   Mary E. (Marshall)............784
   Sue (*Tebbs*)......................*2168 b*
   William J........................ ..*660 e*
Andrews, Alice (Harbeson)...2158
   Charles E......................2052
   Charles M......................2054
   Daisie F........................2054
   Emily R. (Marshall)...........826
   Fannie E. (Sloan).............2058
   George Y.......................2062
   James A........................2052
   James.............................2052
   Kate 876
   Laura H........................2052
   Lucien T.......................2060
   Lucy B.........................2048
   Marshall L.....................2054
   Mary D.........................2056
   Mattie J.......................2064
   Mattie..........................2054

Andrews, O. D....................2048
   Rev. R. L...................... 814
   Robert L.......................2052
Archer, *Abram*....................*254 f*
   Lizzie 1262
   William B.......................504
   William S......................1260
Armistead, Bowles E........740, 1270
   Eleanor B......................1846
   Fanny (*Ambler*)..............*50 m*
   Henry. 183
   John B..........................1844
   Louis B........................1840
   Mary M.........................1836
   Stanley 1842
Armstrong, Darling..............1114
   George M.......................1102
   James 370
   Louisa (Porter)................1108
   Matilda (Walker)..............1104
   Robert E. L...................1116
   Sallie L. (McCormick).......1106
   Thomas H......................1110
   Thornton T....................1112
Arnett, (*Newton*).................*162 f*
Ashby, Ann (Smith)..............37
Ashby, *M. L*......................*150 i*
   Nancy (Duke)...................276
Ashford, Thos....................442
Atterbury, Ellen M....... 2024
   J. T.......................... 2024
   Josephine 2024
   Mary B.........................2024
Aylett, *Col. Wm*..................*162 m*
Aynes, John......................342
Bacon Mary L. (*Pickett*).......... *64 g*
Baley, Ann (Marshall)...........19
Baker, Nannie (Ambler)......2114
Baldwin, A. S....................2008
   Charles M......................2000
   Cornelius 2000
   Cor. C.....................*244 l, 1266*
   Family.......................*2000*
   Dr. J. M.......................2008
   Maria 2008
Ball, *family*......................*162 i*
   Judith S. (Marshall)..........236
   Pattie (*Green*)...................*180 h*
Ballow, America..........1136, 386
   Charles 104
   Cynthia 380
   Edward 112, 1150
   Elizabeth 376
   Elizabeth (Barnes)............408
   Emily (Kelso).................1146
   Fannie 1140
   George S......................1142

INDEX.

Ballow, Harry..................1138
   Hattie (McMillan)..............378
   Hattie..........................1148
   Jane (Reading).................414
   Jane (Hope)....................1134
   Lucinda (Bohon)................410
   Malinda (Hacket)...............416
   Martha..........................384
   Mary E. (Logan)................1132
   Mary (Griffin).................412
   Mary J. (Morris)...............1131
   Permelia........................382
   Preston....................334, 404
   Susanna (Bohon)................418
   Susan (Vance)..................1144
   William....................406, 1130
   Dr. William................350, 374
Barbee, Thos..................980, *180 n*
   Family........................*180 n*
Barbour family....50 n, 180 i n, 162 i
Barclay family..............244 o t, 68 o
Barhydt, M. G. (Marshall).....1272
Barnes, Emily.................1154
   F. D............................1126
   Fannie..........................2604
   Gay.............................2602
   Lucie A. (Sayle)...............1128
   Martin..........................1152
   Sallie..........................2600
   Shadrack........................408
   Shadrack C.....................1124
   Shade...........................2606
   Tillie (Neely).................2598
Barnet, Dr. J. R..............2466
   Chas............................150 j
Baron, E. C. (Forsythe)............1224
Barry, Lucy (Marshall)........1014
Bartley, H. M. (Forman).........660 f
Barton, Agnes.................2018
   Bolling W...............2018, 2020
   Chas. M.............524, 2004, 2018
   David R........................2010
   D. W............................802
   Family........................802
   Fannie J........................2014
   Jane C. (Shield)................2006
   Martha W (Shield)..............2008
   Maria (Marshall)..........512, 2002
   Mary E. (Jones).................804
   Mary (Smith)...................1378
   Capt. Randolph.................2018
   Randolph J.....................2018
   Hon. R. T......................2016
   Robt. K........................2018
   Rev. Thos......................802
   William........................802
   W. S...........................2012

Basket, M. (Hackett)..........1158
Basye, (McClanahan)...........122
   Lou (Robinson).................454
Battaille, Mary................102 d
   John, Col......................502 e
   Nicholas.......................102 d
Baxter, Elizabeth.............2424 b
Baytop, Lucy (Taliaferro) 502 e, 102 f
Beatty, Dr. O..................180 m
Beall, family..................1226
Beckwith, family...............162 i
Beirne, M. H. (Thomas).........1588
Bell, David and family........180 m
   Eliza (Bates).................1012 e
   Family........................1012 b
   Harry.........................1012 b
   Judith (Gist).................1012 b
Bennett, R. H..................1660
Benson, Dr. D. B..............162 j
Bentley, Chas. M...............1782
   Frank M........................1784
   John...........................692
Benton, Eliza P. (Jones)........68 k
   Jessie (Fremont)..............68 k
   Sarah (Jacob).................68 k
   Susan V. (Boileau)............68 k
   Thomas H. and family..........68 k
Berry, Henry C.................2442
   Jackson T......................2442
   Jessie S.......................2442
   Sallie C. (Marbury)...........828
   Sally (Kennan).................56 h
   William........................2442
Berryman, Rose................102 g
Betts, A. B....................812
   Katie..........................2050
   Lucy S. (Amdrews)..............2048
   Mary F. (Crow).................2044
Biegler, Cam A.................2280
   Chas. A........................2280
   John W.........................2280
   Martin.........................2280
   Philip.........................2280
   Sue M..........................2280
Birdsong, K. L. (Burnley).....1980
Birney, Anna R. (Marshall)....296
   Family......................68 f, 296
   James G.....................68 f, 296
Blackbeard, Legend............12 j
Blackburn, Dr. C. B...........2164
   Family........................2164
   Frank A..................70 b, 2164
   John D.........................2164
   Marshall.......................2164
Blackford, Chas. M.
         620, 1636, 2650 b c
   Nannie (Withers)...............1634

THE MARSHALL FAMILY.

INDEX.

Blackford, Raleigh C..........1638
  L. M..............2118, 2650 b c d
Blackwell, Ann (Marshall)......500
  Sue (Green)...............*180 j*
  William......................*500*
Blaine, Sam'l..................1068
Blair, F. P...................1012 c
  Col. Jos...................244 t
  Martha (Paxton)...........244 k
Bland, Ben......................632
Blassingame, F................102 f
Bledsoe, Jesse...............1012 c
Blossom, Eliz. (Randolph)......668 b
Bogardus, *family*.............*1702*
  Lou (Maltby)................1702
Bohon, Dan......................410
  William......................418
Boilleau, family..............68 k
Bolling, A. B. (Ambler).........850
  Family................16 w, 150 k
Booker, Ed......................114
Booth, Allen...................2568
  Kate (Taliaferro).........102 g
  Mary B......................2564
  Raswell.....................2566
  R. V........................1088
Boswell, Jo..................1012 c
Bowles, Eleanor..............150 h
Bowman, Dr......................484
Bowyer, M. C. (Brockenbrough)..162 c
Bradford,
  George......................758
  Maria (Marshall)...........1066
  Thomas......................1072
Brant, family.................68 i
Broshear, Dennis..............68 f
  Eliza (Sullivant).........68 f
Braxton, Anna M................1360
  Hon. E. M...................520
  Elliott M., jr.............1362
  Eliza (Brockenbrough)......1354
  Jacq. M.....................1364
  Mary A......................1358
  Sallie M....................1356
  Westar W....................1366
Breckinridge, *Alex............70 f*
  Caro. (Bullock)..............70 h
  Cath. (Waller)..............682
  Cabell......................2430
  Cabell, C...................70 h
  Desha (Maltby)..............1704
  Family..............1704, 70 h
  Fanny (Steele)..............70 h
  Fanny (Young)...............70 g
  Frank P.....................2430
  John (1760)............70 g, 1754
  John C..............70 h, 1754

Breckinridge, John, D. D., (1797)..70 i
  Joseph Cabell (1788).....70 g, 1704
  Let. P. (Grayson)..............70 g
  Let. P. (Parkhill).............70 g
  Mary S......................2430
  Mary (Saterwhite)..............70 h
  Mary A. (Castleman)...........70 h
  Mary A. C....................70 h
  Owen..........................70 h
  Col. Robert..................70 f
  Dr. R. J., (1800).............70 i
  Wm. (1759)....................70 g
  Wm. L. (1803) and family......70 i
Breeden, Ann....................84
  John M.......................84
Brent, *Chas. S.............2424 b*
  E. L. (Hart)..............2424 b
  Family....................2424 b
  Hannah (Payne)......1012 d, 2424 b
  Hugh................1012 c, 2424 b
  Innes.....................2424 b
  Margaret (Young).........2424 b
  Lizzie (Marshall).........2424 b
  Sarah B. (Lewis).........2424 b
  William......................50 p
Brockenbrough, *Alice........162 m*
  Alex. (emigrant)............70 f
  Arthur S..................162 g h
  Austin and family.........162 h i
  Ben. W. and family........162 g
  Carter.....................1354
  Ed.......................162 d m
  Eliz. (Phelps).............162 f
  Eliz. (Woodward)...........162 k
  Ella (Knox)................162 m
  Family....................162 e
  Frank H...................162 e
  Geo. L....................162 h
  Henrietta (Nelson).........102 j
  Jane (Colston).............162
  John F. and family.........162 i
  John B. and family.........162 d
  John L.....................1354
  Judge John W..............162 c
  John N....................162 g
  Judith W. (McGuire).......162 e
  Littleton and family......162 l
  Louisa G. (Sems)..........162 e
  Lucy (Shackelford)........162 k
  Lucy C.....................1354
  Mary (Tucker).............162 k
  Mary R. (Hawkins).........162 h
  Mary S. (Newton)..........162 e
  Moore, F. and family......162 k
  Robert L. and family......162 e
  Sarah J. (Colston)........162 f
  Sarah R. (Maxwell)........162 h

THE MARSHALL FAMILY. 391

INDEX.

Brockenbrough, Thos. W............162 g
  Dr. W. A. and family......... 162 h
  Col. William (emigrant)......162 c
  William and family............162 d
  William, S. R....................162 f
  Judge William and family.....162 g
  Willoughby and family..........162 d
Broderick, Jos..........................660 k
Brooke, Annie.........................1850
  Courtenay (Selden)..............150 i
  Elizabeth (Marshall)............200
  Family...................50 p., 150 p
  Fanny (Adams)..................216
  Frank 1854, 764
  Frank E.............................50 p
  George........:..........60, 208
  Humphrey.........................204
  John.................................762
  John L............................150 i
  Lewis................................210
  Lucy (Davis)......................212
  Martin P............................64 b
  Mary................................758
  Mary L. (Byrd)...............150 i l
  Mary (Burwell)..................214
  Mathew...........................150 i
  Robert..............................766
  Whiting............................206
  Wilhelmina.....................1852
Brown, Rev. John....................70 k
  Mary (Green)....................180 j
  Mary A. (Forman).............660 c
Browning, Eliza M................2288
  Geo. T..............................922
  Granville M.....................2290
Bruce, Eli.............................64 i
  Ellen (Morson).................1428 b
  Geo..................................64 i
  Pauline (Duke)..................956
Bryce, Mamie (William)........1548
Buck, Rev. C. E....................1226
Buckner, Sue (Taliaferro).......102 e
  Wm................................102 e
Buford, Abraham.....68 g, 70 b, 280 b
  Annie.............................2384
  Basil D.....................2390, 972
  Blanche............................984
  Charles......2386, 286, 973, 2382
  Charlotte..........................976
  Family............................280 b
  George.............................986
  Harry..............................2202
  Hattie............................2380
  Henrietta (Barbee).............980
  Henry.............................874
  Col. John.......................280 b
  Gen. John........................950

Buford, John S....................2392
  Louis M....................2388, 974
  Lucy..............................982
  Mary (Duke)....................280
  Samuel...........................280 b
  Susan M. (Edson)..............978
  William..........................280 b
Bull, Anna (Jacquelin)..........196 g
Bullock, Dr. Jos....................70 h
Bullitt, Aga.........................2238
  Alex. S.........................2240
  Jas. B..........................2236
  Keith............................2244
  Mildred A.....................2242
  Myra............................2246
  Col. Thos. W...................900
  William M.....................2234
  William C................180 n, 900
Burch, M. C. (Breckenridge) 70 h, 1704
Burgess, R. (Warfield)..........184 d
Burkadike, Eliza..................50 l
Burke, Florence (Marshall)....894
Burnes, Sue E. (Tebbs).........2168
Burnley Blanche.................1990
  Edwin.....................224, 1982
  Furline........................1980
  Dr. Hardin......................796
  Jos. H..........................1996
  Martin D.......................1980
  Mary E.........................1994
  Nannie O......................1988
  Robt. M........................1984
  William........................1992
  Wm. M..........................798
  Wm. G.........................1986
Burwell, Ann C. (Cooke)......772
  Carter..........................158 d
  Claudia H (Marshall).......158
  Eliza (McGuire)..............770
  Eliza (Nelson).................158 c
  Evaline C......................1896
  Geo. H..........................1884
  John P.........................1890
  Lewis (1658)..................158
  Lewis (1764).................158 d
  Lucie............................768
  Mary W........................1888
  Nathaniel.......................774
  Maj. Nat.......................158 c
  Nathaniel, of Carter Hall..158 d
  Dr. Philip....................1886
  Rebecca L. (Ambler)...50 p. 158 d
  Robert C......................158 e
  Susan R. (Henry)............1882
  Thomas........................1894
  William N......................214
  Dr. William N...............1892

THE MARSHALL FAMILY.

INDEX.

Bush, *Cath. (Ambler)* .... *50 n*
   Ella (Marshall) 1082
   Family .... *858 c*
   Philip .... *858 c*
   Sally (Paxton) 858
Butler, Ann E. (Green).. 648
   Edward *648*
   Family *648*
   Jane (*Washington*) .... *150 p*
   Margaret (*Washington*) .... *150 o*
   Pierce *648*
   Maj. Thomas *648*
   Thomas *648*
   W. W. 1304
   Col. Wm. *648*
   Gen. Wm. O. *648*
Byrd, Ann G 1240
   Family .... *1240, 150 l*
   Hannah M 1240
   Lewis W 1240
   Mary B........................... 1240
   Richard C....................... 1240
   Dr. S. P. .... *50 i*
   Samuel P. 1240
   Capt. W. and family..... *150 l, 1240*
Cabell, *Mary H.* (*Breckinridge*) *70g, 170*
Caldwell, *Abram* .... *68 g*
   Rev. Robert *660.f*
Calhoun, *Andrew* .... *180 j*
   Mary (Lewis) .... *248 b*
Cull, Daniel .... *50 q*
   Elizabeth (Norton) .... *50 q*
Camm, Annie L 1616
   Gertrude 1616
   Robert 1616
Campbell, *Alex* .... *244 o*
   Prof. John .... *244 o*
   Dr. J. P. .... *368 e*
   Margaret M. (Pickett) ..... *64 f, 68 e*
   Mary (Smith) 1200
   Nancy (*Soward*) *364*
   Robert and family .... *244 o*
   Sarah B (Preston) .... *70 k*
Carman, *S. K. (Randolph)*... *668 d*
Carpenter, Ben. B 1644
   Bessie 1644
   Elias 1644
   Eliza D 1644
   Emily M 1644
Carrington, *Col. Chas* .... *68 i*
   Edward, *Col* .... *50 p, 160 c*
   Family .... *160 c, 50 p, 68 i*
   George (emigrant) .... *160 c*
Carroll, Chas 1596
   Douglas G 1596
   Col. Gray 566
   John 1596

Carroll, *Judith (Bell)* ....*1012 b*
Casson, S. S. (*Alexander*) ....*722 c*
   Thomas ....*722 c*
Carson, Col. John................*68 q*
Carter, Charles...................*150 h*
   Elizabeth (*Burwell*).............*158 c*
   Fanny (Brockenbrough) ....*162 i*
   Mary (Robinson)............ ...1178
Caruthers, *Maj. Jas.* and *family*....*244 n*
Cary, family ....*1012 b*
   John (immigrant) ....*1012 b*
   Martha..............................*196 g*
   Mary (*Ambler*)....................*50 l*
   Wilson ....*50 l*
Casey, Alex. M 1682
   Frances (Tate) 1670
   Illa L.............................1680
   Col. James B 642
   John ....*150 h*
   John B...........................1678
   Mary M.........................1674
   Sallie F..........................1672
Catlett, *Elizabeth (Taliaferro)*.....*502 e*
   John ....*502 e*
   Mary (*Taliaferro*) ....*102 d*
   Sarah (*Taliaferro*) ....*502 e*
Castleman, D ....*70 h*
Cecil, Henry A 2436
Chalfant, Jose (Marshall).......266
Chamberlain, K. E. (Taylor)...1906
   Elizabeth (Pickett)........ ......*64 e*
Chambers, *Jane (Forman)*.......*660 g*
   Frank T........................... 634
   John 1668
   Gov. John.......................*2424 b*
   Joseph................................*858 d*
   Matilda (Brent).............*2424 b*
Chancellor, Dr. C. A 1248
   Leah S.......................... 1248
Chenoweth, B. D 2298
   H. P 2298
   Margaret (Tate) *1670*
Chesley, Bessie B..............1226
   Claudia L......................1226
   Family *1226*
   Rev. J. H.......................1226
   Margaret L....................1226
   William *1836*
Cheswell, *Mary (Lewis)* . ...*150 i*
Chew, *Eliza*.........................*842*
Chilton, Let. (Smith)............140
   Sallie Pickett...................*64 d*
Chinn, Jas. H 1188
   Joseph W. ....*162 k*
   Margaret (Duke)....................*74*
Choate, *Patience (Maltby)*.........*652*
Chrisman, G. L....................2306

INDEX.

Churchill, Judith................16 w
Clarke, Mrs..........................322
  Dr. H. O........................64 h
Clarkson, Ann D..................152 c
  Caro M. (Stribling)..........152 c
  Eliza L. S. (Marshall).........152
  Family ....64 b c, 152 c
  Henry........................152 c d
  Martha.........................152 d
  Mildred........................152 d
  William...................64 b, 150 c
Claybrooke, Edwin................162 f
Cloyd, Elizabeth.................68 h
Cobb, Samuel.....................150 n
Cochrane.................................
  James and family..............68 q
  R. L.........................1078
Coke, Reb. F. (Marshall).........506
  Richard C.....................150 l
Coleman, Anne H. (Taylor)......782
  Browning.....................2288
  Burbridge.....................184 b
  Chas. F......................1760
  Chas. L........................676
  Claudia......................1444
  Daniel........................184 b
  Family........................184 b
  Fannie (Randolph)...........668
  Harry H......................1764
  Harry W.......................678
  Maj. James....................672
  James.........................184 b
  Julia (Tebbs)...............2168 b
  Col. Lewis M..................560
  Lewis M.....................1446
  Lloyd R....................184 b c
  Lloyd R.....................2288
  Lucy M. (Smith)..............670
  Maria E.....................1762
  Martha (Ambler)..............50 p
  Mary O.......................184 d
  Maud........................1442
  Hon. Nic. D...................184
  Nic. D......................2288
  Robt. L. (Taylor).............782
  Sue M. (Dickinson)...........674
  Capt. Thos. B................184 b
Colston, Alice....................624
  Ann B. (Camm)..............1616
  Annie (Michie)........2650 a, 604
  Annie F. (Minor).............618
  Edward..................162, 608
  Eliza F. (Gildersleeve).....1614
  Eliza (Williams).............594
  Elizabeth M.................1570
  Jane B......................1568
  Jane.........................596

Colston, Jane (Howard).........1618
  John ·M...................170 b, 174
  Laura H......................622
  Lucy.........................606
  Lucy A.......................172
  Mary I. (Thomas).............164
  Mary W. (Leigh)..............598
  Marie L. (Rogers)............622
  Gen. Raleigh E...............170 c
  Raleigh T....................170
  Raleigh.................600, 616
  Rawleigh......................52
  Sophia H....................1572
  Susan S.....................1566
  Susan (Leigh)................166
  Susan L. (Blackford).........620
  Thomas M................168, 1620
  William B....................602
Compton, S. G...................162 i
Conger, H. (Randolph)..........668 b
Cooke, Aletha (Meade).........1880
  Anna K......................2414
  Geo. K......................2422
  D. J. G.....................1004
  John R......................2416
  Lizzie......................1872
  Maria P. (Kennedy).........1874
  Mary H......................2418
  Million (Green).............180 k
  Nannie E....................1876
  Nat. B......................1878
  Philip P.....................772
  Thos. T.....................2412
  Wm. L......................2420
Coppie, St. J...................1092
Corbin, C. C. (Byrd).......150 l, 1240
Cousins, Jos..................244 s
Cowherd, B. R................1922
Craddock, Elizabeth......50 l, 196 j
Craig, S. (Bush)..............858 c
  Pattie E. (Green)............648
  Dr. William and family....180 i
Crenshaw, Virg. (Taylor).....1900
Crittenden, G. B..............70 b
Crockett, D. S...............2036
  Prior F.....................2036
  Willie V....................2036
Crooke, H. B..................660 k
Crow, Abel B.................2044
  Asa L. (2)..................2044
  D. R........................2044
  Lucy A......................2044
  Mary F......................2044
Crutchfield, C. (Marshall)...2440
  Virg. (Marshall)............2440
Cummins, David................904
  W. H........................302

INDEX.

Cunningham, E. (Woolfolk).....912
Currie, *family*..................282
  James..................64 d, 282
  Mary (Duke)..............282
Custis, Bettie (Ambler)..........850
  Edmund..................850
  Eleanor (Lewis)..........150 h
  Family..................850
Dabney, Lela (Taylor)...........1916
Dangerfield, F. L...............1214
  Frank L..................1214
  Mary.....................1214
  Sarah....................1214
  William.................103 d
Dare, Jane (Chesley)..........1326
Darnell (Smith)....................38
Daviess, Col. J. H.................78
Davidson, Jas. D. and family..68 l, 244 s
Davis, Eben N....................68 m
  Dr. J. M................2168 b
  Pres.....................212
  Robert A................1658
Davison, A. J..................1794
  Cary A..................1794
  Fontaine...............1794
  Marshall...............1794
  William R..............1794
Dawe, Eliza (Hampton)..........64 j
  Phil. R................64 j
Dearing, James....................304
DeBell, Baldwin.................1646
  Catherine W...........1640
  Clarence..............1640
  Joshua................1640
DeGrand, U. (Colston)............170
Desha, Ellen (Pickett).........64 e
  J. B..................64 g
  Margaret (Clarke)......64 h
Dewees, S. (Duke)................962
Dickinson, Maj. A. G.............674
  A. G..................1770
  Fannie R..............1772
  Harry M...............1776
  Nannie................1768
Dimmitt, Dr. Ad..................628
  Fanny (Davis).........1658
  Kate B. (Fee).........1656
  Julia M. (Herndon)....1654
Dinmock, Mabel (Maltby)........65 c
Dix, S. (Alexander)............68 p
Dodge, Jane M..................2222
  Robert F..............2222
  Theodore..............2222
Donahoo, L. C. (Forman)........660 j
Doniphan, *Gen. A. W*...........103
  George...........360, 2512
  Maria L. (Felix)......2510

Doremus, E. (Bogardus).........1702
Dorsey, Eliza (*Warfield*).......184 d
Douthat, A. H. (Stribling).....1324
  A. H..................1416
  Eleanor...............1320
  Elizabeth.............1408
  Family........150 j, 244 b
  Fielding, L.......1410, 550
  Jacquelin M..........1326
  John.................1420
  Kate.................1422
  Lizzie...............1318
  Mary (Marshall)...588, 1322
  Mary W...............1414
  Robert P.............1412
  Robert..............150 j
  Robert........514, 1328, 1330
  Susan H..............1418
Dubois, Rebecca (Jans).........672
Dudley, Eliza (Marshall).........868
Duer, A. A.....................1308
  Agnes B..............1308
  Fannie B.............1308
  Duer, Hen. A.........1308
  Isabel...............1308
  John.................1308
  Margaret L...........1308
  Thos. M..............1308
Duerson, Ella (Duke).............944
Duff, Sir Wm...................180 k
Duke, Abram B....................940
  Alice................938
  Basil...........970, 2362
  Dr. Basil.............74
  Basil, of James K....942
  Gen. Basil...........960
  Bettie (Todd)........928
  Chas. B..............966
  Calvin M............2368
  Caroline (Smith).....944
  Carrie..............2308
  Charlotte (Strahan)..946
  Charlotte J. (Taylor).288
  Charlotte (Sharp)....932
  Frank K.............2374
  Harry T..............964
  Henry H.............2370
  Henry B.............2300
  Henrietta (Keenon)...952
  Henry...............2356
  James C.............2302
  James K....280, 956, 2296, 2310, 2354.
  Jane (Taylor)........288
  Dr. John M...........284
  John M.........934, 962
  Julia B.............2372

INDEX.

Duke, Katie (Chenoweth) 2298
  Lottie (Chrisman) 2306
  Louis M.........................968
  Lucy (Steele)..................958
  Lucy A. (Buford)...............286
  Lucy S........................2318
  Madge (Roberts)...............2312
  Mary B.........................948
  Mary C...................971, 2306
  Mary W. (Henry)................278
  Mary....................2304, 2352
  Mattie........................2316
  Capt N. W......................282
  Pattie (Buford)................950
  Richard.......................2358
  Sallie F......................2302
  Stephen........................936
  Judge Thomas M.................276
  Thomas M......................2364
  William...................2314, 944
  Wm. W........................2300
Duncan, Electa (Maltby)..........652
Dunn, Adie (Ballou)............1138
  Eleanor (Green)...............180 h
Durr, F. G. 1168
  Kate..........................2640
  Mary..........................2642
Durrett, A. E. (Wortham).......2624
  Chas. M.......................1742
  Eliza (Mitchell)...............396
  Eliza M.......................1736
  Emily (Barnes).................402
  Emma B........................2626
  Frank..........................110
  Frank.........................2622
  Fannie J. (Sayle).............1122
  Geo. A........................1154
  Harry S.......................2630
  Kate (Hawkins)................2631
  Lucy (Sesson)..................400
  Lucy M........................1738
  Lucy (Sayle)............2584, 2632
  Martin M......................1732
  Mary H. (Townsend)............2620
  Mary P........................1740
  Nina..........................2628
  Richard C.....................1734
  Richard......................660 g
  William..................662, 1744
Dushane, M. (Jones)............2022
Duval, Hanson R................1594
  Henry R.......................1594
  Lot............................356
  Rieman G......................1594
Dye, Mary (Forman)............660 d
Eagan, Lou (Paxton)...........244 p
Edloe, Kate (Marshall)..........522

Edmondson, Sallie [Paxton]...244 r
Edson, Aga B..................2394
  Maj. Theo......................978
Edwards, Dr. Ben. and family..180 i
  Lucretia (Green)...........180 j, 424
Egborn, M. (Nelson)...........1254
Elder, Lizzie (Durrett).......2630
Elgin, Sam'l...................440
Elliott, Bessie (Morris)......1808
English F. (Strader)..........2436
Ernst, W.....................858 d
Essex, Anna B. (Hoffman)......1956
Etherton, Jos..................358
Evans, Amelia (Marshall).......872
  Cecile........................2076
  Eug. E........................2076
  Maggie W......................2076
Ewing, Elizabeth..............2538
  Gertrude......................2530
  John....................1060, 2536
  Preston.......................2532
  Sallie M. (Marshall)...........554
  Susan.........................2528
  Tillie........................2534
Fairfax, Lord...................58
Families, Adams.................32
  Alexander.........72 c, 722 c, 2208
  Ambler........................50 l
  Bell........................1012 b
  Birney........................296
  Blackburn....................2164
  Breckinridge............70 h, 1704
  Brent.......................2424 b
  Brooke........................50 p
  Buford.......................280 b
  Bush.........................858 c
  Butler........................648
  Byrd..........................1240
  Carrington.....................160
  Chesley.......................1226
  Clarkson................64 b, 150 c
  Coleman........................184
  Currie.........................282
  Custis.........................850
  Fishback......................64 c
  Fisher........................50 q
  Forman........................660 b
  Fry....................180 l, 1012 c
  Gist........................1012 b
  Gray..........................64 g
  Green........................180 h
  Johnston.....................272 g
  Jones........................228 b
  Keith...........................16
  Kennan........................56 h
  Langhorne...................1012 b
  Lewis................150 g, 243 b

THE MARSHALL FAMILY.

INDEX.

Families, McClanahans............20
McClung............................72
McDowell..........................68 d
  " Mary E....................68 l
  " & Reid......................68
Madison............................228 c
Maltby..............................652
Monceur............................50 n
Morgan.............................962 c
Morris..............................68 c
Neil.................................884 b
Nicholas............................50 o
Paxton..............................244 k
Pickett..............................64 b
Pocahontas............150 i j, 16 w
Poindexter..........................733
Randolph....................668, 16 p
Reid.................................296
Robinson.............................20
Scott...............................64 c d
Slaughter...........................64 b
Smith............................196 j, 32
Starling............................254 f
Stringfellow........................64 b
Stribling...........................64 c
Strother............................228 d
Sullivant...........................254 c
Taliaferro.................102 d, 502 e
Taylor..............................56 h
Tebbs..............................2168
Waller...............................682
Warfield............................184 d
Washington..........................150 o
Wilford.............................722
Willis...............................852
Farrar, Nellie M. (Duke).........2302
Fee, Darlington E..................1656
  Fannie M.........................1656
  Kate D............................1656
  Jesse D...........................1656
Felix, Josiah S....................2510
Fernandes, M. (Duke)...............2296
Fishback, family...................64 e
Fisher, Eliza J. (Colston).........168
  Family.............................50 q
  Kitty (Marshall)..................2456
Fitzhugh, Luc. (Marshall)..........576
Fleming Ad...................1642, 1650
  Chas. M...........................626
  Eliza M. (DeBell)................1640
  Emily M..........................1652
  Fannie M. (DeBell)...............1646
  Fannie H.........................1642
  George...........................184 b
  Col. John.........................16 w
  Julia (Carpenter)................1644
  Marshall.........................1642

Fleming, Mary (Lewis)..........150 i
  Sue (Lewis)................150 k, 1240
  Wm. H............................1642
  Wm. P............................1648
Florence, Wm........................42
Fontaine, M. A. (Lewis).........150 g
Fontleroy, L. L. (Brockenbrough)..162 h
  Martha (Taylor)................150 j
Ford, family.......................16 g
Foree, Chas. M....................2042
  J. P. Judge......................808
  Pryor............................2040
  Sallie J.........................2038
  Sue B. (Crockett)...............2036
Forman.
  Ann (Henry)....................660 j
  Ben R..........................660 i
  Chas. and family........64 h, 660 l
  Dr. Chas. W..............70 b, 660 j
  Elizabeth (Taylor).............660 f
  Elizabeth (Marshall)............660
  Ezekiel, sr....................660 b
  Ezekiel (1770).................660 c e
  Rev. Ezekiel...................660 i
  George (1811)..................660 g
  Geo. L. (1810).................660 l
  Harriet (Perrie)...............660 l
  Jane (Forman)..................660 h
  Jane (McDonald)................660 k
  John, sr.......................660 b
  John (1775)....................660 d
  John S. (1813) and family....660 g
  Joseph (1775)................660 d k
  Joe (1812) and family....660 h, i, k
  Mary (Paxton)..................862
  Mary (Throckmorton)...........660 b
  Mary (Lewis)...............660 c, l
  Matilda (Huston)...............660 j
  Samuel..........................364
  Samuel (1778)..................660 d
  Samuel (1818)..................660 l
  Thomas.........................660 b
  Thomas (1740)..................660 c
  Thos. S. (1808) and family...660 e
  Thos. W. (1798)................660 b
  Throck (1814)..................660 h
  Whiteman W.....................660 j
  William (1804).................660 k
Forsyth, Charlotte E.............1224
  Rev. R. W......................1224
Franklin, Ch. (Taliaferro).......1258
Fremont, J. C. and family........68 k
Frogg, Capt. John................228 f
Fry, family......................1801
  Mildred A. (Christian).180 m, 900
Garner, S. N. E..................1124
Gibson, Ella (Barton)............2020

THE MARSHALL FAMILY. 397

INDEX.

Gildersleeve, B. L...............1614	Green, Letitia (Barbour)........180 i
Emma 1614	Dr. Lewis Warner......180 j, 70 b
R. C..................................1614	Lewis W..............................1700
Gill, Geo.............................990	Lily....................................1690
Gillespie, James......................68 f	Martha (Craig)...................180 i
Gilmore, Jos........................244 p	Martin P. B.........................2110
Gist, family.....................1012 b c	Mary K..............................1694
Givens, E. (Lewis)................244 b	Moses M 832
Glasgow, Kate (Paxton)........244 o	Gen. Moses and family......180 k
Glenn, Phœbe (Forman).........660 k	Nancy (McClanahan)........118
Jennie (Ballow).................1150	Nancy 434
Goodloe, Ann (Craig)............180 i	Nannie T...........................1698
Goodwin, Cor......................244 t	Nicholas ....180 k
Rev. E. L.........................1218	Pattie C..............................1696
Family 1218	Peachy (Johnston).............180 c
Margaret L.......................1218	Pierce B............................1688
Maria L............................1218	Robert (1695)....................180 h
Mary F...........................1218	Robert ....180 h
Gordon, Anne C. (Thomas)......610	Sally (Barclay)..................180 c
Anne S. (Blackwell) 500	Sarah (Neal)......................430
Jane ....254 f	Sarah (Sneed)....................180 j
W. G.................................162 j	Susan (Weir).....................180 c
Grant, Clarisse (Bennett)......1660	Col. Thos. M.......................648
Julia B. (Stephenson).........1662	William.........180 c h j, 1012 d k
Mary..................................2502	Judge Wm. H....................180 i
Noah................................. 630	Capt. Wm.........................180 h
Richard..............................2504	William.............................420
Thomas 2500	Wm. O. B..........................1692
Grasty, M. A (Brockenbrough)..162 e	William and family..........180 j
Graves, E. (Poindexter) 738	Willis ....116 a b, 180 c h
Gray, Abbie (Pickett)..............64 g	Dr. Willis D.......................180 i
Family ....64 g	Mrs. William....................116
Her. M. (Lewis)...............660 m	Greenlee family ......68 l m n q s
Lucy (Brockenbrough)........162 g	Gregg, Annie (Thomas).........1598
M. C.................................162 h	Gregory, Roger.....................150 o
Grayson, A. W. S..................70 g	Grieffe, E. (Langhorne).......1012 d
Greathouse, Mary (Marshall)...878	Griffin, Ann C. (Lewis).........150 i
Green, Bessie (Tracy)...........1686	Cyrus..................................150 k
Bettie (Huling).....................426	Pierce 412
Gen. Duff and family ...180 j, 424	Grigsby, Elizabeth...............244 v
Duff......................180 h, 150 p	Jane (Paxton).........68 l, 244 u s
Elizabeth (Smith)...............116 b	John....................................244 u
Elizabeth ....180 h i	Grymes, Lucy and Sue...........158 d
Ellen (Semple)...................428	Guisenbury, Jane (Marshall).....17
Family ....180 h	Gwathmey, Brooke ....150 i
F. W................................180 h	Ellen (Fry).......................1012 e
Henry 422	Gwatkin, C. B. (Marshall).....1274
Henry...........................116 a b	Hackett, Ben.......................1158
James ....180 k	Eliza..................................1160
Jane..................................432	Frank.................................1164
Judge John.........................180	James...............................416
John D..............................650	Mabel................................2636
John A.............................1684	Mattie B...........................1170
John..................................116 b	Nellie...............................2634
Col. John............................180 j	Preston 1162
Joseph................................180 h	Richard 1166
Rev. Joshua........................180 c	Susan 1168

INDEX.

Hall, A. P 2478
  Chas. H 2478
  Mary E 2478
  Sarah O. (Smith) 142
Hamilton, W. T .... 660 f
Hammond, Lou (Coleman) 672
  S. F .... 102 j
Hampton, T. R .... 64 j
Handley, Sallie (Robinson) ... 1186
Hansford, Sue (Marshall) 372
Hanson, Jane C 164
  John 164
Harbeson, Amy A 2158
  Ben.. 856
  Ben, jr 2156
  Geo. B 2156
  Jas. P 2158
  Jas. P., jr 2158
  John M 2156
  John M 2162
  Joseph H 2162
  Lawler 2154
  Lida G 2162
  Mary P 2162
  Mary L 2156
  Mary (Wilson) 2160
  Mary 2158
  Mathew L 2156
  Rosanna 2162
  Wm. P 2162
Hardin, Col. J. J .... 70 b
Harris, *Abagail (Johnson) ...... 272 g*
  Ann (Marshall) 222
  Frederika (Harbeson) 2162
Harrison, Car. (Douthat) 1326
  Cary and family .... 1012 e
  Judith C. (Fry) .... 180 m
  M. B. (Burwell) 1886
Harry family 1226
Hart, Henry C .... 2424 b
  Capt. Nat .. .. 1012 c
Harvie, Ann F 540
  Ellen S. (Ruffin) 530
  Emily 542
  Gen. J. B 154
  John M 528
  Mary M 526
  Susan M. (Wade) 536
  Virg. (Patrick) 534
  Wm. W 538
Harvey, Geo. H 818
  Judith M. (Evans) 2076
Harwood, Agnes (Lewis) .... 150 j
  Nannie (Lewis) .... 150 l
Houghton, L. H. Pickett .... 64 k
Hawkins, Jas 2342
  Dr. J 2631

Hawkins, John .... 228 f
  Maria L. (Smith) 142
Hawthorne. Carrie (Ambler)..2134
Hays, Dr. Wm 776
  W. F 1898
Hebron, D. L 1080
Helm, W. P 1278
Hemphill, K. (Jolliffe) 1856
Hendrick, Pat. L. (Fleming) ...1642
Henry, John F., Dr 278
  Dr. J. W .... 660 j
  Lizzie (Marshall) 1090
  M. W 1882
  Sue (Madison) .... 228 e
Herndon, Fannie 1654
  John C 1654
  Laura (Marshall) 790
  Leonard H 1654
Heron, Courtenay (Pickett) ..... 64 d
Hickman, Carrie (Duke) 944
  Cath (Marshall) 250
  David 437
Higgason, Lucy Burwell ...... 158 c
  Mary A. (Woolfolk) 914
Hill, Mattie (Marshall) 820
Hite, Cor. B 1266
  Cor. B .... 196 g
  Family 1266
  Fannie M. (Willis) 852
  Mary (Davison) 1794
Hoffman, E. M. (Marshall) 1962
  Essex M 1956
  Family 672
  Maria L 1956
  Mary K 1956
  Robt. T 1956
  Ruthana 1956
  Sarah E 1956
  Wm. A 1956
Halloway, John .... 11 j
Holt, C. J 1314
  Frank A 1314
  Jas. L 1314
Holt, Marg't L 1314
  Susan L 1314
Hope, Nic 1134
Houston, *Maj. S. and family...244 m*
  Gen. Samuel .... 244 m
  Rev. S. R. and family .... 244 p
  Wm. P .... 244 o
Howard, Con. R 1618
  Gertrude 1618
  Jane 1618
  John .... 70 k
  Mary 1618
  Nancy (Ballow) 406
Howell, Mary (Lewis) .... 150 l

THE MARSHALL FAMILY. 399

INDEX.

Howland, C. (Russell)..............2028
Hughes, Sallie (Marshall).........680
Hunt, J. W.............................960 c
Hunter, W............................102 f
Huston, W. B.......................660 j
Innis, Robert........................150 l
Ireland, Nancy (Key)...............16 r
Irvin, Sarah (McDowell)..........68 gr
 Anna (McDowell)..................68 f
 William..............................216
Isham, Mary..........................16 p
Jackson, Gov. Claib................64 j
 Dumpsey.............................64 j
Jacobs, Ade (Poindexter)........738
 Isabella D. (Taylor)...............778
Jacquelin Family............50 l, 196 j
James, John T.......................494
January, Clem. (Wall)............316
 Elizabeth.............................84
 Matilda E............................84
 Peter..................................84
 Samuel............................318, 92
 Thomas...............................314
Jans, family..........................672
Jenkins, Millie (Marshall).......2482
Johnson, Flora......................162 g
 Nancy (Langhorne)............1012 c
 Reb. (Marshall)...................98
Johnston, Gen. Albert S........272 g
 Arch.................................272 g
 Eliza McClung....................272
 Family..............................272 g
 Dr. John............................272 g
 Lucy (Ambler)...................242
 Robert..............................438
 Stoddard...........................272 g
Jolliffe, Alex. B...................1858
 David M...........................1856
 Fannie M..........................1858
 John M.............................1858
 Jos. J...............................1858
 Lucy B.............................1858
 Samuel H.........................1856
 Thos. P............................1858
 Wm. B. and Wm. H..........1856
Jones, Agnes H. (Butler).......1304
 Alice................................1464
 Anna M............................2000
 Ann C. R..........................2024
 Basil B.............................1472
 Cary................................1302
 Cary R. (Marshall)......726, 1292
 Chas. M............2034, 1998, 800
 Claudia B.........................1468
 Elizabeth (Lewis)...............150 g
 Family.............................228 b
 Fannie B. (McIlhany).......1296

Jones, Fannie L. A. M. (Barton) 802
 Feilding L.........................1302
 Frank H...........................2026
 Fred. B............................2030
 Gabriel............................228 b
 Col. Hilary.......................568
 Hilary P..........................1462
 James F..............508, 806, 1300
 James K..........................1470
 Josiah S..........................1298
 Lucy M...........................1466
 Mabel F..........................1302
 Marian E.........................2022
 Robert L.........................1300
 Strother.......................228 b, c
 Susan C..........................2032
 Thomas B........................2022
 Thomas M.......................1294
 W. C. and family..............68 k
 W. S........228, 2028, 804, 1300
 Rev. W. S.......................1298
 Willie T. (Marshall)...........576
Jordan, Cath. (Paxton).........244 p
Keenon, Adam C..................2336
 Bessie C..........................2340
 Edgar.......................2338, 952
 James D..........................2332
 Jennie.............................2334
 Mary D. (Shoemaker).......2330
Keith, Alex........................16 q, s
 Anderson.........................16 q
 Elizabeth.........................16 q
 Family.............................16 q
 George............................16 q
 Isham..............................16 q
 Parson James.............16 n, l, p
 James..............................16 q
 John................................16 q
 Judith..............................16 q
 Legend........................16 n, w
 Mary R (Marshall)...............16
 Mary...............................16 q
 Peyton............................16 q
 Thomas.......................16 q r
Kelso, W. T........................1146
Kennan, Fanny (Marshall).......56
 Family..............................56 h
 Mollie..............................56 h
 Sallie...............................56 h
 William............................56 h
Kennedy, A. E....................1874
 Joseph...........................2168 b
 Lizzie P..........................1874
 Laura (Tebbs)...............2163 h
 M. H..............................1874
 P. E...............................1874
 Reb. W..........................1874

THE MARSHALL FAMILY.

INDEX.

Kennedy, Lucie E. (Soward) 364
Kennon, Wm. ....150 l
Kenton ....180 h
Kenny, Wm. M. 2308
Kerfoot, S. A. (Pickett) ....64 k
Kerrick, Barnes 786
Key, family ....16 r, s, t
Keys, Sus. W. (Ambler) 848
Keyworth, (Pickett) ....64 f
Kincaid, Geo. B. ....70 b
   Wm. B ....70 b
King, Mary (Taliaferro) ....102 e
Kirk, Capt. Robt ....68 q
Kirkland, Agnes (Barton) 2018
Kirtley, Fannie (Buford) .....280 b
Knight, Katie (Barton) 2016
   Prudence 364
Knowlton, Julia A. (Marshall)2458
Knox, Lieut. Robt ....163 m
Landon, E. (Wellford) ....722 d
Langborn, Mary ....102 f
Langhorne, D. B. ....1012 d
   Elizabeth (Brent) ...1012 c, 2424 b
   Family ....1012 b
   John D ....1012 d
   John.. ....1012 c d
   Judith F. (Marshall) 1012
   Maurice ....1012 c d
   Sarah B. (Waller) .....680, 1012 d
Larabie, Dan'l 2250
   Elizabeth 2250
   Mary 2250
   S. E. 2250
Lashbrooke, Jane (Wood) 1668
Lawrence (Marshall) 323
Lee, Anna K. (Marshall) 258
   Claude 1436
   Rev. H. B 1436
   Harry B 1436
   Rob 1436
Legends. Blackbeard.. ....12 j
   Keiths ....12 n
   Markham ....12 j
   Randolph ....16 n
Le Grand, Lucy (McDowell) .....68 e
Leigh, B. W 166, 1554
   Ed. C 1556
   Eliza M 1564
   Mary S. (Robinson) 614
   Raleigh C 1558
   Thos. W 1562
   W. R 1560
   Lieut. Wm 598, 612
Lewis, Addison ....150 k, 1240
   Agnes (epitaph) 150
   Ann ....150 l
   Bettie (Carter) ....150 h

Lewis, Charles T. (1830) ......660 m
   Col. Chas. ....150 m n, 248 c
   Chas. (1760) ....150 h
   Chas. (1721) ....150 l
   Dangerfield ....150 h
   Eleanor (Douthat) ....150 j
   Eliza (Marshall) ....248 c
   Elizabeth (Brooke) ....150 i l
   Elizabeth (McIlvane) ....660 m
   Family ....150 g, 248 b, 660 l
   Fanny (Taylor) ....150 j
   Fanny (1744) ....150 m
   Col. Fielding ....150 g h o
   Fielding of Weyanoke ....150 j
   Forman ....660 m
   Gabriel J ....150 g
   Maj. Geo. and family ....150 h
   George and family ....660 c
   George (1832) ....660 m
   Henry Howell ....150 h
   Howe'l (1771) ....150 i m
   Isaac, sr ....660 c
   Isaac (1796) ....660 l, 2424 b
   James ....150 j l
   Jane (Anderson) ....150 n
   Jane (Greathouse) ....660 l
   John (1745) ....150 g
   "   (1669) ....150 g
   "   (1747)..150 i n, 244 b c 150 g
   "   (1720) ....150 l
   "   Pioneer ....248 b
   Judith (McGuire) ....150 i
   Lawrence (1767) ....150 h
   Margaret (Marshall) 150
   Mary F. (Alexander) ....660 n
   Mary C. (Peyton) ...160 c d, 150 i
   Mary (Cobb) ....150 n
   Mary (Lewis) ....150 o
   Meriwether ....150 n
   Mildred (Lewis) ....150 n
   Miriam (Madison) ....228 e
   Nannie (Duke) 966
   Nicholas ....150 n
   Reb. (Innis) ....150 l
   Dr. Reubin ....150 n
   Robert ....150 n
   "   (1769) ....150 i
   "   (1739) ....150 m
   "   (1694) ....150 m
   Gen. Robert (1620) ....150 g
   Sallie (Griffin) ....150 k
   Sam'l ....150 h, 248 b
   Sarah (Lewis) ....150 n
   Susan (Byrd) ....150 k
   Thomas ....248 b, 150 l
   Warner ....150 i, 1240
   Maj. William ....150 g

THE MARSHALL FAMILY. 401

INDEX.

Lewis, Capt. William............150 n
  William ....248 b
  Zack....................................150 n
Link P. T.............................. 68 m
Logan, Aga. (Marshall)......896, 898
  Annie P. (Bullitt)..................900
  Caleb 264
  Elizabeth Paxton ....244 k
  Gordon 1132
  Mary K. (Cummins)............904
  Myra M 902
Logsdin M. E. (Blackburn)....2164
Lord, E. S. (McDowell)..........68 g
Love, Jas ....244 l
  Patsey (Lewis)....................248 b
Lovell, Robt. and family........13
Lucas, Hannah (Sullivant)....254 b
  John..................................162 k
Luke, Ann (Anderson)..........248 c
  Jane ....244 c, 248
Lyle, Polly (McDowell)..........68 e
  Esther (Paxton).................244 o
  Joseph .... 72 e
Lynd, Rob't ....858 d
Lynn, Marg't (Lewis)............248 b
Lyne, Sue (Starling)............254 f. g
Lyon, M. A. (Chesley) 1226
McAfee, Hon. J. J................2438
  Julius S............................2438
McAlister, F. E. (Marshall)....1010
McCampbell, James................68 p
McCarty, J. M......................660 h
McClanahan, Aga. (Elgin) 440
  Alice (Vaughan)..................124
  Alice..................................20
  Ann 444
  Ann (Robinson)..................448
  Clara (Hickman)..................437
  Elijah (1714)........................68 l
  Family 20
  Hannah (Greenlee)..............68 l
  John..................................120
  John..................................20
  Nancy..............................120
  Peggy (Johnston)................438
  Sally Ashford 442
  Susan (Robertson)..............126
  Thomas 20, 436, 118
  William, Rev......................20
  William ....128, 445 o
McCandlish, family................150 l
McClung, Alex. K ....274, 70 b
  Arch ....72 d
  Anna M 926
  Betsy (Paxton)..................244 r
  Charlotte (Woolfolk) 270
  Elizabeth (Browning) 922

McClung, Elizabeth (Stuart) ......72 d
  Esther ....72 d
  Harrison T........................2282
  James ....72 f, d
  John A., Dr........................272
  John........................72, b, c, d. f
  John W 920
  Joseph ....72 d
  Julia L..............................2286
  Margaret (Tate) ....72 d
  Mary (1735) (McDowell)..68 d 72 f
  Mathew ....72 f
  Nellie M............................2284
  Phœbe ....72 d, 180 e
  Phœbe (Paxton) ....244 m
  Polly................................72 d
  Reb. (Steele)......................72 d
  Susan 924
  Thomas 268
  Judge William....................72
McCormick, C. R 1106
  Homes 1860
  John................................1860
  Kate (Jolliffe) 1858
  William............................1860
McCown, Rev. B. H................950
McCue, S. (McDowell)............68 q
McCullough, I. (Taliaferro)......102 h, i
McDonald, M. (Thomas)........1590
McDowell, Abram (1793)......68 g
  Agatha (Birney)............296, 68 f
  Ann (Caldwell)..................68 g
  Betsy (McDowell)..............68 g
  Brant..............................68 i
  Caleb (1774)......................68 h
  Caleb..............................68 h r
  Charles ....68 g r
  Elizabeth (McGavock)..........68 h
  Eliza (Gellespie) ....68 f
  Eliza (Rochester)................68 g
  Eliza (Wolfe)....................68 j
  Eliza P. (Benton)................68 k
  Ephraim (emigrant)............68 d, n
  Dr. Ephraim......................68 h
  Family ....68 d
  Irvin, Gen ....68 g
  Isabella (Campbell)............68 b
  Col. James (1760)..............68 c
  James (1739)....................68 h n
  Col. James........................68 h
  Gov. James........................68 i, n
  Dr. James..........................68 i
  John (1714)......................68 d
  Maj. John (1757) ....68 e
  John A. (1789)..................68 q
  John............................68 f, 180 e
  Col. Jo. (1768)..................68 g, r

INDEX.

McDowell, *Gen. Joe*..............68 q
   Jos. J ....68 q
   Lucinda (*Brashear*).............68 f
   Lucy Marshall......260
   Mag. (*Reid*) ....68*d, o
   Mag. (*Wallace*)................68 h
   Margaret (*Sullivan*)........ 68 g, r
   Margaret C. (*Venable*)....68 j
   Margaret (*Mitchell*)...........68 m
   Martha (*Buford*).......68 g, 280 b
   Mary Marshall 68
   Mary (*Thompson*) ....68 f
   Mary B. (*Ross*)................68 i
   Mary E (*Greenlee*).............68 l
   Dr. Nashe.....................68 e
   Sallie B. (*Wycliffe*) ....68 i
   Sallie C. P (*Thomas*).........68 i
   Samuel (*1735*)...............68 d, r
   Samuel (*1764*)................68 f
   Sarah (*Wallace*)..............68 d
   Sarah (*McDowell*) ....68 e, h. n
   Sarah (*Sullivant*)..............68 g
   Sup. P. B. (*assie*) ....68 l
   Sus. P (*Carrington*) ....68 i
   Sus. (*Taylor*) ....68 j
   Thomas. and family.........68 j
   Judge W. (*1762*)............68 e
   Gen. William................228 f
McGavock, D......................68 h
   Elizabeth (*Moore*)............68 o
   James ....68 h
McGuire, Agnes B............1862
   Bettie (Ambler) 848
   Burwell 1866
   Dand, H 770
   Rev. E. C...........150 h, 848
   Homes 1864
   Jane S. (Jones).............1300
   Rev. J. P.....................162 e
   Lucy (Smith)...............1860
   Mary 1870
   Rebecca 1868
   Robert L.....................150 j
McIlhany, Hugh...............1296
McIlvane, Wm.................660 m
McKee, W. C..................1170
McKnight, Lucien 656
   Martin M...................1714
   Virgil 1716
McMurran, Geo. K............2406
   Ger. V.......................2409
   John B......................2400
   Mary A......................2408
   Robert L..............1002, 2404
   Samuel......................2402
   Wm. R......................2410
McNaught E. (*Taylor*) ....68 j

McNutt (*Paxton*).............244 q
Mackey, A. E. (Marshall)......368
Macon, Mary (Marshall) 62
   Sarah A......................50 m
   Wm. H ....50 m
Madison, Eliza ....228 f
   Gabriel ....228 e
   George ....70 b, 228 e
   Jas. (*Bishop*) ....228 e
   John ....228 e
   Lucy ....228 f
   Margaret (*McDowell*).......68 e
   Roland ....228 e
   Thomas......................228 e
Magill, E. D. (*Smith*) ....196 g
   L. W. (*Brockenbrough*)......162 d
   Mallory, K. (*Brockenbrough*)..162 l
Maltby, Anson................1704
   Edith F......................1702
   Elizabeth 1702, 1706
   Family.......................652
   Frances M..................1704
   Lafayette 652
   Louis B......................1702
   Martin M...................1702
   Dr. Martin M..............1702
   Marion......................1704
   Mary B......................1704
   Timothy 652
Manly, Ida (Marshall) 822
Marbury, Alex. M...........2108
   Feudall 828, 2106
   Wm. L......................2104
Markham, Eliz. (Marshall).......12
   John ....12 h
   Legend ....12 j
   Lewis........................12 l
   William.....................12 l
Marshall.
   Rev. A. B..................... 2 h
   Adelaide 1830
   A. Eloise 1970
   Agatha (Logan).............264
   Agnes H. (Helm)...........1278
   Agnes H. (Taliaferro) 502
   Agnes R.....................838
   Albin H....................1962
   Alex. J......................238
   Alex. K......................68
   Dr. Alex. K., of Louis.......260
   Dr. Alex. K., of John 636
   Dr. Alex. K., of C. T.......868
   Dr. Alex. K., of J. K.......878
   Rev. Alex. S................. 2 h
   Alice B..............1546, 1834
   Alice (Carroll) 566
   Alice H....................1290

THE MARSHALL FAMILY. 403

INDEX.

Marshall, Angelina W............1960
Ann C.....................890, 1374
Ann G. (Byrd).....................1240
Ann L..................1285, 2226
Ann L. (Jones).................508
Ann (Smith)......................14
Anna B. (Berry)................2442
Anna C. (Cochrane)............1078
Anna M...........720, 1806, 2482
Anna M. (Braxton)..............520
Anna M. (Jones).................228
Anna M. (Wilshire).............2450
Annie, of T. A...................1096
Annie M..........................1978
Ashton, of J. E..................1402
Ashton, A..........................546
Basil M..........................1512
Bell (Roloson)..................2444
Belle............................1484
Ben. H.............................696
Benjie..........................2458
Betsy L. (Newton)................586
Betty (Buford)...................874
Beverley H......................1820
Birney...........................1008
Brent............................2424
Burwell..........................1430
Cannie S.........................1424
Cath. T. (Marbury)...............828
Catherine........................1958
Charles of Chas.................2432
Charles of M. P..................654
Charles of R. M..........1722, 708
Charles of Thos............64, 352
Charles of T. C.................2482
Col. Charles.....................826
Charles A. of Chas..............2102
Col. Chas. of A. J...............826
Col. Chas. A..................2 b 188
Chas. C. of Chas.................236
Chas. C. of C. C...........2078, 820
Chas. of Jas....................1796
Charles Ed................2446, 1440
Chas. L. of Jas..................198
Chas. L. of J. E................1396
Chas. L. of W. C................1074
Chas. M....................2082, 2432
Chas. S....................726, 1292
Chas. S. of J. C................2486
Chas. T. of A. K..........248, 2174
Chas. T. of T. A................2460
Chas. T. of J. A................1332
Charleton........................2424
Charlotte (Duke)..................74
Clara............................2440
Claudia B.......................1480
Claudia H. (Jones)?..............568

Marshall, Claudia (Morson)....1428
Courtenay (Marshall)...590, 734
Dabney..........................1120
David B.........................1306
David M.........................1476
David P. B......................1274
Dorcas (Powell)..................330
Edith...........................2440
Edward of C. T...................866
Edward of W. S..................2452
Edward C. of E. C................582
Edward C. of J. A...............1334
Edward C. of John................160
Edward C. of John...............1502
Edward C. of J. K................570
Edward C. of Louis...............266
Edward C. of Thos...............1338
Edward C. of J.A................1322
Edw'd L.........................2188
Edw'd P...................1486, 1516
Eleanor....................908, 1322
Eleanor W.......................1284
Eliza of Humprey.................300
Eliza of J. A...................1342
Eliza of J. R...................1966
Eliza A. (Taylor)................218
Eliza B.........................1522
Eliza C. (Marshall)..............182
Eliza C. (Grant).................630
Eliza C. (Young).................824
Eliza (Robertson)................518
Eliza J. (Armstrong).............370
Eliza L. (Anderson)..............870
Eliza (Jameson).................2068
Eliza (True)....................2454
Elizabeth (Armistead)............740
Elizabeth (Ballou)...............104
Elizabeth (Colston)...............52
Elizabeth (Ewing)...............1060
Elizabeth (Durrett)..............662
Elizabeth (Hebron)..............1080
Elizabeth (Hoffman).............1956
Elizabeth (Neal).................348
Elizabeth (January)...............92
Elizabeth M (Reading)..........1394
Elizabeth F. of Robert..........1718
Elizabeth of J. B...............2424
Ellen (Barton)...................524
Ellen of J. M...................2456
Eloise..........................1970
Elsie L.........................2572
Emmaline........................1818
Emily of T. C...................2482
Emily K.........................2488
Emily M. (Fleming)...............626
Emily R.........................2092
Eugine..........................2210

THE MARSHALL FAMILY.

INDEX.

Marshall, Ewing............1432
  Fannie (Chambers)............634
  Fannie (Maltby)............652
  Fannie A. (Dimmitt)............628
  Fannie E. (Cecil)............2436
  Fannie E. of Chas............2432
  Fannie G............1976
  Fannie J. (Holt)............1314
  Fannie L............1242
  Fannie M............684
  Fayette............910
  Fielding L. of Thos............506
  Fielding L. of F. L............1274
  Fielding L. of Thos............1316
  Francis B............1370
  George of Geo............324
  George of Wm............94
  George C............1066
  George H............1972
  George T............1282
  George W............784
  George Willis............372
  Hannah............2460
  H. D. lineage............10
  H. L. lineage............11 o
  Harry T............2100
  Helen............1098
  Helen............1306
  Helen of W. S............2452
  Henry L............892
  Henry M. of J. M............200
  Henry M. of H. M............746
  Henry M. of Thos............1540
  Henry W............2448
  Hester (Marshall)............690, 730
  Hester of H. M............742
  Hester of Jas............1794
  Hester of R. M............742
  Hettie (Ballou)............112
  Horace............1090
  Hudson S............2094
  Senator Humphrey............88
  Gen. Humphrey............1010
  Humphrey of Geo............323
  Humphrey of Hum............2440
  Humphrey of T. A............1026
  Ida............2206
  Rev J. H............? h.
  Dr. I. M. of Knoxville............11 m
  Jacob............2486
  Jacquelin A. Dr............152
  Jacquelin of J. A............1332, 516
  Jacquelin of E. C............588, 1322
  James of Chas............2096
  James of J. M............194
  James of John............80, 644, 722
  James of R. M............706

Marshall, James B............*............1008
  James D. J............1514
  James Ed............548, 1398
  James J. of C. S............1822
  James K. of A K............250
  James K., Col............584
  James K. of Jas K............556
  James K. of J. K............1438
  James K. of John............158
  James K. of E. C............1488
  James M............58
  James M. of A. J............834
  James M. Capt............2456
  James M. of H. M............738
  James M. of Jas............1800
  James M. of Thos............702
  James S............2066
  James T............872
  James W............186
  Rev James............? g
  Jane of Chas............230
  Jane of John............84
  Jane of T. G............794
  Jane (Agnes)............342
  Jane (Durrett)............110
  Jane (Sullivant)............254
  Jennie............2186
  John of Ireland............10
  John of the Forest............12
  John Ch. Justice............50
  John of John
    82, 156, 638, 544, 1244, 1508, 17
  John of Jas. M............196
  John of Ed C............576
  John of Jas. K............552
  John of Geo............328
  John of H. M............*68 f*, 748
  John of C. S............1824
  John of J. L............2204
  John of R. M............1730
  John of Thos............500, 178
  John A............732
  John B............2424
  John C............262
  John H............1400, 2462
  John J. of Hum............296
  John J. of Wm............226
  John L............876
  John N............1288
  John R............1482, 788
  John J. Col............2434
  John T............1962, 1964
  Josephine............2232
  Judith (Brooke)............60
  Judith B. (Harvey)............818
  Judith............1792, 2550
  Julia S.*(Breckinridge)............2430

THE MARSHALL FAMILY. 405

INDEX.

Marshall, Julianna (Bland)......632
Kate (Sanford).................2428
Kate of W. S..................2452
Kate C........................882
Kate T........................1372
Katherine.....................2554
Kitty.........................2456
Lelia P.......................1478
Letitia (Booth)...............1088
Letitia L.....................2556
Lewis of C. T.................2460
Lily T. (Green)............... 832
Lily..........................1306
Lindsay.......................1974
Lizzie (Smith)................15
Lizzie of George..............1118
Lizzie (Ambler)...............1710
Lizzie (Waller)...............686
Logan M.......................1724
Louis Dr......................70
Louis of E. C..........906, 2230
Louis C.......................896
Louis H. Capt.................894
Louis J.......................2426
Louis of R. M.................1728
Louis of Wm...................96
Lucy of Geo...................332
Lucy of Jas...................1790
Lucy (Ambler)............16 e, 66
Lucy (Booker).................114
Lucy (Duval)..................356
Lucy (Bentley)................692
Lucy (Casey)..................642
Lucy (Burnley)................224
Lucy (Lee).................... 1436
Lucy (Marshall)..........178, 246
Lucy (Marshall)..........192, 232
Lucy A. (Coleman).............184
Lucy B........................792
Lucy M 1817
Lucy S........................2070
Lucy S. (Marshall)......706, 810
Lucy E. (Richmond)............2484
Lucy P. (McKnight)............656
Lucy P. (Morris)..............710
Mae...........................2176
Margaret......................2084
Margaret L. (Smith)......480, 510
Margaret L. (Hite)............1266
Margaret L. (Duer)............1310
Margaret P. (Bradford)........1072
Maria of C. A.................682
Maria (Paxton)................244
Maria (Powell)................338
Maria J. (Andrews)............814
Maria L.......................786
Maria N.......................1280

Marshall, Maria W..........558, 1474
Marion L......................1340
Markham.......................19
Marie L. (Allin)..............1434
Marie L. (Marshall)...636, 1100
Martin P................182, 234
Martin P. of C. C............. 816
Martin P. of M. P.............2074
Martin P. of R. M.......716, 1720
Martin P. Wm..................344
Martin........................2548
Martin of T. A................1062
Martin of Wm............102, 354
Mary (Marshall)..........589, 1322
Mary of Humphrey..............2440
Mary of Thos..................700
Mary (Archer).................504
Mary (Etherton)...............358
Mary (Ballou)............334, 404
Mary (Harvie).................154
Mary (McClanahan).............20
Mary (Marshall)...........54, 88
Mary (Whittington)............90
Mary A. (Coleman).............560
Mary A. (Doniphan)............360
Mary A. (Douthat).............514
Mary A. (Robinson)............106
Mary B. (Coppie)..............1092
Mary C. of John...............1510
Mary K. (Green),..............180
Mary Jane.....................196 j
Mary L. of J. L...............1962
Mary L. of E. C...............578
Mary L. of E. C...............2228
Mary M. of J. E...............1406
Mary M. of Jas................1802
Mary M. of John...............638
Mary M. (Marshall).......734, 548
Mary M. (Mitchell)............880
Mary M. of R. M...............718
Mary M. (Reeves)..............2480
Mary P. (Foree)...............808
Mary R........................2086
Mary W. (Douthat).............550
Mary W. of M. P...............658
Mary W. B. (Yates)............1268
Matilda (Powell)..............336
Matilda (Young)...............1086
Matilda P. (Bradford).........1072
Matilda.......................2548
Mattie M......................1076
Mildred P.....................1344
Minnie G. (Alexander).........2208
Myron B.......................1264
Nancy (Daviess)...............78
Nancy (Ballow)................350
Nancy, of John................86

THE MARSHALL FAMILY.

INDEX.

Marshall, Nanette (Turner).....1028
Nannie (Norton) 564
Nannie, of Thomas 1774
Dr. Nat. B..................554
Nellie N. (McAfee) 2438
Dr. Nic. T..................364
Norman T....................1504
Oscar S.....................2 h
Paulina (Morris) 346
Paxton......................690
Peggy (Smellan).............22
Philip T....................1404
Phœbe A., of M. P...........666
Randolph....................1346
Reb. F. (Nash)..............1276
Reb. C...............1264, 1506
Reb. P. (Douthat)......1328, 1330
Reb. P. (Marshall)......516, 580
Reb. P. (Stribling).........574
Richard C............1264, 1544
Richard S.............588, 1322
Richard.....................1430
Robert, of R. M.............714
Robert D....................1322
Robert A....................790
Robert M., of James ..192, 1798
Robert M., of John 728
Robert M., of M. P..........660
Robert M., of R. M..........1726
Robert L., of Charles.......2098
Robert P....................1070
Robert T..............830, 1708
Rev. Robert ....*2 g*
Roberta.....................824
St. Julien..................1264
Sallie (Wilkes) 694
Sallie E....................1426
Samuel, of A. K.............252
Dr. Samuel..................864
Samuel T....................1516
Samuel W.............1816, 1264
Rev. Samuel V.............*2 g*
Sarah (Lovell)..............13
Sarah D.....................1712
Smedes......................2452
Sophia G....................1274
Susan (Ambler) 202
Susan (McClung).............72
Susan (Massie)..............664
Susan (Skenker).............240
Susan A. (Marshall) 2478
Susan A.....................1536
Susan B.....................1804
Susan L. (Armistead)........1270
Susan L.....................1264
Susan M. (Betts) 812
Susanna (Masterson).........108

Marshall, Susie, of Humphrey..2440
Symmes......................2424
Theo........................2080
T. H........................1306
Thornton F..................368
Thomas, of Westmoreland....11
Thomas, Col.................16
Thomas, Capt................56
Thomas, Gen.................176
Thomas, of C. A.............680
Thomas, of F. L.............1272
Thomas, of H. M.............736
Thomas, of James............190
Thomas, of J. K.............562
Thomas, of John.............150
Thomas, Col, of Thos........512
Thomas, of Martin...........2552
Thomas, of Thos......1312, 1542
Thomas, of R. M.............712
Thomas, of Samuel...........2172
Thomas, of William !........100
Thomas, of H. M.......--590, 734
Thomas A., Judge............298
Thomas A., of Martin........366
Thomas A., of T. A..........2458
Thomas A, of T. A....1018, 1094
Thomas A., of C. T..........2460
Thomas F., of Louis.........256
Thomas C....................2482
Thomas G....................222
Thomas J., of J. C..........2486
Virg. C.....................1520
Walton H....................1286
William, Rev................18
William, of John............724
William, of Thos............62
William, of Wm........98, 220
Dr. William.................340
William, of H. M............744
William, of J. A............522
William A...................2190
William B...................822
William C., of T. A.........1084
William C., of J. A.........1336
William C., of Martin.......362
William C., of W. C.........1368
William C.............1246, 2558
William F...................1968
William L.............258, 2072
William L., Capt............688
William H., of C. M.........2432
W. Smedes...................2452
Col. *Wm., of Mecklenburg..11 g, h, i*
Wm. J., of Henderson......*11 i*
William, of Ireland.......*2 h*
William, of Va.,..........*10*
Yelverton...................1338

THE MARSHALL FAMILY. 407

INDEX.

Mason, Anna (Ambler) ...842
   Claudia ...1448
   Hatley N ...1448
   James M. ...*842*
   John ...2112
   Rev. J. K ...1448
   Landon ...2112
   Lucy J ...1448
   Lucy ...2112
   Randolph ...2112
Massie, Alice ...1746
   Col. Jas. W. and family ...*68 i*
   Nathaniel ...664
Masterson, Chas ...108
Maupin, Agnes M ...1252
   Chapman ...1252
   Margaret L ...1252
   R. W ...1256
   Sallie W ...1252
Maury, Ann T. (Hite) ...*196 g, 1266*
Mayo, Ann²(Carrington) ...*160 c*
Meade, Philip ...1880
Meng, Chas ...*2168 h*
Merriwether, J (Lewis) ...*150 m*
   Lucy (Lewis) ...*150 n*
   Nicholas ...*150 m*
   Thomas ...*150 o*
Metcalfe, *A. S. (Taylor)* ...*660 g*
   Eli ...*64 h*
   Elizabeth (Pickett) ...*64 e*
   Fannie (Harbeson) ...64 i, 2156
   Hiram ...*64 i*
   Maria (Pogue) ...*64 i*
   Sabina (Bruce) ...*64 i*
Michie, Dr. Theo. A ...604, 2650 a
Middleton, Jose ...2526
   Thos ...2522
   William ...2524
Miles, Ellen (Marshall) ...1018
Miller, *Hannah (Moffett)* ...*68 q*
   James ...*68 q*
   Rev. John and family ...*68 i*
   Letitia (Marshall) ...366
   Margt. (Breckinridge) ...*70 i*
   Mary (Burnley) ...798
Milton, (Taylor) ...*56 h*
Minor, Prof. J. B ...618
   John B ...1628
   Mattie ...1624
   Nannie C ...1630
   Raleigh C ...1630
   Susan ...1626
Mitchell, Chas ...2216
   Chas. W ...880
   Chas S. ...*176 a*
   Edward ...2218
   Jas. T ...2212

Mitchell, *James (1714)* ...*68 m*
   Kate ...2220
   Lydia (Pogue) ...*64 j*
   Thos. W ...2214
Moffet family ...*68 q*
   Margt. (McDowell) ...*68 g*
Monceur family ...*50 n*
Monfort, Dr. J. G ...*2 q*
Monroe, Hen. (Marshall) ...2460
Montgomery, Anna (Durrett) ..1732
   Ann (Lewis) ...*248 b*
   R. H ...*162 h*
   Robt ...*1012 e*
Monteer, Phœbe (Dye) ...*660 d*
Moore, *Andrew and family* ...*680*
   Harriet L. (Coleman) ...*180 c e*
   Mary A. (Marshall) ...1008
   Morgan, Cal. C ...*960 c*
   Family ...*960 c*
   Henrietta H. (Duke) ...960
   Susanna ...*56 c e*
Morford, E. (Pickett) ...*64 h*
Morris, Anna ...1810
   Family. ...*58 c*
   G ...346
   Grace ...1808
   Henry ...1808
   Hester (Marshall) ...58
   Lucy ...1814
   Dr. Robt ...710
   Robt ...1808
   Robt ...*58 c*
   Susan ...1812
Morrison, Mrs ...312
Morsell, Rev. J ...*1226*
Morson, *Alex* ...*1428 b*
   Alice (Robinson) ...1600
   Claudia H ...1428
   Family ...*1428 b*
   J. B ...1428
   Jas. M. ...*1428 b*
   Sallie M ...1428
   Thos. S ...1428
Morton, Hannah (Duke) ...284
Murat, Achille ...*150 i*
Murrell (Brockenbrough) ...*162 d*
Murry S. (Lewis) ...*248 c*
Myers, Susan (Marshall) ...362
Nash, C. R ...1276
   Reb. C ...1276
Neal, John ...348
Neil *family* ...*884 b*
   Jane M. (Dodge) ...2222
   Lucy (Williams) ...2224
   Robt. E ...884
Nelson, Agnes H ...1254
   Prof. Alex ...*68 o*

THE MARSHALL FAMILY.

INDEX.

Nelson, Alex. T................1254
  Ann (Brockenbrough).........162 k
  Dr. Benj. and family.........162 j
  George E......................1254
  Mildred B.....................1254
  Thos..........................160 c
Newton, Bessie..................1532
  Ed. M.........................1530
  Jacq. A.......................1534
  Jas. K........................1524
  Margt. (Forman)...............660 j
  Mary W........................1526
  Robt. P.......................1528
  Willoughby.....................586
  Hon. Willoughby and family.162 e
Nicholas family..........50 o, 150 h o
  Robt. C........................50 o
  Mary L. (Veech)...............1430
Noel, Aug. W. (Marshall)........788
  Julia (Brooke).................764
Norris, Norman..................2628
Norton, Claudia.................1448
  Courtenay.....................1460
  Courtenay (Lewis).............150 h
  Rev. Geo. D. D.................564
  Geo. H.........................564
  Hatley........................1458
  Jas. K........................1452
  John (immigrant)...............564
  John H.........................50 n
  Maria G.......................1450
  Nannie B......................1456
  Thos. M.......................1454
Oakhill..........................50 b
Oliver, Sarah (Taliaferro).....102 g
Osborne, Ida (Pickett)..........64 g
Overall, D. (Marshall)..........344
Owsley, Ann (Craig)............180 i
Page, Dora (Burwell)............774
  Gov. John.....................158 c
  Lucy (Burwell)................158 e
  Maria.........................1890
  Mary (Newton).................162 f
Parcels, Helen (Marshall).......2452
Parker, Eleanor (Butler)........648
  W. S.........................2168 b
Parkhill, Chas..................70 h
Parks, Margt. (Alexander).......72
Parsons, Col. Lewis............180 i
Patrick, Geo. S................1380
  Jacq..........................1382
  Dr. Spicer....................534
  Susan (Poindexter)...........1380
  Wm. H.........................1384
Patton, (Preston)...............70
Paxton, A. M....................858
  Alex........................244 l, o

Paxton, Anna M..................2166
  Arch..........................244 l
  Aurelia.......................244 l
  Betsy (Houston)...............244 m
  Elisha, and family............244 q
  Gen. E. F................2018, 244 q
  Family........................244 k
  Hannah (Caruthers)............244 n
  Hugh..........................244 l
  Isabella (Lyle)...............244 m
  Isabella (Alexander)..........244 r
  James....................70 d, e, 244 m
  James A........72 d, e, 180 e, 244
  Maj. Jas. and family..........244 p
  Dr. James.....................244 r
  Rev Dr. John D................244 r
  John (1721)...................244 k
  Jonn.........................244 k l
  Jordan........................244 p
  Jos.....................244 l, m, n, r
  Lydia (Blackburn)..A..........2164
  Margaret P. (Houston).........244 p
  Margaret (Baldwin)............244 l
  Mary E (Barclay)..............244 o
  Mary (Harbeson)...............856
  Mary (Greenlee)...........244 q, 68 l
  Phœbe A. (Marshall).....188, 860
  Phœbe M......................2170
  Phœbe (Love)..................244 l
  Phœbe (McClung)................44 o
  Polly (1784)..................244 l
  Thomas (1720)..............244 r, t, u
  Tillie (Tebbs)...............2168
  William (1732)................244 h
  William, and family...........244 m
  William M.....................862
Payne, Bessie W. (Jones).......1294
  Charlotte (Duke)..............940
  Duval...................1014 d, 2424 b
  Eliz. B. (Langhorne)..........1012
  Rice, W.......................1294
Pelham, Henry...................988
Pembroke, Earl of................2 a
Penn, A. (Marshall).............100
  John B.......................2334
Pepper, Fanny (Allen)...........920
Perrie, E. S. (Forman)..........660 l
Perrine, Julia (Pickett).......64 g
Perry, Jenet (Marshall)........2432
  Joseph........................70 b
Peyton, John...................150 i
  Reb. (Marshall)...............160
Philips, C. T.................2056
  M. T.........................2054
Phister, Sarah P. (Duke).......970
Pickett, Ann (Brooke)...........64
  Ben. O........................64 g

THE MARSHALL FAMILY. 409

INDEX.

Pickett, Betsy (Scott) ....64 c
  Caro. (Currie)..........64 d, 282
  Chas. E. (1822)..............64 k
  Cornelia ....64 g
  Darwin.........................64 h
  Family ....64 b
  Geo. B.........................64 d
  Gen. Geo. E...................64 e
  Jas. C. (1793)................64 f
  Capt. Jas. F..................64 j
  Jas. S.........................64 e
  Jas. T.........................64 k
  John (1744)...................64 b
  Col. John...................64 e, f
  John ....64 g, k
  J. Desha (1820)...............64 f
  Judith (Slaughter)............64 b
  Lillie (Johnston).............64 c
  Lucy (Marshall)................64
  Margaret C....................64 g
  Martin ....64 b
  Mary Ann (Marshall)..........18
  Mary E. (Wormley)............64 k
  Mary O. (Jackson)............64 j
  Mary R. (Forman).......64 h, 660 l
  Mildred (Clarkson)......64 b, 152
  Pattie.......................64 e, j
  Reubin........................64 b
  Robert ....64 e
  Sallie M. (Metcalfe)..........64 h
  Sabie (Smith) 44
  Steptoe ....64 d
  Thos. J....................64 f, 68 e
  Dr. Thos. E...................64 g
  William ....64 b, e, f, h, j
Pitcher, J. S.................102 g
Pocahontas..............16 w, 150 i j
Poague, family..................64 j
Poindexter, Alice (Marshall)...738
  Family 738
  Henry 1380
  Mary M 1380
  Spicer.......................1380
Pollard..........................78
  John.........................162 j
Pope, Ann (Washington).......150 o
Porter, E. E.................1108
  Peter B......................70 g
Posthlewaite, M. (Buford)......973
Powell, Gertrude 616
  J..............................330
  L. D....,...................1890
  L. (Marshall) 336
  Louis 1674
  M. L.........................1674
Power, Sus. (Taliaferro).....102 d
Powers, Eliza M..............2518

Powers, Margaret H............2520
  Mary M 2514
  Susan D 2516
Preston, family...........68 h, 70 f
Price, Alf....................162 i
  Eliza (Price)................298
Putnam, John..................150 h
Quarles, B. (Marshall) 2066
Ramsey, E. (Taliaferro).......102 f
Randolph, A. C...............1882
  Ann C. (Barton).............2018
  Edgar F.....................1754
  Edmund........................16 q
  Edward.......................668 b
  Elizabeth 1748
  Ephraim.....................668 c
  Family ....16 p, 668
  Gabriel (Brockenbrough)...162 h
  Henry.........................16 q
  Isham.........................16 p
  Jas. F......................1748
  James ....668 d
  Sir John......................16 q
  John, of Roanoke..............16 p
  Joseph ....668 b
  Legend ....16 n
  Lewis........................668 c
  Lucy A......................1752
  Mary (Lewis)................150 l
  Mary I. (Keith) ....16 n, p
  Peyton........................16 q
  Richard, of Curls.............16 p
  Gov. Theo. F.................668
  Theo. F.....................1748
  Thos., of Tuckahoe ......16 p, w
  Thos. M.....................1750
  William, of Turkey Island...16 p
  Raworth, Olive (Smedes)...2464
  Rawson, Mary (Waller).......682
  Read, Mildred (Warner).....150 o
  Sarah (Green)...............150 h
  Reader, Thos A..............1226
Reading, Chas. L.............1394
  Joseph 1394
  Katie M. (Marshall).........1084
  Russell......................1156
  Sarah A 1956
  Sarah 1394
  William................414, 1394
Reaney, Belle (Marshall).......570
Reid, Agnes (Alexander).......72 d
  Family ....68 d o, 296
  Sarah (Alexander)...........72 e
Reeves, Emily M.............2480
  Geo. W......................2480
  Katie 2480
  Susan A.....................2480

THE MARSHALL FAMILY.

INDEX.

Reynolds, L. M..... 2178
  Maria (Ward).... *1054*
Rice, N. L. Dr..... *68 k*
Richards, F. (Green)..... *180 k*
Richmond, Fannie D..... 2484
  Hattie..... 2484
  Wm..... 2484
Ricketts, Rev. R. S..... *64 h*
Riddell, M. J. (Bush)..... *858 d*
Ridgley, Reb. (Warfield)..... *184 d*
Rittenhouse, E. (Barton)..... *802*
Roane, (Brockenbrough)..... *162 c k*
Robb, Ann (E. Marshall)..... 238
  Sarah (Tyler)..... *1246*
Roberts, Edwin..... 2312
  Theresa (Marshall)..... 1306
Robertson, (Harrison)..... 518
Robinson, Agnes C..... 1612
  Alex. L..... 1178
  Dr. A. M..... 454
  Ben. N..... 1902
  Cary..... 1604
  Chas. N..... 1184
  Judge Conway..... 614
  Conway..... 1608
  Eliz. M..... 1602
  Family..... *20*
  Gaward..... 448
  Harrison..... 1352
  Jacq..... 1350
  James..... 390
  Jas. T..... 1902
  John..... 126, 446, 1186
  Leigh..... *1428 b*, 1600
  Louis M..... 456
  Louisa..... 1182
  Lucy C..... 1188
  Dr. L. H..... *162 j*
  Max..... 452
  Robert..... 1348
  Susan..... 1610, 394
  Thomas..... 106
  Warner..... 392
  William..... 388, 450, 1180, 1606
Rochester..... *68 g*
Rogers, Ann (McIlhany)..... *1206*
Rolfe, John..... *16 w*
Roloson, R. W..... 2444
Ross, Col. John..... *68 p*
Rossiter, C. E. (Smith)..... 1212
Royall, Geo..... 1000
  Helen M. (Cooke)..... 1004
  John..... 290, 998
  Mary A. McMurran)..... 1002
  Wm. I..... 1006
Ruffin, Col. F. G..... 530
Russell, Bessie (Marshall)..... 1094

Russell, Mary G. (Jones)..... 2028
Sanford, C. M..... 2428
  John..... 2428
  Julia B..... 2428
Saterwhite, T. P..... *70 h*
Sayle, Alice..... 2593
  Ben. B..... 2584
  D. L..... 1128
  Durrett..... 2588, 2608
  Ervin..... 2594
  Jennie..... 2590
  John..... 2596
  Lucy..... 2592
  Medora..... 2612
  Melissa..... 2610
  Minnie..... 2614
  Robt..... 2582
  Towns..... 2586
  William..... 2580
Sayre, J. (Randolph)..... 1748
Scott, Gov. Chas..... *1012 c*
  Family..... *64 c d*
  Judge John..... *64 d*
  Mary (Pickett)..... *64 h*
Scudder family..... *660 b*
Seabrooke, J. (Forman)..... *660 b*
Selden, Robt..... *150 i*
Semmes, T. M. and family..... *162 e*
Semple, Gen..... 428
Shackelford, *Lucy C. (Brockenbrough)*..... *162 l*
  Mary (Marshall)..... 196
  Vincent..... *162 k*
Sharp, J. (Ambler)..... 850
  J. (Burwell)..... 1894
  William..... *850*
Shelby, S. (McDowell)..... *68 h*
Sherrard, J. (Alexander)..... *2208*
Shelton, Anna (Marshall)..... 816
Sheppard, M. E. (Harbeson)..... 2158
Shield, C. H..... 2006, 2008
  Geo. N..... 2008
Shoemaker, R. A..... 2330
  Sarah A..... 2330
Skenker Thos..... 240
Slaughter family..... *64 b*
Slevin, Mary (Buford)..... 974
Sloan M. F..... 2058
  W. T..... 2058
Smedes, Alice M..... 2472
  Anna (Vosberg)..... 2468
  Edward..... 2464
  Ellen (Vosberg)..... 2470
  John M..... 2474
  Olive..... 2464
  Thos..... 2464
  Susie (Barnett)..... 2466

THE MARSHALL FAMILY. 411

INDEX.

Smedes, Wm. C............2464, 2476
Smellan.................................22
Smith, Abram.....................68 p
  Agatha (Marshall).............70
  Agnes J.............................1228
  Alice..................................1236
  Alice (Strong)....................1210
  Ann (Florence)....................42
  Aug.....................14, 38, 1200
  Col. Aug..........................196 g
  Betsy (Fry).....................180 m
  Carrie...............................1234
  Chilton H.........................1204
  Claudia M. (Cheslee).........1226
  Claudia. W. L. (Chesley).....1226
  Courtland H.....................1212
  Dr. D. B............................1216
  Edward..............................496
  Eleanor (Vass)....................470
  Eliza A. (Bowman).............484
  Eliza................................2342
  Eliza A. (Brockenbrough)...162 k
  Elizabeth (Brown)................40
  Elizabeth (Soward).............364
  Emily S.............................488
  Family........................32, 196 j
  Frank L.....................472, 1208
  Gladys.............................1200
  Gen. Green C......................954
  G. C., jr...........................2350
  Harry...............................1216
  Harriet, E. B......................476
  Harry B...........................1230
  Rev. H. M.........................670
  Horace.............................1860
  Jacq................................1200
  James.................................44
  Jane S.............................1208
  Jane (Madison)................228 e
  Gen. John.......................196 g
  John...............15, 36, 1140, 1200
  John, A. W........................142
  John Thos..................480, 510
  J. D.................................2346
  Joe....................................30
  Julia (James).....................494
  Julien H............................478
  Lawrence.........................502 e
  Lela................................1860
  Lena...............................2348
  Lucy M...........................1756
  Margaret V.......................1202
  Margaret L. (Forsyth).......1224
  Margaret (Forman)...........660 d
  Maria L. (Goodwin)..........1218
  Marshall, J................492, 1232
  Mary S..............................474

Smith, Mary J....................1206
  Mary (Smith)..................1216
  Mary B...........................2344
  Mary R...........................1758
  Mary C. (Breckinridge)......70 g
  Mathew.............................34
  Nancy (Pickett)................64 j
  Reb. B. (Marshall).............196
  Richard H.......................1378
  Robert W...................1220, 482
  Sarah P...........................1200
  Sarah V. (Dangerfield).....1214
  Sarah (Brockenbrough)...162 k
  Stover C...........................486
  Susanna.............................46
  Susan (Preston).................70 k
  Thos.......................32, 56 a, b
  Thos. M................140, 144, 1222
  Thos. S............................490
  Treadwell.......................1860
  William.............................37
Smoot, K M. (Jones)..........1298
Snowden.
  Rachel (Randolph)..........668 c
  Sarah R. (Marshall)..........826
Sooter, Ada (Marshall)........352
Soward, Anna (Forman).....660 l
  Col. Alf...................102 e, 364
  Family...........................364
  Elizabeth (Marshall)........364
  Gen. Richard..........102 e, 364
Speed, Thos. and family.....180 l
Spottswood, Mrs..............150 h
Stanley, N. C. (Jones).......1302
Stanton, Az. (Forman).......660 h
Starling, family................254 f
  Lucy T. McDowell............68 g
  Mary (Payne)..................150 g
  Sarah (Sullivant)............254 b
  Samuel M.......................150 g
  William...................68 f, 258 f
Steele, John A...................958
  John..............................70 h
  Mary D..........................2360
  Rachel (Randolph).........668 e
  William..........................72 d
Stevens, John..................1870
Stevenson, Hon. A. E........180 j
  S. C. (Colston)................608
  Eben............................1662
  Mary C. (Marshall)..........864
Stewart, Jennie................2088
  W. H..............................824
Stith, Wm.......................16 q
Stockdell, A. (Taliaferro)...102 f
Stone, Helen (Higgason)....914
Strader, Humphrey..........2436

INDEX.

Strader, J. B................................2436
    Jessie...2436
Strahan, Caro. (Warner)........2326
    David..2324
    Rev. F. G....................................946
    Jas. D..2328
    Mary (Warren)......................2322
Street, Mary B. (Wellford).......722 d
Stribling, Carrie M................2150
    Claudia B..................................1490
    Eliza J..1500
    Family.....................................64 b, c
    Gray C......................................1498
    Henry C............................1494, 574
    Jas. K...1496
    Mary D......................................1324
    Mildred P. (Marshall)..........552
    Robt. C......................................2152
    Robt. M.....................................1492
    Dr. R. M....................................150 e
    Col. R. M........................1324, 854
    Dr. William............................152 d
Stringer, Theresa (Jones)........800
Stringfellow, family....................64 b
Strong, Alice...........................1210
    Anne..1210
    Frank L.....................................1210
    Wm. E.......................................1210
Strongbow..2 d
Strother, family.........................228 b
    Jane (Lewis).........................248 b
    William...................................1378
Stuart, Eliz. (Paxton)............244 m
    Mary..72 d
    Robert.......................................72 d
Sullivant, *family*..................*254 b*
    Jane (Neil)..................................884
    Joseph.....................................254 e
    Lucas.......................................254 b
    Michael...................63 g, 254 b, d
    William S..................................254
Summers, *Ann (Metcalfe)........64 i*
    Marian (Colston)...................602
Sutherline, Jane E. (Smith)...1208
Swallow, Anna (Woolfolk)......916
Tabb, E. M. (Wellford)...........722 d
Taft, Nellie (Duke)....................964
Taliaferro, Agnes M..............1256
    Gen. A. G....................*102 g*, 502
    Ann..502 e
    Ben (1728)..............................102 h
    Charles (1737)........502 e, 103 h
    Eleanor W..............................1254
    Elizabeth................................502 h
    Family....................102 d, 502 e
    Frank......................................502 e
    Geo. C. (1792)........................102 e

Taliaferro, *James (1746).........102 f*
    James.......................................102 g
    John (immigrant)................502 e
    John (1687)...........................102 d
    John C. (1784).......................102 e
    John (1753)............................102 f
    Col. John, and family..........102 f
    Lawrence (1721).......502 e, 102 d
    Lawrence W. (1800)..............102 f
    Leah S......................................1250
    Lucy M. (Buckner)..............102 e
    Lucy (Hunter).......................102 f
    Lucy (Lewis).........................150 m
    Margaret L............................1252
    Marshall (1809)....................102 f
    Martha (1749).......................102 f
    Mary A...................................1248
    Mary W. (1798)........364, 102 e
    Mat. A. (Soward).................102 e
    Matilda B. (Marshall)..........102
    Nicholas (1757)....................102 d
    Nicholas (1806)....................102 f
    Peter (1740).........................102 h
    Philip.............................*102 f, 502 e*
    Rev. Philip.............................102 g
    Richard (immigrant)..........102 d
    Richard (1700).........502 e, 102 h
    Richard (1731).....................102 h
    Robert (1635).......................502 e
    Sarah (Dangerfield)............102 d
    Thomas...................................102 g
    Wm. A....................................1258
    William (1726)....................102 d
    Dr. Wm. T. (1795).....102 f, 502 e
    Gen. W. B................502 e, 102 g
    Zachariah..........502 e, 102 h, i
Tarleton, *Isabel (Miles)..........1018*
Tate, John C.............................1670
    Nancy (Duerson)....................940
    Robert......................................72 d
Taylor, *Ann (Cary)............1012 b*
    Alf...1904
    Alice M....................................1912
    Anna K. (Royall)....................290
    Arch, and *family.................150 j*
    Ashby......................................1908
    Col. Bennett............................606
    Bessie H. (Gill).......................990
    Bettie (Duke)..........................276
    Burnley..................................1926
    Chas.......................................1900
    Charlotte.................................992
    Clarence W............................1936
    Edmonia (Levy)....................63 k
    Edw'd C.................................1582
    Ed. K.......................................1934
    Elizabeth................................1902

THE MARSHALL FAMILY.

INDEX.

Taylor, Elizabeth (Scott)..........64 d
  Emily M. (Taylor)............1918
  Family...............660 h, 56 h
  Fannie 1952
  Florinda (Jones).........56 h, 804
  Gar. B.......................1940
  Geo. K 76, 782, 1948
  Georgeanna 294
  Griffin... ....56 h
  Harrison................288, 994
  Hattie A.....................1910
  Isabel D.....................1900
  James M................1950, 778
  Jas. W.......................1918
  Jane (Marshall)...............654
  Jane B.......................1584
  John D........................56 h
  John D........................996
  John J.......................1942
  John R..............1580, 780, 1918
  Joseph C.....................1900
  Lewis R......................1578
  Maria R. (Marshall)...........238
  Mary (Smith).................492
  Mary (Pelham)................988
  Mary D.......................1924
  Mary A.......................1946
  Maud E.......................1918
  Nannie C.....................1932
  Pattie J.....................1574
  Percy A......................1930
  Raleigh C....................1576
  Reb. L. (Marshall).....1708, 1944
  R. Ashby.....................1908
  Robt. and family.............660 f
  R. T.........................1920
  Roberta B....................1922
  S. R.........................1246
  Sally...................292, 1928
  Susan (Weller)................68 k
  Sue (Brent).................2424 b
  Thos.........................1954
  Thos. B.......................68 k
  Virg. E. (Marshall)...........582
  Virg. M......................1918
  Walter M.....................1900
  Warren P.....................1914
  Wm. M........................1916
  W. D....................1938, 218
  Wirt E.......................1906
  Col. Wm. and family..........68 j
  William of Cal...............68 k
Tebbs, A. S....................2168
  Alice A. (Forman)............660 l
  Family......................2168 b
  Laura G......................2168
  Mamie........................2168

Terrell family..................150 g
Thayer W. B....................1672
Thomas, Alice (Brockenbrough) 162 d
  Alice W......................1592
  Anna G. (Duval)..............1594
  Annis (Hackett)..............1166
  Annie C......................1590
  Basil G......................1586
  Douglas H....................1592
  Gov. Francis..................68 i
  Howard B.....................1588
  John G.......................1598
  John Hanson.............610, 164
  John H.................1588, 1592
  John M.......................1598
  Mary M.......................1590
  Mary N. (Marshall)............506
  Mary R. (Carroll)............1596
  Perry.........................64 i
  Raleigh C....................1590
  Reginald C...................1590
Thompson, Amy 2158
  Geo. C........................68 f
  L............................2054
Thornton, Betsy (Taliaferro)...102 g
  Cath. (Marshall)..............190
  Mary ....102 d
Throckmorton, Harriet (Talia-
  ferro)................102 f, 502 e
  Jane (Forman)................660 b
  Joseph ....660 b
  Thos.........................150 j
Tilford, Robt.................102 e
Todd, Barbara.................2292
  Eliza (Butter)...............648
  Robt.........................180 i
  Thos.........................928
Tompkins, Chris................70 b
Tonsey, V. (Bush).............858 c
Townsend, R. S...............2620
Tracy, Rose (Marshall).........354
  Thos. E.....................1686
Triplett, Illa (Green).........650
True, Eliza...................2454
  Ellen 2454
  John W......................2454
  Marshall 2454
Turner, Eliza (Marshall)......1332
  Lucy E.......................1796
  Marshall.....................2490
  Mary E. (Marshall)............876
Tyler, Lucy (Newton)..........162 f
  Sadie R. (Marshall)..........1246
Utterback, Ad. (Marshall)....2486
Valmey, Duchess of............170
Vance, Sam'l..................1144
Vardeman, O. (Marshall)........94

THE MARSHALL FAMILY.

INDEX.

Vass, J. C.....470
Veech, Lizzie (Marshall).....1430
  Richard.....1430
Venable family.....68 p
  Prof. C. P. and family.....68 j
Vossburg, Capt.....2468, 2470
  Wm. S.....2470
Waddell, Susie (Duke).....2300
Wade, Rev. A.....536
  Dr. Carter.....1390
  Ellen H.....1388
  Wm. H.....1392
Walker, C. S.....1104
  Chas.....70 b
  Mary E. (Pickett).....64 j
  Mary (Lewis).....150 n
  Peachy (Fry).....180 l
  Sarah (Paxton).....244 r
Wall, Fanny M.....84
  Geo. W.....84
  Samuel G.....84
  W. K.....316
Wallace, Caleb.....68 d, h
  Samuel.....70 b
Waller, Edward.....686
  Family.....686
  Henry.....1776
  Henry.....70 b, 686, 1012 d
  Rev. Maurice.....686
  Phœbe F.....1778
  Sarah B.....1780
  Sus. L. (Marshall).....1316
  Sus. P.....686
  W. S.....686
Ware, Lizzie (Woolfolk).....916
Warfield, family.....184 d
Warner, Cath. (Lewis).....150 g
  Elizabeth (Lewis).....150 g
  Mildred (Washington).....150 o
Warren, Isaac.....2326
  Samuel.....2322
Warrington, M. (Burwell).....1890
Warwick, C. McDowell.....68 j
Washington, Bettie (Lewis).....150 h, i
  Family.....150 h, o
  Sallie (Maupin).....1250, 1252
Waters, Lizzie (Green).....180 j
Watkins, Laura W. (Andrews).....2052
  M. W.....814
Watson, Ann B. (Buford).....280 b
  Jas L.....68 m
  John.....280 b
Watts, Margaret (Jones).....228 b,d
Weaver (Smith).....30
Wedderbane. B. (Taliaferro).....102 g
Wellford, family.....722 b, c, d
  Mary A. (Marshall).....722

Weller, John B. and family.....68 k
West, Bettie (Forman).....660 j
West, Sarah (Brockenbrough).....162 g
Whetcroft, family.....176 d
  Julianna (Marshall).....176
White, Elvira C. (Marshall).....894
  Prof. Jas.....68 p
  Lizzie (Paxton).....244 q
  Mary (Morris).....58 c
Whiteridge, Alice L. (Thomas).....1592
Whiting (Washington).....150 p
Whittington, Ann.....308
  Charlotte (Cummins).....302
  Elizabeth.....306
  Isaac.....310
  Kate (Dearing).....308
  Thomas.....90
Wilkes, Ed.....694
Williams, Alf. B.....1548
  Blanche (Burnley).....796
  Bettie (Marshall).....712
  Ed. D.....1550
  Ethel V.....1548
  G. W.....660 j
  Lucy (Green).....180 j
  Robert E.....2224
  R. A.....594
  Ros. B.....1552
  Capt W. W.....2224
Williamson, Rob. (Newton).....162 f
Willis, Ann M. (Ambler).....852
  Ann (Green).....150 p. h
  Ann R. (Burwell).....158 d
  Byrd, and family.....150 h
  Family.....852
  Harry.....150 p
  Maria.....158
  Thomas.....852
Wilson, Cath. (Marshall).....1264
  Dan. M.....2160
  Harbeson.....2160
  Mamie.....2160
Wiltshire, Geo. P.....2450
  Lucy B.....2450
Winchester, family.....176 d
Windsor C. (Franklin).....1258
Winn (Smith).....34
Winston, M. C. (Marshall).....62
  Jennie (Cooke).....1878
  Col. John H.....2168 b
  Sattie E. (Taylor).....780
Withers, Samuel.....1634
Wolffe. T. B. and family.....68 j
Wood, Ann (Chambers).....1668
  Andrew.....1668
  Dolly (Forman).....660 c
  Hattie S. (Taylor).....660 g

INDEX.

Wood, *Mag.* (*McDowell*) .... *68 d*
   Rebecca (Marshall) 262
Woodson, J. (*Lewis*) .... *150 m*
Woodward, Phil .... *162 k*
Woolfolk, Ada S 2266
   Alex. M 2252, 916, 2274
   Anna S 2270
   Carrie M 2276
   Chas. E 018
   Clinton S 2272
   Eva 2260
   Horace 2254
   Julia (Larabie) 2250
   Juliet (Roberts) 2278
   Lizzie 2258
   Rev. Lucien 912
   Lucien 2256, 2264
   Mary 2262
   Susan M 2268

Woolfolk, Thos. H 270
   Rev. W. M 914
Wormley, R .... *64 k*
Wortham, Mary (Durrett) 2622
   W. T 2624
Wyckoff, E. (*Forman*) .... *660 b*
Yates, J. R 1268
   Mary M 1268
   Rev. Robt .... *16 q*
   Rev Wm .... *16 q*
Yost, Bettie (Marshall) 256
Young, A. B 2090
   D. L 824
   Dr. John C .... *70 g*
   Kate M 2562
   Thos. A 2560
   Capt. Thos .... *2424 b*
   Judge Upton 1086